Barbarians of Wealth

Barbarians of Wealth

Protecting Yourself from Today's Financial Attilas

Sandy Franks
Sara Nunnally

WILEY

John Wiley & Sons, Inc.

Published by John Wiley & Sons, Inc., Hoboken, New Jersey.
Published simultaneously in Canada.

For general information on our other products and services or for technical support, please contact our Customer Care Department within the United States at (800) 762-2974, outside the United States at (317) 572-3993 or fax (317) 572-4002.

Wiley also publishes its books in a variety of electronic formats. Some content that appears in print may not be available in electronic formats. For more information about Wiley products, visit our web site at www.wiley.com.

Library of Congress Cataloging-in-Publication Data:

ISBN   978-0-470-76814-3 (cloth); ISBN   978-0-470-94657-2 (ebk);
ISBN   978-0-470-94658-9 (ebk)

Printed in the United States of America

10 9 8 7 6 5 4 3 2

This book is dedicated to my husband Mark, my son Zachary, and my daughter Rachael, who have supported me not just in writing this book but in all my endeavors and who serve as my source of inspiration and pride; to my mother and father, who are without a doubt the world's best parents; and to my brothers and sister, who keep me smiling.
— SANDY FRANKS

For my great loves . . .
— SARA NUNNALLY

Contents

Foreword

Authors Sandy Franks and Sara Nunnally have chosen a loaded word for their title: *barbarian*. It can mean so many different things to so many different people that we must begin by wondering what it means to the authors. In anticipation of the next 1,000 words, the answer is: I don't know; but I can take a guess.

There is no disputing that the way of the world includes many things that might be labeled barbaric. Some of them will seem wrong to readers. Others will seem necessary. And some will even seem desirable. Most of the civilized world felt that water-boarding a prisoner was not only reprehensible but illegal and barbaric. Former U.S. President George W. Bush, however, said that he was glad he had allowed it.

And how about Goldman Sachs' handling of its credit derivatives? Is it barbaric to create an investment that you know will blow up on your client? Is it barbaric to create special instruments for the Greek government so that it can mislead investors and regulators as to how much debt it is carrying?

What is barbaric and what isn't?

Barbarism most commonly means *uncivilized*. But that doesn't take us very far. The Greeks accused everyone who was not Greek of being a barbarian. The word itself is believed to be onomatopoetic; the Greeks thought foreigners sounded like they were babbling, "Bar . . . bar . . . bar." The Romans had much the same view of foreigners. So did the Chinese. So universal is the description of foreigners as barbarians that we could come to believe the word is not actually pejorative. Maybe it could be replaced with *stranger*, or *people unlike us*.

But there is another aspect to the word: the uncivilized side of it. This kind of barbarian is not just foreign, either to the Greeks or to the authors of this book. Nor is he the innocent savage of Rousseau's imagination. This barbarian is the fellow you don't want to meet in the jungle or in the boardroom. He will ambush you in the forest of Teutoburg, throw you down a well in Calcutta, or rip you off with hedge fund fees.

A barbarian is not only unlike us; he is also wild, savage, untrustworthy, and violent. So when we think of the barbarians of finance, we have to include the Little Bighorn in our thoughts. A financial barbarian is not a noble savage. He is a ruthless cutthroat and a cad.

But what does that mean, exactly? The mark of a barbarian is that he is literally uncivilized. Being civilized originally referred to living in a town. Uncivilized people, like the Irish before the Viking invasions, don't have towns. So they don't have the rules and refinements that city life requires. At least, that's the idea. Hunters and gatherers, by this definition, are not civilized. A hunter is a killer. A gatherer takes what he finds. In the world before the agricultural revolution, a hunter/gatherer probably needed little encouragement to hunt his fellow men and to gather up their possessions and their women.

Living in a civilized, sedentary community, by contrast, required new codes of behavior. The instinct for reciprocity probably predates city life and even the species itself. It was easily applied to property. A hunted animal belonged to no one. A domesticated animal needed an owner. If you couldn't control an animal and exploit it, it wouldn't have been worthwhile feeding him. We can imagine that owners could only anticipate that their property rights would be respected if they respected others' property. Thus a general rule evolved that hadn't been necessary in the uncivilized world.

Obviously, people don't want to be robbed or cheated. So there we have our definition: A barbarian is someone who is uncivilized, meaning he is either unaware of or unwilling to abide by the rules of civilized life. Thus, a barbarian of finance is one who doesn't honor the codes of civilized financial behavior. He lies. He cheats. He steals. He doesn't do unto others as he would have them do unto him.

No need to put too fine a point on it. Most people try to provide a fair service for a fair exchange. "Do unto others . . ." is a good policy for business as well as life, generally. And yet there are plenty of barbarians too—people who lie, cheat, and steal whenever it suits them.

Note that the rules of civilization are often confused with the rules laid down by the barbarians themselves. When Attila swept over modern-day Turkey, he subdued town after town. He killed those who opposed him. He made slaves of others. He replaced existing governments, whatever they were, with another one—his own. Henceforth, he was the law; he made the rules; the tax collectors were his own men. These rules were not reciprocal; they were simply imposed.

This brings up another essential distinction between civilization and barbarism. Civilized life depends on cooperative, mutually respected rules. Barbarism depends on coercion. Civilization works by persuasion; barbarism functions by brute force. A group of people might agree to contribute to a fund for their mutual protection, for example. Forced tribute, however, even if is it supposedly for the protection of the payers, is barbaric.

Once he got to the gates of Constantinople, Attila seemed unstoppable. The Eastern Empire enjoyed Rome's protection. But in the fifth century, Rome was too weak to defend even its second most important city. So instead of fighting off the Huns, the Romans bought them off.

What marked Attila as a barbarian was not the fact that he didn't wear a toga or a business suit. It was that he did business in an uncivilized way. So do many people today. In 2008 and 2009, Wall Street nearly melted down. Instead of abiding by the contracts and agreements in place at the time, the U.S. government and Wall Street itself colluded to gazump them. The feds seized some of America's biggest corporations while Wall Street was bought off.

Readers will be surprised by the extended focus on history in this book. The authors are not announcing a new theory of history, nor are they elaborating on an old one. Nor are they merely trying to fill the gaps in our historical knowledge.

Instead, the role of the barbarian is illustrated by a broad display of history, almost as if we were watching a historical epic at a 3-D theater. We discover, for example, much about Attila's troubled relations with the declining Roman Empire. We are also reminded of the extent of his reach into Europe and what a close call the Battle of Châlons was.

The slide of events shows the slippery interplay of barbarism and civilization. The Vikings did great mischief to England, Ireland, and Scotland but were then absorbed into more civilized life. In fact, they contributed greatly to civilizing the English! The Norsemen formed towns which then became trading centers. And it was they who began the sea-borne commerce that would later be essential to Britain's empire.

While the English came to terms with the Vikings, the men from the North were also harassing the Franks on the continent. After failing to take Paris, Rollo, a renegade from Denmark, settled in what is today Normandy. Scarely five generations later, his great-great-great-grandson William invaded England. During four years of ruthless conquest he almost exterminated the local aristocracy, stole its lands, and established a Norman command hierarchy in its place. This land-based Norman aristocracy was fiercely independent, jealous of its rights, and resistant to the tribute (taxes) imposed by William's descendants. It largely created the English system of government which the colonists brought to America and from which the U.S. Constitution and other foundational documents are derived.

Then, in their bid for independence, was it barbaric for the colonies to allow Robert Morris to prey on English shipping? Morris was the biggest financial backer of the American Revolution. Arguably, he did it not because he was a great fan of democracy. The revolutionary government gave him cover to steal property from the English. His private fleet captured 1,500 British vessels, making Morris one of the richest men in the colonies.

The authors tell these stories, some from ancient history and some from yesterday's newspapers. The reader can draw his own conclusions.

—William Bonner, President of Agora Publishing,
Author of *Empire of Debt, Financial Reckoning Day,*
and *Mobs, Messiahs, and Markets*

Acknowledgments

I would like to thank my mentors Bill Bonner and Mark Ford for teaching me the value of good ideas. They have shared with me many valuable business and life experiences, for which I will always be grateful.

I would also like to personally thank Sara Nunnally for taking on this tremendous challenge with me. I've always enjoyed her viewpoints and welcome her ideas. She's a wonderful researcher and writer.

Of course there are many more people to thank for their support, and my list could truly never be considered complete. I can only acknowledge some of them on this page, including the great thinkers and writers of my company, the Taipan Publishing Group: Justice Litle, Adam Lass, Byran Bottarelli, Zachary Scheidt; Kent Lucas, Michael Robinson, Michael Sankowski, Joey McLiney; and Chip Biggs.

I also need to acknowledge other members of my company, the Taipan Publishing Group, including Jeanne Smith, Erin Beale, Jeffrey Little, and the many other staff members who work vigorously to make the Taipan Publishing Group a wonderful company.

My list of acknowledgments wouldn't be complete without mentioning Laura Davis, Daryl Berver, and Dan Denning, who have become my most cherished friends.

And last but certainly not least, I couldn't have undertaken this task without the encouragement and support of my husband, Mark, and my children, Zachary and Rachael, for which I am most grateful.

—SANDY FRANKS

I would like to thank Taipan Publishing Group for giving me the curiosity to foray into the history of wealth and its disappearance, and the abundance of time needed to accomplish such a task. I'd also like to thank all my dogs for keeping me company on the couch throughout the whole process.

—SARA NUNNALLY

Introduction

On April 16, 2010, the Securities and Exchange Commission (SEC) charged Goldman, Sachs & Co. and one of its vice presidents for defrauding investors by misstating and omitting key facts about a financial product tied to subprime mortgages as the U.S. housing market was beginning to falter.

In an e-mail to a girl he was dating, Fabrice Tourre, a Goldman Sachs trader named in the SEC suit, writing about the mortgage investments he was trading, described them as "Frankenstein turning against his own inventor."[1]

His invention was Abacus 2007-AC1, a security backed by subprime loans. Tourre created the security when the market was on an upswing. However, led by greed, Tourre continued selling the securities after the market turned downward.

When credit rating agencies started downgrading the securities, Goldman Sachs executives were more than pleased because they were secretly betting against them. Goldman Sachs executive Donald Mullen wrote, "Sounds like we will make serious money."[2]

Unlike many people, we weren't surprised when the SEC filed charges against Goldman Sachs. That's because we knew the firm was capable of dirty investment deeds. The truth is Goldman was a major player in subprime derivatives that brought down the world economy.

However, Abacus 2007-AC1 isn't the only risky mortgage-related financial product Goldman sold to institutions. You can go back to April 27, 2006. That's when Goldman created the mortgage security known as GSAMP Trust 2006-S3.

Goldman's GSAMP Trust 2006-S3 security was made up entirely of subprime loans. Goldman Sachs bought the loans from several different mortgage companies throughout the United States that had granted thousands of non-creditworthy borrowers millions of dollars in mortgage loans.

But Goldman Sachs isn't the only financial firm that deserves blame for wreaking havoc on the global economy. There are others that are just as guilty.

This is one of the compelling reasons we decided to write *Barbarians of Wealth*. In this book, we'll show you how reckless decisions and actions by certain people and companies severely cripple the financial prosperity of the American public. In many ways their actions are no different from the barbarians of the Dark Ages.

Economic Destruction

After the fall of the Roman Empire, Europe was invaded many times by various barbaric tribes including Attila the Hun; the great Charlemagne; the Mongols (from Asia), led by Genghis Kahn; and the Vikings, invading pirates of the sea.

These barbaric tribes plundered villages throughout Europe, destroying homes, farms, and often entire villages. In their wake, they left masses of people impoverished, with all hopes of personal prosperity crushed. They were ruthless. And the destruction and devastation they caused was for their own personal gain.

Almost 15 centuries later, modern-day barbarians have left a path of economic destruction far greater than that caused by hurricanes or earthquakes.

Who are these modern-day barbarians of wealth? One is the U.S. banking industry, including the Federal Reserve. The decisions they make on monetary policy and interest rates affects the entire U.S. economy and therefore the wealth of many hardworking Americans.

By the first half of 2010, the Fed had already spent $2 trillion to bail out Wall Street's banks and the U.S. mortgage market. Our national debt now stands at $12.8 trillion. And it will probably only get worse.

But we can't talk about the Federal Reserve without talking about its leaders. Just as each barbaric tribe had a leader, so do these modern-day barbarians. For the banking industry, we name Alan Greenspan as a modern-day barbaric leader.

In his imperious "wisdom," Greenspan lowered interest rates, which created an era of rampant credit. As he lowered interest rates, capital costs were dramatically reduced and suddenly the worst business plans and most feeble management could appear brilliant. Institutions took on more risk than they were capable of properly managing. Many Americans began purchasing well beyond their means.

Alan passed his low interest rate philosophy down to his modern-day barbarian heir, Ben Bernanke. This era of mass credit reached a level so great that when the credit bubble it created burst, millions of people lost their jobs, and home values were destroyed, as well as trillions in 401(k) retirement plans.

Other modern-day barbarians of wealth are the major Wall Street institutions such as Goldman Sachs, J.P. Morgan, CitiGroup, AIG, and a host of others, including credit rating agencies such as Moody's, Standard and Poor's, and Fitch.

These investment firms helped transform illiquid financial assets into standardized, liquid, marketable securities such as mortgage-backed securities, which we now know contributed to the global financial recession of 2008.

The combined size of these derivatives grew almost 30 percent in the first half of 2007, when it reached a size of $370 trillion.

And what about Washington's role? Or, more specifically, what man was near the top of political power and was also a major principle of a Wall Street firm? None other than Henry Paulson, named runner-up for *Time's* Person of the Year 2008 for his knee-jerk reaction to inject $700 billion into the financial system. Before taking office as

Secretary of the Treasury, Paulson was CEO of Goldman Sachs. By the way, all three successive CEOs of Goldman Sachs followed Paulson into government.

The cronyism doesn't stop there. Timothy Geithner, current Secretary of the Treasury, was Paulson's protégé. He allegedly, while head of the Federal Reserve Bank of New York, had AIG keep quiet some details about its payments to banks (like Goldman Sachs and Société Générale) during the financial crisis.

Of course, no listing of modern-day barbarians of wealth would be complete without adding members of Congress. In this book, we pinpoint certain members of Congress such as Christopher Dodd, head of the U.S. Senate Banking Committee, who acted more on his own behalf than that of his constituents.

Dodd received privileged VIP loans from Countrywide Financial, loans that the people he represents could never receive. And Countrywide Financial was the first mortgage to go under in the credit crisis.

Defend Your Wealth

Sun Tzu said in his book *The Art of War*, "It is only one who is thoroughly acquainted with the evils of war that can thoroughly understand the profitable way of carrying it on."[3] You can't fully understand the motives of modern-day barbarians until you have at least looked back at the barbarians of the past. The first four chapters of this book detail the exploits and invasions of the most ruthless and cunning barbarians of the Dark Ages. Because we live in a civilized society, you might think that because we are 1,000 years removed from the Dark Ages, our advanced era cannot support the cruelty and greed of Attila or the Vikings. To believe so puts your wealth and prosperity at risk.

Today's stakes are very high: our economic world as we know it— the very foundation of our society. The tools the modern-day barbarians use are no longer trebuchets or Mongolian bows. They're computer programs and toxic assets. But they're designed to leave you penniless and dumbfounded as surely as a barbaric invasion.

These modern-day barbarians are "thoroughly acquainted with the evils of war," and they definitely know how to make it profitable.

Barbarians of Wealth is a walking tour through the history of our economy. Along the journey, you'll learn about the people and events that shaped our financial future and how those actions have impacted your future financial well-being. The list of modern-day barbarians is long and their actions detailed.

Knowing how these barbarians—both from the past and the present—operate gets you one step closer to regaining your financial freedom.

But *Barbarians of Wealth* wouldn't be complete without offering you specific strategies you can undertake to protect your financial future. We've dedicated the last section of this book to showing you not only how to protect what prosperity you have left, but how to win back the wealth today's financial barbarians have stolen from you.

Putting these strategies in place can make an appreciable difference in your financial life.

Part One

GREAT BARBARIANS
OF HISTORY

Chapter 1

Attila the Hun: The Scourge of God

Attila! One of the most notorious barbarians of the Dark Ages, his name struck fear into the heart of the Western world. A Roman historian called him "a man born to shake the races of the world, a terror to all lands."[1] Saint Jerome called the Huns the "wolves from the North."

His enemies called him the Scourge of God.

Attila was even rumored to have killed his own brother in a staged hunting accident. This Hunnic king's brutal raids and constant plundering shook the foundations of the Roman Empire, and brought the great city of Constantinople to its knees—twice.

And each time, Attila left with hoards of cash and thousands of pounds of gold in tribute as Rome was forced to buy peace.

Attila was power-hungry and ruthless. He said, "For what fortress, what city, in the wide extent of the Roman Empire, can hope to exist, secure and impregnable, if it is our pleasure that it should be erased from the earth?"[2]

As Attila and his Huns marched on Constantinople, the historian Callinicus wrote:

> The barbarian nation of the Huns, which was in Thrace, became so great that more than a hundred cities were captured and Constantinople almost came into danger and most men fled from it. . . . And there were so many murders and bloodlettings that the dead could not be numbered. Ay, for they took captive the churches and monasteries and slew the monks and maidens in great numbers.[3]

More favorable historians would tell you that Attila was not swayed by the riches his pillaging brought. Renatus Profuturus Frigeridus, a Roman historian, said Attila was "renowned for the arts of peace, without avarice and little swayed by desire."[4]

But that doesn't hold much water. Under Attila's rule, Eastern Rome's tribute to the Huns doubled in 435, and then tripled in 443.

Attila knew how to negotiate with an iron fist. He was a master at breaking the spirit of those he conquered. Paying Attila the ransom he demanded was easier than suffering more devastation and despair.

For example, the Eastern Empire had already been paying tribute to the Huns with an annual payment of 350 Roman pounds. In 435, Attila and his brother marched into Roman territory, threatening to take more land unless their demands were met.

The two brothers met with the Romans on horseback outside the city of Margus, intimidating the Romans enough to force a new treaty with even better terms: 700 Roman pounds in tribute, and eight solidi ransom for every Roman prisoner taken by the Huns. (There are 72 solidi to a pound.) The Huns were also awarded the right to trade on the banks of the Danube.[5]

Attila's Retaliation

Edward Gibbons, author of *The Decline and Fall of the Roman Empire*, wrote, "The kings of the Huns assumed the solid benefits, as well as the vain honors, of the negotiation. They dictated the conditions of peace, and each condition was an insult on the majesty of the empire."[6]

But instead of keeping its promise, Eastern Rome reneged on the treaty.

Even more foolhardy, in 440, even as Attila was threatening invasion, the bishop of Margus allegedly went out and robbed the graves of some Hunnic royalty, taking the treasures back within the city walls of Margus. This gave Attila the excuse to attack a market across the Danube, raze the fortress at Constantia, and demand the bishop and the stolen treasure be turned over.

Rome did not turn the bishop over, or return the Hunnic grave treasures. If this pretense of stolen treasure was true—and Gibbons asserts that it was not, writing that the Huns' attack was unprovoked—this was probably the Eastern Empire's worst decision. The Huns came in force, Attila's sweeping invasion driving the Romans back out of the Balkans.

Richard Gordon, author of "Battle of Châlons: Attila the Hun Versus Flavius Aëtius," published in the magazine *Military History*, wrote, "Attila's warriors sacked Belgrade and numerous other centers . . . defeating Roman armies three times in succession and penetrating as far as the outskirts of Constantinople itself."[7]

The Huns' retaliation overwhelmed Eastern Rome's defenses. Crossing the Danube, thousands of Huns struck swiftly, sweeping in for 500 miles, pushing the Romans back as far as Constantinople.

The Huns now had thousands of captives who, at eight solidi apiece, were very valuable. Thrace and Macedonia were pillaged and stripped of all their riches. This was enough to cause the Eastern Emperor Theodosius to sue for peace.

And yet after this resounding defeat, Rome still did not honor its peace treaty. At dispute were captives on both sides. Rome would not pay for all the prisoners taken, nor would they turn over Attila's subjects who had fled.

Attila showed no mercy. He would be paid the money he demanded. In 442, he attacked again, laid waste the military city of Ratiaria, and besieged Naissus with battering rams and towers.

Priscus of Panium, a contemporary of Attila and author of *Fragmenta Historicorum Graecorum*, told of this siege, chronicling, "Then the enemy brought up scaling ladders. And so in some places the wall was toppled by the rams and elsewhere men on the battlements were overpowered by the multitude of siege engines."[8]

The city fell. Attila's terms were paid willingly.

The Cost of Peace—Attila's Cash Cow

Peace was Attila's cash cow. He was now exacting a tribute of 2,100 Roman pounds, plus a 6,000 pound fine. Roman hostages were now ransomed for 12 solidi. This single attack on Constantinople cost Rome the equivalent of $107.6 million and a huge parcel of land in Thrace.[9]

This amount was devastating for the crippled empire. After fighting Africans at Carthage, the Visigoths in Gaul, and Attila at Constantinople, Rome was quickly running out of cash. The tripling of its annual tribute to the Huns forced Rome to levy a war tax.

Priscus wrote, "Those registered in the senate paid, as the war tax, sums of gold specified in proportion to their proper rank, and for many their good fortune brought a change in life. For they paid under torture what those assigned to do this by the emperor assessed them."[10]

Roman senators auctioned off their wives' jewels and the rich decorations of their houses, such as heavy silver tables and gold vases. What a humiliation for the Great Empire! Gold in hand, the Huns left Constantinople in shambles and continued their push west into the rich, ripe Balkans.

That was their game—attack and pillage, then demand tribute. Attila and the Huns believed that exacting tribute was the ultimate form of superiority.

In all, it's estimated that between 443 and 450, Rome paid Attila 22,000 pounds of gold.[11] That's $387.2 million, or $55.3 million a year— or a daily payoff of more than $151,500. The Huns were very rich indeed.

This type of barbarism—smart military tactics with crafty negotiation— nearly bankrupted the Roman Empire.

What's truly barbaric about all the loot and plunder Attila won— aside from the cruel and ghastly acts that decimated huge city centers—is that only Attila's select cadre of commanders and generals reaped the benefits of the Huns' barbarism.

Golden goblets and silver platters, gem-crusted armor and jeweled swords—these chieftains wore their wealth. Gibbons wrote, "The Huns were ambitious of displaying those riches which were the fruit and evidence of their victories: the trappings of their horses, their swords, and even their shoes, were studded with gold and precious stones; and their tables were profusely spread with plates, and goblets, and vases of gold and silver, which had been fashioned by the labor of Grecian artists."[12]

Not only that, but when the Huns settled in Gaul and began a diverse economy based on trade and labor, Attila collected food and tribute from his own people.

Taxes and tribute ... sound familiar?

Today's barbarians do the same thing. They even have the swords.

Take Hank Paulson, for example, the former CEO of Goldman Sachs and the seventy-fourth Treasury secretary. He was also *Time* magazine's Person of the Year 2008[13] for his knee-jerk reaction to inject $700 billion into the financial system.

Paulson told banks they would be forced to take the money, whether they wanted it or not. In a memo given to the banks, he wrote, "If a capital infusion is not appealing, you should be aware that your regulator will require it in any circumstance."[14]

And what did Paulson and the government get in exchange? Stock in the companies, and a lot of interest on the bailout loans, as we saw when financial institutions released earnings for 2009. Citigroup had to pay $8 billion in pretaxes for paying back its TARP loans early. That led to the company posting a loss of $7.14 billion for the last quarter of the year.[15]

We'll talk more about Hank "the Hun" Paulson in later chapters, but his barbaric tactics forced businesses to carve up their companies in tribute to the government's economic plan. Not unlike Attila holding his sword to the throat of Constantinople, requiring a tripling of his annual tribute, is it?

Aëtius and Attila—A Double-Headed Coin

Much as modern-day barbarians share their tactics (and wealth) with a select circle of friends and partners, Attila discerned that befriending a powerful Roman soldier could help him expand his empire.

He found that partnership in Aëtius, a young political hostage of both the Goths and the Huns. Political hostages were a means of making sure both sides held up their ends of the deal. The lives of the hostages were at stake. One false move and the boy Aëtius would have been killed.

For three years, Aëtius was with the Goths under King Alaric I. Then the boy, who was the son of a Roman soldier and a wealthy Roman woman, was sent to the Huns, in the care of King Rua—none other than Attila's uncle.[16] There it is said he learned his ruthlessness, but also forged a great friendship and trust.

Aëtius even sent his son Carpilio to be educated in Attila's camp.

Later, in 433, Aëtius sought out the safety of the Huns after marching against his Roman rival Bonifacius. Though Aëtius lost the battle, Bonifacius was killed, leaving Aëtius as the strongest Roman general in the Empire. This promotion wasn't looked on favorably by Rome, and Aëtius was forced into a short exile for the death of Bonifacius.

The Huns welcomed him, remembering his time with them as a hostage and his trust in sending his son to learn from them.

Aëtius returned from exile backed by 60,000 Huns,[17] and forced the Empress Placidia to grant him clemency. Placidia was half-sister to Honorius, Western Rome's emperor until his death in 423. Honorius left no heir, which sparked a bit of a struggle for the throne.

This 60,000-strong show of solidarity wasn't the only example of how Aëtius and the Huns got on. The Roman general even engaged the Huns to help defeat the Burgundians in Gaul in 437. More than 20,000 died at the hands of the Huns, and Aëtius rose to great acclaim in Rome.[18] In 449, Aëtius signed an agreement with the Huns, allowing some of them to settle in Pannonia, or modern-day western Hungary, and parts of eastern Austria, down into Serbia, Croatia, and Slovenia.

One can make an interesting comparison between the relationship of Attila and Aëtius and the relationship between Hank "the Hun" Paulson and China. During his time as CEO of Goldman Sachs, Paulson traveled to China 70 times,[19] creating extremely close ties that some might suspect constituted a conflict of interest during his time as Treasury secretary.

Paulson spearheaded U.S.-China relations and led the U.S.-China Strategic Economic Dialogue. At the Shanghai Futures Exchange, he told people, "An open, competitive, and liberalized financial market can

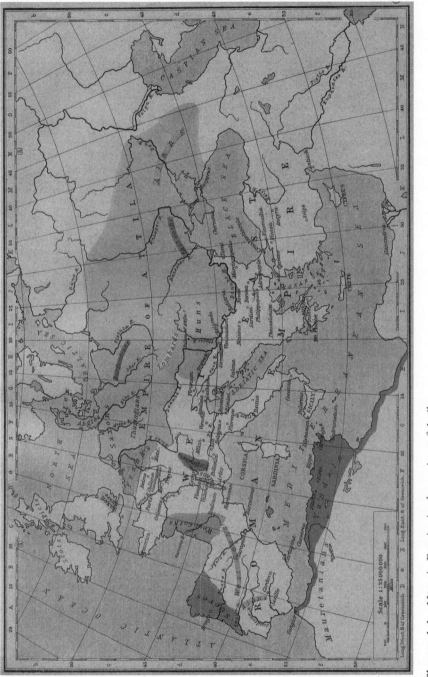

Figure 1.1 Hunnic Empire in the region of Attila

SOURCE: Perry-Castañeda Library Map Collection, from William R. Shepherd, *Historical Atlas* (1911; 8th ed. Barnes & Noble, 1956), taken from www.emersonkent.com/map_archive/attila_empire_450.htm.

effectively allocate scarce resources in a manner that promotes stability and prosperity far better than governmental intervention."[20]

Like a double-headed coin—a sort of "Heads, I win; tails, you lose" scenario.

Meaning, don't interfere. And that's what got both Attila and Paulson in trouble in the end. It was Attila's biggest—some say only— flub as king of the Huns, and how his terrifying horde of barbarians faded away into nothing more than a fantastic history for spirited Hungarians.

The Battle of Châlons—Attila's Fate is Sealed

It wasn't just for Attila's honor that the Huns marched against Western Rome, though the temptation of Rome's riches would've been enough.

A succession battle in the Frankish kingdom widened the rift between Rome and Attila. After Clodion, king of the Franks, died with 20 years of what could be called peaceful reign under his belt, his two sons fell to fighting over the kingdom. Fatefully, the younger son, Meroveus, sought the help of Aëtius and Rome, while the older son courted Attila.

This was a key alliance for the king of the Huns, as it provided a safe passage across the Rhine—and, as Gibbons puts it, an honorable pretense for the invasion of Gaul.[21]

With a sure foothold across the Rhine, Attila would be able to sweep down on the Western Empire, or west into Visigoth territory. Either way, Attila's position would open the floodgate for plunder and pillaging aplenty for his Huns.

As Attila raised the call, tens, perhaps hundreds of thousands of eager tribes lined up for what looked to be an easy rout of the Old Empire—and a huge payday. They took Cologne, Mainz, and Worms on the banks of the Rhine. "Advancing in three columns through modern-day Belgium, the Huns spread terror and destruction," wrote Richard Gordon in *Military History*. "Town after town was destroyed, including Metz, Cambrai, Strasbourg, Rheims, Amiens and Worms. Paris was saved only because the Huns considered it too small to be worth the trouble of a siege."[22]

It was a masterful first strike, and Attila and his Huns were weighed down with plunder. However, it was at this point that things started turning against the barbarian king.

During this first sweeping invasion that Gibbons describes as a "promiscuous massacre,"[23] Aëtius was beseeching the Visigoths under the rule of King Theodoric to join him against Attila. Theodoric had refused—until the Scourge of God reached Orléans, a scant 100 miles away from Visigoth lands in western France.

Theodoric thought it better to forget the past injustices between his people and Rome in favor of preservation. With Attila, there would be slaughter.

As the Huns marched on Orléans, Aëtius and Theodoric rushed to the city. Orléans was held by King Sangiban, and Aëtius doubted the king's loyalty. This was the land where Rome had settled the Alans, whose distant homelands between the Caspian and Black Seas were now under Attila's rule.

Aëtius was right to fear, for just as he and the Visigoths arrived at Orléans, King Sangiban was opening the city to Attila and the Huns.

In a quick attack, Aëtius and Theodoric diverted the Huns, who prudently retreated to the open fields of Châlons, just east of Paris. This is where Attila could have chosen to quit the field, having gained an enormous amount of wealth, and hightail it back across the Rhine.

But Attila turned, and sealed his fate.

Pride over Prejudice—Attila's Only Defeat

The two sides aligned for battle on the flat plains, with only a small hill on Attila's left flank as a point of advantage. Rome and her allies arranged themselves with the Alans in the middle, where they could be watched, with Theodoric and his sons to the right and Aëtius and the Romans to the left.

Attila arranged his troops with his fearsome Huns front and center, with the Gepids on his right and the Ostrogoths on his left, facing the singular hill. It was this hill that would be the first fight of the battle. Theodoric's son Thorismund, armed with heavy cavalry, advanced on the hill, warding off the Ostrogoths and the Huns, though both sides took heavy casualties.[24]

Next, Attila—at the center of his host of warriors, standing on the front line—charged the Alans at the center of Aëtius's and Theodoric's armies, and quickly turned on the Visigoths, separating Theodoric from Aëtius. Thorismund was quick to respond from his hilltop vantage and charged into the flanks of the Ostrogoths who had partially surrounded his father's army. The charge broke the lines, and the Ostrogoths wheeled around to retreat, with the Huns barely escaping to the safety of the wagons.

From here, it was pure mayhem. Historical sources give conflicting versions of the rest of the battle. One says that Attila successfully cut off Theodoric from the Roman army, and that the Visigoth king was killed in battle, poetically and tragically speared by Andages, an Ostrogoth noble, and trampled by his own horses.[25]

Another says that Theodoric and his son Thorismund thwarted Attila's attack, forcing him to retreat to his wagons by nightfall. The Visigoth king was accidentally thrown from his horse, and his death was not noticed until later that evening.

Though Attila was forced back to his wagons, he would not back down. Even the Visigoths' historians likened Attila to a lion encompassed in his den, and after several attempts to avenge his father's death were thwarted by showers of arrows, Thorismund was talked into leaving the field of battle. Aëtius allowed Attila to retreat after it was clear that the Huns would never back down. Rather than risk his Roman army, Aëtius let Attila slink back to Hunnic territory.

This allowed the Roman general to have all the spoils of victory for himself, and also headed off any Gothic pride at victory on the battlefield. Aëtius knew that if Attila remained a threat, the Visigoth threat would always remain checked.

The scene at Châlons was one of pure carnage. Gibbons wrote:

> The number of the slain amounted to one hundred and sixty-two thousand, or, according to another account, three hundred thousand persons; and these incredible exaggerations suppose a real and effective loss sufficient to justify the historian's remark, that whole generations may be swept away by the madness of kings, in the space of a single hour.[26]

These kinds of numbers don't matter to a barbarian like Attila. The number of coins in his treasury matters, or the number of wives at his camp. But ruthlessness overpowers prudence in Hunnic culture, which is why, only one year after the Battle of Châlons, Attila invaded Rome again—and this time, the barbarian Visigoths did not come to Aëtius's aid.

The only card Rome had to play was negotiating for peace, and an embassy was quickly dispatched to Attila. In this embassy was none other than the future Pope Leo I, then a bishop, who successfully bribed Attila with enough gold and the promise of the deliverance of his bride Honoria to make him go away.[27]

The Death of Attila

In early 453, as he took a young bride named Idilco to his bed, Attila suffered a nasal hemorrhage and drowned in his own blood at the age of 49.[28]

Priscus reports:

> Worn out by excessive merriment at his wedding and sodden with sleep and wine he lay on his back. In this position a hemorrhage which ordinarily would have flowed from his nose, since it was hindered from its accustomed channels, poured down his throat in deadly passage and killed him. So drunkenness put a shameful end to a king famed in war.[29]

This is a stunning end to one of the most notorious barbarians of all time.

Of course, controversy surrounds his death: Was he poisoned? Did his new bride kill him?

A full 80 years after Attila's death, Count Marcellinus, a Roman chronicler, wrote, "Attila, King of the Huns and ravager of the provinces of Europe, was pierced by the hand and blade of his wife."[30] And more recently, Michael Babcock asserted that the Emperor Marcian was behind Attila's death, in his 2005 book *The Night Attila Died: Solving the Murder of Attila the Hun.*[31]

After his death, the Huns fell into disarray as Attila's sons squabbled over the riches the Hunnic Empire had gained under their father's rule. Within a year, the ferocious Huns were defeated and scattered across the Pannonian plains. They would not bother Rome again.

Whether from natural causes, overindulgence, a young bride's fear, or political will, Attila's death highlights the transient nature of the barbarian's rise to wealth and power. His smash-and-grab tactics allowed for only momentary gain that simply vanished in the wind in the absence of real prosperity.

And indeed, his barbarism sucked the prosperity out of every land his Hunnic feet touched.

Today's barbarians of wealth have learned a lot from Attila. Have we not seen the Hank "the Hun" Paulson smash and grab $700 billion to allegedly rescue the financial system from imminent collapse? Have we not seen the nationalistic President Hugo Chavez force international companies to give up their stakes in lucrative oil fields off the coast of Venezuela?

We've seen AIG throw a lavish retreat for its employees as the financial world collapsed around them. We've seen Attila-like investment banks heap multimillion-dollar bonuses on their CEOs while raking in taxpayer-funded bailouts.

Yes, barbarism was never the same after Attila, though the world would soon come to know barbarians of a different ilk—ones with silk tongues and righteous causes, ones with the might of empires behind them.

Ones like Charlemagne—Charles the Great, the Father of Europe.

Chapter 2

Charlemagne: The Clandestine Barbarian

When you think of barbarians, you think of rough bands of brigands, pooling their resources to ravage the countryside and harry the larger empires. Pillaging and plundering—mob warfare—come to mind. The Goths, the Mongols, the Huns, the Vikings . . . The tribes you hear about would as soon cut your throat for your gold necklace as look at you, or would burn your little thatch hut and haul off your virgin daughter.

You don't normally think of such historical heroes as Charles the Great—known as Charlemagne.

Why would you? His campaigns were made under the cross, in the name of Christianity, and his deeds have earned him the moniker "the Father of Europe." He united many warring tribes under his banner and expanded the Carolingian Empire down into Italy, ushering peace and prosperity across middle Europe.

But he achieved these successes through constant campaigning, snuffing out rebellion, and bringing his enemies to heel. That's why we call him the *clandestine barbarian*.

The triumphs of Charles the Great marked the brightest spot of the Dark Ages, and his vassal kings were wealthy beyond belief. He himself was known to despise rich clothing or costumes, and rarely wore bejeweled attire, choosing instead to dress more like a commoner.[1] But Charles knew the power of wealth on display and lined his banquet tables with plates and cups of silver and gold.

Charlemagne exhibited many of the traits we see in modern-day politicians, whom we also call barbarians of wealth. He knew the power of campaigning. He also recognized that he had to keep his vassal kings' appetite for wealth satisfied, or they would rise up and try to overthrow him. They respected strength of arms and money, so he bribed them with riches from his dynastic expansions.

This isn't much different from how politicians behave when campaigning for votes from their constituents—or the backdoor deals they negotiate with one another and with corporate lobbyists in order to get bills passed. Consider the deal made between Senate Majority Leader Harry Reid and Senator Ben Nelson to get the sixtieth vote needed to pass President Obama's health care reform bill.

Ben Nelson (D-NE) was induced to cast the decisive vote in exchange for a special provision exempting his state from a mandate imposed on states to pay for Medicaid expansion. This is one example of modern-day bribes used by our political leaders. In later chapters, we'll learn more about the dirty deeds of our modern-day politicians. For now, let's return to Charlemagne's rule as the clandestine barbarian.

Charlemagne ruled with an iron fist—or rather, a steel sword. Born sometime in the 740s (the specific date is still under debate; some historians say 742, while others say 747 or 748), he was the grandson of Charles Martel—Charles the Hammer—a masterful military general.

The Hammer was responsible for subduing the eastern duchies of Bavaria and Alemannia, and the southern duchies of Aquitaine and Provence. He successfully protected the western provinces from the invading Muslim armies that occupied modern-day Spain.[2]

Charlemagne's father, too, was handy with the sword. Pepin III (a.k.a. Pepin the Short, or Pippin) rose to power under the last of the

Merovingian kings, Childeric III, who was essentially a figurehead, wishing instead for a monastic life.[3] (You may remember that Aëtius, the Roman general who drove out Attila and the Huns in the Battle of Châlons, supported the younger Frankish prince for the throne in 451, while Attila supported the older, after the death of King Clodion. According to some sources, that young prince—who succeeded to become king of the Franks, as Rome declared victory at Châlons—was named Meroveus.)[4]

Childeric was considered an impotent power, and for all intents and purposes, Pepin ruled the Franks as the *mayor of the palace*—which means he had control of the armies and magnates.

As tensions grew in southern Italy with the Lombards, Pepin had Childeric deposed by the Pope, and his first action as king of the Franks was to march on the Lombard king Aistulf, who had expanded into Roman territory. Pepin was victorious and the ancient capital of the Western Empire, Ravenna, was returned to the papacy.

Needless to say, Charlemagne had some big shoes to fill—and the clandestine barbarian was more than up to the challenge.

The Piety of Charlemagne

His kindness and control were key characteristics of Charlemagne. Everything from his plain dress to his piety was conservative and, perhaps, reverent. Charles the Great even put huge amounts of the gold and silver won in his campaigns into the hands of the church to build monasteries and places of worship. He fairly lavished them with riches.

In Charles's time, there were 600 monasteries throughout his lands,[5] and as he defeated the rebellious barbarians, like the Saxons, he forced them to be baptized—under pain of death. Then the newly conquered Christians had to pay tithes (just like every other Frank) to the church, and forfeit large plots of land "for the benefit of the missions," according to Thomas Shahan and *The Catholic Encyclopedia*.[6]

And with all of Charlemagne's conquests, there was always a flow of money into the government and through to the church.

With the gold and the wealth that the kings and princes of Spain presented to Charlemagne, the emperor built the Church of Saint James during the three years that he remained in the country. He established a patriarch and canons there, according to the rule of Saint Isidore the confessor. He built the church nobly, decorating it with bells, silken cloths, books, texts, crosses, calixes, and other ornaments.

With the rest of the gold and silver that he brought from Spain he constructed many churches on his return to France. These include the Church of Our Lady Saint Mary and the Church of Saint James in Aix-la-Chapelle; more churches of Saint James in Béziers, in Toulouse, and in Gascony, in the city of Axa (Dax); the Church of Saint John of Sorges, on the pilgrims' road; a sixth Church of Saint James, in the city of Paris, between the Seine and Montmartre; as well as innumerable churches and abbeys that he built and founded throughout the world.[7]

In contemporary times, we can see a similar relationship between Alan Greenspan and Wall Street.

Greenspan was the chairman of the Federal Reserve from 1987 through 2006. In 1987, the markets were crashing. After he was nominated, the bond markets experienced their largest one-day drop in half a decade. Then the stock markets went haywire. The Dow Jones Industrial Average lost 22.61 percent on the infamous day dubbed Black Monday, October 19.[8]

Alan "the Great" Greenspan responded to this crisis by saying that the Fed would "serve as a source of liquidity to support the economic and financial system." This response would reappear as a trump card for any crisis during his tenure, such as when he flooded the system with dollars during the Asian financial crisis in the late 1990s.[9]

Another way Greenspan shoveled money into Wall Street's coffers was by playing with interest rates. After the tragedy of September 11, 2001, and the revealing of several corporate scandals that also rocked the markets, Alan the Great slashed interest rates bit by bit until in 2004, the Federal Fund rate was only 1 percent.[10] And that allowed markets easy access to money.

Between 2004 and 2007—when the house of cards came crashing down—the Dow Jones Industrial Average gained 27 percent. That's 9 percent a year. And from Black Monday in 1987 until Greenspan left office on January 31, 2006, the Dow Jones has gained 525 percent, or 27.6 percent a year.

To many, this behavior seems appropriate, but when the market gets too big and demanding, soon there's not enough money to satisfy it, and the pendulum swings.

This happened to the Frankish kingdom after Charlemagne's death. His character was so big, and his influence so wide-reaching, that his successor, Louis the Pious, could not live up to the kingdom's—and church's—expectations.

This is the heart of clandestine barbarism: The union and stability of Charlemagne's empire depended on the life of a single man: he initiated the dangerous practice of dividing his kingdoms among his sons; and after his numerous diets, the whole constitution was left to fluctuate between the disorders of anarchy and despotism.[11]

The Christian Kingdom

Charlemagne's campaigning efforts also led to a rapid expansion of Christianity. He often forced newly subdued tribes to be baptized, and then taxed them in support of the church. Derek Wilson, author of *Charlemagne: A Biography*, wrote, "Any leader who comes with armed support in the name of a compelling faith is sure of a following. The faith that underpinned Charlemagne's reign, and that would become the most powerful the world has ever seen, was militant Christianity."[12]

This wasn't just an expedient way of subduing the masses. Charles believed it was his divine mission to bring Christianity to the pagan peoples. He just did this at the point of his sword.

Susan Wise Bauer, author of *The History of the Medieval World: From the Conversion of Constantine to the First Crusade*, wrote:

> First, Charles wanted to expand his empire to the north; the land around the Rhine was rich, and the Saxon tribes were not well united.... The following year [in 773], he crossed the Alps, set on punishing [the Lombard King] Desiderius for his plots and aiming to claim Italy for his own.[13]

Rome was in trouble. It was surrounded by the Lombards, who were intent on making this city their capital. They'd been chipping away at the old empire for decades. Indeed, in Charles's father's time, the Lombards had captured the old Western Roman Empire's capital of Ravenna.

The Pope, Stephen II, was forced to call on Pepin III, Charlemagne's father, to expel the Lombards from papal lands. He was successful, but Lombardy was never truly brought to heel in Pepin's time.

Charlemagne found himself at the edge of a conflict that would determine his place in history. Christianity was the unifying factor for his empire. His rule encompassed a vast variety of cultures and languages. Faith was a commonality that helped Charles the Great keep his people loyal—and they adored him for it.

This made a relationship with Rome and the Pope extremely important—but it was a balancing act. Charlemagne, however devout he was, did not want to appear to be under the thumb of the Pope. In fact, it was a Frankish ideal that the king ruled over all his subjects, including the clergy.

So it was in late 773 that Pope Hadrian I beseeched Charles the Great to save Rome from the designs of the Lombard king, Desiderius. Charlemagne responded quickly—far more quickly than Desiderius expected, as the Pope's summons came after the campaign season, and the Franks would have to cross the daunting Alps with winter coming on.

According to Derek Wilson, Desiderius thought the winter weather would do the work for him. "At the very worst," he wrote, "Desiderius would be obliged to agree to a truce and make promises that he would have no intention of keeping. But Desiderius was in for more shocks than one."[14]

Rather than withdrawing as winter set in and the snow piled up around the Lombard capital of Pavia, Charlemagne dug in and besieged the city. It was a long wait through bitter-cold months, and as spring worked its way north in 774, Desiderius still saw Charles' armies camped on his doorstep.

But it wasn't until full summer that the Lombard king called for a truce. Einhard, Charlemagne's biographer, wrote, "Charles did not cease, after declaring war, until he had exhausted King Desiderius by a long siege, and forced him to surrender at discretion."[15]

Unlike his father, Pepin III, Charlemagne assumed control over Lombardy, taking the Iron Crown for his own. With the threat of

Lombardy removed, the Pope was indebted to the king of the Franks, and their friendship was mutually beneficial: The king was the protector of the church, while the Pope provided that religious cohesion that helped Charlemagne rule his many peoples.

We see this protector role played out centuries later by Alan "the Great" Greenspan. Alan was *the* protector of Wall Street investment banks and corporations. As Chairman of the Federal Reserve, Alan began to slowly pull apart the Glass-Steagall Act, which had kept banking and commercial banking activities separate.

Alan justified his unraveling of that act by suggesting that the greedy fat cats on Wall Street could regulate themselves in a type of "establishment radicalism," so termed by Richard Eskow.[16] In return, his Wall Street comrades would sing his praises. He would become known as "the Maestro."

The Saxon Wars

The Saxon wars were about three things: border security, money, and ideology.

The relationship between the Franks and the Saxons was one of constant conflict. At times there was peace, and Saxony was part of Francia. At other times, there was war.

After the fall of the Western Roman Empire, the Franks became Christianized. The Saxons held on to their own beliefs, a pagan religion that worshiped (in part) the Irminsul, or "great pillar," that symbolically connects earth and heaven.[17]

Their paganism was a large part of Charlemagne's justification for war. After his first few battles with the Saxons, Charles divided the territory up into missionary districts. He instituted rules, and established churches and monasteries. But the Saxons' quid pro quo was to submit to Charlemagne and, when his back was turned, go back to their old ways of living. This caused the king to tighten the thumbscrews.

His next round of religious laws was much more pointed: Christianity or death. Indeed, in 780, Charlemagne decreed that the Saxons must submit to baptism or be put to death. And in 782, the king himself marched into Saxony to institute harsh codes of conduct meant to stamp out pagan practices. The local population rebelled—a decision that received even harsher retribution.

Charlemagne had 4,500 Saxons slaughtered because they continued to practice their own pagan rituals.

But religion wasn't the only reason the Franks and the Saxons were at odds. The Saxons' territory followed the Elbe River to the Saale River, and crossed west, nearly to the Rhine, which happens to be the border of the Frankish kingdom.

Also spurring on the Franks against the Saxons was the plunder. Derek Wilson writes, "They also needed to achieve success, for success meant booty, which they needed in order to pay their followers and ensure their own mounting prosperity."[18]

And the Saxons were a fairly rich culture, being barbarians themselves. . . . In fact, when Charlemagne first invaded Saxony and struck down the Irminsul near modern-day Obermarsberg, he carried away the gold and silver found there as sacrifices to the idol.

Einhard again comments on the Saxon Wars, saying, "The memory of man cannot recall any war against the Franks by which they were so enriched and their material possessions so increased."[19]

In all, Charlemagne launched 18 campaigns against the Saxons, and the conflict came to an end in 804, more than 30 years after it began. The Saxons were subdued, Christianized, and paying tithes to build and support the church.

The Conquest of Lombardy and the Imperial Throne

Of all the territories Charlemagne brought into his fold, Lombardy was the most strategically important, followed closely by Saxony. If the conquest of the Saxons was the epitome of Charlemagne's expansion of Christianity, his defense of Rome was its salvation.

You see, this clandestine barbarian arrived in Rome at a time when the old Eastern Empire was in turmoil. The Emperor Constantine VI was killed by his power-hungry mother, Irene. Many leaders from other empires didn't take well to his murder, even though he wasn't a competent ruler. They also didn't take well to having a woman on the throne in Constantinople. They started to look west, and saw Charlemagne.

Wilson writes, "The Muslim emperor [Sultan Harun al-Rachid] had always conducted business with Constantinople, but he was no less scandalized than the leader of Latin Christendom by a woman's usurpation of the Byzantine throne and now regarded Charles as the only spokesperson for Christian Europe."[20]

Charlemagne was met by Pope Leo III outside the Rome—a high honor, as previously the king of the Franks had been met only by a delegation a mile from the city and was forced to camp beyond the city wall.

Pope Leo III crowned Charlemagne Emperor of the Roman Empire. It was Christmas Day, 800, an auspicious day indeed, and the congregation in Saint Peter's cried, "Hail to Charles the Augustus, crowned by God the great and peace-bringing Emperor of the Romans!"[21]

There's no good account as to whose idea it was to give Charlemagne the imperial crown. But it is clear that Rome and its peers in the Muslim world and in the Holy Land believed the Old Empire's throne to be vacant. As noted, a woman sat on the throne in Constantinople, which meant to most leaders of the time that no one sat on that throne. The Pope believed the crown of the Empire was his to give—and he chose Charlemagne.

And what do you think was the first thing this clandestine barbarian did as emperor?

He sent to Byzantium to propose an allegiance of marriage to Irene. This is an old move by Charles. In his early rule with his brother Carloman, Charles attempted to surround his brother's territories (that blocked his way to Rome) by marrying the Lombard king's daughter, Desiderata. And two decades before, Charles and Irene had been in negotiation to marry their children, Constantine and Rotunda. That arrangement had fallen through, though.

Now, he was again attempting to unite the Old Empire using the same tactic. Byzantium's reaction to this proposal was to replace Irene with Nicephorus I, one of her ministers.[22]

Charlemagne is reported to have said, "Oh, would that pool were not between us; for then we would either divide between us the wealth of the east, or we would hold it in common."[23]

This was not some sort of love letter to Irene—far from it. In fact, once she was replaced, Charlemagne dropped all attempts at marriage.

No, Charles the Great's drive was wealth and power—gold, silver, and Christianity.

Modern-day barbarians of Wall Street may not be obsessed with religion as was Charles the Great, but they are certainly obsessed with wealth and power. And that power resides with a select few investment banks.

During the fallout of the recession of 2007, Washington talked about stricter regulations on the financial industry to prevent an economic disaster of that magnitude from happening again. Yet just the opposite has occurred.

President Obama and his team have proposed and submitted to Congress legislation that would rein in the size and scope of investment banks such as J.P. Morgan, Goldman, and Citigroup. But Anil Kashyap, in an article in the *New York Times*, says, "The law is sufficiently ambiguous as to be practically unenforceable."[24]

A New King Is Crowned

Essentially, for Charlemagne, his crowning translated into rule over all Christian peoples, including those in Byzantium. Though he may not have been able to bring the whole Frankish army against Constantinople, taking the Eastern Empire by force, he was strong enough to chip away at the barbarian peoples that lay between the two kingdoms.

The victory against the Avars was proof of this, and obliged the East to keep a wary eye on Charlemagne. But for the Pope, and church leaders to follow, the coronation ushered in great cooperation between government and the church.

Durant wrote in his *History of Civilization*:

> He allowed the clergy their own courts, decreed that a tithe or tenth of all produce of the land should be turned over to the Church, gave the clergy control of marriages and wills, and himself bequeathed two-thirds of his estates to the bishoprics of his realm. But he required the bishops now and then to make substantial "gifts" to help meet the expenses of the government.[25]

In a way, this kind of cooperation echoes the relationship between the Federal Reserve and both the Federal government and the U.S.

financial system. Chairmen, like Alan Greenspan, can tithe some of its funds to ailing financial systems, and even keep interest rates low in order to keep money flowing cheaply. But the Reserve remains independent—even as the U.S. government nominates the chairman.

Talk about hand-in-glove!

When the Pope needed someone to bail him out, the Carolingian dynasty was always there to do it. Charlemagne had the might of arms and the religious conviction to collaborate with Rome to spread Christianity at the point of his sword.

At the time he was crowned emperor, Charles the Great was already in his fifties, considered an old man for his time. He had long since stopped leading his own armies into rebellious territories, or against new barbarians threatening his realm. The Frankish Empire had expanded about as far as it could.

He died on July 8, 810, a few months after an unsuccessful siege of Venice, his army forced to withdraw after rampant disease whittled his ranks. His middle son, Charles the Younger, was to hold Austrasia and Neustria, Saxony, Burgundy, and Thuringia, and had some success against the Bretons, and in Saxony, but he died suddenly of a stroke on December 4, 811.[26]

Only Louis the Pious outlived his father to rule the Frankish kingdom as emperor—and it was not a solid reign.

Charlemagne's character was so formidable that none could live up to his persona. We've noted before that Charlemagne had some big shoes to fill, and he did so with more than a little panache. But when he died, he left a massive hole in the kingdom of the Franks—and in the protection of Christianity.

A long life, and a long rule, helped establish his fame almost immediately upon his death—good for history, not so good for Louis the Pious. Louis had to deal not only with internal factions that were loyal only because of the strength of Charlemagne's character—and the riches his campaigns brought them—but also with a new and evasive threat.

They came by sea, raiding coastal villages, pillaging, and burning, before escaping back on their ships.

They were the Vikings.

Chapter 3

The Vikings: Savage Pirates, Savvy Traders

The Vikings have been characterized, demonized, and passed off as uncouth, dumb raiders. In reality, they were more fearsome than any tale, and smart. They were the Huns of the sea. Wolves, they've been called, freebooters, and their rise to power was savage and quick.

They were raiding and taking lands for their own on two fronts, the British Isles and Northern France, and even making forays into the heavily defended Mediterranean Sea. Their raids were quick and brutal, striking quickly, loading their longships with booty and plunder, and making their getaway before the local militias could even mobilize.

History has convoluted the Viking's past with idealistic sentiments, calling them "noble savages."

But their start was far more savage than noble.

Norsemen—men from the North. Their first raids smashed into England in the 790s. The first known killing blow came in 789 in the harbor of the Island of Portland, on England's southern coast. Three Viking ships landed and a horde of Vikings waded ashore. As the island's official came down the beach to meet them, believing them to be traders, he was swiftly shot down with arrows, dying instantly.[1]

The next encounter England had with the marauding mobs of sea wolves was at St. Cuthbert on the Island of Lindisfarne. Thomas J. Craughwell, author of *How the Barbarian Invasions Shaped the Modern World*, references an anonymous monk, writing in his *Anglo-Saxon Chronicle* for June 8, 793:

> And they came to the church of Lindisfarne, laid everything waste with grievous plundering, trampled the holy places with polluted steps, dug up the altars and seized all the treasures of the holy church. They killed some of the brothers, took some away with them in fetters, many they drove out, naked and loaded with insults, some they drowned in the sea.[2]

The Vikings carried away the relics and bones of St. Cuthbert, along with all the treasure in the monastery.

You may be thinking that a monastery wouldn't yield much plunder for a band of sea wolves, but you'd be wrong. Britain had been experiencing a wonderful renaissance, where education and religion were revered.

In fact, one of England's most renowned monks was invited by Charlemagne to be a personal tutor to his children and spiritual adviser to the king of the Franks himself. I'm speaking of Alcuin, who wrote of the Lindisfarne massacre:

> Woe on the day that brought to all men sorrow,
> When the heathen host from the far verge of the world
> Came rowing swiftly sudden on our coasts,
> Dishonoring our father's reverend graves,
> Fouling the churches consecrate to God.[3]

But let's get back to the wealth the monks had. Craughwell reported, "This religious devotion ... expressed itself in lavish gifts to churches, monasteries, and convents. Gospel books received golden covers. Shrines of the saints were plated with silver and studded with precious stones. Bishops presided at Mass holding croziers of intricately carved ivory."[4]

This was the soft underbelly of England, and the Vikings exploited that to no end. Immense treasure guarded only by pious monks who saw their riches only as the glorification of God, not booty for the barbarians. But it was these easy gains that sparked an invasion that changed the course of these British Isles. And it wasn't only there that the Vikings made a big impact.

Consider: The northern coast of France is named *Normandy*, its populations called *Normans*, or northmen. And this term doesn't just mean from the north of France. It means Norsemen: Vikings.

It's hard to overestimate the brutality with which these sea wolves raided unsuspecting seaside towns. Craughwell's anonymous monk wrote, "The pagans from the northern regions came with a naval force to Britain like the stinging hornets and spread on all sides like fearful wolves, robbed, tore and slaughtered ... priests and deacons, and companies of monks and nuns."[5]

The Vikings' sole purpose, at first, was to raid and pillage. War bands were the unspoken rule in the Viking civilization: You either joined or were conquered. Jonathan Clements, author of *The Vikings: The Last Pagans or the First Modern Europeans?* wrote, "The war band was an organism that lived to acquire possessions—it would roam in search of a territory of its own. . . . A war band was not so much a parasite upon a community as an outlet for a community's bad seeds."[6]

And when these bad seeds hit the seas, they struck with deadly force. In the ninth and tenth centuries, they ruled the North Sea and the English Channel. Two centuries of terror, 200 years of Viking domination.

Conquest and Colonization

Robert Ferguson, author of *The Vikings: A History*, wrote:

> A degree of activity that the annalists saw fit to describe as the "devastation of all the islands of Britain" probably implies the existence as early as the 790s of a base in the north from

which the raiders could easily reach targets further west round the coast of Scotland, and to which they could return without risking a North Sea crossing each time.[7]

Further evidence of their colonization comes from Jonathan Clements, who also asserts that the Vikings' base had much to do with strengthening their hold over the seas. He believes that the sea wolves targeted their victims because they were on previously established trade routes. "They knew what they were looking for because they had been there before. They knew whom they were robbing, because perhaps only months earlier, they or their associates had been trading with them."[8]

This change in tactics did not decrease the cruelty with which the Vikings treated the local populations. But it did usher in a new kind of lifestyle.

Prior to the Viking age, Scotland and Ireland were largely agrarian, and there were no large city centers, no large ports for trade. Usually the monasteries were the centers of towns and villages, and life revolved around education, religion, and farming. England's economy had come a bit further, with a money-based economy already in place.

But the British Isles had no ships or navy. This all changed with the Vikings, and the sea wolves may even be responsible for Britain's evolution into a major sea power, eventually allowing for the British Empire's expansion far and wide.

The Vikings introduced a new concept: the town or city as a thriving, outward-looking commercial center where goods were manufactured or stockpiled for eventual shipment to markets overseas, and which received goods from foreign markets in return. Thanks to the Vikings, the Irish began to participate in this early medieval global economy.

But in addition to trading centers, the Irish needed currency. The Vikings supplied that, too, establishing a mint to produce the first coins in Ireland. It was the Vikings, then, who guided the Irish as they took their first steps away from their insular, pastoral life and into the international marketplace.[9]

A New Economy

This introduction into a new economy is not dissimilar to a latter-day Viking's exploits. I'm talking about Robert Morris, the second U.S. Senator ever elected, and known as the "financier of the American Revolution."

During that war, Morris's private merchant fleet captured about 1,500 British vessels. These privateer vessels were really just pirate ships, and Morris helped sell the stolen booty when his catch came into port.

With his newfound wealth, he nearly single-handedly funded the Revolutionary War, and established the first national bank, the Bank of North America in 1782. This bank was the first attempt at using credit to fund government and private initiatives.

Unfortunately, Morris's bank was forced to close under suspicion of fictitious credit and large foreign interest. Morris was, in essence, a Viking pirate who brought money and trade to the early United States.

And the Vikings, like Morris, worked only for themselves.

We'll discuss Robert Morris again in later chapters. Suffice it to say that the Vikings' new strategy in the British Isles and Ireland brought a new age of commerce, but not without its harsh downfalls and characteristic Viking domination. For when the sea wolves came ashore and established their trading centers, they expected the local populations to recognize their rule. And that rule was ruthless and cutthroat.

David Willis McCullough, author of *Wars of the Irish Kings: A Thousand Years of Struggle*, wrote, "Although the foreigners arrived as raiders and kidnappers, they later became businessmen who established busy ports (founded as winter camps) both to carry out trade and to provide embarkation points for raids on other lands, notably Scotland and northern Britain."[10]

The Last King of England

But trading wasn't the only thing on the sea wolves' minds. They wanted conquest. And the British Isles would have made an outstanding point from which to launch raids against Europe and explorations across the Atlantic to places like Iceland and Greenland, as well as keep connections with their homeland in Scandinavia.

Thomas Craughwell asserts that the Vikings had a stranglehold on England. "Archaeologists have found evidence of the Vikings making themselves at home in England," he wrote, "with hints that they planned to destroy English Christian society and put a Norse pagan one in its place."[11]

By 870, there was only one kingdom left, and the Vikings were on the verge of transforming England into a Scandinavian outpost.

The last king was Alfred of Wessex. His family home at Chippenham was besieged, and Alfred fled into exile at Athelney, an island in the marshes of Somerset. There, the last king plotted to take back his kingdom and push the Vikings out.

Five months later, King Alfred returned and launched an attack, and forced the Viking Guthrum to surrender after a two-week siege at Chippenham, the very home Alfred was forced from less than a year earlier. The terms of surrender favored Alfred.

Craughwell reported, "In a document known as the Treaty of Wemore, Alfred and Guthrum agreed on their respective spheres of influence in England. . . . Alfred's territory was all of southern England or Wessex, and about half of central England, or Mercia. This territory included two important cities: Winchester, Alfred's capital, and Canterbury, the heart of the Church in England."[12]

Alfred later captured London. The treaty also called for Guthrum to demobilize his army and be baptized. These he also did, taking the name Aethelstan.

This point in the story takes us to the Vikings' incursions into northern France.

The *Oxford History of Medieval Europe* states, "The raiding Vikings seem to have been sensitive to changing circumstances, moving to the area of northern Europe which would offer the most profits, in booty or tribute."[13]

Initially, the men from the north were traders, sailing merchants who plied their trade up and down France's rivers, like the Seine that leads right to Paris. France was beyond wealthy. Craughwell calls France, "fabulously wealthy, with everyone from barons to archbishops embracing the new capitalist economy."[14]

The Normans—the Norsemen

Thomas Cahill, author of *Mysteries of the Middle Ages: And the Beginning of the Modern World*, relates this story:

> In the early tenth century, a band of Norwegian Vikings, led by a Dane called Hrolf the Ganger ("Rollo" in subsequent French literature), settled around Rouen in the lower Seine valley.
>
> In short order they carved out for themselves a sizable province, henceforth called Normandy—home of the Northmen, or Normans. The tall, straw-haired, cold-eyed, calculating warriors, more adept at battle than any of their neighbors, would soon extend their reach far beyond Normandy.[15]

But there's more to this story. Rollo was an exile from Denmark. His father had offended the king of Denmark, and upon his father's death, the king set out to kill Rollo and his brother Gurim.

Gurim was hacked to death, but Rollo escaped, and was named an outlaw. The only thing for Rollo to do was become a pirate. He hooked up with a group of sea wolves that had been harrying England and modern-day Holland, and he was with the group of Vikings that laid siege to Paris in 885.

It wasn't the first time Paris had been attacked by the Vikings, but it was the largest Viking assault the city had known. The city had been attacked in 845 and twice in the 860s, and each time, the Viking hordes had accepted a bribe or tribute paid in thousands of pounds of gold and silver for peace.[16]

Of course, we know Rollo didn't leave France altogether. He and his Viking army retreated to a bleak and nearly uninhabited part of northern France. There he saw his chance to create a kingdom of his own.

Dudo of St. Quentin, a Frankish historian, gave an account of Rollo's view of what would become Normandy:

> This land is plentifully furnished with an abundant supply of all the fruits of the earth, shady with trees, divided up by rivers filled with fish, copiously supplied with diverse kinds of wild game, but empty of armed men and warriors. . . . We will

subordinate this land to our power. And we will claim this land as our allotment.[17]

Indeed, from this point, the Vikings had a huge advantage in northern France. The fledgling community was able to strike out and harry Burgundy and the lower Seine basin. Their attacks became so frequent that Charles the Simple, in 911, ceded the entire province of Normandy to Rollo.

William the Viking Conqueror

Within two generations, these Vikings had assimilated into the French culture. They spoke French, married locals, and converted to Christianity. This integration gave birth to none other than William the Conqueror, the great-great-great grandson of Rollo.

And here's the irony. In England, Harold the II became king after the death of the childless King Edward the Confessor. William, Duke of Normandy, claimed to be a legitimate heir to the English throne, as he was a bastard cousin of Edward, who supposedly promised that William would inherit the throne.

At the same time, a Viking, Harald Hardrada, was persuaded that he was the rightful king of England, with a totally implausible claim that he was promised the throne through some treaty between Canute (the Danish King of England before Edward) and Magnus, the king of Norway.

Hardrada rounded up 300 longships and 7,000 warriors and invaded England in September 1066, a scant month before the Battle of Hastings. King Harold rushed to defend York and was successful, though his army was worn out from chasing and battling the Viking usurpers.

The army only had two weeks of rest before the threat from the Normans. Six hundred ships were about to land at Hastings, with the Viking Duke of Normandy at their helm: William the Conqueror.

Craughwell wrote, "With great brutality, within five years William subdued the entire country. He killed or scattered almost all the English nobility, giving their lands to Normans."[18]

The Vikings had finally conquered England. William embodied both the wealth and sophistication of the French and the ruthlessness of the Vikings. Once he established his rule in England, he introduced feudalism, forcing the locals to become little more than slaves to his schemes.

This is not unlike the powerful combination between early government and financial institutions' marriage with early Wall Street. Folks in the government willingly took massive risks with the early markets, banking the gains for themselves as the everyday American felt the sting of harsh taxes and the aftermath of banking bubbles. We'll talk more about this connection in later chapters.

Chapter 4

Genghis Khan: Mighty Warrior

Genghis Khan was a hair's breadth away from being called the Conqueror of the World. During his reign, he conquered more land than did Alexander the Great and the Roman Empire combined. This fame was foretold by certain omens.

There was a legend of his divine birth from a gray wolf. It is also said that he was born with a blood clot grasped in his fist.[1] This sign meant he would become a great leader, but to get there, he would have to hack his way to the top.

A warmonger and a true barbarian, he never stopped fighting, never stopped expanding his empire. His Golden Horde held such strategic trade routes as the Silk Road, and his warriors penetrated as far south as India, as far west as Vienna, and as far east as Japan. Genghis Khan, consummate warrior, exacting leader, changed the course of history forever.

When Genghis-Khan rose from the grade of childhood to the degree of manhood, he became in the onslaught like a roaring lion and in the melee like a trenchant sword; in the subjugation of his foes his rigour and severity had the taste of poison, and in the humbling of the pride of each lord of fortune his harshness and ferocity did the work of Fate.[2]

But while Genghis was indeed ruthless, he was also calculating, systematically killing off or subduing all his rivals on his way to becoming Khan of all the Mongol tribes. Genghis's Mongol army and its political structure was a machine fueled by victory and plunder. And once he hacked his way to the top, he instituted some long-lasting laws and systems that kept his empire going for another 150 years.

That's staying power, and it has some historians rewriting history to put Genghis in a better light.

There are some historical references that say Genghis Khan despised luxury, that all riches and spoils were held in common, that all his soldiers were his brothers, that he ate the same food as the shepherds, and so on. And while all of these things might have been true, they were also convenient politics, a great counterweight to the Chinese excess that was flaunted to the Mongols' south.

This practice is not unlike the nationalist leaders in today's modern world who have grabbed up all their assets to purportedly distribute wealth more evenly (think Chavez and Putin with their energy resources).

But we're getting way ahead of ourselves. To better understand this barbarian's vengeful and cunning nature, we have to understand the Mongol lifestyle in which he grew up.

Consider this passage from *History of the Mongols: From the 9th to the 19th Century*, by Sir Henry Hoyle Howorth, written in 1876:

> The history of the Mongols is necessarily a "drum and trumpet history." It deals chiefly with the conquests of great kings and the struggles of rival tribes, and many of its pages are crowded with incidents of butchery, and a terrible story of ravage and destruction.

It is in the main the story of one of those hardy, brawny races cradled amidst want and hard circumstances, in whose blood there is a good mixture of iron, which are sent periodically to destroy the luxurious and the wealthy, to lay in ashes the arts and culture which only grow under the shelter of wealth and easy circumstances, and to convert into a desert the paradise which man has painfully cultivated.

Like the pestilence and the famine, the Mongols were essentially an engine of destruction; and if it be a painful, harassing story to read, it is nevertheless a necessary one if we are to understand the great course of human progress.[3]

His personal history—aside from those myths and legends about his birth—is not that unusual for the thirteenth century on the Asian steppe.

The Mongols were originally only one tribe of many that held the harsh territory between the mountains of Tibet and the winters of Siberia. There were the Tartars, the Naimans, the Merkits, and the Kereyds, along with a number of smaller tribes.

Indeed, the Tartars were the fiercest of all the nomadic tribes in Mongolia. So fierce were they that even after the Mongol tribe came into power, people called them Tartars. The chronicler Matthew Paris alluded to this in his thirteenth-century account, saying they were a "detestable nation of Satan that poured out like devils from Tartarus so that they are rightly called Tartars."[4]

Their lives were hard. The steppe was unyielding in many ways: constant winds, treeless, bitterly cold in winter, difficult to farm. The tribes were nomadic, searching out grazing lands for their animals.

With such an unforgiving landscape, tribal wars often occurred over simple goods and the best grass, and raids were even more frequent. In J. A. Boyle's translation of *Genghis Khan: The History of the World Conqueror*, Ata-Malik Juvaini wrote, "There was constant fighting and hostility between them. Some of them regarded robbery and violence, immorality and debauchery (*fisq ve fujur*) as deeds of manliness and excellence."[5]

The Capture of Hoelun

Genghis, or Temüjin, as he was named by his parents, had to overcome a lot of adversities. While still a young boy, he was betrothed to a girl from his mother's clan. In order to help pay the bride price, Temüjin had to work for his future father-in-law. Temüjin was only eight years old, and his indenture started immediately.

But it was interrupted by something awful. On his way home, Temüjin's father, Yesügai, came across a camp of Tartars, the Mongols' sworn enemies. Such was the custom, however, that a traveling man alone could seek shelter and food from anyone, and it would be given. Yesügai could not go around the camp undetected, so he marched up and asked for their hospitality.

Here it must be said that Yesügai had previously raided Tartar camps and ransomed prisoners, and rumor has it that some of those prisoners were sitting around that fire.

Thus it was that when the Tartars passed him some food and drink, it was poisoned, and Yesügai, who had made it all the way back to his own people three days later, fell sick and died.[6]

Temüjin was eight.

The hardships didn't end there. After Temüjin's father died, the tribe abandoned him and his mother, his siblings, and Yesügai's other wife and children. And as soon as word got out to the other tribes in the area that the Borjigin clan was leaderless, they would descend and rip the tribe to pieces.

Interestingly, they didn't kill Temüjin, thinking he and his family would die in the harsh steppe or be killed by a rival tribe. But the small group eked out a living, scrounging for food and shelter for nearly four years until one fateful day.

Temüjin, only 12 or 13, and his brother Qasar (or Khasar) killed their half-brother Bekhter. Some histories say this slaying was because of an argument over food.

In one story, Bekhter took an animal from Temüjin, who had killed it for food, and kept it for his own family without sharing. That would have made the killing one for survival. Another story has Bekhtar rivaling Temüjin to be head of their little clan.

As punishment for this act of violence, the Tayichi'ud (sometimes called Tarqutai) clan, whose land the family was squatting on, came and took Temüjin captive.

Thomas Craughwell explains that Temüjin was put in a *cangue*, which is like the stocks. The prisoner's neck and wrists are locked between two pieces of wood so that he cannot lie down and must rely completely on his captors for eating, drinking, and relieving himself.

As a prisoner, Temüjin was passed around the Tayichi'ud tribe, and one family took pity on him, taking the cangue off at night. It is to the head of this family, Sorqan Sira, that Temüjin owed his escape.

The story goes that during a festival, the watching of the prisoner was left to a scrawny boy; Temüjin overcame him by smashing the cangue into his face, and made a run for it.

Temüjin hid in the Onon River, but was spotted by Sorqan Sira, who told the boy to lie still and he would not tell the rest of the Tayichi'ud where he was. By morning, when no one had found Temüjin, he crept back to Sorqan Sira's tent. The family helped him out of the cangue and gave him dry clothes and food.

Temüjin made his escape in the back of one of Sorqan Sira's wool carts.[7]

It is these events—the hardships and small kindnesses—that shaped Temüjin's character, and it is his character that drew to him bands of warriors. Temüjin's character really showed after he was old enough to claim his wife. She was taken from him in a raid by the Merkit tribe. The family had been camping at the base of a sacred mountain called Burgan Qaldun when 300 Merkit warriors descended on them, scattering the family in every direction.

The Merkit found Börte hiding in an ox-drawn cart and took her away. Temüjin sought the help of his father's old *anda*, Toghril. In a daring counterattack, Temüjin, with his own small clan and a large band of Toghril's warriors, descended on the Merkit tribe that was camped on the Khilok River in the middle of the night. The Merkit were driven out and their chief captured.

And then the world saw Temüjin's ruthless side.

He made the Merkit chief identify the warriors who had attacked him and his family. Temüjin had them killed—but the blood-letting didn't stop there. Craughwell wrote, "Then he assembled the dead men's wives and sorted them into two groups, those who would make suitable concubines, and those who were better suited as slaves."[8]

The Making of Genghis Khan

This is the start of how Temüjin became Genghis Khan. And because of this past, we can see how Genghis Khan, while a brilliant strategist, was a suspicious man, stingy with his trust, and merciless in his revenge.

Leo de Hartog, author of *Genghis Khan: Conqueror of the World*, asserted that Temüjin's suspicion made him hold tightly to his own authority and protect his position and those most loyal to him.

Hartog wrote, "As was the case with all his contemporaries, Genghis Khan worked exclusively for himself, his descendants and his closest companions. There is no evidence that he entertained any ideas about the welfare of the whole nation, not even in the form that such ideas were expressed in the Yasa."[9]

Yasa, or *Yassa*, was Genghis Khan's code of law—and it was firm.

For example, the punishment for the crimes of adultery, murder, perjury, and the theft of a horse or ox was death. The office of Khan was to be by election rather than hacking your way to the top as Genghis himself did.

There were also strict laws for warriors.

Edward Gibbons wrote that each warrior was responsible—under pain of death—for the safety of his fellow warriors, "and the spirit of conquest breathed in the law, that peace should never be granted unless to a vanquished and suppliant enemy."[10]

Temüjin was already known as a great warrior, and this drew other warriors to him. He also used his influence to split other tribes and bring the defectors into his fold. According to Craughwell, "Temüjin's followers had grown to such numbers that he could put 30,000 Mongol riders in the field."[11]

Paul Ratchnevsky, author of *Genghis Khan: His Life and Legacy*, wrote, "Vengeance was a moral duty, approved by Heaven, and Genghis was convinced of his right to exact vengeance."[12]

By 1206, Temüjin had become Genghis Khan, the first Mongol ruler over all the tribes in the steppe. He had hundreds of thousands of warrior beholden to him, held together by the thin thread of his own character.

Genghis was smart. He knew that the only way to hold on to his horde's loyalty was to buy it with riches. Warriors flocked to Genghis' banner because of the promise of reward, according to George Lane, author of *Genghis Khan and Mongol Rule*.[13] David Morgan, author of *The Mongols*, wrote of Genghis' dilemma:

> Unless something decisive was done with the newly formed military machine, it would soon dissolve into quarrelling factions again, and Mongolia would revert to its earlier state.
>
> This we believe is at least one explanation for the beginnings of the Mongols' astonishing career of conquest. A superb army, potentially invincible in the field in thirteenth-century conditions, had been successfully created.
>
> But if it was not used against external enemies, it would not remain in being for long. The only matter that required a decision was in which direction the armies were to advance.[14]

The Bow Is Strung: Genghis Sets His Sights on China

And when it struck, it first aimed its blows at opulent China. China had been interfering with Mongol tribes for centuries, trying to keep the barbarians warring with each other so that they would be less of a threat to China itself. Genghis struck right for the weak link in China's dynasty—Xi Xia.

This state was closest to the Mongol tribes, and Genghis knew that the more powerful Jin state would not come to its aid. By 1209, Xi Xia had fallen to the Mongols. This was the first mistake of the powerful Jin dynasty. With Xi Xia now under Mongol rule, there was nothing stopping Genghis from taking Jin lands. In three short years, Genghis had brought the Jin dynasty to heel, and his ever more effective siege tactics helped him sack the Jin capital city, Yanjing, modern-day Beijing.

While the Mongol's knowledge of siege technology grew, it was the Mongol bow that struck fear into the hearts of those who would be conquered. This bow was said to outshoot the English longbow by more than 130 yards![15]

When it came to conquest of the enemy, though, Genghis pulled no punches. Amy Chua, author of *Day of Empire: How Hyperpowers Rise to Global Dominance—And Why They Fall*, wrote, "The Mongols were also utterly ruthless in battle. They poured molten silver into the eyes and ears of their enemies. . . . Genghis Khan himself allegedly said that happiness was 'to crush your enemies, to see them fall at your feet—to take their horses and goods and hear the lamentation of their women. That is best.' "[16]

And that's exactly what Genghis and his hordes of Mongol warriors did, eventually conquering all the lands between Vienna and the Sea of Japan!

That means the Mongols controlled trade between the East and the West. The Silk Road—in part—was under their control.

The Empire Grows Fat

These raids brought back immense riches—and changed Mongolian lifestyles for good. The nomadic tribes who had determined the status of a chief by the fact that the man had iron stirrups was now transformed into a lavish existence.

In his article "The Mongols and the Silk Road," John Masson Smith Jr. wrote, "The Mongols gained an appreciation of the wealth, especially in foodstuffs and textiles, now available to them through plunder and extortion, taxation and exchange."[17]

Food and textiles, extravagant tents, were all on display in the new Mongol society. With the capture of the Silk Road, wealthy Mongols now had new enterprises to invest in, and heavy caravans of silk trolled the trade highway from the Far East to the Muslims' Samarkand (see map, page 51). And by the middle of the thirteenth century, Chinese silk could be bought in Italy.

The Old Silk Routes

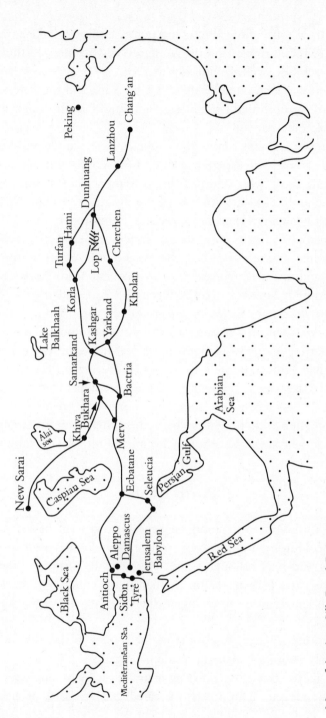

Map of Ancient Silk Road Route

SOURCE: Silkroad Foundation, silk-road.com/maps.

New trade routes flowed into and out of Europe to take advantage of these newfound riches, and the Mongols' trade centers on the Volga and the Black Sea swelled with wealth.[18]

Genghis was long gone by then, but his Yassa and the fierceness of his Mongol warriors held fast to their roots, and Genghis's descendents reaped a plentiful harvest.

But during Genghis's time, the struggles were bloody and brutal.

"Most of those who experienced the Mongol onslaught and survived, and certainly those who heard of the invasion second or third hand," wrote Lane in his *Genghis Khan and Mongol Rule*, "were quite willing to believe that Chinggis Khan was indeed the 'Punishment of God.'"[19]

This barbarian nation, one that collected armies like souvenirs on their nomadic journeys, sucked the wealth out of its surrounding neighbors and hoarded it away in its own coffers. But in its greed, the Mongol Empire bored a hole between the East and the West that opened the floodgates of trade, and it was the later Mongol Empire, under Kublai Khan, that became a political force to be reckoned with.

Another technique of Genghis Khan was to absorb the conquered armies. David Morgan quoted the author of *The Tartar Relation*, written in the 1240s, as saying that Genghis "had acquired the invariable habit of conscripting the soldiers of a conquered army into his own, with the object of subduing other countries by virtue of his increasing strength, as is clearly evident in his successors, who imitate his wicked cunning."[20]

Putin Khan

That didn't stop him from completely annihilating some of his enemies. He had a cold heart, and according to Ratchnevsky he customarily disgraced the leaders of his opponents. "He mocked Gurbesu of the Naimans, humiliated Terken-khatun and had all the children of the shah of Khwarazm killed, even the youngest, the favourite son of the sultana," Ratchnevsky wrote.[21]

Interestingly, we can see some of these traits in the behavior of a modern-day political barbarian, Vladimir Putin.

Putin Khan—while heralded by many of his own people as a great reformer, and one who vastly increased the standard of living in

Russia—has a knack for trouncing political opponents and crushing alleged rebellions in unhappy Soviet satellite states (read: Chechnya) that have continued to plague his political career.

In a scathing report on Putin's achievements as president, Bret Stephens of the *Wall Street Journal* wrote in July 2007:

> Russia has become, in the precise sense of the word, a fascist state. It does not matter here, as the Kremlin's apologists are so fond of pointing out, that Mr. Putin is wildly popular in Russia: Popularity is what competent despots get when they destroy independent media, stoke nationalistic fervor with military buildups and the cunning exploitation of the Church, and ride a wave of petrodollars to pay off the civil service and balance their budgets.
>
> Nor does it matter that Mr. Putin hasn't re-nationalized the "means of production" outright; corporatism was at the heart of Hitler's economic policy, too.[22]

Juvaini, as translated by Boyle, said a similar thing about Genghis Khan, writing:

> And so it has come to pass that the present world is the paradise of that people; for all the merchandise that is brought from the West is borne unto them, and that which is bound in the farthest East is untied in their houses; wallets and purses are filled from their treasuries, and their every-day garments are studded with jewels and embroidered with gold; and in the markets of their residences gems and fabrics have been so much cheapened that were the former taken back to the mine or quarry they would sell there for more than double the price, while to take fabrics thither is as to bear a present of caraway seeds to Kerman or an offering of water to Oman.[23]

The treasures of the Mongolian Empire came at the destruction of other peoples. The nomadic, warlike tribes had nothing, and set out to grab what they could from their neighbors, using their fierceness and uncompromising cruelty. They succeeded, so much so that Genghis Khan's family became a stalwart name in the new aristocracy, and

continued into the twentieth century. George R. Goethals and his colleagues reported in the *Encyclopedia of Leadership* that rulers of other
nations, such as Tamerlane in Turkey and Ivan IV in Russia, attempted to
make a familial connection to Genghis in order to prove their right
to rule.[24]

Edward Gibbons reminds us that in the first 68 years after Genghis
Khan's death, his successors subdued almost all of Asia and a good part of
Europe.[25]

The Mongols had created the largest contiguous empire the world
had ever seen—subduing the great Chinese dynasties, vanquishing the
great Persian strongholds, and terrifying the gentrified European
nations.

Their great history—started by that cunning, crafty, and ruthless
man, Genghis Khan—fizzled after 150 years. But Genghis's political
tactics and his ruthless authority have filtered down into some modern-
day political barbarians, as we'll see in later chapters.

Part Two

BANKS: THE BARBARIANS OF MONEY

Chapter 5

The Brotherhood
of Power

Think of the banking system as we know it today, and one automatically assumes the United States created the central banking system that most countries use.

But the earmarks of a central banking system can be traced back to the medieval era. One of the first known central banks is that of the *Taula de Canvi* (Municipal Bank of Deposit) in Barcelona, which opened for business on January 25, 1401.[1] The bank was created as a place to safely keep the deposits of private citizens as well as the government. By 1433 Taula de Canvi had 1,460 clients and more than 600,000 pounds on deposit.[2]

But as systems evolved, and they always do, another precursor of what we would recognize as a central banking system developed in the Dutch Republic sometime around the early 1600s. During that time,

800 to 1,000 different coins were in circulation. That presented a problem because the coins could easily be debased.[3]

The Dutch government made several attempts to curb the problem by creating new regulations, including assigning each coin a certain value. A mint ordinance was also established that allowed certain bankers, called *kassiers* (later translated to *cashiers*), to use coins with less silver content when settling debts.

By 1609, the Dutch government had created the Bank of Amsterdam, which was allowed to guarantee the quality of coins deposited in or withdrawn from the bank. The government also banned kassiers from operating with debased coins.

A few years later, we see this early form of a central banking system evolve even further in Sweden. In 1656 the Palmstruch Bank was founded by Johan Palmstruch.

Interestingly enough, although Johan was born in Sweden, as a young adult he moved to Amsterdam. While there, he was jailed when it was determined that he was not able to pay his debts. Perhaps that could have been a warning sign of things to come, as Johan would eventually bring an entire economy to its knees.

You see, when Johan returned to Sweden, he submitted a proposal to its ruler, King Charles X Gustav, to create a central bank to help the country with its enormous debt problem. Sweden's economy was ailing because of the tremendous amount of debt the country had incurred fighting the Thirty Years' War and the extravagant spending by Gustav's predecessor, Queen Christina.

But in addition to the debt, the country's currency, known as *kopparplatmynts*, which were heavy nuggets of copper, was quickly depreciating.

In his proposal, Johan called for the use of paper-based banknotes to replace the kopparplatmynts. However, King Gustav denied Palmstruch's proposal for a central bank. After all, how is it possible that little pieces of paper could represent currency or even hold value? But Johan didn't give up.

Johan wrote a second proposal, which he sent to the King. Once again the King rejected Johan's proposal. But on his third proposal, Johan promised to pay half of the bank's profits to the crown. That sealed the deal and the bank was created.

Although the bank was a private entity, it was the king who had the authority to choose the bank's managers and how the bank would operate, including whether it would be allowed to issue Johan's proposed banknotes.

Now paper notes weren't necessarily new. Records show that paper notes were used earlier in China around 1374. The notes were called *Ta Ming T'ung Hsing Pao Ch'ao*.[4]

However, paper notes hadn't surfaced again until Johan proposed the idea to the King of Sweden. In fact, Sweden is credited with issuing Europe's first paper-based banknotes.

Prior to this development, most debts were settled in coin or were paid in kind, or in goods or labor. Financial transactions between merchants and citizens were done using the heavy copper kopparplatmynts. The idea of using paper notes, which were admittedly much easier to carry around and handle, was a new one.

Eager to try this new system out, the king granted Palmstruch's bank permission to produce paper money. The first notes issued by the bank were called *Palmstruch issues*.[5] The notes were printed on thick, white, handmade paper with the word *banco* as the watermark. Because of their intricacies, they were difficult to forge.

Additionally, the notes could be exchanged for a predetermined number of coins that the bank would carry in reserve. Plus, the bearer of the notes could use them to purchase goods in the marketplace or to conduct other financial transactions. It didn't take long for the Swedes to accept the idea of using paper notes in lieu of kopparplatmynts. The system was working exactly as Johan had envisioned.

However, as you might suspect, a system so easy to use, and so easily adopted by the public, held a hidden flaw that would soon be exploited by Johan Palmstruch.

Whatever good intentions Johan might have started out with, they soon turned to what was good for his own well-being. Johan's bank (also known as Stockholms Banco) was forced into bankruptcy because he had issued more banknotes than the amount of coin reserves on hand.

The state was forced to intervene. The incident became Sweden's first banking crisis. Palmstruch, who was responsible for the huge losses, was condemned to death, but later received clemency from the king.

In 1668 a new bank was created, known as the Riksbank.[6] All of Palmstruch Bank's privileges were transferred to the newly created Swedish Riksbank. However, because of the earlier crisis that grew from overprinting banknotes, Riksbank was strictly forbidden from issuing banknotes.

But that decision didn't last long. Three years later, in 1701, Sweden reversed that decision and the Riksbank began issuing banknotes, which were called *transport bills*.

The transport bills were used well into the eighteenth century. However, an old problem popped up again: Counterfeit transport bills were circulating throughout the country.

To curb the problem of banknote forgeries, the government decided that Riksbank should create its own paper on which the transport bills would be printed. So the Tumba Bruk paper mill was founded in Tumba, an area just outside of Stockholm, with the sole purpose of milling paper to be used for the banknotes.

From Failed Banknotes to a Failed Fiat Money System

In 1694, England followed in Sweden's footsteps and established its own central bank, the Bank of England, to purchase government debt.

When King William and Queen Mary took over the royal throne, England's finances were in disarray. During the reign of Queen Elizabeth I, England had spent a huge amount of money helping Holland fight off the mighty Spanish. The country's finances were weakened from over 50 years of fighting. As a result, pressure grew for the creation of a national bank. The government received many proposals from prominent citizens on how to create an institution that could stabilize the nation's economy.

Sir William Paterson, who made his fortune in foreign trade with the West Indies, also knew something about banking from his time in Amsterdam. In 1691, Paterson submitted a proposal to the government as to what procedures it could undertake to create the bank, but his proposal was rejected.

Not able to accept rejection, Paterson submitted a second proposal to William and Mary outlining his plan, which included loaning the

1,200,000 pounds to create the bank. The king and queen accepted his proposal. In 1694 through an act of Parliament the bank was given its royal charter.[7]

The bank was given the official name of the Governor and Company of the Bank of England. It was privately owned by a group of about 20 people who lent money to the government to fund the bank's start-up. In return, they were granted the right to receive interest at the rate of 8 percent annually along with an annual management fee.

Paterson became one of the bank's directors. His merchant friend Michael Godfrey became the deputy governor, while another London merchant, John Houblon, served as the bank's first governor.

The bank could lend money, issue banknotes, and, most importantly, provide funds to the government. The bank could also organize the sale of government bonds when funds needed to be raised. It also acted as a clearing bank for government departments, facilitating and processing their daily transactions. The bank was able to stabilize England's economy for several years.

The bank was privately owned and operated until it was nationalized in 1946.[8] In 1997 the Bank of England became an independent public organization, wholly owned by the government of England and charged with setting monetary policy for the United Kingdom. The bank managed the government's accounts and made loans to finance spending during times of both peace and war.

Short on Funds

For a long time, it looked as if the Bank of England would run smoothly, but in 1825 things changed dramatically. After the end of the Napoleonic Wars, England's economy was experiencing a major boom. Areas in Latin America were being built, and London investors began investing in all things related to that region.

In addition, the Bank of England's loose monetary policy was helping fuel an economic boom. Banks were lending money freely. There was rampant speculation in shipping lines, canals, and textile-spinning factories.

But eventually the boom got out of hand as investors began to wildly drive up the price of stocks. Credit began to subside and companies found it difficult to get loans. By April 1825 things worsened and the boom ended.

Companies began filing bankruptcy and many banks began to fail. Six banks in London were closed along with 60 other banks spread throughout England. By November a panic broke out as many large firms had gone under. The Bank of England responded by increasing its paper issues. But that only prompted a decline in its specie reserves—in fact, the reserves reached critical levels.[9]

The bank received help from one of the richest people in England, Nathan Rothschild. Nathan was one of five sons of Mayer Rothschild. Born in a German ghetto in 1777, Nathan Rothschild grew to become the main force behind the growth of the Rothschilds' wealth. He was sent by his father to Manchester to start a branch of the Rothschild empire in England.

By 1808 Nathan opened N M Rothschild & Sons and the business eventually became the largest financial powerhouse in London. It had so much influence, power, and money that Rothschild was able to supply enough coin to the Bank of England during the 1825 crisis.

This wasn't the only time England would need Rothschild's help. In 1815, Nathan was able to provide funds to General Wellington to fight the Battle of Waterloo. The battle was critical to London's financial success. If England were to lose, its bonds would become worthless. If England were to win, the bonds would rise in value. For investors it also was a make or break moment.

But this also proved a pivotal time in Nathan's climb to great wealth. You see, in earlier years, Nathan and his brothers had built up an underground intelligence network that supplied them with breaking news and information at a much faster pace than anyone else could achieve, including the government.

Nathan used this network to track events that were happening during the battle. But he also used that information to make a critical financial decision. With their money tied up in bonds, investors waited for word of whether General Wellington had prevailed in the battle. They weren't privy to Nathan's advance information network. They thought the odds were against Wellington.

A popular legend says that when Nathan walked into the London stock exchange, investors went into an immediate panic, assuming Rothschild would confirm their suspicions that Wellington had lost. Thinking the bonds were worthless, many started selling. Nathan began buying every English bond he could find. Later, to everyone's shock, it was announced that Wellington had indeed defeated Napoleon, and the value of the bonds rose again.

In one day, Nathan's wealth increased to levels most of us could never imagine. Reports suggest he grew the family wealth twentyfold that day.[10]

Rothschild became the biggest holder of England's debt. Nathan is quoted as saying, "I care not what puppet is placed on the throne of England to rule the Empire. The man who controls Britain's money supply controls the British Empire, and I control the British money supply."[11]

The Rothschild empire would expand beyond London to the United States. The Rothschild Bank of London would become one of the original member banks of the U.S. Federal Reserve, created by the Federal Reserve Act of 1913.

Tally Sticks Serve as Fiat Money System

Long before the Bank of England was created, the country was using a money system that was the forerunner of our modern fiat currency system.

In the Middle Ages, the tally stick system was used for counting and record keeping. A tally stick was nothing more than a piece of wood (sometimes bone) on which a single notch was cut to represent a transaction or number. Because so few people could read, a notch cut into a stick was the easiest way to visually represent a transaction.[12]

When King Henry I, son of William the Conqueror, took the throne of England in 1100 A.D., he reformed the tally stick as a method for paying taxes, which were due around Easter each year.

King Henry's sticks were made of polished hazel or willow wood, with the notches cut along one edge. The notches varied in size, equaling specific denominations. The tally stick was then split in half lengthwise, so each piece still had a record of the notch.

Splitting the sticks in half lengthwise prevented either party from adding more notches. After the tally stick was split, one half was given to the taxpayer as proof that taxes had been paid. The other half remained with the King's exchequer (tax collector).

Anytime the two parties wanted to verify the transaction, the two pieces of split wood were put back together, much like pieces of a puzzle. If the two halves fit together properly, both sides knew the tally stick was authentic.

But King Henry used the tally sticks for more than taxes. It didn't take him long to realize he could issue tally sticks in advance in order to finance England's own spending, particularly for wars to further expand his empire.

In other words, these newly created tally sticks, which represented future taxes due, could be used as a form of payment to the king's own creditors. In turn, the creditors could either collect the tax revenue directly from those who were assessed to pay taxes or use the same tally stick to pay their own taxes to the government.

The tally sticks could also be sold to other parties in exchange for gold or silver coin at a discount, which was calculated based on the length of time remaining until the tax payment was due.

The selling of future taxes due through the newly issued tally sticks created a huge market for government debt. No one questioned whether the debt could be paid. After all, this was the King of England and his word was all that was needed.

This kept the market for government debt strong, and in fact the system worked well for England for several years. But as we saw with Johan Palmstruch, power- and greed-driven systems eventually collapse.

That's exactly what happened with England's tally stick system when King Charles II became England's ruler. When he took the throne, his monetary powers were greatly reduced. King Charles had to ask Parliament for money, especially if he wanted to raise taxes. At the time, the country was still suffering the financial effects of the Dutch War.

Whenever Parliament granted him permission, he would then sell the tally sticks (the governments' future tax debt) at a discount to goldsmiths, who acted as bankers since they were already in the habit of issuing receipts for gold and other precious metals that were deposited in their vaults for safekeeping.

Since the tally sticks represented the king's obligation and were payable to the bearer, the goldsmiths could hold on to the tally sticks and present them for future payment. Or they could sell the sticks.

But King Charles grew tired of asking Parliament for permission to raise money.[13] So he bypassed Parliament altogether and started issuing tally sticks as he pleased. However, the more sticks he issued, the more he expanded England's debt.

In fact, it was this massive expansion that brought down King Charles II. Each time the king issued more tally sticks, the goldsmiths would only buy them if a larger discount were offered, which the king granted. Now caught in a vicious cycle, the king would further increase the number of tally sticks in circulation, and greater discounts were offered each time.

However, the future payments due per the number of new tally sticks sold soon exceeded the monarchy's tax revenues. England would soon be bankrupt.

Charles was forced to remedy the situation by declaring the debt illegal. He stopped payments on all tally sticks that were eligible for redemption. The tally sticks that now filled the goldsmiths' vaults were reduced to mere pieces of wood.

If only we could learn from these mistakes. Once again, we see that systems not backed by hard assets are susceptible to failure greater than their inventors could imagine. Yet these systems continue to be used. Look no further than the United States' current monetary system.

It is not much different from England's medieval tally stick system. Our currency is backed by nothing more than the word of our government. And yet the United States continues to increase the amount of money in circulation. Our national debt has grown to astronomical amounts. One wonders if our fiat currency is doomed to failure.

We can't say for sure what the outcome will be, as our fiat currency has only been around for 38 years.[14] But we can certainly use past failures as a guide, including Sweden's Palmstrucher's banknotes and England's tally sticks.

Yet these countries were not the only ones to experience great monetary failure. France, too, would soon find itself struggling from economic despair brought on by a failed monetary system.

France's National Debt Becomes a Bargaining Tool

Other central banks began to spring up throughout Europe. For example, the Banque de France was established by Napoleon on January 18, 1800, to stabilize the country's currency after the French Revolution.

The original statutes restricted the bank's scope of activities to the city of Paris. The statutes also did not give it protection from competition from similar establishments already in existence. Napoleon was trying to avoid the mistakes that occurred with the earlier banking system established by John Law.

John Law, son of a Scottish goldsmith, lived in various cities throughout Europe before settling in France. At age 14, John worked in his father's business. But Law had a keen interest in banking and economics and continually studied both subjects. In fact John developed a theory about money, which he wrote about in a text entitled *Money and Trade Considered with a Proposal for Supplying the Nation with Money*. Law is also credited for two other works, *Essay on a Land Bank* and *Money and Trade*.[15]

John believed that countries should create two separate types of institutions. One would be a bank for national finance. The other, a state company for commerce, would exclude all private banks. He believed this would create a monopoly on finance and trade, which would be run by the state. The profits the state made from these activities would then be used to pay off the national debt.

John also believed the main role of any government was to increase prosperity for its citizens. And the best way to achieve this goal was to increase the amount of money in circulation. Since gold and silver coins were in limited supplies anyway, Law theorized that larger amounts of paper money in circulation would increase commerce and thus make a country much wealthier.

John needed only a place to put his ideas on banking, economics, and monetary policies into practice. He turned to France, which had racked up a national debt amounting to three billion *livre* (the French currency at that time) from the Spanish War of Succession.[16] With King Louis XIV now beheaded, the new regency that stood in place of the king was willing to listen to John Law's ideas on how to reform France's monetary system.

In October 1715, John put before the Duke of Orléans his proposal on how the country could rebuild its wealth, using a new type of money system not seen before. The duke allowed John to put his theories into practice and granted him the privilege to start a private bank, Banque Générale Privée.

This new bank was allowed to issue paper money, which was backed by the French government's debt. This new paper money was also granted the status of legal tender. Up until this time, French citizens used gold or silver coins as well as copper and brass in their day-to-day financial activities.

Now of course, it stands to reason that the citizens of France were weary of this new form of paper money. So John encouraged the duke to mandate that any notes issued by the bank could be redeemed for gold and silver coins. The duke also agreed to make the new paper money acceptable for payment of taxes. Lastly, the duke also ordered that all public funds must be deposited in Banque Générale Privée.

But starting a bank was only part of John's plan. He was also granted a charter to create a company with the exclusive rights for trade and development in the Louisiana and Canadian territories France owned.

As part of its charter, the Mississippi Company would take over most of the financial functions for the French government in the new territories. In addition, the charter required John to bring 6,000 French citizens and 3,000 slaves to settle the new territory.[17]

The Mississippi Company was also allowed to issue shares in the company in exchange for a portion of France's debt. For many, this deal was simply too good to pass up. After all, the company was there to develop the land into French territories, not to mention the trade monopoly it enjoyed. Investors bought in. The Mississippi Company's share price skyrocketed. It was a resounding success. Of course, John Law became a very wealthy man.

In 1718, the two entities John had created, the Banque Générale Privée and the Mississippi Trading Company, were combined into one under the name Banque Royale. The duke bought out all the stockholders in the bank and made it an institution owned by the state. In return for his work on behalf of the new government, the duke of Orléans appointed John Law Controller-General of Finances.

The Bubble Caused by Banque Royale

The French government's interest in developing the Louisiana territories arose from previous expeditions it had sent to the New World. Those expeditions came back with reports of riches in this new land that equaled those of Mexico. Explorers claimed the region was abundant in silver and furs. They also claimed the land would be good for growing tobacco and other crops that were hugely popular with French citizens.

However, the reports were misleading. The new land was harsh and almost uninhabitable. But eager for the investors to buy shares of the newly formed Mississippi Company, John depicted life in the area as a new kind of Paris. Hearing the stories of mass amounts of silver and conditions similar to Paris, investors couldn't wait to buy shares in this new company.

The shares were originally issued at 150 livres but quickly rose to 10,000 livres in just a few short months. When the company issued a dividend in 1720, the share price rose to 18,000 livres.[18]

Since a 10 percent deposit was all that was needed to enter into this new market, people from all working classes were lining up to buy shares of the Mississippi Company. This was their chance to escape from poverty.

But as we know from other too good to be true, frenzy-driven speculations, things can end as abruptly and as suddenly as they began. And that's exactly what happened with the Mississippi Trading Company.

You see, a handful of keen investors realized that the stories of getting rich in the new territory were more exaggeration than actual truth. In 1720, two royal princes decided it was time to sell their shares in the Mississippi Company.

For many people who were anxiously awaiting the riches from their investment, this early selling of shares by the royal princes signaled something was wrong. An avalanche of investors began selling their shares of the Mississippi Company. Prices began spiraling downward.

The Mississippi Company had lost 97 percent of its market capitalization.[19]

Angry with what was happening and trying to save what little of their money was left, crowds mobbed the Banque Royal, demanding gold coins for their paper notes as had been promised to them. But Banque Royale did not have enough reserves of gold or silver coins on hand to match the notes it had issued.

Banque Royal had greatly overinflated the supply of banknotes in circulation. In other words, there were more notes in circulation than the bank could ever redeem for gold or silver.

In a desperate attempt to avoid an all-out collapse of the bank, John printed an additional 1,500,000 livres worth of paper notes. But it was too late. The notes were worthless and the public was outraged. Banque Royal had no choice but to declare bankruptcy.[20]

The crisis was so well known and widespread, this poem appeared in newspapers throughout Paris:

> My shares, which Monday I bought
> Were worth millions on Tuesday, I thought.
> So on Wednesday I chose my abode;
> In my carriage on Thursday I rode;
> To the ballroom on Friday I went;
> To the workhouse next day I was sent.[21]

John Law, the man behind the great paper note scheme, was forced to leave Paris forever. After the run on the Banque Royale, France threw away the paper-based currency system John Law had helped the country create. The French economy was in shambles.

However, similar to the 2008 credit crisis that crippled the world for months on end, this 1720 crisis reached far beyond the borders of France. People from all over Europe had invested money in the Mississippi Company, which represented the dream and promise of great fortune. Unfortunately, those promises couldn't be kept. Companies and private citizens alike lost money on the deal. Some were forced to declare bankruptcy.

Now, you could say these incidents are isolated to Europe, and that by the time the United States created its banking system, the imperfections would have been worked out. But you'll be surprised to learn that just a few weeks after George Washington signed legislation to create the Bank of the United States, a panic took hold that almost wreaked havoc on the already ailing economy.

Origins of the U.S. Banking System

The United States began its central banking system in the early nineteenth century with the formation of the Bank of the United States in 1790. The bank's first home was at Carpenters' Hall, where it rented space until it moved into its own building, erected between 1795 and 1797.

The bank was formed to help pay for the debt the country incurred fighting the Revolutionary War. But it was also needed because, as we saw with various European countries, the country was using several different forms of currency.

Alexander Hamilton, serving as George Washington's secretary of the Treasury, was the main proponent of creating a central bank to help create a standard form of currency for all states to use.

In 1790, Hamilton proposed the funding and charter of a national bank, which would be called the Bank of the United States and modeled to some extent after the Bank of England. The Bank of the United States would accept deposits, issue banknotes (as loans or to show proof of deposits), discount commercial paper, and make short-term loans to the government.

The size of the bank building alone would make it the nation's largest bank. It was approximately five times the size of the handful of other commercial banks that had already been established in America. There weren't many banks at the time, because Britain had used its authority to prevent the development of financial rivals in the colonies.

This new bank would also control the nation's money supply. Hamilton argued that the nation needed a federally chartered bank to attract foreign investment, serve as an administrative arm of the federal Treasury, and regulate the country's money supply.

Regulating the money supply was a critical issue. That's because at the time there were only three state chartered banks that could issue banknotes. But the notes were limited to local distribution and use.

The new bank would not only hold the nation's federal reserves, but would also use the funds to pay down the country's debt, which had risen considerably because of the war. The national debt was sitting at around $80 million. The Treasury was basically empty. By 1795 federal revenues were not enough to pay for government expenses.[22]

Hamilton also argued that the bank should be a source of capital for new businesses, which would help develop the nation's ailing economy. That meant the Bank of the United States would become a primary commercial lender.

However, not everyone agreed the country needed a central bank. When the legislation was presented before him, Thomas Jefferson, serving as secretary of state, voted against creating a central bank.

At the time, Jefferson was one of the richest men in America. Upon his father's death, he inherited 5,000 acres of land and several hundred slaves. Being a landowner, Jefferson wanted to build a national economy that relied on the "fruits and labor of the land."

Jefferson didn't agree with Hamilton's vision of a central bank, especially a bank that issued paper notes. Nor did Jefferson like the idea of ordinary citizens being able to borrow money. Jefferson was a smart man and realized borrowing money could lead to tremendous debt. He also knew how debt could destroy a man's wealth—and not just a man's wealth, but a country's as well.

In papers sent to President Washington, arguing against creating a central bank system, Jefferson wrote that the Constitution doesn't grant Congress the power to create a bank:

> The incorporation of a bank and the powers assumed [by legislation doing so] have not, in my opinion, been delegated to the United States by the Constitution. They are not among the powers specially enumerated.[23]

To his fellow congressmen, Jefferson wrote of many reasons why he couldn't back a central bank. For example, to John W. Eppes, a representative and senator from Virginia, Jefferson wrote,

> The trifling economy of paper, as a cheaper medium, or its convenience for transmission, weighs nothing in opposition to the advantages of the precious metals . . . it is liable to be abused, has been, is, and forever will be abused, in every country in which it is permitted. [24]

To Thomas Law, Jefferson wrote:

The idea of creating a national bank I do not concur in, because it seems now decided that Congress has not that power (although I sincerely wish they had it exclusively), and because I think there is already a vast redundancy rather than a scarcity of paper medium.[25]

To Albert Gallatin, a member of the House of Representatives, Jefferson wrote:

The Bank of the United States...is one of the most deadly hostility existing, against the principles and form of our Constitution....An institution like this, penetrating by its branches every part of the Union, acting by command and in phalanx, may, in a critical moment, upset the government.[26]

But Hamilton fired back, claiming Congress had the right to decide what means were necessary and proper. Washington sided with Hamilton.

On February 25, 1791, President George Washington signed the bill authorizing the nation's first national bank. The bank was funded with $10 million in start-up capital, which was financed by selling stock.

This was a huge amount of money, especially considering that the country's only three state-chartered banks had a total money supply of just $2 million. Of the $10 million, the federal government would own $2 million worth of shares, and own 20 percent of the board seats. This gave the U.S. government substantial control of the bank. Individual private investors would buy the remaining shares.[27]

The bank was granted a 20-year charter. The bank would have the right to issue notes or currency up to $10 million. Those notes could be used to pay taxes.[28]

Thomas Willing, former president of the Bank of North America, as well as mayor of Philadelphia, secretary to the congress of delegates at Albany, and a judge of the Supreme Court of Pennsylvania, was named the new bank's first president.

The new board met to hammer out rules and regulations. But they also quickly began selling the national debt in the form of U.S bonds, which were paying an interest rate of 6 percent.

As for private investors, shares (or *scripts*, as they were called back then) of the Bank of the United States were offered in very tightly structured payment system. Investors would have to come up with $25 in coin for the initial payment. They would then have to make an additional four payments, made up of coin and in the form of the newly created bonds.

Early investors wasted no time buying the newly issued shares of the Bank of the United States. The initial offering was priced at $25 a share. Within days the price skyrocketed to $300. It eventually settled at $150 a share.[29]

However, the country had never seen such an incredible rise and fall in share prices before. Investors began to worry and a slight panic managed to work its way into the market. Hamilton wrote to Rufus King, director of the Bank of New York and a fellow senator, that a bubble was developing in conjunction with his new central bank funding system.[30]

To prevent an economic collapse, Hamilton immediately authorized $150,000 worth in purchases of the U.S. debt. He was openly signaling to the public and investors that the United States fully backed the bond market.

This calmed investors' fears and the markets settled nicely. But unfortunately, another panic would set the market off yet again. This time, it would be at the hands of a very influential businessman and market manipulator.

The First Bank Bubble

William Duer was born in England in 1743 and came to America at the age of 30. Duer was a member of the Continental Congress and a signer of the Articles of Confederation. He also held a position on the board of the Treasury, to which his friend Alexander Hamilton had appointed him.

Duer had already made himself quite a fortune supplying the royal navy with masts for their ships. While living in New York, he purchased a tract of timberland above Saratoga, on the Hudson, known as Fort Miller. On a return visit to his native country, Duer secured a contract with the Royal Navy to make masts for its ships. After he purchased the land near Fort Miller, he then erected a sawmill and began producing the masts.

But this was not his only source of income. Duer had already gained a reputation among businessmen as a speculator in land, stocks, and international trade.

By 1791, Duer had resigned his Treasury position and entered into a partnership with Alexander Macomb, one of New York's richest and most prominent citizens. Macomb, like Duer, made most of his fortune speculating on land and other types of commodities and assets.

The two agreed to combine Macomb's money and Duer's insider connections with the Treasury Department to make a fast fortune. It is said that while serving at the Treasury, Duer did not hide his deals or intentions of making money in almost any manner possible.

In fact, some claim that Duer would purposely leak news stories about companies he was investing in to the press in order to make the share prices rise. These claims are probably true. Wealthy businessmen ruled the country. As you'll see in Chapter 15, the Continental Congress was made up of landowners, businessmen, and rich merchants who were dubbed demigods.

There were no regulatory agencies to monitor their actions. They had absolute freedom to conduct business in any way they saw fit. This is why Duer could leak stories to the press.

Acting on rumors that the Bank of New York was to be bought out by the Bank of the United States, Duer began buying shares in the bank, certain that the price would rise. But being a trader already familiar with hedging techniques, while at the same time buying shares in the Bank of New York in hopes of the stock rising, Duer was also betting the stock would go down.

Using funds in his own private account, Duer was shorting the stock. If the buyout didn't take place as rumors suggested, Duer and Macomb's combined account would lose, but Duer would come out a winner in his private account.

The two men's interest in buying shares in the Bank of New York set off bank mania. More rumors began circulating about other bank mergers.

Duer was hooked on speculation and the fortunes it could bring him. With so much interest in bank mergers on the part of investors far and wide, Duer began to buy additional bank securities on contract, with a promise to pay within two weeks. Duer was positive the securities would rise and the money he had committed on contract could easily be repaid.

If prices had risen as Duer anticipated, he probably would have become the richest man in America. But there's never any certainty in the markets. The bank merger didn't take place. Stock prices began a rapid downward spiral. Duer couldn't repay the money he had borrowed to purchase the additional securities. Duer's debt problem was self-inflicted and one that would prove difficult to resolve. As share prices continued to fall, the people he had borrowed money from lined up to collect what was owed to them.

Duer was arrested on March 23, 1792, and sent to debtors prison. Because Duer had created an arbitrary bull market in bank stocks, the news of his arrest set off a panic on Wall Street. The loss was estimated at $3,000,000, and impoverished many in all classes.[31]

Concerning the crisis, Alexander Hamilton wrote to Thomas Randolph, "At length our paper bubble is burst. The failure of Duer soon brought on others and these still more, like ninepins knocking one another down, till at that place the bankruptcy is become general."[32]

As he had done previously to calm the markets concerning the dramatic rise of the share price of the newly created Bank of the United States and purchased bonds, Hamilton did so again immediately following this most recent panic in order to restore confidence in the markets.

This temporarily calmed the markets. But after a brief rally, prices fell. Hamilton bought an additional $50,000 worth of Treasury securities, pledging $100,000 more if necessary. This worked, and by late April, investors who had fled the market were now back in, buying shares.

Duer remained in debtor's prison until his death on May 7, 1799. Duer was never able to pay off his debts. As the markets recovered, few people ever mentioned his name again. Although he was banished from memory, speculation in the markets remained.

It would become a method of choice not just for individual investors but for Wall Street institutions as well. One of the biggest and most well-known institutions is Goldman Sachs. As you'll see later in this book, Goldman not only created speculative and extremely risky mortgage-backed securities, it also betted against their demise while touting them as recommended buys to other institutions.

That's why on April 15, 2010, the SEC charged Goldman Sachs with securities fraud. The SEC says Goldman failed to disclose to investors a "conflict of interest" in subprime investments that it sold as the housing market was collapsing.

Naturally, Goldman denies the charges. The firm says the SEC charges are completely unfounded. Based on the research we've uncovered for this book, Goldman appears to have a history of borderline fraudulent schemes. That's why we call Goldman the "dirtiest barbarian of all."

Chapter 6

Race to the Bottom Line

I n the television show *I Love Lucy*, Desi Arnaz would often say to his wife, "Lucy, we've got a problem." Well, we've got a problem right here in the United States—a big bank problem.

In the United States, the Federal Deposit Insurance Corporation (FDIC) insures deposits at 8,124 banks and savings associations with $13.1 trillion in assets, which includes $9 trillion in customer bank deposits.[1]

The biggest banks in the United States are:

- Bank of America
- JPMorgan Chase Bank
- Wachovia Bank
- Citibank
- Washington Mutual Bank
- SunTrust Bank
- U.S. Bank
- Regions Bank

- Branch Banking and Trust Company
- National City Bank
- HSBC Bank USA
- World Savings Banks, FSB
- Countrywide Bank
- PNC Bank
- Keybank
- ING Bank, FSB
- Merrill Lynch Bank USA
- Sovereign Bank
- Comerica Bank
- Union Bank of California

Many of these institutions were considered too big too fail. However, according to (FDIC) statistics, 25 banks failed in 2008. That's more bank failures in a single year than through the previous seven years. But the problem got worse the very next year—five times worse: In 2009, there were 140 bank failures. The biggest bank failure was Washington Mutual (WaMu) in 2008 with a staggering $300 billion in assets.[2]

Although that failure rate is alarming, more banks failed during the Great Depression. Between 1929 and 1933, roughly 9,400 banks failed. The FDIC says bank failures during that time resulted in losses to depositors of about $1.3 billion.

The problem was so bad that President Roosevelt was forced to close all U.S. banks to prevent any further runs on banks.[3] Figure 6.1 shows the dramatic number of bank failures during times of economic crisis.

A bank is closed or considered to be in default when it is unable to meet its obligations to depositors and others. When a bank fails, the FDIC seizes the bank's assets and then operates the bank for a short time as a federal bank as it attempts to sell it to a stronger bank. The FDIC reimburses customer deposits from its Deposit Insurance Fund (DIF).

The DIF is financed by the insurance premiums paid by member banks. At the end of 2007, the amount of money held in the DIF was around $52.4 billion. However, with the dramatic increase in bank

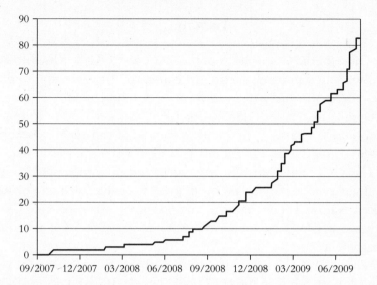

Figure 6.1 U.S. Bank Failures During Financial Market Crises
SOURCE: Economicreason.com.

failures, by the end of 2009, the FDIC fund moved into the red, ending up with a deficit of $20.9 billion.

But if you think that's bad, then consider that over the next four years, the bank failures triggered by the financial crisis are expected to cost the FDIC $100 billion.[4]

Now one way the FDIC could raise money to cover this deficit is by asking some of the institutions to prepay their insurance premiums for the next three years. The FDIC estimates doing this would net the agency about $45 billion. Unfortunately, that's not enough money to cover the expected losses. So the agency will have no choice but to get the money it needs from the government.

The government knows the FDIC is short on funds. That's why, in 2009, Congress approved a bill that would allow the FDIC to borrow the money it needs from the U.S. Treasury to cover the losses.

Now in general, banks have a greater tendency to fail during an economic crisis than at any other time. But the current situation deserves further examination to determine what is the root cause of the problem.

Mismanaged

The Office of the Comptroller of the Currency (OCC), which charters, regulates, and supervises all national banks, did an interesting study on bank failures that had happened from 1979 through 1989.

During that time 1,956 banks failed. That was also during the savings and loan crisis, with the peak number of bank failures occurring in 1989 coming in at 534 failures.[5]

The OCC found that "management-driven weaknesses" played a significant role in the decline of 90 percent of the failed and problem banks it evaluated. The two main internal problems noted were "overly aggressive activity" and "uninformed or inattentive board of directors or management."[6]

What the OCC is telling us is that those banks failed because managers assumed more risk than the bank could handle. If we take a quick look back in time, we see that during the Great Depression, banks failed because they got caught up in speculative securities trading, which is another way of saying that banks took on more risk than they could handle.

In its review of bank failures, the Congressional Budget Office (CBO) wrote:

> Although many of the problems that beset banks were externally induced, the primary responsibility for bank failures rests squarely on the shoulders of bank managers and boards of directors. This responsibility does not negate ineffective regulation or unforeseen economic developments as causes of failure, but the bank manager is the agent who reacts to economic conditions and the regulatory environment.
>
> Some managers made mistakes because they reacted incorrectly to a barrage of unusual factors. In some cases, managers simply failed to diversify asset portfolios, and boards of directors did not insist on reasonable loan practices.
>
> Managers of failed banks often pursued aggressive loan policies without reasonable precautions against default. As a result, many bank managers who failed to deal effectively with increased competition and adverse economic shocks presided over the demise of their institutions.[7]

The FDIC concurred with the CBO. It also suggested the staggering number of losses came about because at the time, banks frequently assumed more risk than they were capable of handling.

In the bank failure review reports written by the OCC, CBO, and FDIC, all three agencies came to the same conclusion: assuming too much risk. But what about the most recent bank failures?

In its fourth quarter *SRC Insights* review, the Federal Reserve Bank of Philadelphia suggests that bank management practices and aggressive risk tolerance are "again called into question."[8]

In its review, the Federal Reserve Bank of Philadelphia found that "common factors in recent failures reveal that management deficiencies and ineffective board oversight were noted in the majority of material loss reviews."

One area in particular highlighted in this report is commercial real estate (CRE). In reviewing the losses, the report states that in institutions that failed through the third quarter of 2009, the average CRE concentration, measured as a percentage of total risk-based capital, was well above the supervisory criteria defined in the 2006 interagency CRE guidance.

Just like what happened on Wall Street, banks became obsessed with increasing their bottom lines. In that obsession, they abandoned risk management policies and procedures in pursuit of the almighty dollar.

Now, many experts suggest that loose risk policies can't be solely attributed to the dramatic number of bank failures during the savings and loan (S&L) crisis. Some critics say Regulation Q had a profound impact on the industry.

Regulation Q

During the Great Depression, lawmakers thought they could improve the country's economic growth if they forced companies to invest their money in areas that would have a greater impact on the overall economy, such as new manufacturing plants and equipment.

Lawmakers were also interested in limiting excessive rate competition for deposits by banks. They felt that more competition among banks, based on interest rates, would provide banks with too much capital that they could then use to invest in risky loans. So lawmakers developed a variety of laws that would make it more attractive to use the funds in ways that would spur economic growth.

One of those laws was Regulation Q, which put a ceiling on the interest rate banks could pay on savings and commercial checking accounts. The law was meant mostly for retail banks but in the early 1960s, Regulation Q was amended to include savings and loan institutions.

But a clever banker found a way around this regulation. In the early 1970s, Bruce Bent, president of the Reserve Fund, Inc., introduced the first money market fund to the public.

Under Regulation Q, banks couldn't pay interest on checking accounts, but they could pay higher rates of interest on money market funds because the regulation didn't apply. Money market funds were a huge hit with the public.

Americans were more than eager for a product that paid a higher interest rate than the one set by Regulation Q. Bent's fund took off. He started the fund with just $300,000 in assets in 1972, and within three years, the fund had grown to $390 million in assets.[9]

We can't talk about Regulation Q without examining the savings and loan industry. At the time, savings and loans were the primary place people tucked their money away in a savings account. But they were also the main lenders for home mortgages. As a side note, at the time, 30-year fixed-rate mortgages were the norm. Adjustable rate mortgages didn't exist.

Basically, if a savings and loan made a 30-year mortgage loan in the 1960s, by the 1980s, the outstanding balance on those loans was still on their books. That's because the money was lent out over a 30-year period.

So how did savings and loans make money if they had to carry a loan for 30 years? It was all about the *spread*—the difference between the interest rate a bank paid on money it borrowed, either from the government or from other banks (short-term rates), and the (higher) rate it charged its customers who borrowed money.

However, if inflation kicked in above the amount of the interest rate on the loan, the savings and loan would lose money. If short-term interest rates moved sharply higher, the value of the long-term assets (their mortgage portfolios) would then drop.

But when it came to individual savings accounts, savings and loans faced a problem with Regulation Q. That's because the interest rate the government was paying on Treasury bills was as much as 15 percent.

So anyone who had their money in an account at a savings and loan, which was capped at 5.25 percent by Regulation Q, could pull their money out and buy Treasury bills paying a much higher rate of interest. And people did exactly that.

But this put the savings and loan institutions into deep trouble. They couldn't raise the interest rate on savings accounts, and therefore couldn't attract more customers to deposit money. And those deposits were essential, representing money they could turn around and lend to out to other banks.

This dramatic decline in money on deposit at savings and loans eventually caused the industry to collapse. In 1981 and 1982 combined, the S&L industry collectively reported almost $9 billion in losses.[10]

By 1986, 441 savings and loan institutions with $113 billion in assets had failed.[11] Another 533 institutions had roughly $453 billion in assets with only 2 percent of total capital reserves on hand.

Between 1989 and 1992, the federal government bailed out hundreds of insolvent savings and loans, costing taxpayers millions of dollars. Some experts say that roughly 1,000 savings and loan institutions failed.[12]

What's worse is they couldn't turn to the Federal Savings and Loan Insurance Corporation (FSLIC), the equivalent of the FDIC, because it didn't have enough funds to cover the losses. The FSLIC became insolvent. The crisis resulted in losses of $150 billion.[13]

Take a look at Figure 6.2, which shows the huge losses suffered during the savings and loans crisis.

There's no question, the United States has had a history of a tremendous number of bank failures. And what's odd is the problem seems to be restricted to the United States.

Consider that during the Great Depression, the number of bank failures in Canada was zero. Were they just lucky? Probably not. Canada has had bank failures but not as many as the United States. For example, the number of bank failures in Canada during the 1980s savings and loans crisis was two. And the bank failures in Canada during the recession of 2007: zero.[14] In fact, the *Financial Times* calls Canada's banks "the envy of the world."[15]

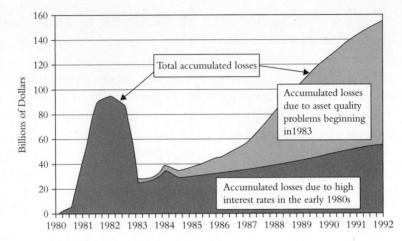

Figure 6.2   The Huge Losses Caused by the Savings and Loan Crisis

SOURCES: Library of Economics and Liberty, "Savings and Loan Crisis," www.econlib.org/library/Enc/SavingsandLoanCrisis.html.

European countries have also had bank failures, but again, not as many as the United States has experienced. In 1931, Austria experienced the failure of Creditanstalt Bank while France experienced the failure of Banque Nationale de Credit.

The *Business Pundit* compiled a list of the 25 biggest bank failures on record:

- New Frontier Bank, Greeley, Connecticut, with $670 million in assets.
- The Bank of Credit and Commerce International, Karachi, Pakistan, with $20 billion in assets.
- Integrity Bank, Alpharetta, Georgia, with $350 million in assets.
- Herstatt Bank, Germany, with $33.4 billion in assets.
- The Hokkaido Takushoku Bank, Ltd., Japan, with $33 billion in assets.
- Southeast Bank of Miami, Miami, Florida, with $200 million in assets.
- New York's Bank of the United States, New York, with $200 million in assets.
- Franklin Square National Bank, Long Island, New York, with $63 million in losses.

- Home Bank of Canada, Canada, with $140 million in assets.
- The Creditanstalt, Vienna, Austria, with assets of $181.4 billion.
- Bright Banc Savings Association, Texas, with $5 billion in assets.
- Long-Term Credit Bank of Japan, with $19 billion in assets.
- Goldome, New York, with $9.9 billion in assets.
- Silverado Savings and Loan, Texas, with $5 billion in assets.
- Gibraltar Savings, Beverly Hills, California, $13.4 billion in assets.
- Northern Rock, UK, with $200 billion in assets.
- Sachsen LB, Germany, with $567 billion in assets.
- Net Bank, Atlanta, Georgia, $2.5 billion in assets.
- MCorp, Texas, with $2.8 in assets.
- Bank of New England, New England, with $21.8 billion in assets.
- American Savings and Loans, Stockton, California, with $107.5 million in assets.
- First Republic of Texas, Texas, with $33.4 billion in assets.
- Continental Illinois National Bank and Trust, Illinois, with $40 billion in assets.
- Washington Mutual, United States (assets not listed in report).
- IndyMac, Los Angeles, California, with $30 billion in assets.[16]

Of this list, the United States has 16 of the worst bank failures in history. But not only have we had a history of bank failures, we also have a long history of bank bubbles and panics, starting with the Panic of 1819.

Panic of 1819

The Panic of 1819 was deep and far reaching. At the time, it was the first major crisis the country faced. Unemployment skyrocketed, banks failed, mortgages were foreclosed, and agricultural prices fell by half.

What caused this economic collapse? Most experts say many reasons, but the one cited most often is irresponsible banking practices. Doesn't that sound eerily similar to modern-day bank failures?

Let's take a more detailed look at what happened. At the time, the federal government had borrowed large amounts of money to finance the War of 1812. Since there was no national bank, as the First Bank of the United States' charter had expired in 1811, the government had to borrow the money from various state banks.

These banks were allowed to use their own currency, and in most instances, the currency they issued was not backed by gold or silver coins. In addition, currency speculators were hoarding gold or silver. Since there were no restrictions in place, more banks popped up, which meant more paper currency in circulation. More paper currency in circulation naturally led to higher rates of inflation.

At the same time, domestic manufacturing grew. Rapid expansion and rising inflation triggered higher prices in goods.

Something needed to be done. So politicians granted a charter to the Second Bank of the United States in 1816. The bank was patterned after the First Bank of the United States and established branches throughout the Union.

But instead of curtailing the activities of the many banks that existed in the country at the time, the new central bank encouraged the banks to continue what they were doing because it meant higher government revenues.

However, just two years later, the Second Bank of the United States realized that inflation was rising too high and the money supply far exceeded the coins available for redemption. So it called in many of its outstanding loans and began reducing the money supply.

Many state banks could not repay their loans, and as a result they failed. The central bank also stopped issuing new loans. This created a large-scale panic. Bank runs ensued. Depositors rushed to banks to have their notes converted to coin, but it was too late.

The country was now in a severe recession. The South suffered because its economy was mostly agricultural-based. Commodity prices fell. In turn, the South decreased the supply of manufactured goods it was purchasing from the North, which had established itself as a manufacturing-based economy.

State-chartered banks rallied back against the Second Bank of the United States and wanted their states to impose restrictions on the bank's operations. In fact, the state of Maryland went so far as to impose a tax on the bank's operations. However, James McCulloch, the cashier for the Baltimore branch of the Second Bank of the United States, refused to pay the taxes.

Neither side was willing to budge. So the case was presented before the Supreme Court in *McCulloch v. Maryland*. Maryland's argument was that the federal government did not have the authority to establish a bank, because that power was not delegated to it in the Constitution.

In Chapter 5, we learned that when Alexander Hamilton faced opposition for the First Bank of the United States, he argued that Congress had the powers to do what was needed, except such powers as were specifically *denied* it in the Constitution. President Washington had sided with Hamilton and the bank was formed.

Maryland lost its case. According to the Court, the chartering of a bank was a power implied from the power over federal fiscal operations. In the Supreme Court's decision, Supreme Court Chief Justice John Marshall declared that the tax imposed by the State of Maryland against the Second Bank of the United States was unconstitutional.

The Panic of 1819 was the first of several major economic downturns in the beginning years of the United States. Another notable panic was that of 1837.

The Panic of 1837

In the years 1830 to 1835, the country was thriving. It was a time of rapid expansion of wealth. The population had grown from about 10 million people in 1821 to 16 million in 1837.[17]

But as we know, periods of rapid expansion also give rise to heavy, often negligent speculation. Heavy speculation leads to more risk taking, often more than people and companies can properly manage. Such was the case during the 1830s. Amazingly similar to the way heavy housing speculation was a factor in the recession of 2007, land speculation triggered the Panic of 1837.

Leading up to the panic, bank credit was rampant. Previously, when a merchant needed credit, he got it directly from the person or company he was doing business with. But as the economy grew, merchants stopped relying on merchant credit and instead used the credit they received from banks for their regular business activities. From January 1834 to January 1836, banking capital rose to $251,000,000.[18]

But it wasn't just merchants using this new, easy source of credit. Private citizens were using credit to buy land in the western states. In fact the federal government had encouraged private citizens to buy land by selling millions of acres of public land in western states like Michigan and Missouri.

You see, at the time, state governments were spending money developing railroads and canals to support a growing population in these areas.

Illinois went from a population of 60,000 to 400,000. Indiana grew from 170,000 to 600,000. Ohio saw growth from 600,000 to 1,400,000. The new infrastructure systems being built would make it easier for those areas to be settled.[19]

Investors and speculators buying land in these areas did so with the anticipation of these regions becoming popular places to live. The price of public land was fixed by law at $1.25 an acre and was open to any purchaser.

This meant private citizens could buy land from the government, then divide it up into parcels that would quickly increase in value, as the new transportation systems being built would bring a huge population of settlers to the once isolated areas.[20]

Government land sales skyrocketed, which in turn created a massive land speculation bubble. From 1820 to 1829, annual government land sales had averaged less than $1.3 million. However, by 1830 land sales exceeded $2.3 million, and sales continued to explode.

In 1831, land sales skyrocketed to $3.2 million and continued to increase dramatically over the next four years. In 1835, government land sales rose to $14,757,600, and in 1836 they touched $24,877,179. Land sales were now 10 times greater than they had been five years earlier.[21]

Inflation was also becoming quite noticeable. Along with a sharp increase in credit, banks were also issuing their own currency. In 1830, total banknote circulation was equivalent to $61 million. By 1837, it jumped to $149 million. So much available paper money led to a higher inflation rate. Land prices began to creep up.

In 1836, President Andrew Jackson and his administration decided the best way to slow down the growing land and credit frenzy was to issue an executive order known as the Specie Circular, which required that payment for the purchase of land be made exclusively in gold or silver.

However, many banks didn't have enough gold or silver reserves on hand. Since there weren't enough coin reserves on hand for people to pay for the land, and paper money could no longer be used, the Specie Circular caused a dramatic decline in land purchases. Land sales dropped to one-quarter of the previous year.

By 1837, banks had stopped gold and silver coin redemption for paper money. With no coin to back it, paper currency lost its value, triggering a nationwide panic.

Out of 850 banks in the United States, 343 closed entirely. With tighter credit and no gold or silver coins available, many states that had invested heavily in canals and railroads were forced into bankruptcy. Hundreds of banks and businesses failed. Thousands of people lost their lands.[22]

Henry Clay, who previously served as secretary of state under John Adams, blamed the economic troubles directly on Jackson's Specie Circular order. Clay had been against the order from the onset.

On January 11, 1837, speaking before members of Congress, Clay predicted the Specie Circular would cause a general panic throughout the country if the administration's actions were not reversed.

Clay told Congress that the circular would place such value on gold and silver coins that people would hoard them and the coins would disappear from circulation altogether. He couldn't have been more right.

By the time Martin Van Buren took office, a full-fledged recession gripped the entire country, which would last roughly five years. On the eve of his inauguration, workers in New York protested high food and fuel prices. Congress passed a federal bankruptcy law removing about $450 million in debt from a million creditors.[23]

The factors that contributed to the Panic of 1837, including massive real estate speculation and rampant credit, are also factors that contributed to the recession of 2007.

But we can't talk about the recession of 2007 without mentioning the role Wall Street played. As you'll see in later chapters of this book, credit derivatives and mortgage-backed securities were investments invented by Wall Street.

The risks associated with those securities were all but ignored. Goldman Sachs, one of the creators of the securities, was well aware of the risk while at the same time recommending them to other institutions.

Goldman, recognizing that mortgage-backed securities could easily go down in flames, was shorting them in anticipation of a downturn in value, which is exactly what happened. Goldman wasn't alone. J.P. Morgan and Citigroup were also heavy into mortgage-backed securities.

We'll dive into those securities in other chapters. For now, let's take a look at one other important economic crisis that hit our country.

The Panic of 1893

The Panic of 1893 was a nationwide economic crisis set off by two of the country's largest employers: the Philadelphia and Reading Railroad Company and the National Cordage Company.

But we can also blame the panic on the government, which in 1890 established the Sherman Silver Purchase Act, named after Senator John Sherman of Ohio, which required the Secretary of the Treasury to purchase 4.5 million ounces of silver each month.[24] Unfortunately, this act assigned a value to silver that was far greater than what public markets paid.

Most of the silver was being mined from western states, and some people saw the act as being in favor of miners and against farmers in the south. Some suggested the act was a step toward abandoning a gold standard.

While there was no formal gold standard, gold had been accepted as the normal means of redemption of paper notes. We must also consider that the Treasury had been stockpiling gold, which perpetuated the sense of a gold standard.

By April 1892, a growing depression in Europe resulted in British investors selling their American investments and redeeming them for gold. This continued for several months and by April 1893, the secretary of the Treasury reported that the nation's gold reserves had dipped below their traditionally acceptable level of $100 million. This created a nationwide distrust of the Treasury.

Depositors withdrew their money from banks. People were rushing to redeem their paper money for gold and silver coins. They were also weary of the government's inability to balance specie reserves for paper money.

A panic began to take hold. That panic reached fever pitch when two of the country's most heavily traded companies filed for bankruptcy. It shocked investors because both were considered too big to fail.

Amazingly, 117 years later, companies such as Lehman Brothers, Bear Stearns, Merrill Lynch, and AIG were also considered too big to fail. But fail they did. And they received bailout money from the government or were bought out by those who received funds.

Prior to the Panic of 1893, money had flowed freely into the construction of railroads. Lines were being actively built in the South, Southwest, and Northwest. Lines such as the Atchison, Topeka, Santa Fe, and Missouri Pacific were expanding rapidly.

From 1883 to 1890, over 39,000 miles of line were laid. The amount of money required to finance those lines is estimated to be around $780 million.

As you might suspect, the iron and steel industry was expanding in step with the building of the rail lines. The country was shifting from an agricultural base to an industrial one. The U.S. Census of 1890 found that the majority of Americans no longer lived or worked on farms. They were migrating to cities. As populations grew in these new areas where rail lines were being built, bank credit was steadily extended.

Just as tech stocks were the all the rage in the 1980s, so were railroad companies in the late 1800s. The New York Stock Exchange exploded, with new shares issued increasing by as much as 900 percent. In 1892, record volumes were set on the New York Stock Exchange with the announcement that the Philadelphia and Reading (P&R) Railway would lease the New York Central and Lehigh Valley railroads.

The P&R was constructed to haul coal from the mines in northeastern Pennsylvania's coal region. The *coal region* is a term used to refer to an area of northeastern Pennsylvania in the central Appalachian Mountains comprising Lackawanna, Luzerne, Columbia, Carbon, Schuylkill, and Northumberland Counties, and the extreme northeast corner of Dauphin county: Philadelphia. According to one source, "Almost immediately the company was profitable as coal replaced wood burned in stoves and furnaces to keep homes warm. The company expanded its rail lines reaching up to New York City. By 1891, the company was the largest in the world, valued at $170 million."[25]

But their fortunes wouldn't last long. On February 20, 1893, with capital worth $40 million and debt equaling more than $125 million, the company filed for bankruptcy. How could this have happened to one of America's most favored stocks?

It was nothing more than a rampant bubble in railroad building. Railroads were overbuilt. Companies were eager to buy one another out in a race to be the biggest and richest rail company. They raised money for the projects by issuing shares and bonds to the public.

But the boom in railroads was based mostly on speculation. Many railroads borrowed heavily to make costly improvements. Their attempts at quick expansion cut into revenues. Their profits dwindled and ultimately the companies were unable to pay their debts.

But unlike General Motors and Chrysler, there would be no bailout from the government, no taxpayer money to help them rebuild. They would have to make it on their own.

Another highly favored and heavily traded company was the National Cordage Company, a rope mill owned by J. M. Waterbury. In those days, ropes were made by hand. The strands were spun and twisted by a wheel and spindle, which was turned by a plant worker. During this time the annual production of cordage mills in the United States was about 120,000 tons valued at $24 million.[26]

The National Cordage Company was capitalized with 15,000 shares that sold at a par value of $100 each. Shares of the company were the most actively traded stock at the time.[27]

Because it operated as a trust, it controlled 90 percent of the market. Trusts were just beginning their reign in corporate America. One of the first and largest trusts was the Standard Oil Company, created by John D. Rockefeller. The trust comprised major oil refineries in Cleveland, Pittsburgh, Philadelphia, and New York. Just as Standard Oil controlled the oil market, the National Cordage Company dominated the market for raw materials and machinery necessary to produce the rope.

Fantasies of unlimited wealth filled the heads of the National Cordage Company's board of directors. Acting much like the Wall Street barbarians of the twenty-first century, the board created fictitious earnings reports to drive up the mania surrounding the company's shares.

As competition moved in, the company struggled to maintain its position. In January, the company's stock was selling for $147 a share. However by May, the stock had plunged to $10 a share.

On May 5, 1893, the National Cordage Company, with $20 million in capital and $10 million in liabilities, filed for bankruptcy. The company was so strapped for cash it could not repay a $50,000 loan it took out to buy stock.[28]

The bankruptcy of the Philadelphia and Reading Railway, followed closely by that of the National Cordage Company, touched off a Wall Street selling panic known as Industrial Black Friday. Banks everywhere began frantically calling in loans, and western and southern banks withdrew substantial deposits from New York–centered banks.

Seven weeks later the price of silver fell to 77 cents an ounce, down from 92.2 cents just a week before. An American silver dollar was now worth a measly 58 cents. Many of the western silver mines closed, and a large number were never reopened.[29]

By May 15, stock prices reached an all-time low. Many major firms, such as the Union Pacific, Northern Pacific, and Santa Fe railroads, were forced to declare bankruptcy. In total, some 50 railroads went under. The railroad companies owned roughly 27,000 lines of track. Since the railroad companies touched other major industries, businesses far and wide began failing. More than 30 steel companies collapsed because of the railroad failures.

Unemployment steadily grew, rising from 1 million in August 1893 to 2 million by January 1894. By the middle of that year, the figure had reached 3 million. Over the course of this depression, 15,000 businesses, 600 banks, and 74 railroads failed.

The severe unemployment led to wide-scale protesting, which in some cases became very violent. Some companies were forced to pay their workers with IOUs. Commodity prices declined dramatically.[30]

In *The Robber Barons*, Matthew Josephson described the financial crisis as a "rich men's panic."[31] It was an era where men like Cornelius Vanderbilt made their fortunes.

By the middle of 1897, signs began indicating that the economy was stabilizing. In fact, between 1897 and 1923, the country once again experienced overall prosperity. New sources of power pushed industrial expansion again.

Agriculture also experienced improvements because of the use of the internal combustion tractor and other types of mechanized farm equipment. Between 1910 and 1920, gross farm income rose from $7.4 billion to $15.9 billion, and the value of farm property shot up 400 percent.[32]

Large corporations and consolidations dominated the business landscape. By 1904 there were 236 giant industrial corporations with total capital of more than $6 billion.[33]

The United States officially went on the gold standard in 1900. New discoveries and increased mining expanded the gold supply, allowing the government to issue more banknotes.

In 1903 the United States encouraged Panama to separate from Columbia and form a new republic. Then, under a treaty signed late in the same year, the United States was given the right to build and control a canal through Panama.

Overall, the national economy boomed during World War I (1914–1918). It seemed as if the country had reached a period of everlasting prosperity. The mood of the general public was one of optimism and confidence in the U.S. economy. Most people believed that national prosperity would continue indefinitely.

For five years prior to 1929, rising prices typified the stock market. During this period, investors enjoyed an enormous bull market. Companies such as Merrill Lynch were reaping the benefits of the decade's prolonged economic boom.

In his 1928 acceptance speech for the Republican Party nomination for the presidency, Herbert Hoover said, "We in America today are nearer to the final triumph over poverty than ever before in the history of any land. The poorhouse is vanishing from among us."[34]

However, by September 1929, stock prices began to fluctuate. Unfortunately, most market analysts dismissed this as temporary. But the warning signs were there. In a matter of months the country would fall victim to one of the deepest depressions to date.

And the warning signs were before the American public in 2007. In fact, had any institution or government agency questioned the $377 million single-day loss of Merrill Lynch in 1987, which was caused by speculative trading in mortgage-backed securities, perhaps the recession of 2007 might not have happened.[35]

In the end the barbarians prevailed. The lessons that should have been learned in 1987 were quietly ignored. Once again the country would find itself struggling to survive. Retirement dreams would be lost, quite possibly forever.

Chapter 7

Say Goodbye to Gold

D elicately displayed in Turin, Italy, at the Turin Museum, is an Egyptian treasure map made of frail papyrus paper. The map is known as *Carte des mines d'or* and can be traced as far back as 1320 B.C. The map is filled with hand-drawn pictures of gold mines, miners' quarters, and roads leading to mountains filled with gold. It is the oldest known geographical map in the world.[1]

Gold has always held value to us as a society, even before it was used for money. Early cultures associated gold with gods. Incas refer to gold as "tears of the sun." King Tutankhamen's inner coffin is made of pure gold. When Howard Carter, the archaeologist who discovered the king's tomb, weighed the coffin, it tipped the scales at 110.4 kilograms (about 240 pounds). Its value would be roughly US$1.7 million.

King Croesus of Lydia (what is now Turkey) minted the first gold coin around 550 B.C. Gold was used as money in ancient Greece. Even Plato and Aristotle wrote about gold. The Romans mined gold extensively. They created waterwheels and ore systems to separate gold from rock and water.

Gold was the ransom coveted by Attila the Hun. Attila made the Romans pay him $387.2 million worth of gold. Charlemagne provided churches with gold to finance the building of monasteries and great houses of worship including the Church of Saint James in France.

In the Middle Ages, gold was used mostly for jewelry and plates, although some coins were made of the metal. Because of its unique composition, gold could be easily melted and formed into jewelry and coins. The craftsmen who formed the gold into jewelry were called *goldsmiths*. Those who turned gold into coin were called *moneyers*.[2] When their work was completed, wardens appointed from the London Goldsmith Company inspected it for purity of gold used.

As more gold was used for jewelry, statues, plates, even coins, people found it difficult to store their precious items made of gold in their homes. So they turned to the goldsmiths for help. Goldsmiths had already developed storage areas for the gold they used for their creations, so it only made sense to ask the goldsmiths to warehouse their golden treasures. The goldsmiths acknowledged the gold they took in by issuing receipts. Eventually the receipts became a form of money. Those who owned items made of gold or gold itself no longer had to pull the gold out of storage. Now they could simply pay for their purchases with their newly issued receipts. Whoever was paid with such receipt could then go to the goldsmith and redeem it for the appropriate amount of gold.

The receipts became a wildly popular form of currency. It was more convenient and safer to carry receipts than heavy gold and silver coins. The system the goldsmiths created was a *reserve system*, meaning their paper money receipts were fully backed by gold.

To avoid unnecessary trips to the goldsmiths, depositors began endorsing the gold deposit receipts to others, by their signature. Over time the receipts were made to the bearer, rather than to the individual who deposited the gold with the goldsmith. This made the receipts transferable to another individual without the need for a signature. However, this practice made it much more difficult to identity a single individual's deposit of gold with the goldsmith.

Goldsmiths became even more important when Charles I seized the gold in the Royal Mint, citing it an unsafe place for the metal to be housed. The goldsmiths then became an important part of the monarchy. For example, in 1663, Charles II borrowed £1,300,000 from the goldsmiths to build a sailing fleet.[3]

Goldsmiths weren't regulated or audited. They received blind faith from the citizens who trusted that the inventories of gold they housed were accurate and equal to the number of receipts handed out. However, acting no different from their modern-day barbaric banking counterparts, the goldsmiths used this unchecked trust to their advantage.

The goldsmiths found that only a small fraction of depositors or bearers ever came in and demanded their gold at any given time. Driven by their thirst to become rich quickly, the goldsmiths began to issue more receipts than the actual gold reserves they had on deposit in their storage vaults.

This practice of issuing more receipts than the actual supply of gold on hand gave birth to our modern-day banking methods of lending out more money than deposits on hand. This is what we call *fractional reserve banking* and it is the core of our twenty-first century banking system.

The goldsmiths were a smart and cunning bunch. Eventually they came to realize they could actually control the supply of receipts in circulation and, in turn, the local economy itself. For example, when goldsmiths made money easier to borrow, then the amount of money in circulation expanded. Money was plentiful, and people took out more loans to expand their businesses. But when goldsmiths would tighten the money supply, they also made loans more difficult to obtain.

Naturally, when money was tight, some people could not repay their previous loans nor could they take out new loans. They had no choice but to declare bankruptcy. Goldsmiths would take possession of their assets. Goldsmiths gradually accumulated more and more wealth and used the money to buy more gold. Is it any wonder, then, that over time, goldsmiths evolved into bankers?

One of the richest and most powerful goldsmiths the world would come to know was Mayer Amschel Bauer. He was born in Frankfurt, Germany, in 1743. His father was Moses Amschel Bauer, a well-known moneylender, coin dealer, and goldsmith. Mayer's father taught him the money lending and coin business. After his father's death, Mayer went to work as a clerk at the Oppenheimer Bank in Hannover, where he was awarded a junior partnership.

Mayer eventually returned to Frankfurt and bought the shop his father had started. Mayer expanded the business from coins and money lending to antiques and textiles. He hung a red shield over the door. Shortly after returning to Germany, Mayer changed his name to Rothschild, which was the German word for *red shield*.

In 1770 Mayer Rothschild married Gutele Schnaper. Together they had five sons and five daughters. Their sons were Amschel, Salomon, Nathan, Kalmann (Karl), and Jacob (James), and Mayer taught them the business of banking just as his father had taught him.

After teaching his sons about the money business, Mayer sent four of them to different European capitals to expand the family's business outside of Germany. Nathan was sent to London, James to Paris, Saloman to Vienna, and Karl to Naples. Mayer kept the eldest son, Amschel, at home with him so that he could continue the business in Germany.[4]

Later the Rothschilds would play an important role in developing America's central banking system, known as the Federal Reserve.

The Government's Main Bank

As central banks evolved, they kept the goldsmiths' tradition of receipts or paper money being redeemed for gold (or silver coins). Most banks were private and not owned by a government.

Originally, central banks were formed to help finance the debt of their respective governments, but they could issue private banknotes as well. Because they worked with an extensive network of other banks, this meant they had access to large amounts of cash reserves.

In many respects, they became banks for bankers. And they were certainly the government's bank. In times of crisis, their governments could turn to them for additional sources of cash.

Central banks were also critical storehouses for gold. This was important because when central banks were established, most currencies (U.S. and foreign) were backed by gold.

Being on the gold standard meant that each country defined the value of its currency in terms of a fixed weight of gold. Part of the charter used to establish a central bank required the bank to hold large amounts of gold reserves in place so that at any time, as needed, the country's currency could be converted into gold.

The Bank of England adopted the gold standard in 1717. The United States did so in 1834. Other major countries joined the gold standard in the 1870s. In 1834, the United States fixed the price of gold at $20.67 per ounce

Being on the gold standard also meant the amount of money banks could supply was constrained by the value of the gold they held in reserve. Although considered a rudimentary system, it did serve as a sort of check and balance. The money supply could *not* grow beyond what was held in reserves. Economic policy discussions had to be made with consideration to a country's gold supply. Gold was the center of a country's economic might. It defined a country's wealth.

Gold's Domination

Just as in the early years of the United States' dual banking system, most countries used a dual coinage system. The favored metals used were gold and silver. Before most countries adopted the gold standard in the early 1900s, both gold and silver were accepted as the primary coinage and the metal for which banknotes could be redeemed.

England was one of the first countries to abandon a dual coinage system in favor of a single metal, that being gold. In 1821 England enacted the gold standard, making its money backed by gold. All international trade imbalances were settled with gold. This, of course, created a strong incentive for governments to stockpile gold. Germany followed suit in 1871 with its gold standard, followed by France in 1876 and Japan in 1898.[5]

The U.S. Coinage Act of 1873 officially withdrew silver as a recognized coin. Prior to this time, the United States used both silver and gold coins; both kinds of coins were legal tender and could be used to pay debts. The idea of two coins was introduced by Alexander Hamilton and enacted into law in 1792 under the Mint Act.

In that earlier act, denominations of coins were specified including the use of copper cents. The law also specified the ratio of silver in coins, which was set at 15 to 1. Gold, too, was set at 15 to 1.

However, in 1834, the silver ratio was changed to 15.988-plus to 1, to curtail exporting gold to other countries.[6] Unexpectedly, this caused a preference for gold, as silver coins were perceived as being undervalued.

In the Coinage Act of 1873, the amount of gold used for gold coins was set. Section 14 of this act states that gold coins of the United States shall be one-dollar pieces at the standard weight of 25.8 grains and shall be a legal tender in all payments. However, the act did maintain that silver dollars could be used for international trade. It wasn't until 1900 that the United States dropped silver entirely.

On March 14, 1900, the United States enacted the Gold Standard Act, which defined the value of all forms of money. This act called for the dollar to be made up of 25.8 grains of gold, nine-tenths fine, and that this would be the standard value. It also stipulated that all notes could be redeemed for gold coins and that the secretary of the Treasury is to set aside a reserve of $150 million in gold coins to be used for redemption purposes.

The threshold of safety for the reserves was set at $100 million, and if the Treasury was to fall short of this mark, it must then issue government bonds paying 3 percent interest.

As countries converted to a single metal, gold became the most precious commodity and countries began mining it extensively. In the first half of the nineteenth century, total gold production was valued at $787 million. By the beginning of the second half, the value jumped to $6.9 billion.[7]

In the United States, gold discoveries were happening at breakneck pace. In 1848, James Marshall discovered a lump of gold at Sutter's sawmill in California. This sparked a gold frenzy like none seen before. Production of gold in California exploded from $36 million in 1848 to $56 million in 1849.[8]

The Comstock find in Nevada was the next big gold discovery. This find produced an astonishing $470 million worth of gold.[9] Other countries were finding gold as well. Australia and New Zealand mines produced $65 million in gold. Russia was mining $25 million worth of gold. Johannesburg in South Africa was founded as a result of the 1886 gold rush. Canada's Yukon Territory was developed as result of a gold rush that started in 1897.

Barbarians Hoard Gold

In 1901, Augustus Saint-Gaudens was considered the finest sculptor in America. He had studied his craft in Paris and Rome and apprenticed in New York. His first statue was that of Admiral Farragut in Madison Square Park. Saint-Gaudens was considered a master of portraits.

That same year, Saint-Gaudens was asked to join as a member of the Commission for the Improvement of the District of Columbia. The plan was to extend the Washington Mall from the Washington Monument to the Potomac basin, allowing an area for the Lincoln Monument to be built.[10]

President Theodore Roosevelt was a great admirer of Saint-Gaudens' work and asked for his help in redesigning the nation's coins, including a $20 gold piece.

Saint-Gaudens gladly accepted the assignment and went to work creating his design. He designed the front side of the coin with Lady Liberty holding on to the torch of freedom as well as an olive branch. On the reverse side, he created an image of a bald eagle flying past the sun. Roosevelt considered Saint-Gaudens' design a classical masterpiece.

During March and April 1907, the U.S. mint in Philadelphia struck 24-proof coins. In November 1907 the production of regular-issue $20 Saint-Gaudens gold coins began.

Unfortunately, the American public would not have long to enjoy the coin. On March 9, 1933, Roosevelt signed the Emergency Banking Relief Act. This act gave the president the power to make it illegal for American citizens to own gold in any manner. He ended all production and circulation of all American gold coins. The order required that all persons deliver all gold coin, gold bullion, and certificates to a federal reserve bank or branch on or before May 1, 1933. His order read:

> By virtue of the authority vested in me by Section 5(B) of The Act of Oct. 6, 1917, as amended by section 2 of the Act of March 9, 1933, in which Congress declared that a serious emergency exists, I as President, do declare that the national emergency still exists; that the continued private hoarding of gold and silver by subjects of the United States poses a grave threat to the peace, equal justice, and well-being of the United States; and that

appropriate measures must be taken immediately to protect the interests of our people.

Therefore, pursuant to the above authority, I herby proclaim that such gold and silver holdings are prohibited, and that all such coin, bullion or other possessions of gold and silver be tendered within fourteen days to agents of the Government of the United States for compensation at the official price, in the legal tender of the Government.[11]

The executive order meant that Americans had to surrender gold coins, gold bullion, and gold certificates. The public had 25 days to turn their gold in to a Federal Reserve Bank. Failure to comply with the act was punishable with a fine of $10,000 or 10 years in prison or both.

At the time of the order, America held the largest gold reserves of any nation. That's because in order to finance World War I, European nations had gone off the gold standard so they could print more money.

Unfortunately, more dollars in circulation brings on inflation (an overinflated money supply). By increasing the money supply, European nations triggered inflation, which drove large amounts of the world's gold to banks in the United States. But this also made their national currencies worth less, especially against the U.S. dollar. The United States had not abandoned the gold standard, so investors could park their gold in U.S. banks where it maintained its value.

So why did Roosevelt make it illegal for Americans to own gold? One obvious reason is that Roosevelt wanted to gain complete control over the country's money if he was going to bring the United States out of the Depression. Earlier, the Federal Reserve had raised interest rates in order to slow down the rampant speculation in the market.

Some reports suggest the market was overvalued by as much as 40 percent. The increase in rates caused a chain reaction of companies cutting back on the manufacturing of durable goods. As mentioned earlier, the country was already suffering from a banking crisis. People lost faith in banks and lending declined. As companies cut back and the bank crisis took off, consumers cut back on their purchasing.

This caused prices to decline. Falling prices led to deflation. J. Bradford DeLong of the University of California at Berkeley and NBER says deflation during the Depression ran as high as 50 percent.[12]

Roosevelt and his administration thought that the only way they could fight deflation was through inflation. That meant they had to put more dollars into circulation. But the plan wouldn't work if the amount of dollars the United States could print was limited to the equivalent of the amount of gold reserves on hand.

The American public was already skeptical of the government's ability to get the country out of the Depression, so many people were holding gold as a hedge against inflation. Remember, back then, dollars were simply the name we gave to the instrument that allowed people to redeem their banknotes for 1/20 of an ounce of gold. For Roosevelt to inflate the money supply, he had to confiscate privately owned gold.

But there was another important line item in his executive order that would allow him to put as many paper dollars in circulation as he deemed necessary. Section 4 of the order states: "Upon receipt of gold coin, gold bullion or gold certificates delivered to it in accordance with Sections 2 or 3, the Federal Reserve Bank or member bank will pay therefore an equivalent amount of any other form of coin or currency coined or issued under the laws of the United States."[13]

Now he could issue paper currency to the public in exchange for their gold. Roosevelt took control of gold in every sense. For example, he made it unlawful to export gold for payment abroad, unless done so through the Treasury. And in his last move to control 100 percent of the country's gold reserves, he signed a resolution that nullified the gold clause in all government and private deals. In other words, no one, not even companies, could make a claim for gold.

Attila the Hun extracted gold from the Romans by the battles he won. Roosevelt simply did it through an executive order. And in the process he made the U.S. government richer. Shortly after banning gold from the hands of the American public, he raised the price of gold from $20.67 an ounce to $35. That simple stroke of the pen now made the government's reserves of gold worth $2.8 billion.

The problem is that dollars or paper-based currency are always at risk of inflation, whereas gold is not. Being on a gold standard means governments can't create money nor can they spur inflation. This has been true in earlier times when kings realized they could extend the money supply simply by adding a bit more lead to the melting pot when making coins. As the percentage of lead increased, the value of the coins decreased, causing the first cases of inflation.

We've experienced this in the United States. The purchasing power of the money in your wallet or bank account has steadily declined, and it's because inflation has taken hold. James Bovard further argues that under government-controlled fiat money, after nearly a century of war, waste, wealth-theft, and welfare, with many families now needing two incomes to live decently, the dollar today is almost worthless.[14]

Worthless Money

Thomas Jefferson once said,

> If the American people ever allow private banks to control the issue of their currency, first by inflation, then by deflation, the banks and corporations that will grow up around them will deprive the people of all property until their children wake up homeless on the continent their Fathers conquered. . . . I believe that banking institutions are more dangerous to our liberties than standing armies. . . .[15]

Jefferson couldn't have been more right. The bankers—that being the Federal Reserve—had controlled the monetary policies since the board was created in 1913. But they did not act alone. As we'll see in later chapters, Wall Street corporations have influenced the Fed's decisions. The Federal Reserve controls a currency that is simply green-colored pieces of paper, the supply of which they can increase or decrease in a single day's decision. Once allowed to open the spigot, they can't shut it off.

But those decisions come with dire consequences. We saw this happen in earlier times, with Sweden's Palmstrucher notes, John Law's Banque Royale catastrophe, and England's tally sticks. One of the problems with fiat currencies is they are backed by nothing more than the word of their governments. What's more, there are no limits on how much paper money a government can create.

Imagine, for a moment, holding a dollar bill in your hand that was worth some amount of gold. For the simple reason that it is backed by gold, that dollar would hold tremendous value to you. Do you feel the dollars you hold in your hand, ones that are created out of thin air, are worth something as great as gold? For that matter, would bankers with their fractional reserve banking system lend gold-backed money so freely? Would Wall Street corporations invest it more wisely?

The point is this: Today, we don't value money as much as we did when it was backed by gold. Nor do the policy makers who control its destiny. In fact, they've done more to destroy the dollar and our chances of complete prosperity than anyone else.

As of the writing of this book and according to usdebtclock.org, the national debt (total amount of money owed by the U.S. government) is $12.5 trillion. The debt has continued to increase at an average of $3.9 billion a day. The estimated population of the United States is 308 million. That means each person's share—every man, woman, and child—is $40,875.

The people who fund the national debt, meaning those who buy government bonds, are mostly foreign countries, with China topping the list at $899 billion, followed by Japan at $765 billion.[16] Here's the scary thing: If China were to stop buying U.S. debt, our currency would plummet as fast as a rock. That means the money you are holding in your hand would be virtually worthless.

Figure 7.1 shows how much our government debt has grown since 1940, and the amount it is expected to grow in the years ahead.

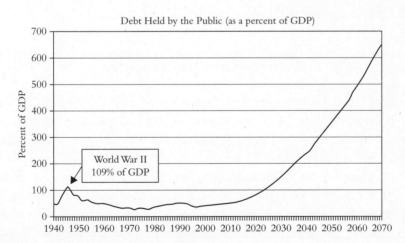

Figure 7.1 Growth of National Debt

Right now the U.S. dollar has the privilege of being the world's reserve currency. But is it possible that one day, we could lose that status? The British pound was once the favored currency. It took 60 years for it to lose its reign as the world's reserve currency.

In a *USA Today* article, Bill Gross, a managing director of PIMCO, a global investment management firm, says, "The financial world is supporting the U.S. debt and the dollar because there's no reasonable alternative at the moment, but it may not be able to overlook the nation's fiscal condition forever. When debt to GDP reaches 90 percent, as it looks like it will, interest rates rise, growth slows and bad things happen. That's the potential going forward."[17]

Already China has expressed reservations about buying more U.S. debt. In the *UK Telegraph*, Cheng Siwei, former vice chairman of the Standing Committee and now head of China's green energy drive, said, "If they [United States] keep printing money to buy bonds it will lead to inflation, and after a year or two the dollar will fall hard. Most of our foreign reserves are in U.S. bonds and this is very difficult to change, so we will diversify incremental reserves into euros, yen, and other currencies."[18]

It's only been recently that world leaders have expressed concern over the worth of the U.S. dollar and our debt problem. No one questioned our leaders nor the Federal Reserve and their monetary policies. In fact, before the U.S. dollar became the world's reserve currency, gold reigned supreme. Unfortunately, that reign was short-lived.

Twenty-One Days in July

In May 1944, 150 workers convened at the Mount Washington Resort in Bretton Woods, New Hampshire. They had just two months to repair the damages from years of neglect and refurnish the once elegant hotel. Roofs had collapsed from the weight of heavy snow, wallpaper was peeling off the walls, and everything needed a fresh coat of paint.

The repairs were being made because special guests were coming to the hotel for what would later be considered one of the world's most important gatherings. I'm speaking, of course, about the Bretton Woods

International Monetary Conference, which took place in July and lasted approximately 21 days.

Representatives from 44 nations attended the meeting, including the United States, the emerging superpower of the world, and the United Kingdom. The Soviet Union attended but did not sign the final agreements. India and China were there as well, but were not considered a major contributor to the negotiations because back then they were not huge economies.

Also in attendance, and one of the lead speakers, was recognized economist John Maynard Keynes, who argued on behalf of the British Empire.

Why was this meeting being held? Well, there were several reasons. One was that starting around World War I and continuing through to World War II, many of the countries attending began controlling their imports and exports by imposing high trade tariffs. The tariffs made it much more difficult to sell goods in other countries.

But that's not all. At the time of the meetings, the major players—the United States and England—were working under different currency structures. Britain had abandoned the gold standard to finance World War I and never returned to it. For Britain, a return to the gold standard would make their exports too expensive, which would naturally cause less demand for their products, which in turn would leave their manufacturers sitting with idle factories.

On top of this, because Britain had depleted its gold reserves to finance the war, it had no incentive to return to the gold standard. John Keynes, speaking on Britain's behalf, referred to gold as a "barbarous relic."

To further complicate the situation, some European countries remained pegged to the sterling pound silver. And all the while, the United States remained on the gold standard. The meeting at Bretton Woods gave world leaders the opportunity to create a stabilizing international currency.

That's exactly what happened. At the meeting, the 44 nations created an international basis for exchanging one currency for another. The nations agreed that gold should be the money used to settle all trade deficits between nations.

But in lieu of gold, U.S. dollars could be used to settle the trade deficits. The central bank of the foreign nations could demand gold from the U.S. Treasury. Because the United States accounted for over half of the world's manufacturing capacity and held most of the world's gold, the leaders decided to tie world currencies to the U.S. dollar. However, the United States could pay for its trade deficits either in gold or in dollars. It was the only nation allowed to do so.

The group created a fixed exchange rate where countries pegged their currency to the dollar and the United States fixed the price of gold at $35. Fixed exchange rates provide greater certainty for exporters and importers and usually offer fewer chances for speculative activity.

The Bretton Woods conference also led to the creation of the International Monetary Fund (IMF), whose purpose was to monitor exchange rates and lend reserve currencies to nations with trade deficits. All signers of the agreement became members of the IMF.

The International Bank for Reconstruction and Development was also born from the meeting, now known as the World Bank. At that time the bank's main objective was to provide funds to countries that needed to rebuild from the war.

Nowadays, the bank's role is to provide low-interest loans, interest-free credits, and grants to developing countries for a wide array of purposes that include investments in education, health, public administration, infrastructure, financial and private sector development, agriculture, and environmental and natural resource management.

The details worked out at Bretton Woods were adopted by the United States and other participating nations in 1945.

In *Money Meltdown* by Judy Shelton, the author gets it right about Bretton Woods when she writes, "Bretton Woods clearly ran into problems and identifying and fixing what went wrong presents a formidable task. But there can be no disputing that much was right about the Bretton Woods approach. The United States flourished under the system as did Europe, Japan and other developing countries around the world."[19]

So why did then President Nixon abandon the system that helped most citizens around the world achieve *real* prosperity? The answer lies in what happened in August 1971.

Too Much Gold

On August 15, 1971, without warning, President Nixon announced during a Sunday evening televised address to the nation that U.S. dollars would no longer be baked by gold. That marked the day in history in which no circulating paper anywhere was redeemable in gold. His decision was called the "Nixon shock" because he made it without consulting any of the other countries that signed the Bretton Woods agreements.

But undoing the agreements worked out at Bretton Woods opened the door for inflation in every major country, including the United States, Japan, the United Kingdom, and Italy. The U.S. inflation rate, which had been 1.5 percent at the beginning of the 1960s, had risen to 5 percent. At the same time, unemployment was also up from 3.5 percent to 5 percent

What happened? Well for one thing, the United States was spending a lot of money fighting the Vietnam War. The Defense Department estimated the war cost $140 billion in direct military outlays between 1965 and 1974. Of course, this is not the only time our country has spent a tremendous amount of money for defense purposes. Figure 7.2 shows just how much military and defense spending has grown over the years. The National Priorities Project calculates that since 2001 our government has spent over $1 trillion on wars.

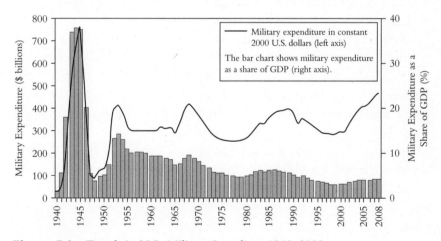

Figure 7.2   Trends in U.S. Military Spending, 1940–2008

But it wasn't just money spent fighting the Vietnam War that caused a spike in inflation. At that time, we were also buying a huge amount of imports from European nations as well as providing foreign aid to help rebuild Europe. As a result, European countries were building up huge reserves of American dollars.

Those countries started exercising their rights to convert their dollars into gold. By 1960, U.S. gold reserves had declined by 9 percent.[20] But at the same time that countries were redeeming their dollars for gold, the U.S. Treasury was printing more dollars. As gold reserves declined and the dollars in circulation increased, this meant that each new dollar was backed by a smaller and smaller amount of gold.

It was also around this time that the price for gold in the private market began to rise above the $35 level set by members of the Bretton Woods agreement. In order to keep the price at $35, the central banks of the United States, England, West Germany, France, Switzerland, Italy, Belgium, the Netherlands, and Luxembourg acted together to keep the price of gold from rising. They formed the London Gold Pool. London had always been the world's premier gold market. Most of South Africa's gold was shipped to London for sale; even Russian gold found its way onto the London gold market.

However, concerns about the value of the U.S. dollar began to creep up again among European nations, who began to worry that the U.S. Treasury wouldn't have enough gold reserves on hand and that the new dollars they printed would be worth less.

One of the first heads of state to recognize that the U.S. dollar was not as good as gold itself was General Charles de Gaulle, then president of France. President de Gaulle realized that the policy of exchanging central bank dollars for gold would eventually break down because the United States was increasing the supply of U.S. dollars at a faster rate than the production of newly mined gold.

In 1965 de Gaulle demanded gold in exchange for the U.S. dollar reserves the Banque de France had built up over the years. De Gaulle is quoted as saying, "What the United States owes to foreign countries it pays—at least in part—with Dollars that it can simply issue if it chooses to."[21]

Not a man to toss words around, de Gaulle sent the French navy across the Atlantic to pick up $150 million worth of gold from the

United States.[22] In 1967, when the Arab-Israeli war broke out, demand for gold skyrocketed. De Gaulle withdrew his commitment to the London Gold Pool altogether.

Now Nixon had a problem on his hands. If France was willing to ask for its gold, then other countries would soon follow. So to prevent a run on U.S. gold, in 1971, Nixon stopped France and any other country from requesting gold for their U.S. dollars.

In essence, Nixon cancelled the dollar–gold exchange rate established 27 years earlier. The United States would settle its trade balances with U.S. bonds or U.S. currency, but not with gold.

What Nixon did was free the United States from ever having to provide a redeemable alternative to its paper currency. Once Nixon abandoned the fixed price of gold set by the Bretton Woods agreement, gold jumped from $35 an ounce to as much as $850, as shown in Figure 7.3.

But Nixon did more than affect the price of gold. The window was now open for the United States to print as much money as it needed. In fact, from January 1971 to December 2008, the U.S. money supply increased 16.8 times. However, at the same time, the purchasing power of those dollars dropped 81 percent.[23]

Richard Nixon demonstrated to the world that we could create an endless supply of new paper money. That money supply can grow so

Figure 7.3 Price of Gold, 1971–2008 (Dollars per Ounce)
DATA SOURCE: Worldgoldcouncil.com.

big that it could destroy a nation's wealth. And yet something as important as the money supply doesn't get much media attention.

It seems as if no one warns the public to be aware of how much money is in circulation. Even the Federal Reserve is in on the act. Figure 7.4 shows the growth of the money supply in the United States over the past five decades. Notice that the line begins to rise rapidly at about the time Nixon takes the United States off the gold standard.

When a currency system is not backed by gold, there are no restraints in place on the amount of money that can be created. Look at our current economic situation. Our government has been throwing money at the problem as if money grows on trees. And that's one of the major problems with a paper-based system: It can grow unchecked.

There's also another problem with this type of system: It allows for unlimited creation of credit. This increase in credit is mistaken for economic growth. Consumers begin buying things they wouldn't ordinarily buy with cash. Instead they use credit—and often overextend themselves.

Business owners do the same thing. Their businesses grow, their stock prices rise, and everybody starts buying equities that are overvalued.

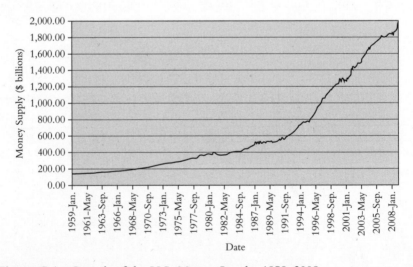

Figure 7.4 Growth of the U.S. Money Supply, 1959–2008
Source: Board of Governors of the Federal Reserve System, federalreserve.gov.

Fiat systems mask the problems associated with too much credit. Could the housing boom have taken root if credit weren't so easily available to anyone who asked? Would subprime mortgage derivatives have mushroomed into a trillion-dollar industry if institutions hadn't been willing to take on more risk?

When Nixon removed us from the gold standard in 1971, he set in motion an inflationary period that was one of the worst our country had ever faced. Since being removed from the gold standard, we've had market bubbles in all kinds of sectors including commodities, Internet start-up companies, and real estate. Each one of these bubbles was followed by a market collapse.

The thing is, while we can create an endless supply of money, we cannot endlessly increase the supply of gold. This is what makes gold so valuable.

Unfortunately, the endless supply of money makes every dollar you earn less valuable. If you are putting money away in a savings account, CD, or money market fund, you are slowly losing what you have saved, and over the years you could lose the bulk of what's left.

Inflation will only continue to grow. The best way to protect yourself from inflation is to buy gold and other precious metals like silver. However, you need to not only protect your wealth but to grow it as well. A way to do just that is to invest in commodities and resources that are high in demand.

For example, China has gone from being the world's twentieth largest oil consumer to number two behind the United States.[24] This change comes as the favorite mode of transportation in China shifts from the bike to the car. But in order to support this demand, more roads, bridges, and other infrastructures need to be built. China will need to import resources and materials to keep pace. Thus, buying in-demand commodities is a great way to substantially grow your portfolio. In Chapter 18, we explore these options in more detail.

Chapter 8

The Gatekeepers

The year is 1913. It's a cold winter evening. But the temperature is not foremost in the mind of President Woodrow Wilson at this moment, for he has a much greater task before him. Waiting patiently for the president are a handful of members of Congress who helped put together the document the president is about to sign. Wilson picks up his pen and places his signature on the Federal Reserve Act of 1913.

For a select group of members of Congress and a handful of bankers, this moment was one of the greatest in America's history. But for most Americans, it would signify the end of wealth and prosperity. How can the signing of a single act be so wide-reaching and controversial?

Because the act, no matter how well intended, allowed a powerful cartel of men to determine the country's monetary and economic policies. Many of those policies have led us to where we are right now, struggling to recover from a recession that started in November 2007.

Before we can see how we ended up with unemployment hitting 10 percent, pending home sales falling, 308,524 properties foreclosed in

February 2010,[1] and consumer sentiment still frail, we need to look back at the history of the Federal Reserve.

In Chapter 5 we learned about the first Bank of the United States, which was really an early form of the Federal Reserve System. When the bank's charter expired in 1811, the country didn't see another type of central bank until 1816, when the Second Bank of the United States was chartered.

Even so, state-chartered banks, which were allowed to issue banknotes, dominated the country's banking system. In 1863, Congress passed the National Banking Act, whereby state banks were assessed a heavy tax if they wanted to continue to issue banknotes. Since the cost of the tax was more than the banks could bear, many closed shop. Only nationally chartered banks could issue notes without being taxed.

The country's banking system didn't really change much until around 1907 when a panic rocked Wall Street. This panic, as we've seen from previous panics, triggered a run on banks. The Knickerbocker Trust Company of New York collapsed entirely as depositors withdrew their money, leaving the bank exhausted of funds.[2] The next bank run was on the Trust Company of America. That was followed by a run on the Lincoln Trust Company.

Some reports suggest that the panic was the work of John Pierpont (J.P.) Morgan in order to create a monopoly of investment banks that he could control. How true this is, we can't be sure.

The Federal Reserve of Minneapolis attributes the cause of the panic to financial manipulation from the existing banking establishment. They recognized what bankers would gain. In a report, the Minneapolis Fed wrote, "If Knickerbocker Trust would falter, then Congress and the public would lose faith in all trust companies and banks would stand to gain, the bankers reasoned."[3]

In an interesting move—and one that resembles current-day bank bailouts—President Roosevelt enlisted the help of J.P. Morgan to restore order. Roosevelt gave J.P. Morgan $25 million in government funds to inject liquidity back into the banking system.[4] Notice how the funds were used: to *inject liquidity back* into the system.

This is certainly eerily familiar to what happened in the recession of 2007. Credit froze due to fears of counterparty risk. Banks began failing. Risky loans had to be written off, further reducing the banks' capital.

The government handed the banks money to lend. But instead of lending, the banks began hoarding the cash.

According to a comprehensive study by RateFinancials Inc., a New York–based independent forensic research firm for institutional clients, the firm found that the top 50 regional U.S. banks aren't healthy and, despite a 12 percent increase in capital, still aren't lending to businesses that need credit. The banks are hoarding cash.[5]

In the 1907 panic, J.P. Morgan received $25 million. Oddly enough, in the recession of 2007, J.P. Morgan received $25 billion from the government.

But what most readers don't realize is that—according to a *Business Insider* recorded phone interview with a J.P. Morgan executive—the company had no intention of lending out the $25 billion of taxpayer money the government gave it to help restore the U.S. economy. The Morgan executive claimed the government bailout money would be used by the firm for acquisitions. The *Business Insider* quoted the executive as saying,

> I would not assume that we are done on the acquisition side. . . .
> I think there are going to be some great opportunities for us to
> grow in this environment, and I think we have an opportunity
> to use that $25 billion in that way and obviously depending on
> whether recession turns into depression or what happens in the
> future, you know, we have that as a backstop.[6]

Is it any wonder we call J.P. Morgan a modern-day barbarian of wealth? Small businesses are the backbone of our economy. They employ over half of private-sector employees. Small businesses have generated 64 percent of new jobs over the past 15 years.[7]

If small businesses can't borrow money to make their payroll or for expansion purposes, they have no choice but to lay people off, adding to the already high unemployment rate.

So while J.P. Morgan sits on a bucket load of cash, most Americans and other businesses are struggling to survive day by day. We'll learn more about J.P. Morgan in later chapters. For now, let's returning to the 1907 panic.

In the aftermath, Congress passed the Emergency Currency Act of 1908, in which the National Monetary Commission was created. The

Commission was made up of nine members of the Senate and nine members of the House of Representatives. The title of chairman of the commission was awarded to Senator Nelson Aldrich of Rhode Island. The commission's job was to investigate what changes were necessary to fix the country's banking system.

The commission wasted no time in getting started on the project, but much like anything else undertaken by the government, it took the group four years to put together their findings.

During that lengthy process, Senator Aldrich traveled throughout Europe for almost two years to study the bank systems of European nations. Upon his return, he invited scholars and several heads of major banks to attend a meeting he was hosting at a little island that lay midway between Savannah, Georgia, and Jacksonville, Florida.

Jekyll Island was the winter retreat for some of America's most elite families, including J.P. Morgan, William Rockefeller, Joseph Pulitzer, George Baker, and James Stillman.

On November 22, 1910, Aldrich and his clan of moneymakers met at the very exclusive, upscale Jekyll Island Club resort.

Those invited included Aldrich's personal secretary Arthur Shelton; former Harvard University professor of economics Dr. A. Piatt Andrew; J.P. Morgan & Co. senior partner Henry P. Davison, who was generally regarded as Morgan's personal emissary; National City Bank of New York president Frank A. Vanderlip; and Kuhn, Loeb & Co. partner Paul M. Warburg.[8]

The meeting was not publicized and was shrouded in secrecy—and the group wanted it that way. You see, for years, the American public had voiced concern about a full-fledged central banking system. They had already seen a number of bank failures. So any major announcement of a group of private bankers, scholars, and wealthy businessman meeting to prepare legislation on how to control the country's bank system would have been met with mass skepticism.

This group of mighty men knew the magnitude of the task before them. While Senator Aldrich was there to prepare to present a plan to Congress to overhaul the nation's banking system, the other members of the group were there to make sure their interests would be left intact. What they drafted in secrecy would eventually become the basis of a plan to control the monetary fate of the people of the United States.

Born into Banking

Of all members in attendance at the Jekyll Island meeting, Paul Warburg is credited as the chief architect of the bill signed by President Woodrow Wilson. Warburg was certainly no stranger to banking. He was born into a family of Jewish bankers in Hamburg, Germany. The first bank his family set up was known as M.M. Warburg & Company, established in 1798. His father, Moritz Warburg, ran the Warburg Company.

The Warburg family had been involved in banking in Europe for over 300 years. In medieval times, Christian religions forbade charging interest on loans. Fees or penalties could be charged, but not interest. The same thing was true of the Jewish religion with one exception: While the Jewish religion prevented Jewish people from charging interest to one another, they could charge interest to Christians.

The idea of not charging interest on loans among the Jewish population comes from a passage in Deuteronomy: "Do not charge interest on the loans you make to a fellow Israelite.... You may charge interest to foreigners, but you may not charge interest to Israelites, so that the Lord your God may bless you...."[9]

Most of the Jewish population were ostracized from many professions by the church and by various local rules, which forbade them from entering certain jobs. Jews were forced into what were considered lesser professions, such as tax or rent collectors. People in these roles were called money changers.

The money changers were popular at trade fairs in places like Germany. The money changers would hand out receipts that could be used at other fairs, so the receipts became a type of circulating currency.

Because Jewish people could charge interest to gentiles, they inherited the role of bankers. A segment of the Jewish population that was expelled from Spain provided financing for William the Conqueror. With the approval of Pope Alexander II and the Holy Roman Emperor Henry IV, William invaded England in 1066. He brought 2,600 Jews into England with him from Rouen. Therefore, Jews became the first bankers in England.

Paul Warburg's family came from this line of Jewish bankers. His father, Moritz, first learned the business of banking when he spent six months in Amsterdam working in the private bank of Wertheim and Gomperts.[10] While in Amsterdam, Moritz became a correspondent for the Dutch Central Bank.

After apprenticing at Wertheim and Gomperts, Moritz continued his education in banking at the French banking firm of Banque Imperiale Ottomane. It was Moritz's father who helped him gain entrance into the firm because of his ties with the Rothschilds—yes, the same influential and powerful banking family that dominated Europe. It was this connection to the Rothschilds that would eventually provide Moritz a position in the firm created by Nathan Rothschild, N M Rothschild & Sons.

The Rothschilds have been engaged in banking for centuries. Take a look at this timeline, representing seven generations:

- 1760s: The orphaned Mayer Amschel Rothschild starts a coins and metals business in Frankfurt.
- 1789: Mayer is appointed an agent to William IX of Hanau.
- 1798: Mayer's son Nathan leaves Frankfurt to become a textile and general merchant in Manchester.
- 1812: Nathan's brother James establishes a banking house in Paris.
- 1815: The English branch of the Rothschilds supplies gold to the Duke of Wellington's campaign at Waterloo.
- 1820: Nathan's brother settles in Vienna; his brother Karl starts a business in Naples.
- 1836: Nathan dies.
- 1840: N M Rothschild and Sons becomes one of the Bank of England's bullion brokers.
- 1850s: Great houses are built. Bordeaux vineyards of Mouton and Lafite are acquired.
- 1875: Lionel de Rothschild raises financing for British stake in the Suez Canal.
- 1887: Rothschild funds the creation of De Beers diamond dealers.
- 1901: With no male heirs, the Frankfurt dynasty comes to an end.
- 1919: N M Rothschild & Sons chair new daily fixing of the gold price.
- 1926: The company finances the spread of the London Underground.

- 1929: Beginning of difficult years for family; Wall Street crash; rise of Nazi Europe.
- 1960s: Rothschilds look to United States; start of Rothschild Inc.
- 1981: France nationalizes the highly successful Paris House but the family refuses defeat and starts new business.
- 1985: Rothschild advises on British gas privatization.
- 2004: An international banking dynasty, Rothschilds operate banks in 40 countries worldwide.[11]

Over time, Moritz developed M.M. Warburg & Company into a distinguished banking firm, and it was only natural that Paul continue the family's banking heritage. After Paul Warburg completed his education in Germany, where he graduated from the University of Hamburg, he studied in Paris and London.

While in London he worked at an English brokerage house. It's fair to say that while in London and Paris, Warburg learned the inner workings of each country's banking system. After gaining that knowledge, Warburg traveled to America where he took a position in the New York banking firm of Kuhn, Loeb & Company. Warburg became a partner of the firm in 1902.

It's worth pointing out here that bankers, especially those involved in the creation of the Federal Reserve, are just as interconnected as Wall Street firms. For example, in Chapter 11, we will learn that Merrill Lynch hired Howard Rubin to teach it how to trade mortgage securities.

Rubin had learned the art of mortgage securities while employed at Salomon Brothers. Salomon Brothers and First Boston are credited with creating the first collateralized mortgage obligation (CMO) for Freddie Mac. First Boston and Merrill Lynch are tied together through Merrill Lynch when it bought out White, Weld & Company, which had previously been part of First Boston. We'll explore more of these connections later.

Already we know that Paul Warburg's father was connected to the Rothschild family through Nathan Rothschild when he worked at Nathan's firm, N M Rothschild & Company. Paul took a position with Kuhn, Loeb & Company, which was founded by Abraham Kuhn and Solomon Loeb in 1867.[12]

Jacob Schiff, originally from Frankfurt, Germany, and also part of a German family bank dynasty headed by Moses Schiff, joined Kuhn, Loeb & Company after meeting Abraham Kuhn on a return visit to Germany.[13] Schiff eventually emerged as the firm's leader. He secured his position in the firm when he married Solomon Loeb's daughter Theresa. Like Schiff, Paul Warburg married into the Kuhn Loeb family when he married Loeb's daughter Nina.

Speaking of marriages, it's worth noting that Senator Aldrich's daughter was married to John D. Rockefeller. Even more interesting is that Jacob Schiff grew up in a two-family house shared with the Rothschilds.[14] The house was located in Frankfurt's Jewish quarters known as Judengasse.

Under Schiff's leadership, Kuhn, Loeb & Company became the second-largest financial firm in the United States, with J.P. Morgan occupying the top spot. The firm made millions underwriting the building of railroads. In 1901, Kuhn, Loeb & Company controlled 22,000 miles of railroad, and stock worth $312 million.[15]

But Kuhn, Loeb & Company wasn't just making its money from building railroads. It was heavily invested in bank stocks. In his book *Real Money versus False Money: Bank Credits*, T. Cushing Daniel notes that in 1912, the firm had acquired stock interest in 32 banks and trust companies.[16]

This makes one wonder whether Warburg's motive to reform the country's banking system was to further his own wealth or to truly help the American public. Records show that during the period of 1897 to 1906, his firm had purchased $821 million worth of securities related to banks and corporations. In the next six years, Kuhn, Loeb & Company purchased an additional $704 million in securities.[17]

Obviously, creating a central bank run by bankers and wealthy businessmen would help keep Warburg's wealth intact.

Interestingly, Warburg was never silent about his interest to reform the country's banking system by putting a central bank in place. In 1907 the *New York Times* published a four-page article written by Warburg, entitled "Defects and Needs of Our Banking System."[18] In the article, Warburg said that United States currency system was no more developed than that of the Medicis or the Asians, and in all likelihood resembled that of Hammurabi. Warburg also argued that Americans should be offered paper drawn in dollars, endorsed by commercial banks.

In closing his article, Warburg argued for a central bank run by the country's wealthy businessmen. He wrote, "Are we not depreciating ourselves by saying that we should not be able to find a set of business men of sufficiently high standing to form the central and local boards of a central bank?"[19]

Obviously Warburg was a strong proponent of a centralized banking system. He envisioned a reserve bank, which would be owned by private individuals who would profit from ownership of shares. This reserve bank would also be allowed to issue banknotes.

Warburg was well aware of the public's distrust of a central bank. Knowing this prejudice toward central banks existed, Warburg suggested to the Jekyll Island gang that words such as *central bank* should not be used to describe the new bank. The truth is, it was Warburg himself who came up with the name Federal Reserve System. Instead, he suggested it should be called the National Reserve Administration.

For Warburg, this would accomplish the goal of deceiving the American public into thinking it was not a central bank.[20]

Slow Victory

When the men wrapped up their 10-day meeting, they were confident that they had drafted a plan that would be well received by Congress. However, this was not the case.

Members of the newly formed Monetary Commission were asked to review the plan. The committee was politically divided. At the time, there were two major political groups vying for control of Washington.

One was known as the progressive group, which wanted to limit political and economic power that seemed to grow rampant in the boom times. They were particularly interested in reducing the power and influence bankers had over economic decisions. This group was generally associated with small business owners and farmers. The other group was more con-servative and represented mostly the ideals of wealthy businessmen.[21]

Obviously, the plan drawn up by Aldrich and his Jekyll Island group was heavily weighted on the side of bankers. The plan called for a central bank that would be controlled by a board of directors composed mostly of bankers. The plan had the backing of the American Bankers Association and a majority of congressional Republicans.

For progressives, the plan was the exact opposite of what they were hoping to achieve. Running for president on the progressive ticket was the outspoken former U.S. President Theodore Roosevelt, who rejected the plan on the grounds that it "placed the credit and currency of the United States in private hands not subject to effective public control."[22]

Woodward Wilson, a member of the Democratic Party who was also running for president, denounced the plan for the control it gave bankers.

Progressives also criticized the plan because of the 46-member board of directors, only 4 would represent the public. The plan also called for only two of the board's nine-member governing committee to actually represent the interest of the government itself.

However, the strongest criticism of the plan was that the National Reserve Association could issue banknotes at its discretion. Senator William Jennings Bryan of Nebraska, who had been the Democratic presidential nominee in 1896, complained, "Big financiers are back of the Aldrich currency scheme."[23]

But Aldrich's plan did something else. It opened the door to an investigation led by members of the other side of the Monetary Commission. They alleged that the nation's banking power was concentrated in the hands of a few individuals, which the committee called a "money trust." This immense concentration of wealth became a major point of contention for the American public.

In the early 1900s, just as is today, only a handful of investment banks handled most of the country's securities transactions. The firms in operation then were J.P. Morgan; Kuhn, Loeb & Company; the First National Bank; the National City Bank; Kidder, Peabody & Company; and Lee, Higginson & Company. And the amount of money they earned was substantial. The capitalization of these firms totaled $30 billion.[24]

So the commission created a subcommittee led by Arsène Pujo of Louisiana. Pujo was part of the group within the National Monetary Commission that studied foreign banking systems to see if there were indeed ways to improve America's domestic banking system. In 1911, Pujo was appointed to chair the House Committee on Banking and Currency.

On April 27, 1912, Pujo began conducting a series of hearings, calling on well-known bankers such as J.P. Morgan for testimony.

Morgan was considered a hero for saving the banking system during the 1907 panic, but over time, the public began to see him as too powerful and influential. Committee Chairman Pujo was intent on showing the public that their mistrust of Morgan was justified.

Pujo was trying to uncover whether there existed interlocking directorates (a money trust) among insurance companies, railroads, public utilities, and industrial corporations. The American public already believed that a money trust existed and that members of this trust had almost absolute control over how credit was given to other companies and corporations.

Louis Brandeis helped pushed this public perception in a series of articles he wrote that were published in major magazines across the nation. Brandeis had studied law at Harvard. After settling in Boston, he became a successful lawyer, spending a good deal of his time pursuing cases with a political bent. In particular, he enjoyed representing small companies against giant corporations.[25]

Brandeis believed that interlocking directorates were incompatible with healthy competition for credit. In his articles, he referred to interlocking directorates as "the most potent instrument of the Money Trusts."[26]

Morgan was called to appear before the committee to answer questions related to his banking activities. In a session that took place on December 19, 1912, Samuel Untermyer, one of New York's wealthiest lawyers and a member of Pujo's subcommittee, asked Morgan, "A man or group of men who have control of credit have control of money, have they not?" To which Morgan replied, "Yes."[27]

As the proceedings continued, Morgan tried to confuse the Senator by rationalizing that money and credit are not the same thing and that one man cannot control both. He also told the committee that the only thing he considers when lending money is a person's character and that this was a generally accepted practice by most banks.

During the hearings, Pujo offered documents prepared by an expert accountant that showed an increased amount of money was lured into the stock market and that the increase seemed to be drawn specifically to New York, where most of the major financial institutions and banks were located, one of those being J.P. Morgan. [28]

On February 28, 1913, 10 months after the investigation began, Pujo's committee presented their findings. The committee reported that control over the national banking system had become highly concentrated through interlocking directorates and other forms of trusts.

The greatest concentration of power lay with the operations of J. Pierpont Morgan's financial firms and John Rockefeller's National City Bank, which together could name 341 directors on the boards of 112 corporations worth $22.2 billion. At the time, their combined wealth represented 10 percent of the U.S. economy.

For the People

One year after the money trust hearings closed, Morgan, Rockefeller, and others who were considered part of the money trust would remove themselves from their interlocking directorates. But that would not stop them from controlling the country's credit and money supply. They would use their influence and connections to ensure the birth of the Federal Reserve Board.

Although the initial plan (Aldrich's) put before Congress was defeated, Senator Carter Glass (of the Glass-Steagall Act) would submit a plan that would indeed secure the president's signature. However, it would take three drafts of his bill before both Democrats and Republicans found the compromise they needed.

Who is this man who would put the country's monetary decisions in the hands of so few? Glass grew up in Lynchburg, Virginia. His father, Robert, worked in the newspaper business as an editor and eventually became mayor. It could be this early exposure to politics that paved the way for Glass' political career.

At the age of 13, Carter Glass worked for the local newspaper, setting type. At 19 he took a job as an auditor for the Atlantic, Mississippi and Ohio Railroad.

Like his father, Carter would enter the newspaper business. He wrote an editorial piece about a mayoral candidate running against his father, which his father published in the *Petersburg News*. That drew the attention of Albert Waddill, editor of the *Lynchburg News*, who offered Carter a job as the paper's main reporter.

Glass stayed with the paper until age 23, when he received his first political appointment as clerk of the Lynchburg City Council.[29]

In 1902, at the age of 44, Glass was elected to the U.S. House of Representatives. Within two years, he was appointed to the Committee on Banking and Currency and learned everything he could about finance. By the time Woodrow Wilson was elected president, Glass served as the committee's chairman. Glass hired financial expert and economist, as well as recognized financial journalist, Henry Parker Willis, Ph.D., to join his team.

Wilson's election ushered in a Democratic-controlled Congress. In referring to the issue of the country's banking system President Wilson wrote,

> However it has come about, it is more important still that the control of credit also has become dangerously centralized. The great monopoly in this country is the monopoly of big credits. So long as that exists, our old variety and freedom and individual energy of development are out of the question.[30]

With President-elect Wilson in full support of reforming the banking system, Glass had greater leverage in getting his draft of the earlier defeated Federal Reserve bill presented by Aldrich approved. But he needed to know what section of the defeated bill needed revising in order to secure the president's signature.

So a representative of New York bankers was sent to Wilson's residence in Princeton, New Jersey. The representative was given the mandate to find out Wilson's reaction to the dormant Aldrich bill. When asked by the representative for his thoughts, Wilson responded that "the Aldrich bill was probably about 60 or 70 percent correct but that the remainder of it would need to be altered."[31]

But this wasn't enough information for Glass to make any substantial modifications to the bill. So on November 7, 1912, Glass wrote a letter to President-elect Wilson suggesting they meet to discuss the matter of revising the country's currency system.

In his letter, Glass pointed out that he, with Professor Willis, already had a substitute for the Aldrich bill, but that before proceeding, it would be best to met with the president and receive his suggestions.[32]

On December 19, 1912, Senator Carter Glass received a reply from Wilson inviting him and Willis to his home in Princeton, New Jersey. On December 26, Senator Glass traveled directly to the president's residence with his expert on finances, Dr. Willis. The two men sat down with President-elect Wilson and discussed what difficulties needed to be resolved in the draft.

Glass described the meeting as follows:

> For two hours the situation was reviewed and the chairman's memorandum dissected. Toward the end, Mr. Wilson announced it as his judgment that we were "far on the right track"; but offered quite a few suggestions, the most notable being one that resulted in the establishment of an altruistic Federal Reserve Board at Washington to supervise the proposed system. We had committed this function to the Comptroller of the Currency, already tsaristic head of the national banking system of the country. Mr. Wilson laughingly said he was for "a plenty of centralization, but not for too much." Therefore, he asked that a separate central board provision be drafted, to be used or not, as might subsequently be determined, "as a capstone" to the system which had been outlined to him.[33]

In January, hearings would resume and Glass's newly revised plan would be the centerpiece. However, bankers who had already endorsed the Aldrich plan would not accept a plan that did not call for a central bank to be owned and operated by bankers. Professor Willis, who had helped Glass draft his plan, pulled the Senator aside and told him that a banker from New York had suggested to Willis, "There is such a thing as getting a committee chairman who will accept *our* plan."[34]

Our Fate Is Sealed

Knowing opposition was rising against his plan, Glass met again with President Wilson. Amendments were made to the plan. However, both men agreed that they would not make provisions for a central bank. They were proponents of regional banks.

This revised draft, they felt, would certainly be passed. But little did they know, operating out of the limelight, and ever eager to ensure the creation of a central bank, were J.P. Morgan, Secretary of the Treasury William McAdoo, and Edward Mandell House (also known as Colonel House) from Texas, who earlier had helped Wilson win the election, and who was now an adviser to Wilson.

From House's diary we learn that on March 27, 1913, he met with J.P. Morgan and another prominent banker to discuss a currency plan that Morgan had drafted.[35]

House also wrote about his dealings with Warburg: "On December 19, 1912, I talked with Paul Warburg over the phone concerning currency reform. I told of my trip to Washington and what I had done there to get it in working order. I told him that the Senate and the Congressmen seemed anxious to do what he desired, and that President-elect Wilson thought straight concerning the issue."[36]

So the groundwork was being laid to prevent approval of the already once revised plan of Senator Glass. This would not be an easy victory for Glass. But he was confident that with President Wilson's influence, their plan would pass.

At the request of President Wilson, Carter wrote a brief digest of the points of their plan, which the president intended to share at a special extended session of Congress requested by Wilson himself.

Edward House received a copy of the digest and sent it to Paul Warburg for review. Of course, Warburg was opposed to the Glass-Willis-Wilson plan because it called for regional banks and not a central bank headed by bankers. Warburg rejected the revised plan.

Of the criticism by Warburg, Glass wrote, "He simply was unalterably hostile to certain fundamental revisions of the Federal Reserve bill and in plain terms consistently said so."[37]

In fact, in 1913, Paul Warburg made an appearance before the House Banking and Currency Committee in which he gave his opinion of the bill:

I am a member of the banking house of Kuhn, Loeb & Company. I came over to this country in 1902, having been born and educated in the banking business in Hamburg, Germany, and studied banking in London and Paris, and have gone all around the world. In the Panic of 1907, the first suggestion I made was "Let us get a national clearing house." The Aldrich Plan contains some things, which are simply fundamental rules of banking. Your aim in this plan [referring to the Glass bill] must be the same—centralizing of reserves, mobilizing commercial credit, and getting an elastic note issue.[38]

Using every ally to their advantage, the behind-the-scenes conspirators were making sure that the Federal Reserve bill that would be signed by Wilson would include a central bank controlled by bankers. They turned to Treasury Secretary McAdoo to apply pressure to Glass to revise his bill.

McAdoo called a meeting with Glass so the two could discuss the bill. When Carter arrived, he was given a revised bill that included a central board. The bill also allowed the board to issue Treasury notes that could exceed gold reserves. McAdoo informed Glass that bankers enthusiastically endorsed this bill.

Knowing the bill that Glass and Wilson drafted would never be passed, Glass met with President Wilson yet again to revise the bill. Ultimately it would take three drafts before a final bill would be passed by members of Congress and signed by President Wilson. However, along the way, Glass felt the pressure of the bankers and their political allies, and it would prove mighty.

A few days before the bill was passed, Senator Elihu Root denounced the proposed Federal Reserve Act as an outrage on our liberties. He predicted: "Long before we wake up from our dream of prosperity through an inflated currency, our gold—which alone could have kept us from catastrophe—will have vanished and no rate of interest will tempt it to return."[39]

The Federal Reserve Act was passed on December 23, 1913 (by a vote of 298 to 60 in the House of Representatives, and 43 to 25 in the Senate). In the end, the bill signed by Wilson gave the Federal Reserve free control of the nation's currency. It could print money as it saw fit.

But herein lies the danger of giving complete control of our money supply to a banking cartel: When more money is put into circulation, it reduces the purchasing power of each dollar. That alone destroys our chances for prosperity. Merriam-Webster defines *inflation* as "a continuing rise in the general price level usually attributed to an increase in the volume of money and credit."[40]

The Cato Institute blames none other than the Federal Reserve for the decreased purchasing power of our money. The Institute says:

> The value of the dollar has been diluted by progressive additions made to the number of dollars (the stock of money) in circulation. Blame for our nation's erratic inflation, then, belongs squarely on the shoulders of our nation's monetary authority. The Fed's actions are responsible for the rate of growth of the total stock of dollars, and hence are responsible for the rate of dilution of the purchasing power of each existing dollar.[41]

Barbarians Control the Money

In referring to the Federal Reserve, former New York Mayor John Hylan said it best:

> The real menace of our Republic is the invisible government which like a giant octopus sprawls its slimy length over our city, state and nation.... At the head of this octopus are the Rockefeller-Standard Oil interests and a small group of powerful banking houses generally referred to as the international bankers [who] virtually run the United States government for their own selfish purposes.[42]

Even President Wilson came to regret his decision. In 1919, he expressed his profound regret, stating, "I am a most unhappy man. I have unwittingly ruined my country. A great industrial nation is controlled by its system of credit. Our system of credit is concentrated. The growth of the nation, therefore, and all our activities are in the hands of a few men."[43]

But the barbarians who made sure their version of the bill would be passed by Congress rejoiced in what they had done. In an article in *The Independent*, Senator Aldrich wrote, "Before the passage of this Act, the New York bankers could only dominate the reserves of New York. Now we are able to dominate the bank reserves of the entire country."[44]

Jacob Schiff sent Edward House a congratulatory note that read, "I want to say a word to you for the silent, no doubt effective work you have done in the interest of currency legislation and to congratulate you that the measure has finally been enacted into law."[45]

In 1914, the Federal Reserve officially began operations under its newly formed Organization Committee. The committee was made up of the secretary of the Treasury, secretary of agriculture, and Comptroller of the Currency. Their job was to decide what cities would make up the "federal reserve cities" and the assignment of Federal Reserve districts.

On April 2, the committee officially announced the cities that were chosen to include a Federal Reserve Bank in each: Boston, New York, Philadelphia, Cleveland, Richmond, Atlanta, Chicago, St. Louis, Minneapolis, Kansas City, Dallas, and San Francisco.

The Federal Reserve is made up of 12 member banks organized into corporations whose shares are sold to commercial banks and thrifts operating in the previously determined Federal Reserve districts. Shareholders elect six of the nine directors for their regional Federal Reserve Bank as well as its president. The chairman of the Federal Reserve is nominated by the president, and that nomination must be confirmed by Congress.

One of the major components of the system is the Federal Open Market Committee (FOMC), which is made up of the members of the Board of Governors, the president of the Federal Reserve Bank of New York, and presidents of four other Federal Reserve Banks, who serve on a rotating basis.

The FOMC oversees open market operations, which is the main tool used by the Federal Reserve to influence money market conditions and the growth of money and credit.

Eustace Mullins, author of *Secrets of the Federal Reserve: The London Connection*, stumbled across some interesting research. Mullins writes that the top original eight stockholders of the New York Federal Reserve were, in order from largest to smallest as of 1983, Citibank, Chase Manhattan, Morgan Guaranty Trust, Chemical Bank, Manufacturers Hanover Trust, Bankers Trust Company, National Bank of North America, and the Bank of New York.[46]

Mullins also asserts that the original organization certificates show the Federal Reserve Bank of New York issued 203,053 shares, and, as filed with the Comptroller of the Currency on May 19, 1914, the large New York City banks took more than half of the outstanding shares.

Rockefeller and Kuhn, Loeb & Co., who controlled National City Bank, took the largest number of shares of any bank: 30,000 shares. J.P. Morgan's First National Bank took 15,000 shares. Chase National Bank took 6,000 shares. The Marine National Bank of Buffalo, later known as Marine Midland, took 6,000 shares. National Bank of Commerce of New York City took 21,000 shares.

If Mullins is correct, one could say that the money trust reinvented itself as the Federal Reserve. But this also demonstrates what the American public was afraid would happen—that the Fed is a powerful group of bankers who can create money at will and thus have the ability to control a nation's wealth.

A Poisonous Drug

Adam Lass, creator of *WaveStrength Options Weekly*, calls the Fed a poisonous drug. Lass writes:

> There's a dangerous drug in the American investors' blood-stream—and it's driving them crazy. This poison has caused them to abandon any pretense of logic or self-preservation. It induces them (some say deliberately) to invest in the worst companies—companies that couldn't hope to make a profit or improve shareholder standing—and at the worst time, when those shares would otherwise be losing value.
>
> This drug was created to be a "magic bullet" that would "fix" the natural cycles of the economy and the market place, to stamp out the normal rhythms and tropes that allow good companies to thrive and eliminate bad business plans and lousy management teams. Instead, it has destabilized the markets, creating wild asset bubbles and massive crashes.
>
> Rather than increase trust, participation and liquidity, it has created an atmosphere of distrust, disaffection and malaise. And beyond the admittedly insular world of the stock market, it has

cost millions of American citizens their jobs, their savings and their homes. The poisonous drug I am speaking of is the modern U.S. Federal Reserve System.[47]

Lass argues that while the general public is shocked at the secrecy that surrounded the creation of the Federal Reserve, the real horror is how little people actually know about the Fed. Lass suggests that for most of the twentieth century, few investors knew or cared about the Federal Reserve or its policies on bank rates and liquidity.

Lass says, "What little understanding the public knows of the Fed, they learn from the media. But that's dangerous because the media can position the Fed's actions in whatever way best suits their needs to sell papers or what Washington and Wall Street want investors to hear."[48]

Lass points to the reign of Paul Volcker as an example. In 1979 Volcker was picked by President Jimmy Carter as the man to tame runaway inflation. However, it was right about this time that the media—feeling high off its destruction of a sitting president and ever so hungry for fresh meat for the evening broadcasts—began to cover the Fed's "back-room" issues in great detail.

Volcker became a hero to some and a villain to others when he supposedly licked inflation single-handedly by doubling the federal funds rate to 20 percent and pushing mortgage rates over 21 percent. It was a great time to invest in banks. Long-term deposit contracts could earn far more than most stock market investments.

However, it was a murderous time if you needed working capital from those same institutions, and farmers and small businessmen could be seen lining up outside the Fed's Constitution Avenue headquarters, armed with torches and pitchforks.

Volcker's successor, Alan Greenspan, was made far more famous by the media. "Never before could a Fed Chairman be assured of a full court paparazzi press waiting for him every time he stepped out of a limo," says Lass. Greenspan reveled in the attention.

The media called him "The Most Powerful Man in the World," and he appeared to believe them. More importantly, almost every investor believed them. Only later would they regret their decisions. As Greenspan lowered interest rates, capital costs were dramatically reduced, and suddenly the worst business plans and most feeble management could look brilliant.

Some say that this injection of pure logical poison into the investing bloodstream was deliberate, that it was intended to end history by damping down economic cycles and ensuring continuous prosperity forever—the classic stock market ladder to the moon.

Instead it exacerbated those very cycles, creating huge tidal waves in and out of entire asset classes, based not on reliable, time-tested economic concepts but rather on the basis of inverted logic wherein the promise of losses was the sweetest honey, and profits pure vinegar on the tongue. Lass says, "The Fed is a dangerous prod, accelerating a series of cyclic crashes that threaten to utterly destroy our modern economy."

Many analysts and authors agree with Lass's assessment of the Federal Reserve. James Turk, publisher of the *Freemarket Gold & Money Report*, says central banking is not only a barbarous relic of the past, but it has become dangerous as well.

Turk writes,

> Not too many years from now—when the U.S. dollar collapses, as just one in a long list of fiat currencies that have collapsed before it—people will look back and ask themselves how it was possible barbarous institutions like central banks could have hoodwinked so many people into thinking that central banks were a good thing. The answer is that central banks have created the illusions of prosperity.[49]

Turk is absolutely right in his assessment of the Fed. The Fed has created the illusion of wealth. Over the past few years, the United States has racked up more debt than during any previous time in history. To add insult to injury, the Fed has dramatically increased the supply of money. But as the money supply increases, so does inflation, which destroys the value of money.

Since the inception of the Federal Reserve, the U.S. dollar has lost more than 95 percent of its value. Unless dramatic measures are taken, generations of our children will pay for the Fed's mistakes.

Chapter 9

Money for Nothing

There are some numbers that can tell you an awful lot about the economy, such as the rate of unemployment, consumer spending, factory orders, or retail sales; corporate earnings reports; and the gains and losses in the stock market. You can find these numbers in just about any newspaper in the country.

But there are a handful of numbers that tell you the inside story of what's really happening with our economy, numbers that rarely receive front page coverage by the media.

One of these numbers is the money supply. We mentioned this in an earlier chapter but it deserves greater discussion. Why is this important? Because the amount of money in circulation tells us the real value of our dollars, and therefore our real wealth.

The easiest way to understand money supply is to compare it to shopping for antiques. What makes antiques valuable is their age and scarcity. The less of a particular antique is available on the market, and the more it is sought after, the more you have to pay for it.

Conversely, the more of that item that exists, the less valuable it is and therefore the lower its price. The same is true for money. The more money in circulation, the less value each dollar holds.

Economists use three definitions to describe the money supply. One is called M0, and it is the total amount of coins and dollar bills in circulation, plus the money in bank vaults and all of the deposits those banks have at reserve banks. In July 2009, the M0 money supply amounted to $908.6 billion.[1]

But there's more money then what's in someone's wallet or sitting in a bank's vault. The next measure is money deposited in checking accounts and held in traveler's checks, which can be redeemed for money. That is known as M1 but it also includes M0. In July 2009 this totaled $1.6 billion.[2]

The next measure of money is known as M2, which equals all the money deposited in savings accounts, money market funds, and certificates of deposit of amounts less than $100,000, and repurchase agreements (sale of securities coupled with an agreement to repurchase the securities at a higher price on a later date). It also includes all of M1 (which includes M0). This equaled $8.3 billion in July 2009.[3]

Following M2, the next measure of money is M3, which refers to money held in certificates of deposit of more than $100,000, plus M2 (which includes M1 and M0). M3 also includes Eurodollar transfers and money in money market accounts by institutional investors. Eurodollars are U.S.-denominated deposits in banks outside the United States, in countries such as China, Russia, and Saudi Arabia.

Basically, Eurodollars represent (1) money U.S. corporations use to fund their foreign operations, (2) foreign corporations funding foreign or domestic operations, and (3) foreign governments funding investment projects or general balance-of-payment deficits.

M3 historically has been considered the broadest measure of the money supply. According to the National Inflation Association, the last known figure for this amount is $10.3 trillion.

Here's the thing about M3 figures. The Federal Reserve used to regularly track this number and include it as part of its report on the U.S. money supply.

But on March 23, 2006, the Fed announced that it would no longer track this figure. The Fed's press release stated, "M3 does not appear to convey any additional information about economic activity that is not already embodied in M2 and has not played a role in the monetary policy process for many years. Consequently, the Board judged that the costs of collecting the underlying data and publishing M3 outweigh the benefits."

Conspiracy theorists argue the Fed stopped publishing this number because it wanted to hide inflation numbers. Now, we all know that it's the Federal Reserve that controls the money supply. And the biggest problem related to the money supply is inflation. Most of the time inflation occurs because of increases in the money supply. Take a look at Figure 9.1, which shows the growth of the U.S. money supply from 1917 through 2009.

As you can see from Figure 9.1, the money supply remains constant until around 1933. Then it begins to gradually increase. In 1980, it rises higher and stays on that track all the way through to 2009, with the biggest increase occurring right around 2000.

This shows we've had a huge increase in the money supply. So it would stand to reason that an increase in money supply means an

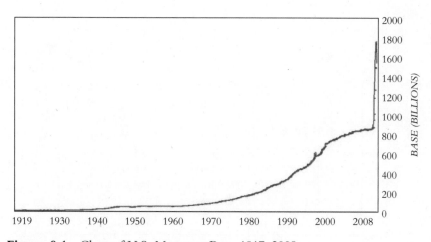

Figure 9.1 Chart of U.S. Monetary Base, 1917–2009
DATA SOURCE: Copyright ©2008 Charting Stocks, www.chartingstocks.net/wp-content/uploads/ 2009/03/money-supply1.gif.

increase in inflation. But let's jump back to the M3 statistics. Look at Figure 9.2, which shows the growth in the M3 money supply.

Notice how much it's grown over the past 40 years. According to the last government reporting of that number, which was in February 2006, M3 grew at an annual rate of 8 percent, but M1 grew by just 0.4 percent and M2 by 4.7 percent.[4]

As mentioned earlier, the government claims that M3 is no longer relevant when accessing the money supply. But their reasoning makes no sense. They suggest M2, which includes deposits of less than $100,000, plus checking accounts and travelers checks, is much more significant measure than M3, which usually represents trillions of dollars. In fact, the last reporting was $10.6 trillion.

How is that not a significant measure? They also claim that reporting M3 takes too much time and money. But it is already incurring the cost of tracking the other money measures, so it would stand to reason that tracking M3 can't be that much more expensive.

So is the government hiding inflation? John Williams, executive editor of *Shadow Government Statistics*, says the growth of M3 does indicate inflation. Williams says, "The current 15 percent-plus level of annual growth in an ongoing estimate of M3—the broadest measure of the U.S.

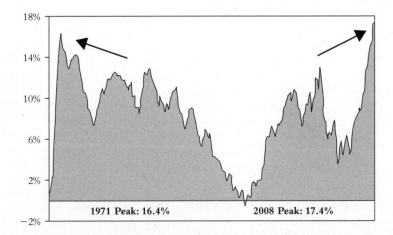

Figure 9.2   Growth of M3 Money Supply

DATA SOURCE: Marketoracle.com; data from *Shadow Government Statistics*, shadowstats.com.

money supply—has not been seen since August 1971, when President Richard Nixon closed the gold window. Such foreshadows increasing monetary inflation pressure in the U.S. economy, on top of existing pressures from oil and food prices and a weakening U.S. dollar."[5]

Williams also argues that by not offsetting the impact of foreign-held dollars going into U.S. treasuries or agencies, the Fed is setting a policy of inflating money growth just as much as if it were injecting the funds itself.[6]

William isn't alone in his belief that we'll see inflation rear its ugly head. G. Edward Griffin, historian and author of *The Creature From Jekyll Island*, agrees. Griffin says:

> Inflation has now been institutionalized at a fairly constant 5 percent per year. This has been determined to be the optimum level for generating the most revenue without causing public alarm.
>
> A 5 percent devaluation applies, not only to the money earned this year, but to all that is left over from previous years. At the end of the first year, a dollar is worth 95 cents. At the end of the second year, the 95 cents is reduced again by 5 percent, leaving its worth at 90 cents and so on.
>
> By the time a person has worked 20 years, the government has confiscated 64 percent of every dollar he saved over those years. By the time he has worked 45 years, the hidden tax will be 90 percent. The government will take virtually everything a person saves over a lifetime.[7]

Justice Litle, editorial director of the Taipan Publishing Group, also agrees we're headed for inflation. Litle writes, "As the 'banksters' rush to pay back TARP funds and clear themselves for year-end bonuses, the world moves closer to a hyperinflationary depression."[8]

Usually when we talk about hyperinflation, we talk about emerging economies such as Zimbabwe, which experienced the highest inflation rate ever seen. So is it possible that the United States, a developed nation, could experience hyperinflation? The truth is, developed nations *have* seen hyperinflation. In fact, we can easily find examples where increases in the money supply eventually led to hyperinflation.

Between 1921 and 1922, inflation in the Soviet Union reached 213 percent. When World War I broke out, the German central bank stopped redeeming its notes in gold and started printing money, which is how Germany financed the war.

By the end of World War I, the amount of money in circulation had quadrupled and the consumer price index had risen by 140 percent. By May 1921 inflation started, and by July 1922 prices rose 700 percent; yet the German central bank continued printing money nonstop.[9]

In 1922, inflation in Austria reached 1,426 percent. From 1914 to January 1923, the consumer price index rose by a factor of 11,836.[10] But Austria released itself from the grip of inflation by following the advice of a prominent economist, Ludwig von Mises.

Von Mises was born on September 29, 1881, in the city of Lemberg (now Lviv) in Austria. He came from a prestigious family, where his father served as a Viennese construction engineer working for the Austrian railroads. In fact, his father received the honorary title *von* from the Austrian government for the work he did on the railroad.

In 1906, at age 25, Ludwig von Mises received a doctorate in law from the University of Vienna. Shortly after receiving his degree, he became chief economist at the Vienna Chamber of Commerce. In 1912, Ludwig's book *The Theory of Money and Credit* was published.[11]

However, one of von Mises' major economic contributions was defeating the inflation that had prevailed in Austria in the late 1920. According to author Mark Skousen of *The Making of Modern Economics: The Lives and Ideas of Great Thinkers*, von Mises was asked by the Austrian government how to end the hyperinflation the country was suffering.

When asked for his help, he told members of the government who had paid him a visit to meet him at midnight at a specific location. Puzzled yet anxious for answers, they agreed and met von Mises at the location of his choice.

When von Mises showed up, they asked him how they could stop inflation. Von Mises pointed to the building they were standing in front of and shouted, "Hear that noise? Turn it off?" The building the group was standing in front of was the government printing press, which had been printing new dollars around the clock. The government heeded von Mises' advice. When they stopped printing more money, inflation ended.[12]

Austria isn't the only country to have experienced high inflation rates. As Figure 9.3 shows, many other developed countries have suffered from extreme inflation. It's a danger the United States faces, especially as government spending increases.

Run, Rabbit, Run

But Litle points out that it's not just the amount of money in circulation that causes hyperinflation. Rather, it has to do with *velocity* of money, or how fast money moves through the system. To understand the velocity of money, let's step back in history for a moment to see where this concept originated.

American astronomer and economist Simon Newcomb developed a mathematical equation to help determine the value of money. In his early years, Newcomb received no formal education. Most everything he knew, he learned from his father, who was a teacher. What his father didn't teach him, Simon learned on his own. However, when studying at the Smithsonian Institute, he was invited to further his education at the Lawrence Scientific School of Harvard University. Those studies helped him receive an appointment as professor of mathematics and astronomy at Johns Hopkins University in 1884.[13]

One of Newcomb's most important pieces of work was conducted around 1885 concerning the supply of money, when he developed a mathematical equation that most economists use to determine money's value: $MV=PT$. In this equation, M equals the actual quantity of money; V signifies the velocity, or the rate at which money circulates (or how long money is held out of circulation); T represents the number of transactions, or exchanges; and P is the level of prices.

Inflation is when the aggregate level of prices goes up, and *deflation* is when the aggregate level of prices goes down. Inflation will occur if V and T remain constant but M goes up—that is, the supply of money increases without any other changes. Inflation can also occur if V goes up (people spend money more quickly) or T declines (the economy shrinks), as the other variables are constant.

The mathematical formula may be somewhat complicated, but Justice Litle providers readers with an easy way to understand velocity as it relates to money. Litle writes,

Country	Month with Highest Inflation Rate	Highest Monthly Inflation Rate	Equivalent Daily Inflation Rate	Time Required for Prices to Double
Hungary	July 1946	4.19×10^{16}	207%	15.0 hours
Zimbabwe	Mid-November 2008	79,600,000,0000%	98.0%	24.7 hours
Yugoslavia	January 1994	313,000,000%	64.6%	1.4 hours
Germany	October 1923	29,500%	20.9%	3.7 hours
Greece	October 1944	13,800%	17.9%	4.3 hours
China	May 1949	2,178%	11.0%	6.7 hours

Figure 9.3 Hyperinflation by Country: Highest Monthly Inflation Rates in History

NOTES: The authors calculated "equivalent daily inflation rate" and "time required for prices to double."

SOURCE: Prof. Steve H. Hanke, February 5, 2009, Cato Institute.

Imagine you're standing in front of a large tree trunk. There is a brightly colored marker on the trunk, and there are rabbits running in circles around the tree itself. Every time a rabbit passes the marker on the trunk, you note it down on your clipboard: one X per pass.

Now let's say you tally up your results and note you made 20 Xs in the space of 60 seconds. Assuming you had your reasons, how could you double the number of Xs in the same amount of time?

There are two ways you could double the number of Xs on your clipboard (to 40 per minute in this case). You could increase the number of rabbits running around the tree . . . or you could go with the *same* number of rabbits and try to make them run *faster*. (Remember, you don't care if it's the same rabbit or a different rabbit when you jot down your X. You're just counting the number of passes.)

The rabbits are analogous to money in the system. Money that's just there is inert. . . . In order to have an effect on the economy, the money has to move. So when money is "hot" and the rabbits are running at top speed, fewer rabbits are needed to fill up the clipboard with Xs. The rabbits speed around the tree very quickly—analogous to high *turnover*, or money changing hands very quickly.

When money is "cold," on the other hand, the rabbits are lethargic, and you need *more* money (i.e., more rabbits) to get a decent number of Xs on the clipboard. If money stops changing hands entirely—as it seemed to have for a brief span in late September and early October—it's like the rabbits coming to a dead stop. They aren't moving at all.

So when the Fed pumps the system full of money, it's the equivalent of dumping more and more rabbits into the equation. As the Fed gets desperate, maybe they round up dozens or even hundreds of rabbits.

The upshot is that the Fed can have a direct impact on the *quantity* of money in the system, but not the *velocity* of money in the system. It can't *make* the rabbits run.[14]

Justice's point is well made. And you can see that point demonstrated in Figure 9.4, which shows that velocity usually peaks right before or during recessions.

But if the Fed has increased the money supply, where is it?

The answer is that banks and corporations are hoarding cash at levels not seen in years. The 30 companies making up the Dow Jones Industrial Average saw cash holdings raise from $279 billion to $498 billion from 2008 to 2009. That's a 79 percent increase in cash holdings.

"Cash accumulation by major U.S. corporations is at an all-time high since the 1960s," says Kenneth N. Daniels, a finance professor at Virginia Commonwealth University. "Firms are hoarding cash ... and the economy will not rebound at the pace or the magnitude to significantly change the unemployment rate over the next 18 months."[15]

It's not just companies on the Dow, either. A majority of companies in the Standard & Poor's 500 stock index increased cash to a combined $1.19 trillion while simultaneously reducing spending, keeping a jobs recovery on hold.[16]

Banks are in on the act as well. In January 2009 some $793 billion of excess reserves were on hand at the Federal Reserve. That is more than

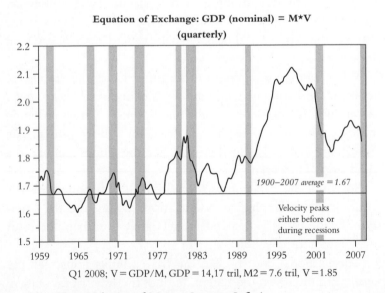

Q1 2008; V = GDP/M, GDP = 14,17 tril, M2 = 7.6 tril, V = 1.85

Figure 9.4   How Velocity of Money Impacts Inflation

SOURCES: Board of Governors of the Federal Reserve System, Bureau of Economic Analysis, HIMCO.

double the amount of money doled out or pledged to financial companies through the Treasury Department's $700 billion Troubled Asset Relief Program.[17]

Citigroup has almost doubled its cash to $244.2 billion in the year since Lehman Brothers Holdings Inc. filed for bankruptcy, the biggest such stockpile of any U.S. bank. In fact, the four largest banks in the United States (Bank of America, Citigroup, Wells Fargo, and J.P. Morgan) had increased their combined liquidity by 67 percent to $1.53 trillion as of September 30, 2009, from $914.2 billion in June 2008. The amount equals 21 percent of the banks' total assets, up from 15 percent a year earlier.[18]

Lending across the U.S. economy contracted 7.4 percent in 2009, the biggest such drop since 1942, according to the Federal Deposit Insurance Corp. That means $1.5 trillion in lending evaporated that year, the Treasury Department estimates.[19]

This contraction mostly hurts small businesses, which account for about 50 percent of all U.S. workers. In addition, small businesses are responsible for more than 50 percent of the nonfarm private gross domestic product (GDP) in the United States.[20]

The problem with hoarding cash is that in order for companies to hire, or for the economy to grow, money needs to circulate in the economy. Consumers don't spend because they don't have the money to do so. For companies, that means reduced sales, and as sales decline, profits drop. As profits drop, layoffs increase.

As more people become unemployed, they are not able to pay their mortgages. Mortgage defaults increase. Soon the economy spirals downward.

In fact, in February 2010, the Mortgage Bankers Association reports that the percentage of home loans 60 or more days past due reached 6.9 percent, mortgages more than 90 days past due climbed to 5 percent, and loans in foreclosure rose to 4.58 percent. This marked the twelfth straight quarter of rising delinquencies.

So as banks and corporations hoard their massive amounts of cash, they're making recovery harder to achieve. Worth noting is an article that ran in the *Financial Times* that might explain why banks and corporations are hoarding money. The article says executives have been told by regulators, particularly those at the Federal Reserve, that "they would have to wait until the economic and legislative picture became clearer before returning funds to investors."[21]

The *Financial Times* also reports that one senior Wall Street executive said, "Regulators are gun-shy at this stage, partly because they fear that giving the green light to healthier banks to return cash to investors would prompt demands from more troubled institutions to do the same." The article says regulators want banks to have more substantial profits on hand before issuing any kind of dividend to investors.[22]

But investment banks like J.P. Morgan and Goldman Sachs have plenty of profits on hand. For 2009, Goldman's net income was $13.4 billion, or $22.13 per share, more than five times 2008's $2.32 billion and exceeding the record $11.6 billion the firm generated in 2007.[23] J.P. Morgan earned $11.7 billion in 2009, more than double its profit in 2008, and generated record revenue. The bank earned $3.3 billion in the fourth quarter alone.[24]

So we have a huge increase in the money supply, yet banks and corporations are hoarding cash at almost record amounts. But let's take a look and see how so much money was generated.

Money for Everyone

In a 2002 speech before the National Economists Club in Washington, D.C., Federal Reserve Chairman Ben Bernanke told his audience, "The U.S. government has a technology called a printing press that allows it to produce as many U.S. dollars as it wishes at essentially no cost. By increasing the number of U.S. dollars in circulation, or even by credibly threatening to do so, the U.S. government can also reduce the value of a dollar."[25]

The Federal Reserve deliberately increased the number of dollars in circulation by keeping interest rates low. That policy started in 2001 when Federal Reserve Chairman Alan Greenspan lowered interest rates to 1 percent. In fact, Greenspan held interest rates at historically low levels for three years.

Freelance financial writer Mike Whitney, in an article for the Market Oracle, blames the entire economic recession and credit fallout on Greenspan. Whitney says Greenspan's "cheap money" policy caused a speculative frenzy in the real estate market that sent home prices through the stratosphere. Whitney writes:

> Greenspan kept the printing presses whirring along at full-tilt while the banks and mortgage lenders devised every scam imaginable to put greenbacks into the hands of unqualified borrowers. Adjustable rate mortgages, "interest-only" loans, and "no down payment" loans were all part of the creative financing boondoggle which the kept the economy sputtering along after the "dot.com" crackup in 2000.[26]

Whitney says the Fed's cheap-money policy caused the housing market to sizzle. In his article, Whitney says that in just six years the total value of real estate jumped from $11 trillion to $21 trillion! He asserts that the explosion in the value of real estate was engineered by seductively low interest rates.

Whitney further argues that low interest rates provide a channel for pumping cheap money into the economy, which inevitably creates equity bubbles. Whitney also suggests that Greenspan knew exactly what was happening and what the fallout would be if he kept interest rates low.

But Greenspan says otherwise—he claims he didn't realize how significant the problems would become. In a *60 Minutes* interview aired in February 2007, Greenspan said, "While I was aware a lot of these practices were going on, I had no notion of how significant they had become until very late. I didn't really get it until very late in 2005 and 2006."

Seems hard to imagine that Greenspan didn't know how significant these practices had become. The man earned two degrees from New York University. He was an economist with the National Industrial Conference Board. He understands economics better than most people. So it stands to reason that as chairman of the Federal Reserve, he certainly understood the consequences of lowering interest rates and creating an abundant supply of money.

After all, the Fed sets the federal funds rate, the interest rate charged when banks lend funds to one another, also known as the short-term rate. When the Federal Reserve raises or lowers this rate, it affects mortgage rates that are tied to short-term interest rates, such as home equity rates and adjustable rates. It's these kinds of mortgages, including interest-only and no-money-down loans, that made it easy for people to buy homes, sometimes homes they couldn't afford.

Yes, low interest rates led to a boom in real estate. But the excess money it created made its way onto Wall Street in the form of extremely risky derivative speculation. According to the Bank for International Settlements, the derivatives market exploded with its value rising fivefold from $127 trillion in 2002 to $684 trillion in 2008. You can see that growth in Figure 9.5.

Greenspan says interest rates were kept low to keep inflation in check. And from all indications, the current Federal Reserve Board intends to keep rates low. James Bullard of the St. Louis branch says the Fed plans to keep interest rates "exceptionally low for an extended period of time."[27]

Thorsten Polleit says keeping rates low is a fatal flaw. In writing about the current recession in his June 2009 Ludwig von Mises Institute article, Polleit says that keeping interest rates low "amounts to fighting the correction of the debacle which has been caused by central banks' downward manipulation of interest rates through a relentless increase in bank circulation credit and the money supply."[28]

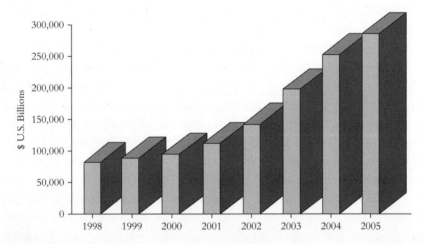

Figure 9.5   Amazing Growth of Worldwide Derivatives Market

Polleit says that the policy of suppressing the interest rate is an attempt to evade the costs of the debt that has been heaped up over the past decades as a result of money production under government-controlled fiat-money systems: If market interest rates no longer fall, or do not stay down, the credit pyramid would come crashing down.[29]

Creating a Mountain of Debt

The policies set by Greenspan and followed through by Bernanke have created a mountain of debt (as seen in Figure 9.6). Since 2007, the U.S. national debt has increased $4.4 billion *per day*. Interest payments on that debt now make up more than 12 percent of the federal budget. That means Washington has to make a staggering $335.3 billion per year in interest payments just to avoid default on that debt.

Other countries such as China and Japan buy most of the debt. China was the number one foreign holder but has recently been unloading its U.S. dollars for other commodities such as gold. Several times, Chinese government officials have expressed worry over our debt. Because China

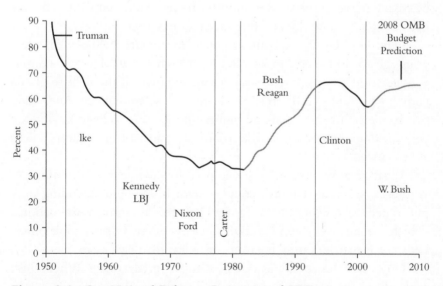

Figure 9.6 Our National Debt as a Percentage of GDP
SOURCE: http://zfacts.com/p/318.html, data from WhiteHouse.gov.

has been anxious to unload U.S. dollars, Japan has gone from the number two spot in owning U.S. debt to number one.

But it's not just foreign countries that own our debt. The biggest holder of U.S. government debt is the United States itself. The Federal Reserve System of banks and other U.S. intragovernmental holdings account for a stunning $4.806 trillion in U.S. Treasury debt.[30] (See Figure 9.6, which shows the growth of our national debt).

Even more alarming is the fact that the Federal Reserve also bought a huge amount of U.S. debt. According to FedUpUSA, of the total $1.1 trillion of net issuance of Treasury bonds, mortgage-backed securities, and long-term debt, the Fed has purchased $861 billion or almost 80 percent.[31]

Why would the Reserve buy its own debt? The Economic Collapse, a financial web site reporting on financial and economic concerns (theeconomiccollapseblog.com), says the reason is that there were simply *not enough buyers*. So the Fed had no choice but to buy it.

Normally, to attract more buyers, the Fed would have to raise the interest rate on the bonds. But if it were to do that, interest rates on everything else would also skyrocket. Since the Fed is the main buyer, in essence, it is keeping interest rates artificially low.

The budget deficit would also rise because the government would be paying higher interest rates on its borrowing. And our debt is already becoming a huge problem—one that requires a solution.

In terms of GDP, our country's debt has risen from 40 percent a few years ago to 50 percent today. But here's what you have to take into consideration when a country has a spiraling debt: If the debt reaches a fairly high level of GDP, investors begin to lose confidence. And when that happens, investors demand higher interest rates to keep buying the debt or, in extreme cases, refuse to buy any more of the country's debt at any price.[32]

What's also worrisome is that it looks like the debt will continue to skyrocket. Obama's bailouts coupled with his stimulus spending only put us deeper in debt. The Treasury Department estimates the national debt has increased over $2 trillion since President Obama took office. Let's not forget he's only been in office less than two years.

How does his spending compare to his predecessor? When Bush took office, the national debt was $5.73 trillion. When he left, it was

$10.7 trillion. That's a difference of $4.97 trillion.[33] If Obama stays in office for four years, can we expect he'll pile on a total of $8 trillion more?

Our national debt continues to plague us. We're already seeing how high debt can send shivers through the market. Consider how the markets reacted to news that Greece could likely default on its debt. Not only that, but the problem could spread to Spain, Portugal, and Italy. The debt-to-GDP ratio in these countries is approaching 60 percent.

European Union leaders are struggling to come up with a safety net that keeps these countries, particularly Greece, from defaulting on their debt. EU Commission President José Manuel Barroso called on European governments to agree on a detailed plan of financial help for Greece.

Worried that Greece won't be able pay its debts, investors are beginning to demand higher interest rates when the country sells government bonds—rates the government says it can't go on paying.

On March 25, 2010, *Forbes* ran an article written by noted economist Nouriel Roubini explaining that at the time the global economy is trying to crawl out of the recession, the eurozone debt crisis has significantly increased the chances of a double-dip recession.

Roubini writes, "The Greek debt crisis has occupied center stage of the economic and political debate. It is not just a Greek tragedy—the contagion could spread to Portugal, Spain, Italy, and Ireland."[34]

Roubini also argues that in a couple of years, the U.S. gross federal debt will exceed GDP and the federal budget will never balance again. This is clearly unsustainable and raises questions about the future of the United States' AAA ratings.

Is it possible the United States could lose its triple-A credit rating? Earlier in March 2010, Moody's, one of the companies that issues credit ratings, expressed concerns over U.S. debt. Moody's said debt affordability is "most stretched" in the United States and Britain among countries with the top AAA rating.[35]

Peter Tanous, president and director of Lynx Investment Advisory in Washington, D.C., sees trouble ahead. He says, "We are heading down a virtually irreversible road where the overall financial picture of the US is going to look very bad."[36]

The Struggle to Be Debt-Free

Of course, this isn't the first time the United States has experienced a tremendous debt problem. It happened during the Great Depression. Between 1933 and 1939, the national debt rose to about 40 percent of gross national product, or GNP, as it used to be called. Roosevelt solved the debt problem by confiscating gold, than raised gold prices to cover the debt. But that ultimately destroyed the value of the dollar.

Now, it's hard to imagine that in this day and age the government would resort to confiscating everyone's gold. But we've got a mountain of debt to pay off. What the government could do is stop selling gold altogether and raise the price of it high enough to cover almost all of the outstanding debt.

Or it could raise taxes. Shawn Tully, writing for CNNMoney.com, says that to keep the debt from wrecking the economy, the United States would need to raise annual federal income taxes an average of $11,000 in 2019 for all families that pay them. That's an increase of about 55 percent.[37]

Let's not forget that every bond the U.S. Treasury issues is backed with a promise of payment from the government out of future taxes collected from U.S. citizens.

Or the government could stop entitlement programs such as Social Security or Medicare and Medicaid. Of course, that wouldn't go over well with many people. But here's the rub: According to the *2008 Financial Report of the United States Government*, future Social Security and Medicare payouts that the U.S. government is committed to now exceed $65 *trillion*.[38] So stopping those programs would definitely impact the national debt.

Another thing the government could do is boost prices and further reduce the value of the dollar. This way the debt is much easier to pay off because as the dollar becomes less valuable, it takes fewer dollars to pay the debt off.

Admittedly these options aren't easy solutions we'd like to see happen. But we didn't get into this problem overnight, so we can't solve it quickly.

The core of the problem lies within the fractional reserve banking system that has developed over the decades. A fractional reserve system allows governments to create money out of thin air. No matter what the government does, our national debt will haunt us for years to come.

The Economic Collapse says there is no mathematical way our debt can be paid off. It says, "If the U.S. government went out today and took every single penny from every single American bank, business and taxpayer, they still would not be able to pay off the national debt."[39]

The sad fact is the United States has had a national debt since the days of the Revolutionary War, with the exception of 1835, when under President Andrew Jackson the national debt was totally paid off. Jackson hated banks. He was born poor but made his own fortune.

Jackson viewed debt as a national curse. Jackson believed it was not only unfortunate, but also dishonest for a government to remain in debt for a long period of time. In his first message to Congress, Jackson said he looked forward to the day when the country could be debt-free.[40]

When he assumed the presidency, the national debt was $48 million, mainly due to the War of 1812. Under his reign, sales of public land generated enough money to cover the government's yearly expenses. Not only did he pay off the national debt, the country had a surplus.

Jackson wanted the federal government to collect only enough revenue to meet its own needs and let any surpluses go back to the American public rather than sit in a central bank.

Unfortunately, what Jackson achieved didn't last long. In 1865 the debt ran up again from financing the Civil War. In 1865, Jay Cooke, general subscription agent of government loans, issued a report about the country's national debt. He projected the debt would grow to $3 billion, representing 15 percent of the wealth of all states or $98.62 per person.[41]

Each person's share of today's debt would equal $41,125.79. That means in 145 years, per person today, the debt has increased 41,601 percent. But in reality not every person is responsible for paying down that debt.

According to the latest information from the Tax Foundation, the IRS reported that in 2007 about 141 million people filed tax returns. However, roughly 47 million people who filed a tax return claimed enough deductions, exemptions, or tax credits that they owed no taxes to the IRS.

Then there's the group of people who filed a tax return and paid very little in taxes because they were making less than $50,000 a year. So that means the real tax burden falls on about 46 million people who pay more in income taxes than anyone else.[42]

So it's those people who, if the government decides to raise taxes to pay off the debt, will bear the burden. If you are one of these taxpaying citizens, that means your share of the debt is $260,869.55, assuming the debt stays where it is right now. But take fair warning: The debt will only continue to grow and so will your share of the burden.

Can we ever return to being a debt-free nation? It's highly unlikely. The barbarians of wealth have put us on a path of financial misery. In the Congressional Budget Office's (CBO) *Budget and Economic Outlook for 2009 to 2019* report, the CBO says the recession will be one of the longest ones the country has faced since World War II, possibly lasting 18 months.

It also expects that this recession will be the deepest, with economic output over the next two years averaging 6.8 percent below normal levels. The CBO says that the deficit will be the largest recorded since World War II. But it concedes that a major source of uncertainty in its outlook is the degree and persistence of turmoil in the financial markets and the impact on the future course of the economy.

The CBO report states:

> Many financial instruments and practices that contributed to the financial crisis came into widespread use only in the past decade, and the scale of the problems and the worldwide linkages of financial markets are significantly different from what they were in previous episodes of financial stress in the United States. Furthermore, the scale and novelty of federal intervention, particularly by the Federal Reserve, and uncertainty about the degree to which those interventions will affect the economic outlook, make it particularly difficult for analysts to use historical patterns to forecast the near future.[43]

Basically the government can't be sure what the outcome will be. The weapons of mass financial destruction that the barbarians of wealth conjured up from their penthouse office suites on Wall Street computer screens have put the U.S. economy in dire jeopardy.

The politicians we turn to for help have only escalated matters by creating a mountain of debt. Their motives are not based on what's best for the people they serve, but what ensures the next vote, the next corporate donation.

James Quinn, senior director of strategic planning for a major university, best describes what has happened to us today:

> Our elected officials no longer represent the people. They represent the 17,000 corporate lobbyists who spend $3.3 billion per year to "persuade" them what is best for their special interests. The ideals of our fledgling Republic have been corrupted by politicians who have sold their souls to corporate and banking interests.[44]

Tallyho, Mr. Quinn.

Chapter 10

The Barbarians' Powerful Ally

On April 16, 2010, an interesting article showed up in *Business Week* but got very little attention from other media outlets. It deserved more fanfare than it received, because it draws attention to the Wall Street barbarians who are just as guilty of bringing down the global economy as the likes of Goldman Sachs, J.P. Morgan, AIG, Bank of America, and Citigroup.

I'm talking about credit rating agencies such as Standard and Poor's, Fitch, and Moody's Investor Services. While the average investor may know the names of these companies, few understand the critical role they play in assessing the investment securities Wall Street corporations sell to the world.

Their ratings make or break securities and are suppose to be unbiased, objective assessments of the creditworthiness of companies, countries, and securities. But what's frightening is that they put their stamp of approval on just about every type of toxic derivative Wall Street created.

According to the *BusinessWeek* article, Moody's placed $43.4 billion of jumbo-mortgage bonds issued before 2005, which had once received the highest ratings, under review for downgrades. In fact, it indicated a total of 3,000 securities may be downgraded. A week earlier, Moody's had said it might downgrade $50 billion of older subprime mortgage bonds.[1]

Scott Buchta of Guggenheim Securities LLC pointed out, "The market has largely ignored this announcement, but should they [Moody's] move bonds from investment grade to non-investment grade it may result in some forced selling."[2]

However, these huge downgrades of the mortgage-backed securities are only just happening, a full 15 months after the crisis hit. Not before, not during, but after.

The American public is well aware of the role the mortgage-backed securities played in the downfall of the nation's largest banks and lending institutions. So for the downgrades to happen now makes little sense and is certainly too late.

If Goldman Sachs is convicted of securities fraud as charged by the Securities and Exchange Commission (SEC), the rating agencies should be next in line to be investigated. That's because for years, companies such as Standard and Poor's, Fitch, and Moody's have been the trusted source for institutional investors to find credit ratings for most of the income-generating securities traded on Wall Street.

In fact, Moody's bills itself as "among the world's most respected and widely utilized sources for credit ratings, research and risk analysis." Standard and Poor's brands itself as known to investors worldwide as a leader in financial-market intelligence. It also says it strives to provide investors who want to make better-informed investment decisions with market intelligence in the form of credit ratings, indexes, investment research, and risk evaluations and solutions. Fitch markets itself as widely recognized by investors, issuers, and bankers for its credible, transparent, and timely coverage.

These aren't the only credit rating agencies—there are several others, including:

A.M. Best (U.S.)
Baycorp Advantage (Australia)
Dominion Bond Rating Service (Canada)
Pacific Credit Rating (Peru)

By definition, credit agencies provide ratings to help aid investors when deciding the credit danger affiliated with certain securities, including derivatives.

But how credible and trustworthy is that advice, when those credit agencies rated toxic mortgage-backed securities as triple-A grade? Take Goldman Sach's mortgage-related security known as Abacus 2007-AC1. This is the security for which the SEC is accusing Goldman Sachs of security fraud. It's also the same security that both Standard and Poor's and Moody rated as AAA, the highest credit level a security can receive.[3]

It gets worse. Moody's rated Lehman Brothers Holdings Inc. A2, and Standard & Poor's rated it A, until it filed for bankruptcy on September 15, 2008. Most of the company's risk exposure was to mortgage-backed securities based on subprime mortgages.

The largest insurer in the U.S. American International Group (AIG) received an A2 rating by Moody's and an A rating by S&P. This is the same insurer that received an $85 billion loan from the federal government in exchange for an 80 percent stake on September 16, 2008, to stay afloat.[4]

Basically, a credit rating estimates the creditworthiness of an individual or corporation or even a country. The credit rating of a corporation or a security is a financial indicator to potential investors of the risks associated with a particular investment vehicle.

Each agency evaluates the financial health of the security or firm it is rating. After it performs its financial evaluation, it classifies the security with a designated rating such as AAA, AA+, BBB, or BB+.

Moody's credit ratings range from Aaa, Aa1, Aa2, Aa3, A1, A2, A3, Baa1, Baa2, Baa3, Ba1, Ba2, Ba3, B1, B2, B3, Caa1, Caa2, Caa3, Ca, to C. Most of the other agencies have similar ratings.

Ratings are divided into two types: long-term and short-term. A long-term rating indicates the agency's assessment of the risk of fixed-income obligations with a maturity of one year or more. Any security rated triple-A means the investment is considered of better quality and carries the smallest degree of investment risk. Ratings of AA or A are either high quality with low risk or medium quality with low risk.

Items rated Baa are medium credit grade with moderate risk. Investments given Ba to B ratings have speculative elements and therefore have higher credit risks. The scale of the ratings continues in this manner all the way down to C, which is the poorest investment grade and carries the highest risk.

Short-term ratings work in much the same manner. The length of time of the investment is usually no more than 13 months. They also receive AAA to C ratings but are also usually footnoted with P-1, P-2, or P-3. The P means *prime* and designates whether the issuer of the investment has superior ability to repay its loans.

So what's the big deal about these ratings? What happens if a company or security is downgraded? Well, for the issuer it means higher borrowing costs, which ultimately affects a company's bottom line. Furthermore, a downgrade usually means the company loses credibility not only with investors but also in its particular industry.

That's not the worst of it. A downgrade also means the bond or security carries a very high risk. A downgrade is a warning for investors to proceed with caution and, depending on the degree of the downgrade, it could mean stay away altogether.

What you have to realize is that credit ratings carry a lot of weight. In the early part of the 1970s, regulators had passed laws that limited financial business transactions to the extent of their rating. For example, a mutual fund couldn't buy bonds rated below a certain level.[5]

New York Times columnist and Pulitzer Prize–winning author Thomas Friedman put it this way in 1996: "There are two superpowers in the world today, in my opinion. There's the United States and there's Moody's Bond Rating Service. The United States can destroy you by dropping bombs, and Moody's can destroy you by downgrading your bonds. And believe me, it's not clear sometimes who's more powerful."[6]

Getting a triple-A rating is like getting a gold star. But one wonders if the agencies are more concerned with protecting the companies they rate instead of acting in the interests of investors.

The SEC suit against Goldman Sachs is a recent example of why investors should be questioning the rating agencies. Some analysts are now starting to do just that.

In the wake of the Greece debt crisis, credit agencies are downgrading their ratings of certain European countries. However, the European Commission has told credit rating agencies to watch their step when judging a country's financial health, saying they would probe their work and could even set up a central agency to take on their job.[7]

What's worth noting here is that these agencies have been in the limelight before, most notably with their high ratings of such disastrous companies as Enron and WorldCom. But those catastrophes have not prevented Wall Street from turning to credit agencies for their ratings.

The credit agencies have always been considered rock-solid and trustworthy. Lawrence J. White, imperatore professor of economics at New York University's Stern School of Business, says:

> Seven decades of financial regulation has propelled these rating agencies into the center of the bond information market, by elevating their judgments about the creditworthiness of bonds so that those judgments attained the force of law.[8]

White also suggests that it was the Securities and Exchange Commission that aided the rise of the ratings agencies by establishing a barrier to entry for other companies to get in.

It used to be that credit rating agencies had to obtain a special designation by the SEC of Nationally Recognized Statistical Rating Organization (NRSRO), which formalized the role of the ratings agencies.

But in 2006, the Senate voted in favor of a bill that was aimed at reforming the credit rating industry. The bill that passed, the Credit Rating Agency Reform Act of 2006, would give the SEC the authority to regulate competition within the credit ratings industry, as well as keep an eye on conflicts of interest. The bill even gave the SEC the right to inspect the agencies.

In addition, the bill changed how agencies received their designation. Instead of using the NRSRO rating, the SEC issued an SRO (statistical ratings organization) designation to agencies that had three years of experience and could meet certain standards developed by the SEC.

Of the more than 130 agencies, to date only five agencies have received this designation from the SEC: Moody's, Standard & Poor's, Fitch, Dominion Bond Rating Services, and A.M. Best. Of those five,

S&P and Moody's hold approximately 80 percent of the credit ratings market.[9]

Although the SEC is charged with keeping a watchful eye over the credit rating agencies, it helped to create a tightly knit group of agencies who dispense ratings at will and often with dire consequences. The subprime mortgage–backed securities serve as a recent example of their failure.

But the agencies have failed us before, crushing the retirement dreams of thousands of Americans.

Crushed Dreams

We only need to go back a few years to see that rating agencies aren't the moral, mighty beings we'd like them to be. Examples of horrific past failures can be found in the collapse of Enron and WorldCom.

Both corporations enjoyed high credit ratings from companies like Moody's and Standard & Poor's. Yet when their shady business and accounting practices were exposed, they wiped out millions in retirement portfolios, thousands of people were displaced, and billions of dollars in market value were erased in a moment's notice.

And what happened to the rating agencies? They walked away unscathed, unlike the accounting firm Arthur Andersen, which at the time was alleged to have known about Enron's problems but did nothing to prevent the firm from continuing its wrongful behavior.

In fact, it looked like Arthur Andersen had aided and abetted Enron in its deceitful practices. On May 2002, Andersen was convicted of obstruction of justice for shredding key documents

These days it seems hard to believe that at one time Enron was considered the premier natural gas pipeline company. The company was an investor's dream stock.

The company was formed in 1985 when Kenneth Lay merged Houston Natural gas with another natural gas company, InterNorth. The merger allowed the newly formed Enron to own 37,000 miles of natural gas pipeline. Over the years, Enron became the largest natural gas merchant in North America.

In 1989 it began trading natural gas commodities. But Lay wanted more. So in 1991 he hired Jeffrey Skilling, an energy consultant from the prestigious economic research firm McKinsey & Company, to help him expand into other resources including water, coal, and steel.

Skilling turned Enron into an extremely aggressive company that bought and sold billions of dollars of electricity and other commodities on a daily basis. Enron went from being a natural gas company to being an energy trading company.

The company was criticized as a profiteer in the energy trading business. But it didn't matter to Lay or Skilling. By 2001 Enron's stock hit a record high of $90 a share, and Skilling was named chief executive officer. Figure 10.1 shows the rapid increase in Enron's share price.

Skilling was inventing markets for the company to trade in, including unused capacity in fiber-optic telecommunications lines and weather derivatives. Its online trading business was hauling in as much as $125 billion per year.[10]

Skilling and Lay built Enron into the seventh largest company in the United States. The company had more than 20,000 employees. In 1993 Enron reported $387 million in profits; in 1994 profits totaled $453 million; in 1995, they totaled $520 million.[11] The company was named the most innovative company in America by *Fortune* magazine.

But the glory wouldn't last. By 2001, problems would begin to pop up. In August of that same year, Skilling would resign as CEO, citing

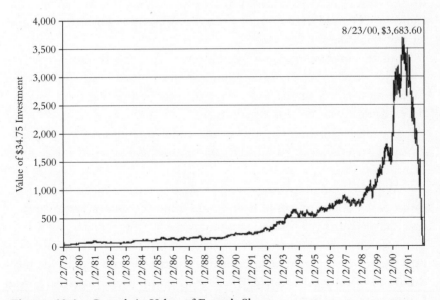

Figure 10.1   Growth in Value of Enron's Shares
DATA SOURCE: James N. Bodurth, Georgetown University.

personal reasons. But he walked away with millions in compensation. Lay took over as CEO. That same year, Enron's vice chairman of the board, J. Clifford Baxter, warned Kenneth Lay that he had found accounting peculiarities.

Those warnings were ignored by Lay. Even as more warnings were reported, Lay continued to ignore them, instead choosing to promote Enron as a credible and trustworthy company.

On December 2, 2001, Enron declared bankruptcy. The company was over $30 billion in debt, $17 billion of which was accounted for by phony partnerships. Enron's investors lost $67 billion as the company's stock fell to 26 cents a share.[12]

One wonders if Enron's rags-to-riches story would have ever happened had the credit rating agencies such as Moody's and Standard & Poor's properly rated the company. This was a question posed by the U.S. subcommittee investigating the Enron's failure.

In 2002, the committee asked John Diaz, a managing director at Moody's Investors Service, why Moody's had said the company's debt was investment-grade, only to see the company default on its bonds four weeks later as it declared bankruptcy.

Diaz said his company was sorry "they hadn't discovered the information that would have allowed us to serve the market more efficiently."[13] He told the committee that if Enron had not misled them, the ratings would have been lower.

But this argument doesn't make sense. As a credit rating agency, Moody's would have performed due diligence on all of Enron's books. Oftentimes, rating agencies are privy to information that most institutions would never be able to access.

The truth is that credit ratings and audit functions are interrelated. Financial statements are a primary information source in making rating determinations.

With this kind of investigative power behind it, it is *not* unreasonable to think the company could have found some accounting irregularities, especially as the firm's own accountant was issuing warnings.

Another red flag for Moody's is the very fact that Enron was forging new paths into energy trading, which at the time wasn't regulated. That should have caused Moody's to take even extra caution before giving Enron its triple-A rating.

Of Enron's wide-reaching failure, Steve Shepard, editor-in-chief of *BusinessWeek* magazine, says, "Enron was really a systemic failure of all the checks and balances we have on corporate governance: integrity of management, board of directors, audit committee of the board, outside accounting firm, Wall Street analysts and ultimately the press. And all of us failed."[14]

"Failed" is an understatement. What's worse is that investors lost their life savings. Retirement dreams were crushed. Yet Enron's failure is only one example of crushed retirement dreams.

The failure of WorldCom was just as bad. WorldCom started as a tiny telecom company and grew to become a name-brand telecommunications company.

But that brand was tarnished when the company's accounting scandal led to one of the biggest bankruptcy filings the country had ever seen.

William McLucas, a lawyer who produced a report on WorldCom's failure, faulted Chairman Bernard Ebbers for creating an environment where top executives browbeat underlings for questioning their authority. McLucas's report also showed that Ebbers participated in company meetings where executives discussed ways to artificially inflate revenue.[15]

Ebbers built WorldCom into the nation's second-largest telecommunications firm. In 1999, its market capitalization peaked at $115 billion and the company's stock was the fifth most widely held stock in the country.[16] (See Figure 10.2.)

But Ebbers didn't act alone in building WorldCom into a giant, nor in its demise. Ebbers consulted regularly with his chief of finance, Scott Sullivan. As it turns out, Sullivan was a master at numbers—or should we say, master at *manipulating* numbers.

Sullivan ordered his subordinates to inflate revenues and hide expenses. When finally revealed, those fraudulent accounting misstatements amounted to the largest accounting fraud in history.

Facing a 25-year sentence, Sullivan became the star witness at the trial of Bernie Ebbers. Sullivan admitted in court that he had lied about the company's finances. In a conference call with analysts in the third quarter of 2001, Sullivan said WorldCom was in a phenomenal industry position. He added, "I think we are set to be successful in whatever the economy throws at us."[17]

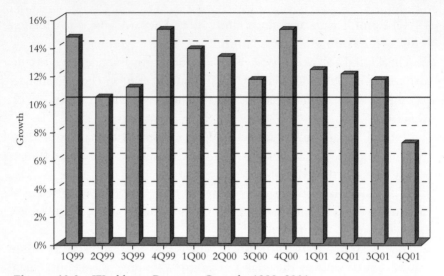

Figure 10.2   Worldcom Revenue Growth, 1999–2001
DATA SOURCE: Big Charts, http://bigcharts.marketwatch.com.

Sullivan was sentenced to a five-year term. At his sentencing, Barbara Jones, the judge who presided over the case, commented that Sullivan was "significantly more culpable" than the other managers who cooperated in the accounting scheme.

Jones said, "In keeping WorldCom going, Sullivan was also preserving his $700,000 salary, $10 million bonus and stock options."[18]

How do credit ratings fit in with the WorldCom disaster? Well, WorldCom received investment-grade ratings up to three months before filing for bankruptcy. In fact, WorldCom had issued almost $12 billion worth of bonds in May 2001 that had an investment-grade rating before it filed for bankruptcy about a year later. Investors in these bonds lost more than 80 percent of their investment.[19]

Not only did the credit agencies not suffer any consequences but they also made out like bandits—or should I say, more like barbarians.

Barbarian Greed

One would naturally assume that credit rating agencies act with the highest principles and are not easily swayed or influenced by anyone for any reason. After all, their ratings are *the* seal of approval for investors. But making this kind of assumption is nothing more than living in a pretend world where people always do the right thing.

The truth is, credit agencies are barbarians in disguise, who are just as motivated by profit as are the companies they rate.

Top executives from Moody's and Standard & Poor's gave testimony before the House Oversight and Government Reform Committee that revealed credit rating agencies relaxed their standards to get business. On October 22, 2008, Bloomberg reported that employees at the agencies privately questioned the value of some mortgage-backed securities that were given creditworthy ratings.[20]

The Committee released a series of e-mails demonstrating that employees of these ratings companies were concerned about the ratings. One e-mail from an employee of Standard & Poor's said, "Let's hope we are all wealthy and retired by the time this house of cards falters."

Upon reviewing the many e-mails the Committee had gathered, House Oversight and Government Reform Committee Chairman Henry Waxman said, "The story of the credit-rating agencies is a story of colossal failure."[21]

Another employee e-mail read, "Seems to me that we had blinders on and never questioned the information we were given. It is our job to think of the worst-case scenarios and model them." The e-mail continued, "Combined, these errors make us look either incompetent at credit analysis, or like we sold our soul to the devil for revenue."[22]

A McClatchy investigation found that as the housing market collapsed in late 2007, Moody's Investors Service, whose investment ratings were widely trusted, responded by purging analysts and executives who warned of trouble and promoting those who helped Wall Street plunge the country into its worst financial crisis since the Great Depression.[23]

McClatchy also claims that Moody's stacked its compliance department with the people who awarded the highest ratings to pools of mortgages that soon were downgraded to junk.

In the end, it probably doesn't matter to the government if the credit agencies are right or wrong with their assessments. Most experts believe Wall Street can't operate without the agencies.

Jeremy Warner, writing for the *UK Telegraph*, calls the credit agencies "untouchable kings." In his December 11, 2009, article Warner writes, "The subprime meltdown is only the latest offence in a serial list of failings, be it the Latin American debt crisis of the 1980s, the Far Eastern crisis of the 1990s, Enron, and just about any other major default you can think of in recent history."[24]

Warner says that in all these incidents, the agencies failed to see it coming. And unfortunately, it's not just subprime derivatives the agencies ruled over—now it's a country's sovereign debt.

As countries struggle to rebound from the crisis, they are throwing piles of money at the problem and rapidly increasing their debt at the same time. And it's agencies like Moody's, Standard & Poor's, and Fitch—the very ones who missed all the previous economic cala-mities—that are determining which countries get triple-A ratings.

Warner argues the reason the agencies have become untouchable is because there are only a handful to choose from. It takes a network of analysts and researchers to rate companies and countries, and it's expen-sive. That's why only a chosen few have remained in the game.

The agencies have a mini-monopoly on the rating business. Warner says, "Undue reliance on this limited choice of credit assessments has accentuated the consequences of any misjudgment."[25]

The *American Chronicle* offers a similar point of view. In a recent issue, it asks, "What is being done today about those credit rating companies that had previously bestowed triple-A ratings on banks with those bogus financial concoctions that were built on mounds of dicey mortgages?"

The answer is nothing is being done. The agencies are still part of the Wall Street cartel. But to save face, they have been downgrading the very investments that once carried their triple-A ratings.

The *Chronicle* points out that the credit rating agencies have recently downgraded more than $600 billion of bad credits that were previously rated AAA. They went from stellar investments to junk—but only after the crisis had become full-blown and the damage was done.

The accusation of credit rating agencies providing a rubber stamp of approval for their clients' securities is absolutely right. The *Chronicle* points out that, for all of their sophisticated mathematical models and financial expertise, the raters are not "disinterested observers."[26]

In a special position report prepared by the Consumer Federation of America (CFA), the organization says, "The high ratings given to these products [securities] made them eligible for sale to even the most conservative of investors, spreading the risks of unsound mortgage lending throughout the financial system, and allowed financial institutions to avoid setting aside adequate capital to compensate for their risks."[27]

The CFA also found that as the structured finance business grew, rating agencies' profitability became increasingly dependent on their ability to win market share in this highly lucrative line of business. Because agencies typically charge issuers for their ratings, the conflicts of interests and pressure to assign favorable ratings were enormous.

The CFA draws attention to one of the biggest problems with the credit rating industry and that is the business model it uses. The company that wants a security rated by a credit agency pays a substantial fee. That in itself can skew the rating, creating a bias toward providing the client a better-than-expected rating.

In the case of collateralized debt obligations (CDOs), the credit rating agencies can make as much as three times their normal rating fees. Generational Dynamics suggests that Moody's made 50 percent of its revenues from these type of ratings.[28] It also found that Moody's commented on its 10-K filings with the SEC that "CDOs should continue to support company growth."

An article in the *Vermont Law Review* shows that as Moody's revenues increased from rating mortgage-backed securities, it changed its business philosophy to favor the securities. The report says one former executive noted that a new dialogue began with Wall Street firms and that the rating process became a negotiation.[29]

As for Goldman's Abacus 2007-AC1, BlackStar News reports that Moody's was able to charge from 0.3 percent to 0.5 percent of the value of the security which would amount to roughly $300,000 to $500,000 in fees.[30]

U.S. Congressman Gary Ackerman says, "Credit-rating agencies use their control of information to fool investors into believing that a pig is a cow and a rotten egg is a roasted chicken. Collusion and misrepresentation are not elements of a genuinely free market."[31]

Vince Farrell of Scotsman Capital Management says,

> What these ratings agencies did is absolutely deplorable. They took the issuers' money and gave them a good rating back. I can

understand how the complexity of this thing can throw you, but there were very smart people who were scratching their head at the time, saying, "How do you take triple B subprime stuff, and through financial alchemy, turn it into triple-A stuff?"[32]

Unfortunately, because of legislative policies, credit rating agencies seem to be immune from liability related to their ratings. This isn't to say they have not been sued in the past. They have, but most often the rulings have been in their favor. For example, Lloyds Bank of England sued Moody's alleging that the latter's ratings lured the bank to invest millions in National Century Financial Enterprises.

In March 2001, Lloyds said it purchased $60 million of NPF XII 2001-1, Class A notes rated Aaa by Moody's. In November 2002, it also purchased $68 million of NPF XII 2000-4, Class A, also rated Aa3 by Moody's.

Lloyds said it lost the value of its investments when the note-issuing company National Century Financial Enterprises went bankrupt amid allegations of a massive financial fraud.[33]

Lloyds said that if it were not for the ratings given by Moody's on the securities, the company would have not put millions of dollars on the line. Unfortunately, Lloyds lost its case against Moody's because the court ruled it did not establish an element of reliance on the ratings report.

Even though Lloyds failed to show the court that it relied on Moody's ratings, it's well known that every institution that uses credit ratings from a rating agency relies heavily on those ratings. Moody's, Standard & Poor's, and Fitch have become their own Wall Street cartel.

An Industry Is Born

John Moody founded Moody's in the early1900s. John started his financial career working for a bank as an errand boy earning $20 a month. But while scanning through the newspapers, John noticed that the number of securities being covered was overwhelming.

He knew the sheer number being reported would make it difficult for investors to follow a particular company or stock. So he decided to create a publication in which he would share his view of the markets with investors.

The manual, *Moody's Manual of Industrial and Miscellaneous Securities*, provided readers with a variety of information and statistics on stocks and bonds of various financial institutions and government agencies, as well as manufacturing, mining, utility, and food companies. Within two months the publication had completely sold out.

But when the market crashed in 1907, John's company didn't survive. He was forced to sell his business. However, John was an entrepreneur at heart and it didn't take long for him to go back into business, publishing financial information for investors. But this time he decided to focus his publication on specific securities. His new book offered investors information on railroad securities.

This edition of John's book didn't just contain information on railroad securities; he also rated each security using a letter rating system. Although John didn't invent the rating system, he was certainly the first person to rate a security.

In 1909 he published those ratings in *Moody's Analysis of Railroad Investments*, which rated 200 railroads. Once again John's publication was a hit with the public.

Four years later, John took the same concept he had used with railroad securities and applied it to industrial utility companies. In 1914, John expanded his rating concept to the bond market. That same year, Moody's Investors Service was incorporated. By 1924, Moody's ratings covered nearly 100 percent of the U.S. bond market.[34]

John Moody has often been referred to as the creator of the credit rating industry for securities and bonds. Seeing the success Moody had with his ratings, the Standard Company began rating bonds in 1916. In 1920 Poor's followed with its ratings. That's also the same year Fitch came into existence. Poor's and the Standard Company merged in 1941 to form Standard & Poor's.

The true origins of ratings can be traced back to mercantile credit agencies, which rated a merchant's ability to pay its financial obligations. Louis Tappan established the first mercantile rating agency in 1841. A few years later, in 1849 John Bradstreet established a firm and created a ratings book. Eventually his firm would become the owner of Moody's Investor Services.[35]

John built Moody's, the nation's oldest and most prestigious credit rating agency, on integrity for providing unbiased, critical information of securities. Today's credit agencies seem to care less about the integrity of the ratings they issue or their credibility. By giving the mortgage-backed securities triple-A ratings, the agencies in essence legitimized these securities.

They led the public into believing the risks were minimal. And all the while, their own profits were soaring. In fact, just as recently as the first quarter of 2010, Moody's reported revenue of $476.6 million for the three months ended March 31, 2010, an increase of 17 percent from the same period the previous year.[36]

But here's where things get really interesting. Just as the agencies provided too little too late with their recent downgrading of mortgage-backed securities, the SEC is acting too late.

Just recently the SEC issued a report that showed significant weaknesses in ratings practices and the need for remedial action by these firms to provide meaningful ratings and the necessary levels of disclosure to investors.

For 10 months the SEC investigated Fitch Ratings Ltd., Moody's Investor Services Inc., and Standard & Poor's Ratings Services to evaluate whether they are adhering to their published methodologies for determining ratings and managing conflicts of interest.

The report states that none of the rating agencies had specific, written, comprehensive procedures for rating mortgage-backed securities or collateralized debt obligations. The SEC also found that significant aspects of the rating process were not always disclosed or even documented by the firms, and conflicts of interest were not always managed appropriately.[37]

So the SEC publishes a report faulting credit rating agencies, but only *after* the agencies have begun downgrading the risky securities; only *after* the credit crisis has wreaked havoc on every economy in the world; only *after* investors have lost millions in retirement accounts.

Is it any wonder that in its report, the SEC deems the agencies worthy of being investigated? Should we be shocked to learn that their findings show the agencies haven't done their job properly?

Perhaps less shocking but even more disappointing is the fact that the SEC, the very agency put in charge of credit rating companies, failed to do its job properly. Senator Ron Paul says the SEC is "a total failure and part of the problem."[38]

In our opinion the SEC qualifies as a modern-day barbarian of wealth. It has failed more times than one likes to recall. Its recent suit against Goldman Sachs, although well intended, is one more example of too little, too late.

Part Three

THE BARBARIANS OF
WALL STREET

Chapter 11

The Scourge of Wall Street

On July 14, 2009, Goldman Sachs, one of the biggest securities firms in the U.S., announced that it had made an astonishing $3.4 billion in quarterly profits, its best-ever performance in the company's 140-year history. The company's quarterly profits had more than tripled from a year earlier.[1]

What makes this achievement even more amazing is that it happened at a time when the United States (as well as the rest of the world) was in the middle of the worst financial crisis since World War II—a crisis so widespread, over 14 million Americans would find themselves unemployed.[2]

But there's more to this profit story that needs telling. You see, just one year earlier, at the height of the credit crisis, Goldman Sachs received $10 billion from the federal government as part of the Treasury's Troubled Asset Relief Program (TARP).[3]

So how is it possible that the same company that received billions in bailout money from the government had a complete turnaround in one year?

What Goldman Sachs didn't say on July 14, 2009, is that it is a prime broker of U.S. government bonds. And this seemingly somewhat simple designation helped it achieve its record-breaking profits.

Looking back to September 21, 2008, we see that Goldman Sachs was granted "bank holding company" status, making it the fourth largest bank holding company in the United States. The company already had the temporary ability to borrow from the Fed through its designation as a Terms Security Lending Facility (TSLF).[4]

A TSLF is a lending facility set up through the Federal Reserve that allows primary dealers to borrow Treasury securities on a 28-day term in exchange for collateral. The eligible collateral could even include mortgage-backed securities with AAA to Aaa ratings.

Now, what you have to understand is that the Fed created the TSLF designation to allow firms such as Goldman to give non-government-guaranteed triple-A rated assets to the Fed in exchange for loans.

However, the trouble with this is that the triple-A assets Goldman Sachs would be giving to the government were not the safe securities they portrayed them to be. In fact, many of the assets were backed by mortgage loans that were failing at incredible speed.

But for Goldman, it didn't matter whether the securities were safe or not. They were in position to profit from them because they were betting they would self-destruct. And to protect their profits, they insured their investments with companies such as AIG.

The interesting thing about Goldman's TSLF designation was that it was only temporary, due to expire in January 2009. But the expiration of that designation didn't really matter because Goldman was in the process of becoming a bank holding company.

As a bank holding company, Goldman Sachs would now have permanent access to borrow money from the Fed. And here's the kicker: It gets to borrow that money at almost zero percent interest.

Basically, what happens when you become a bank holding company is that it is much easier to raise capital than as a traditional bank. Not only that, but a bank holding company can assume the debt of shareholders on a tax-free basis, acquire other banks and nonbank entities more easily, and issue stock with greater regulatory ease. It also has greater legal authority to buy back (share repurchase) its own stock.

In addition to these benefits and privileges, Goldman can take comfort in knowing that as a bank holding company, the federal government will cover any of its losses. That's right: Its losses are backed by the government.

Bank holding companies can also buy other banks. This means Goldman Sachs, if it so desires, can now buy other banks in order to build up its base of deposit money.

Given the number of bank failures that have occurred in the past two years and are likely to continue, it's quite possible the firm could target these banks for acquisition. Prior to receiving bank holding company status, federal regulations prohibited the firm from pursuing such deals. Now it has the freedom to do so.

Another benefit of becoming a bank holding company is that Goldman gets to take advantage of favorable accounting rule changes.

There are some caveats to becoming a bank holding company. One is that the government can scrutinize your every move and impose greater regulatory oversight.

Most experts assumed that when Goldman Sachs was granted bank holding company status, the firm would no longer be able to make the huge profits it had grown accustomed to making because it would come under more intense scrutiny by the government.

However, based on the company's July 14 announcement, the government hasn't slowed down this twenty-first century money machine. But becoming a bank holding company and escaping the wrath of regulators alone doesn't qualify the company as barbaric.

It's the numerous ways Goldman Sachs has plundered the wealth of the American public that makes it a twenty-first-century barbarian.

We'll examine some of those ways, including the 2008 subprime crisis that caused one of the greatest economic recessions the United States has faced in 25 years, and Goldman's involvement in underwriting IPOs for Internet-related businesses during the dot-com bubble of the 2000s.

But first let's take a look at how this firm, founded in 1885, became one of America's greatest barbarians of wealth.

History of Goldman Sachs

One of Marcus's first jobs in the new land was as a peddler with a horse-drawn cart. While living in Philadelphia, Marcus met another Jewish immigrant named Bertha Goldman (no relation to his family). Bertha was 19 when she arrived in the United States to live with her parents, who had migrated here earlier. She and Marcus married soon after.

Marcus's next job was as a shopkeeper. With Bertha's encouragement, the two set up a clothing store on Market Street. However, in 1869, Marcus, Bertha, and their five children moved to New York so Marcus could pursue more fruitful work. Marcus set up a shop on 30 Pine Street and hung up a sign that read, "Marcus Goldman, Banker and Broker."

Marcus began trading in promissory notes in 1869. In the morning, Marcus would purchase promissory notes that jewelry merchants in lower Manhattan and leather goods merchants in an area known as "the swamp" would make their customers sign. Then, in the afternoon, Marcus would sell those promissory notes to commercial banks for a small profit.

This made Marcus a pioneer in the commercial paper business. It also made him a very rich man. By 1880, Marcus's company was making $30 million a year.[5]

It wasn't until his son-in-law, Samuel Sachs, joined the business in 1882 that the company was renamed Goldman Sachs. It expanded into a general partnership when Goldman's son Henry and his second son-in-law, Ludwig Dreyfus, joined the group.

It was Henry Goldman who helped the company step into a broader range of business interests. In 1887, Goldman Sachs developed a relationship with the British merchant bank Kleinwort Sons, which gave Goldman an entry into international commercial finance, foreign-exchange services, and currency arbitrage.

Goldman Sachs now had a name in the business community. Of course it didn't take the firm long to win over business from several Midwestern companies, including Sears Roebuck, Cluett Peabody, and Rice-Stix Dry Goods. Soon after, Goldman Sachs opened offices in St. Louis and Chicago. Henry Goldman was put in charge of expanding the firm's domestic operations.

In 1896, soon after Samuel Sachs's brother Harry joined the company, Goldman Sachs joined the New York Stock Exchange. Goldman now had a firm foothold in the United States and managed to build itself into the company of choice for investment-related businesses.

For years the firm enjoyed recognition as one of the country's premier investment banks. But as we'll soon see, that honor would eventually be tainted with an air of distrust.

Goldman and the Subprime Crisis

In 2007 Goldman Sachs made roughly $4 billion in profits, betting on the collapse of subprime mortgage–backed securities that ultimately brought down the entire U.S. economy. But this is also what qualifies Goldman Sachs as a modern-day barbarian.[6]

You see, what few people realize is that although the company was betting against the sustainability of the subprime market, it was one of the major firms not only creating subprime mortgage–backed securities, but also selling them up and down and all over Wall Street.

In fact, it is Goldman Sachs' creation of the Abacus security that has the company on the hot seat with the SEC. The SEC says Goldman intentionally did not disclose to investors the fact that it was betting *against* the Abacus securities while at the same time recommending them as good buys.

But Abacus isn't the only mortgage-related security that Goldman bet against. To understand this modern-day act of barbarism, we have to go back to April 27, 2006. That's when the company created the mortgage security known as GSAMP Trust 2006-S3. By the way, *GSAMP* stands for Goldman Sachs Alternative Mortgage Products.

Goldman took this newly created security, backed entirely by subprime mortgages, and sold it to other investment institutions and firms on Wall Street, including those directly responsible for managing the pension funds, mutual funds, and retirement plans of millions of Americans.

Subprime mortgages are granted to borrowers whose credit history is insufficient to qualify for a conventional loan. These loans are classified as the riskiest category of consumer loans and are typically sold in a separate market from prime loans.

Borrowers of subprime mortgages pay a higher rate of interest, whereas borrowers of prime loans pay considerably less interest. People who qualify for subprime loans are generally classified as low income or have a poor credit history of repaying loans. That's why they are charged higher interest rates.

Goldman's GSAMP Trust 2006-S3 security was made up entirely of subprime loans. Goldman Sachs bought the loans from several different mortgage companies throughout the United States that had granted thousands of noncreditworthy borrowers thousands of dollars in mortgage loans.

Goldman then divided GSAMP Trust 2006-S3 into several different securities with credit ratings ranging from high risk to low risk. The credit ratings were granted by agencies such as Moody's and Standard & Poor's, who assess the risk associated with securities being sold on Wall Street.

Although most of the loans bundled in the new security were worthless, 68 percent of the issue was rated AAA by both rating agencies. Since most financial institutions don't take the time to read the massive pages of documentation that come along with the securities, they relied mostly on the credit ratings to make their decisions.[7]

We learned about credit rating agencies in Chapter 10 and how they rated these securities with AAA ratings. We also learned that the rating agencies often worked with their clients to provide better than normal ratings because for the agencies, better ratings lead to higher fees.

But you may be wondering why any bank or mortgage company would loan money to someone they knew couldn't afford to repay it. Well, many of these lenders will now tell you they were simply following Congress's desire to reduce discrimination against low-income borrowers.

They say they were acting in accordance with the Community Reinvestment Act, which required lenders to approve a certain number of low-income borrowers for mortgage loans. (In later chapters we'll take a look at this act and how it contributed to the global financial collapse of 2008. We'll also examine how politicians have become twenty-first-century barbarians.)

Unfortunately, less than 18 months after Goldman created this new security, one-sixth of these subprime borrowers began defaulting on their mortgage loans. This caused rating agencies such Standard & Poor's to downgrade their initial credit ratings.[8]

On July 19, 2007, Standard & Poor's issued its RatingsDirect report, in which it lowered its rating on 418 classes of U.S. residential mortgage-backed securities. Those 418 downgraded securities were valued at $2.5 trillion.[9]

In its report, Standard & Poor's wrote that it was taking this action because it believed that losses on these securities would significantly "exceed historical precedents."[10]

Of course, it's hard to imagine that Goldman Sachs didn't know the securities it had created would backfire. In fact on January 12, 2010, a Goldman Sachs executive admitted as much.

According to the *New York Times*, Thomas C. Mazarakis, head of Goldman's fundamental strategies group, acknowledged that the company had bet against particular instruments it had recommended.[11]

And it's those bets against subprime securities that helped the company make a whopping $4 billion in profits in 2007.[12]

But for institutions that bought into the subprime mortgage–backed securities, it was too late. Experts say the recession that started as a result of the subprime securities fallout wiped out $1.3 trillion in U.S. personal wealth.[13]

On a global scale, Steve Schwarzman, chairman of the private equity group Blackstone, estimates that 40 percent of the world's wealth had disappeared.[14]

That makes Goldman Sachs a twenty-first-century barbarian of almost unimaginable magnitude. It's also why we call Goldman the "scourge of Wall Street." But this is certainly not the firm's first barbaric act that destroyed the wealth of thousands of American investors.

We need to look no further than the dot-com bubble of 2000.

The Dot-com Era

Goldman Sachs was the front-runner in the record year of mergers and acquisitions that took place during the dot-com era, underwriting more than a quarter of all deals done. More impressive is how much Goldman earned in fees: just over $2 billion.

Underwriting initial public offerings (IPOs) is a specialty of Goldman Sachs. In 1906 the firm began helping other companies raise money for expansion purposes. Back then one of the firm's clients, United Cigar Manufacturers, needed additional capital to expand its business. It had previously been borrowing money from Goldman Sachs to maintain its inventories.

Goldman suggested to United Cigar's management team that it could get the capital it was seeking if it were to sell shares of the company to the general public. Although Goldman Sachs had never managed a share offering before, it succeeded in marketing $4.5 million worth of United Cigar stock.[15]

On the strength of this success, Goldman Sachs next co-managed Sears Roebuck's IPO that same year. In 1910, Goldman managed public offerings for a number of companies including May Department Stores, F.W. Woolworth, Continental Can, B.F. Goodrich, and Merck.

Ironically, one of Goldman's greatest IPO's was its own. In May 1999 Goldman raised $3.6 billion from the sale of approximately 69 million shares. Today, Goldman is the lead IPO underwriter on Wall Street.[16]

And it's because of that honor of being lead underwriter that so many Internet-related start-up companies turned to Goldman Sachs to help them raise money to fund their businesses.

In the case of the tech stock bubble, Matt Taibbi of *Rolling Stone* magazine accused Goldman Sachs of underwriting a high number of risky Internet IPOs and manufacturing a "collapse in underwriting standards."[17]

We only need to look at a few of the Internet IPOs Goldman Sachs was involved with to see this statement is true.

Take the case of NetZero, an Internet service provider located in California. Founders Ronald Burr, Stacy Haitsuka, Marwan Zebian, and Harold MacKenzie launched the company in October 1998.

At the time, it was the first free Internet service provider. The business premise was simple: Offer free Internet service to millions of users, who would become the prime audience (and eyeballs) for display advertising (banner ads) that was paid for by other companies.

NetZero's advertising-serving technology had over nine patents. NetZero was also the first company to invent real-time URL-targeted advertising based on user Internet surfing patterns.

NetZero seemed to have the perfect business model. All it needed to continue its growth was an extra $115 million in capital. So the founders turned to none other than the leading IPO underwriter, Goldman Sachs. Goldman saw moneymaking potential in NetZero going public and agreed to underwrite the offering. On July 14, 1999, the company filed its papers for the IPO.

Just a couple months later, on September 24, 1999, NetZero shares were available on the NASDAQ index. Goldman Sachs expected the initial shares to trade as high as $9 to $11 a share. It was easy for Goldman to calculate the initial share price because already in 1999, twice as many IPOs had doubled on their first day of offering than in the 25 previous years combined.[18]

But based on pretrading bids from institutions and what Goldman perceived as intense demand for NetZero shares, the firm quickly revised its initial share forecast to $16 a share. On the day NetZero went public, the bidding started out at $27.75 per share.

By the end of the day, the share price closed at 29$\frac{1}{8}$, giving NetZero a value of $3 billion. From the revised offering price of $16, NetZero's shares rose 82 percent in a single day. That made NetZero's founders overnight millionaires. But it made Goldman Sachs just as wealthy.

You see, as the underwriter, Goldman would collect substantial fees managing the deal. Just how lucrative a business is underwriting IPOs?

"Well, an investment bank can charge 5 to 6 percent of the amount raised," says Zachary Scheidt, former hedge fund manager and now editor of New Growth Investor.

Zach says underwriting firms are typically paid very well for their assistance in getting the stock distributed to investors. Typically the underwriting fees are between 6 and 10 percent of the stock price, so if a company is selling 30 million shares at $14.00 per share, the underwriters could split between $25 million and $38 million.

In the case of NetZero, Goldman Sachs could have easily received $150 to $180 million in underwriting fees.

But here's the salt on the wound: As a business, NetZero had already lost more than $15 million. It had only managed to earn around $4.5 million in revenue from its advertising clients, including BellSouth, eBay, Microsoft, and Netscape.

Even as NetZero was trying to build its advertising revenue–based business, the public's perception of Internet banner advertising had already changed. Banners ads were becoming a nuisance and people weren't clicking on them as often as they had when banner ads were first introduced. The novelty had already worn off.

Whether NetZero could actually survive as a legitimate business didn't matter to Goldman Sachs. They weren't underwriting these new dot-com businesses for their value to investors, but for the money they could make managing the deal.

At the height of the Internet dot-com boom, it was possible for any kind of dot-com company to make an IPO of its stock and raise a substantial amount of money even though it had never made a profit.

Underwriting IPOs is a bit of a game on Wall Street. Buyers of IPOs are typically institutional investors. Underwriters generally approach the buyers with information about the stock, the expected price range, and maybe some color as to how much demand there is for the stock.

Buyers will then offer an indication of interest (IOI), stating how much stock they would like to buy when the transaction is completed.

Most IPO transactions are usually priced with the expectation of being a bit below the anticipated market price. This makes the buyers pleased with their transaction but also makes them willing to come back the next time the underwriter has a new IPO to pitch.

Zachary Scheidt says that during his time as a hedge fund manager, he fielded several calls from "breathless brokers" offering the deal of a lifetime if he'd be willing to buy shares in an IPO. Usually they are breathless because their manager just came in and said if they didn't sell 50,000 shares by the end of the day, they were out of a job! Zach adds, "The harder an underwriter pushes to get a deal done, the more I know that the deal is in trouble."

For Goldman Sachs, underwriting IPOs, regardless of whether the company could actually survive or be a great investment for investors, was a business within itself. It was all about the fees they could make.

Barron's called the IPO craze "one of the greatest gold rushes of American capitalism." But inevitably most of these businesses would fail because they were built on poor business models and valued on rapid expansion as opposed to the amount of money they could actually make for shareholders.[19]

As the dot-com mania took hold, on March 10, 2000, the NASDAQ composite peaked at 5,048.62, as shown in Figure 11.1. However, just

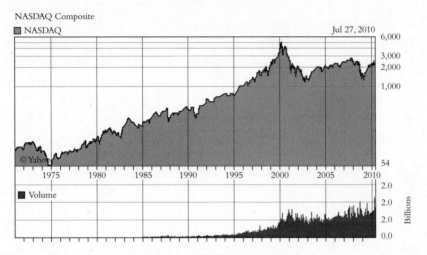

Figure 11.1 By March 2000, the NASDAQ Had Peaked
DATA SOURCE: "Sorting through the Wreckage," March 7, 2003, http://dalesdesigns.net/nasdaq.html.

three days later, on March 13, the composite dropped to 4,879, one of the greatest-percentage premarket sell-offs for the entire year.[20] That initial sell-off triggered a chain reaction of selling that fed on itself as investors and institutions liquidated their positions in dot-com stocks.

By 2001, the tech bubble that was fueled primarily by dot-com IPOs was unwinding at rapid speed. Experts say the crash wiped out $5 trillion in market value of technology companies from March 2000 to October 2002.[21]

Interesting enough on June 27, 2001, NetZero received a NAS-DAQ Staff Determination letter, which basically informed the company it didn't meet the minimum bid price requirement to stay listed on the NASDAQ Index.

Of Goldman Sachs' performance as lead IPO underwriter during the dot-com bubble, Christopher Byron writes:

> If you bought one share, on its first trading day, of every Internet IPO Goldman Sachs has managed since they began with Yahoo! Inc. in 1996, you'd now own shares in dozens of complete flops. In total, your complete portfolio would be down about 8 percent. You'd have been better off hiding your cash under your bed. And this is the most successful firm going.[22]

When Goldman Sachs went public in 1999, the firm named Henry Paulson Jr. as sole chairman and CEO. After the IPO, Paulson put plans in motion to secure the company's position as a major player on Wall Street.

In fact, in a 2002 *BusinessWeek* article, Paulson said, "We want to be the premier global investment bank, securities, and investment management firm. We want to have a disproportionate share of the business of the most important clients in the most important markets."[23]

Certainly Paulson's vision for the company has come true. Goldman Sachs is a major player on Wall Street (there are currently only two others, J.P. Morgan and Citibank). Goldman also had become a recognizable household name.

But its recognition comes not as a shining example of high ethical standards and business practices, but for the barbaric act of robbing thousands of individuals of hard-earned retirement money. Goldman Sachs shall forever be remembered as the company that brought down an entire economy.

And now the company is accused of defrauding investors for not providing full disclosure of its mortgage-backed securities. But Goldman isn't the only modern-day barbarian to reside on Wall Street.

We call Merrill Lynch the evil twin. Here's why.

Merrill Lynch—The Evil Twin

In February 2010, New York state officials began legal action against Merrill Lynch and its former executives on the grounds that they withheld details of huge losses the company was suffering in order for shareholders to approve the merger of Merrill Lynch and Bank of America.

New York State Attorney General Andrew Cuomo was quoted as saying, "This merger is a classic example of how the actions of our nation's largest financial institutions led to the near-collapse of our financial system."[24]

Prior to the merger, Merrill Lynch was already suffering huge losses from the subprime crisis. On January 17, 2008, Merrill Lynch reported a $9.83 billion fourth-quarter loss (2007), which included a $16.7 billion write-down of assets associated with subprime mortgages.[25]

The losses continued. On April 17, 2008, Merrill Lynch reported yet another net loss of $1.97 billion for the first quarter of 2008.[26]

Public outrage against Merrill Lynch worsened on January 22, 2009, when John Thain resigned as CEO of the company after it was reported in major newspapers that he had rushed to pay out $3 billion to $4 billion in fourth-quarter bonuses to top executives before Bank of America's acquisition of the company became final.

Bank of America officials contend that Thain did not disclose to them his intentions to pay the bonuses. Bank of America had already received $25 billion in bailout funds when the credit crisis peaked in the fall of 2008.[27]

But the firm had to request $20 billion in emergency capital, primarily in order to cover losses at its newly acquired subsidiary.[28]

Shareholders revolted and on January 22, 2009, filed a class action suit against Bank of America and Merrill Lynch. Their suit alleges that Bank of America CEO Ken Lewis, ex-Merrill chief financial officer Nelson Chai, ex-Merrill chief accounting officer Gary Carlin, and John Thain failed to warn shareholders of the magnitude of Merrill's losses prior to the Bank of America acquisition.

This isn't the first time Merrill Lynch executives have been sued for fraudulent behavior. Investors sued Merrill Lynch after then–New York Attorney General Eliot Spitzer released e-mail correspondence from Merrill Lynch's top Internet dot-com stock analyst Henry Blodget.

In those in-house e-mails, Blodget was extremely negative about stocks that in his public research he recommended as strong buys. To call it "extremely negative" is being extremely polite. Some of the words Blodget used in these e-mails to describe the stocks were "junk," "crap," and "a disaster."[29]

What motive would Blodget have for privately trashing companies he publicly recommended? By issuing more-than-enthusiastic reports on stocks they privately derided, Merrill could keep the lucrative investment-banking business it enjoyed with those firms.

Brokerage firms generate huge revenue streams from their investment banking operations. Corporations, which do most of their investment banking through brokerage firms, like to do business with firms whose analysts give their stock favorable recommendations.

Some of the dot-com companies Merrill Lynch was working with, and wanted to continue the relationships, included Pets.com, Buy.com, eToys, GoTo.com (now known as Overture), and InfoSpace.

Through most of 2000, Blodget advised investors to buy these Internet stocks. However, by November of that same year, Blodget began publicly admitting that the Internet businesses were in trouble.

Unfortunately, many investors bought the Internet stocks on Blodget's recommendation. As thousands of investors were watching their wealth dwindle on these stocks, Merrill Lynch was making millions of dollars hand over fist.

At the end of 2000, Merrill Lynch & Co., Inc., had grown to become one of the largest financial institutions in the world, with total corporate assets in excess of $400 billion and client assets of nearly $1.7 trillion.[30]

In that same year, the company reported earnings of $3.8 billion, a 41 percent increase over the $2.7 billion figure of the previous year.[31]

Although Merrill Lynch has now merged with Bank of America because of losses it suffered from the subprime fallout that rocked the financial word, if we go back a bit further, we see that Merrill Lynch had previously lost money speculating on mortgage-backed securities.

In April 1987, Wall Street was stunned when the company announced it had lost $377 million. The loss was the largest one-day, one-company trading loss in Wall Street history. After the announcement of the loss, Merrill Lynch's stock fell $2.50 to $35.50.[32]

Here's an interesting twist: The securities that cost Merrill Lynch $377 million in a single day were mortgage-related securities. In this case, the specific type of security was known as interest-only/principal-only (IOPO), a relatively untested new type of security.

As with subprime-backed securities, IOPOs were created by investment firms that would buy mortgage-related bonds and then split them into two parts. The bonds were generally bought from the Government National Mortgage Association (also known as Ginnie Mae).

The two parts are categorized as either interest-bearing or non-interest-bearing. Regardless of whether the part pays interest, its price rises or falls with the resale value of the bond.

Merrill Lynch was selling the interest-paying part of the bonds and holding on to the principal-only part, betting that its value would rise as interest rates declined. At the time, Merrill Lynch's portfolio of IOPOs was worth $900 million.

If you're holding on to principal-only mortgage-related securities, you expect interest rates to go down. Lower interest rates make it easier for homeowners to prepay their mortgages. If you are holding a principal-only mortgage security, then you benefit from the early payoff.

However, if interest rates go up, homeowners can't prepay their mortgage. That means principal-only mortgage securities would take years to generate a return on investment. The longer it takes to make money from the securities, the less valuable they become.

In Merrill Lynch's case, interest rates began to rise quickly, making it difficult for homeowners to make prepayments. That also meant the value of Merrill Lynch's principal-only mortgage security portfolio was beginning to fall.

But instead of liquidating the securities and taking the loss, Merrill Lynch bought up $800 million more of the securities in the hope that an interest rate turnaround would bring enough profits to bail out all its losses.

But rates didn't change, and the losses were staggering. In a desperate (not to mention barbaric) act to save face, Merrill Lynch blamed all of the losses from the IOPOs on Howard Rubin, the head trader for the firm's mortgage-backed securities.

Merrill Lynch released a statement to the press saying the losses were due to significant unauthorized activity. The company dismissed Mr. Rubin immediately after the losses occurred. The Securities and Exchange Commission even barred Rubin from trading securities for almost one year.

It's hard to imagine that Mr. Rubin got in over his head. After all, he was a respected trader and had earned a master's degree in business from the prestigious Harvard Business School.

In addition, he had also served as a portfolio manager at the famous Soros Fund Management. Rubin sat on audit committees of several organizations including Deefield Triarc Capital, Global Signal, Gate-House Media Inc., and Capstead Mortgage Corporation.

Prior to working for Merrill Lynch, Rubin had worked for another Wall Street titan, Salomon Brothers. That's undoubtedly where Rubin gained expertise in mortgage-backed securities, and he took that knowledge with him to Merrill Lynch.

At the time, Salomon Brothers was the biggest mortgage securities dealer in the world. Although it claimed the number one spot, it no doubt learned the business of mortgage-backed securities from First Boston. The latter was the first financial firm to create a security tied to mortgages, known as a collateralized mortgage obligation (CMO).

With mortgage-related securities, investment firms like Salomon Brothers could make money in several different ways. They could make money by setting up the mortgage deals, by earning commissions selling mortgage-related securities to clients, or by trading the securities themselves.

In 1986, Howard Rubin made $25 million for Salomon Brothers from mortgage-related securities. He repeated that performance the following year, earning the firm $30 million from mortgage-related securities.

He then left Salomon Brothers to join Merrill Lynch, which was more than eager to learn the art of making money trading mortgage-related securities.

Rubin was the man to teach it. After all, he'd learned the business from Salomon Brothers and had already shown he could make millions trading mortgage-backed securities.

But one has to wonder, did Rubin act without authorization as the company claimed? Or did Merrill Lynch act as you might expect a ruthless barbarian to and blame someone else for the mistake?

We can find the answer to this question in a *New York Times* article from August 1990. The article points out that Merrill Lynch had quietly settled a claim related to the IOPO securities.

As part of the settlement, Merrill Lynch agreed to release more than $1 million in compensation, plus interest, that it had withheld from none other than Howard A. Rubin. The company also agreed to provide Mr. Rubin with "a general release from all potential claims."[33]

In the article, George B. Yankwitt, the attorney for Howard Rubin, commented, "It is worth noting that these lawsuits are being settled without him paying anything and, indeed, with Merrill Lynch paying him. I consider this a complete vindication of Mr. Rubin's position, which is that he had not engaged in any unauthorized or wrongful trading."

Credit Suisse, First Boston:
The Lesser-Known Barbarian

On July 11, 2001, something unusual occurred among the executive ranks of Wall Street investment firms. Allen D. Wheat, head of Credit Suisse First Boston, was fired. John J. Mack replaced his position.

It turns out Credit Suisse First Boston (CSFB) was the center of a federal investigation into how the firm sold shares of newly issued stocks. The Justice Department had begun a criminal investigation into whether CSFB received kickbacks from buyers of initial public offerings they underwrote.

As we've seen with the barbaric Goldman Sachs, underwriting IPOs is a very lucrative business. The financial firm that manages the deals gets to walk away with 5 to 6 percent in fees. So the more shares sold, the more money raised, and bigger fee payouts to the underwriting company.

The pursuit of money (and power) can change ordinary people into savage beings. It seems this was the case with CSFB, which became a powerhouse in the underwriting of emerging technology companies.

Frank Quattrone was CSFB's ringleader. His group received a share of the revenue from the deals it generated for the firm, but also earned lofty commissions as well. Reports suggest Quattrone was earning roughly $160 million a year during his peak years at the firm.[34]

Quattrone was the centerpiece of the criminal investigation. He was accused of "spinning" the IPO stocks of the companies CSFB was bringing to the market.

Being able to buy the stock at the IPO price gives investors the chance to flip the stock immediately with incredible profits, particularly if the underwriters are setting the initial offering price. Offering these shares to preferred customers is known as *spinning* and is a violation of NASD rules.

Quattrone suspected an investigation might be pending, so on December 5 he sent an e-mail to employees in his division suggesting they should delete "relevant e-mails" regarding their IPO procedures. He was convicted of two counts of obstruction of justice, and one count of witness tampering, which were both later overturned. In January 2002,

Credit Suisse First Boston reached an agreement with U.S. regulators whereby it would pay $100 million in fines to settle the allegations.

Frank Quattrone, the head of CSFB's technology underwriting group, was forced to resign from the company in March 2003.

But, as usually happens when giant corporations settle with regulators, Credit Suisse First Boston admitted no wrongdoing.

Just one year later, Credit Suisse First Boston would yet again be settling charges of fraudulent behavior. In April 2003 the firm participated in what was considered a landmark $1.4 billion settlement between 10 other Wall Street firms, the New York Attorney General, the Securities and Exchange Commission, and other regulatory agencies.

The parties agreed to quietly settle the matter. The deal reached settled a number of related allegations that had been raised against the 10 companies, including pressuring research analysts to issue positive reports on companies that the analysts believed to be worthless stock.

Credit Suisse First Boston's share of the settlement was $200 million in fines and penalties.

But you might wonder how a Zurich-based investment firm wound up as a major player on Wall Street in the first place.

Alfred Escher, a young Zurich politician, founded Credit Suisse in 1856. Escher's goal was to finance the building of a railroad. He had hoped to get the financing from several foreign banks, but failed to do so.

Escher then decided the best way to finance the project was to start his own bank. To raise money, he sold shares to the public, with the expectation of selling about 3 million in shares. But the response was better than he had hoped for: He sold 218 million in three days.

He named his new bank *Schweizerische Kreditanstalt* (translated Swiss Credit Institution, later referred to as Credit Suisse) and opened the doors for business on July 16, 1856.

The bank was a huge success. Credit Suisse helped develop the Swiss monetary system and, by the end of the Franco-Prussian War in 1871, became the largest bank in Switzerland. Credit Suisse branched out from Zurich and by the beginning of World War I, it had 13 different locations throughout Switzerland.

In 1940, Credit Suisse opened its first foreign branch in New York. By the 1960s, foreign exchange deals had become an important part of the financial community. That gave Credit Suisse the opportunity it needed to become a major player on Wall Street.

A Tight Circle

Interestingly enough, not only have the barbarians of Wall Street been tarred by fraud, but they operate within a small network where firms are bought out by each other, and employees move from one company to the next.

But this inner network is not penetrable by the average investor. That means the millions of dollars that circulate from one firm to another, and the strategies they use to generate those millions, stay within the firms operating within this private network of dealmakers.

For example, when we take a closer look at Credit Suisse First Boston's history, we learn that Merrill Lynch and First Boston were both connected to Credit Suisse. In 1978, Merrill Lynch bought out White, Weld & Company, which previously was part of First Boston. As a result of the buyout, White, Weld & Company dropped out of its London-based investment banking partnership with Credit Suisse.

First Boston Corporation stepped in, creating Financiére Crédit Suisse-First Boston, widely known as Credit Suisse First Boston. That was the deal in Europe.

In the United States, a different deal was happening whereby Credit Suisse would wind up with a 44 percent stake in First Boston in 1988. On March 7, 1989, Credit Suisse First Boston lent $487 million to Gibbons and Green, a well-known private equity firm that was doing a leveraged buyout of the Ohio Mattress Company, maker of Sealy mattresses, for $1.1 billion.[35]

At the time, the deal was considered one of the largest on Wall Street, and many experts thought the price was too much for the mattress maker. The amount was more than 20 times Ohio Mattress's expected 1989 earnings.

For First Boston's part, the money it lent was equal to about 40 percent of the company's total equity capital. But it didn't balk at the deal. First Boston went full steam ahead. However, things didn't work out as they had hoped.

Gibbons and Green floated as much as $475 million in junk bonds (high-yield bonds generally rated below investment grade because of a higher risk of default) to help finance the deal. A year later, in 1989, the junk bond market collapsed.

Because First Boston couldn't redeem the millions it had lent to Gibbons and Green for the buyout, it had no choice but to ask for help from Credit Suisse. Credit Suisse bailed First Boston out, which ultimately lead to a complete takeover of First Boston by Credit Suisse.

The incident was known as the "burning bed" deal. At the time, the takeover of First Boston by Credit Suisse was considered illegal under the Glass-Steagall Act, which separated commercial and investment banking activities. Credit Suisse had been classified as a commercial bank, First Boston as an investment bank.

However, in typical Washington-helps-Wall-Street fashion, the Federal Reserve decided the integrity of the financial markets was better served by avoiding the bankruptcy of such a significant investment bank, as First Boston was considered to be, and the deal was deemed appropriate.

In the end, the firm changed the name of First Boston to Credit Suisse First Boston.

However, by 2006, the "First Boston" part of the name was phased out and from that point forward the company was referred to as Credit Suisse.

As we've seen, becoming a major player on Wall Street often comes at a steep price. And while the price is steep for the firms involved, it's almost always devastating to the average investor who invests hundreds and thousands in hard earned money in the securities these barbarians tout as the next hot thing.

Unfortunately, as human beings, our memories are short and we forget more than we forgive. As this short tour through history shows, mortgage-backed securities are not new investment vehicles.

In 1987, Merrill Lynch lost $377 million in a single day trading mortgage-back securities. Twenty-one years later, Bank of America bailed out Merrill Lynch for the losses it incurred once again trading mortgage-backed securities.[36]

But this time mortgage-backed securities didn't just bring down one Wall Street firm; they dragged the entire United States and global economies into recession.

To make matters worse, as one U.S. firm after another lined up for their share of the $700 billion in U.S. government rescue money, it was once again the ordinary investor whom these modern barbarians plunged into despair and destitution.

Over $1.3 trillion in U.S. personal wealth vanished. On a global scale, experts say the economic destruction wiped out 40 percent of the world's wealth.

Chapter 12

Epic Tool of Destruction

O
n March 23, 1989, around 9 P.M., the *Exxon Valdez*, an oil tanker carrying 1.25 million barrels of oil, left the Valdez oil terminal in Alaska for Long Beach, California. The Valdez Narrows is a deep, still-water fjord in the northeast section of Prince William Sound, surrounded by the Chugach Mountains.

Navigating through the Valdez Narrows is exceptionally challenging because of the Bligh Reef, which makes the narrows only about 500 feet wide.

But most tankers have had little problem navigating the area. In fact, tankers carrying oil have passed through the narrows more than 8,700 times in the 12 years since oil began flowing through the trans-Alaska pipeline, with no major disasters and few serious incidents.[1]

Small icebergs from nearby Columbia Glacier occasionally enter the tanker lanes in the narrows, but captains have the choice of slowing down to push through them or moving into another lane if no other tankers are nearby.

Rather than opting to reduce speed, the *Exxon Valdez* crew asked for permission to change lanes to avoid the floating pieces of ice. At 10:49 P.M. the crew radioed that it intended to increase its speed.

But this meant the crew had to navigate a 987-foot-long tanker in a space little more than a 0.9-mile gap between the edge of the ice and the Bligh Reef, and they had to do it at higher than normal speeds. This gave the crew little room for error. Unfortunately, it was more than they could handle. At 12:04 A.M., the *Exxon Valdez* shuddered as it ground to a halt on the Bligh Reef.

Eight of the vessel's 11 cargo tanks were ruptured. Over 10.8 million gallons of oil spilled out into the icy waters, enough to fill 125 Olympic-size swimming pools. In a matter of days, the oil slick grew to about three miles wide by five miles long.[2]

The damage was widespread. The oil spill contaminated a national forest, four wildlife refuges, three national parks, five state parks, four critical habitat areas, and a state game sanctuary, which spreads along 1,400 miles of the Alaskan shoreline.

But that's not all. The oil spread to more than 1,200 miles of coastline, closed fisheries, and killed thousands of marine mammals and hundreds of thousands of sea birds. It was the thirty-fourth largest oil spill in the world at the time and the largest in U.S. waters.[3]

Two decades later, oil—an estimated 55 tons of it—still oozes a foot or so below the surface of many beaches in the area. Shellfish in the western sound have never come back, nor have the otters that depended on them.

Of course, Exxon had to pay for this horrific mistake. In civil charges, Exxon had to pay the State of Alaska and the United States $900 million over a 10-year period. The money would be used for restoration and administered by six government trustees—three federal and three state.[4]

On criminal charges, Exxon was ordered to pay a fine of $250 million. Two restitution funds of $50 million each were established, one under state control and one under federal authority. Despite strong opposition from many Alaskans, $125 million of the balance was forgiven, because of the manner in which Exxon cooperated during the cleanup, and the upgraded safety procedures it put in place to prevent a reoccurrence.[5]

The remaining $50 million was divided between the Victims of Crime Act account and the North American Wetlands Conservation Fund.[6]

Now you might wonder, what does one of the largest oil spills in U.S. waters have to do with Wall Street barbarians? Well, that's where our story takes an interesting turn.

The Smartest Woman on Wall Street

You see, Exxon Mobil didn't have enough cash on hand to cover the damages and fines from the oil spill. It had no choice but to borrow money. So it turned to its longtime banking partner, J.P. Morgan, for help.

But Morgan's hands were tied. The firm was obligated to follow the Basel Accord, a set of bank rules and regulations that require banks to hold a certain amount of their capital in reserves to offset the risks associated with outstanding loans. The riskier the loan, the more money a firm must hold in reserve.

According to the requirement, loans over $9.3 million and up to $43.9 million need a 3 percent reserve. For loans over $43.9 million, the bank must have on hand $1.038 million plus 10 percent of the net amount over $43.9 million.[7] The requirement was created so that banks could only lend out a certain amount of money at any given time.

New girl on the block Blythe Masters, a Cambridge University mathematics graduate and employee of J.P. Morgan, had an idea for getting over this little lending hurdle. If the risk associated with the loan itself could be sold, then the loan could be reclassified as risk-free, therefore freeing up cash reserves for additional lending.

Naturally, the executives at J.P. Morgan loved the idea. After all, if the bank had limits on how much it could lend, that indirectly put a limit on how much profit it could make. This new idea of selling the risk gave the executives at J.P. Morgan the best of both worlds—the ability to make more money for themselves and at the same time extend Exxon the money it needed, which was estimated at around $5 billion.[8]

Of course, J.P. Morgan could have simply told Exxon there was no way it could help the company out. But Morgan didn't want to take that risk because it didn't want to lose the lucrative business it had with Exxon.

Believe it or not, back then relationships were the cornerstone of the commercial banking business. So finding a way to extend Exxon the credit line it needed was of particular importance. And keeping the relationship also meant money for J.P. Morgan, which was earning good money in fees from Exxon.

Now all J.P. Morgan needed was some other company to take on the huge risk associated with lending Exxon that enormous amount of money it needed. Enter the European Bank for Reconstruction and Development (EBRD).

EBRD had sufficient credit to lend to companies with good credit ratings—although, to be sure, lending any company $5 billion comes with huge risk attached. If the company can't repay the money, the backer is on the hook. But EBRD wasn't too worried about the risk associated with lending Exxon Mobil the money it needed. That's because at the time, Exxon was earning roughly $99.6 billion in annual revenues.

Since then, Exxon Mobil has grown to become one of the largest moneymaking companies in the world. In 2008, with $45.2 billion on its bottom line, Exxon Mobil reported the largest annual profit in U.S. history. In 2009, it beat out Wal-Mart for the number one spot on *Fortune's* list of top 500 companies.[9]

On top of this, Exxon had earned an AAA credit rating. Nor was the company issuing large amounts of corporate debt. So for EBRD, all signs signaled go. Of course, we can't forget that EBRD wasn't assuming the risk associated with the Exxon loan for free.

Masters arranged it so that EBRD would receive an annual fee for each year it assumed the risk associated with J.P. Morgan providing Exxon the credit line it needed. The fee EBRD earned was much higher than the money it generated from any other types of loans the firm made.

Now all parties had what they needed. The credit derivative swap had been born.

Not All Derivatives Are Bad

As you've read, the market for credit derivatives barely existed 16 years ago. In 2008, the International Swaps and Derivatives Association

(ISDA) says the market for credit derivatives totaled $93.1 trillion.[10] That's down from its peak of $107.5 trillion in 2007.

The ISDA data shows the market didn't really begin until around 2001, when it was a mere $631 billion in size. (See Figure 12.1.) That means it took the market just six years to expand to 6.7 times its original size.

While we can give Masters credit for creating the first credit-related derivative, the derivative market has actually been around for a long time. In fact, the first known reference to a derivative dates back to around 2000 B.C. when merchants in the Arab Gulf created consignment transactions for goods to be sold in India.[11]

As the name implies, derivatives get (or *derive*) their value from another asset, such as a stock, a bond, or a commodity such as gold. In their most basic form, derivatives are financial contracts that are designed to create market price exposure in an underlying asset. Their purpose is to capture, in the form of price changes, some underlying price change or event.

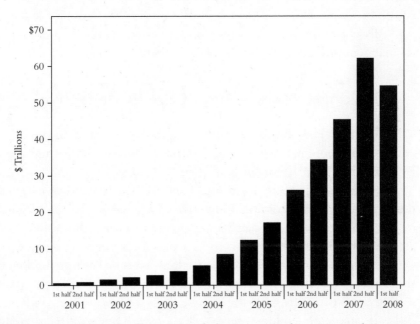

Figure 12.1 Growth of Credit Default Swaps Market—Notional Amounts Outstanding, 2001–2008

DATA SOURCES: © October 2008 Elliott Wave International (www.elliottwave.com); Blooomberg, ISDA.

Basically, the parties who buy and sell derivatives are each making a bet on the future value of the underlying asset. Derivatives also help financial firms manage their risks. Examples include futures, forwards, swaps, and options. They are traded on exchanges such as the Chicago Mercantile Exchange.

Nowadays, banks use derivatives to reduce the risk that the short-term interest rate they pay their depositors will rise, which in turn reduces the profits they make on fixed-interest-rate loans and securities. Electricity producers use derivatives to hedge against unseasonable changes in the weather.

As the derivatives market grew, most analysts, brokers, and economists saw them as sound financial instruments. Alan Greenspan, former chairman of the Board of Governors of the U.S. Federal Reserve System, said:

> By far the most significant event in finance during the past decade has been the extraordinary development and expansion of financial derivatives. These instruments enhance the ability to differentiate risk and allocate it to those investors most able and willing to take it—a process that has undoubtedly improved national productivity growth and standards of living.[12]

Making a Business out of Credit Derivatives

To understand how credit derivatives imploded and brought down an entire world economy, we have to go back to the early 1990s and meet Bill Demchak, a J.P. Morgan employee.

Demchak studied business at Allegheny College in Pennsylvania and then earned an MBA from the University of Michigan. He was assigned to J.P. Morgan's team of math geniuses hired to solve the problem of reducing the firm's risk when it lent money to distressed companies.

Demchak, working with Blythe Masters, who had already brokered the deal with Exxon Mobil, came up with the idea to apply the concept of securitization to the loans. Blythe had already solved the problem with the risk associated with lending money to Exxon with her creation of credit derivatives. Now, however, J.P. Morgan was eager to apply what it had learned from the Exxon deal and use it across multiple loans it had issued.

Securitization is not a new concept. The idea has been around since the 1970s. Securitization works like this: Basically, a banker takes a group of loans, which could be credit card or corporate loans, and bundles them together. The bundled loans are then sliced up into pieces called *tranches*. Each tranche is rated based on its risk of default. Those tranches are then sold to someone else as an investment.

Riskier tranches pay a higher interest rate than safer ones. Safer tranches pay a lower rate of interest. This lets the investor pick the tranche that best suits his needs along with his risk tolerance.

The person who buys the tranche gets the revenue stream it creates. Remember, tranches are loans (and other assets) that are being paid off by the company that borrowed the money. The person who sells the tranche, in this case J.P. Morgan, gets a fee for setting the deal up. In addition to receiving fees, J.P. Morgan is also protected in case the loans are not paid off.

Keep in mind that what we're talking about—this idea of packaging credit risk and selling it to another person—isn't regulated by the government or SEC. These are private deals between each set of parties.

Demchak, working alongside Masters, realized he could slice up the credit risks of the 300 or so corporations J.P. Morgan worked with into tranches, and sell them on Wall Street as a one-of-a-kind investment instrument.

But there was one obstacle to overcome: If Demchak and Masters were going to be successful at selling the credit derivatives to multiple parties, they needed another company to assume the risks, just as EBRD had done in the Exxon Mobil deal. But if they were going to sell the individual risk attached to the loans of their 300 or so clients, theoretically they would need an equal number of parties willing to take on the risk.

That would take too long, not to mention the tons of paperwork to pull off such a feat. So the two cunning financiers found a solution by creating an offshore shell company that would do just that. They called it a *special purpose vehicle* (SPV).

The shell company would assume J.P. Morgan's risk on the 300 or so outstanding loans. Remember, with derivatives, the idea was to separate the risk on the loans from the loans themselves. That's why they needed an offshore company.

But there was another benefit to the SPV. Remember that Basel rule we talked about earlier in this chapter, which required banks to keep a portion of cash reserves on hand to cover the risks related to loans? Well, by being able to remove risks from J.P. Morgan's balance sheet and put it on the SPV, it freed up their cash reserves for lending or investing.

Now everything was in place. The barriers to launching their new product had been removed. J.P. Morgan could now sell its new credit swaps to investors—and sell it did. By 1994, the total value of derivatives contracts on J.P. Morgan's books was estimated to be $1.7 trillion.[13] Not only that, but derivatives were generating half of the bank's trading revenue. It was a huge success for Demchak and Masters.[14]

A Credit Mania Takes Hold

The credit swap idea began to spread like wildfire. Investors were buying them like crazy. Other firms began developing their own credit derivatives. J.P. Morgan even created guidebooks to help other firms understand the credit derivative market.

About the credit derivative market she helped create, Blythe Masters said,

> In bypassing barriers in different classes, maturities, rating categories, debt seniority levels and so on, credit derivatives are creating enormous opportunities to exploit and profit from associated discontinuities in the pricing of credit risks.[15]

To this day, J.P. Morgan has huge amounts of derivatives contracts on its books. The last count showed the value of credit derivatives at around $10.2 trillion.[16]

Soon new forms of the derivatives were being created. As the Federal Reserve cut interest rates and Americans of all working classes started buying homes in record numbers, mortgage-backed tranches became the hot new investment vehicle for institutions of all kinds and sizes.

And as we'll see in a later chapter, it would be none other than Goldman Sachs, the dirtiest barbarian of all, who took them to extremes, even using derivatives to insure the debt of emerging countries such as Greece. And even that has now been called into question.

The *Washington Independent* ran an article in February 2010 with the headline "Is the Greco-European Financial Crisis Goldman's Fault, Too?" The article reports that *Der Spiegel*, a German online publication, says, "Goldman Sachs' tricky derivatives trades may have masked the Greek debt just long enough to screw us all over again."[17]

The fact is that credit derivatives had originally been created to help protect banks against the risk that a borrowing company wouldn't pay its debt. They were supposed to be used in much the same manner as you and I would buy home insurance to protect us against losses that might happen from fire, flood, or theft.

But by the time the greedy fat cats on Wall Street got their hands on them, derivatives had become toxic time bombs. The Wall Street barbarians had brainwashed banks and other institutions into believing credit derivatives were the golden egg of investing. Unfortunately, the institutions bought in big-time and took on more risks than they could handle.

The new contracts could be traded—or *swapped*—from investor to investor without anyone overseeing the trades to ensure the buyer had the resources to cover the losses if the security defaulted.

Wall Street bankers were far more concerned with how fat their bonus checks could become than whether the derivatives they were loading up on their books were at risk of failure. (See Figure 12.2.)

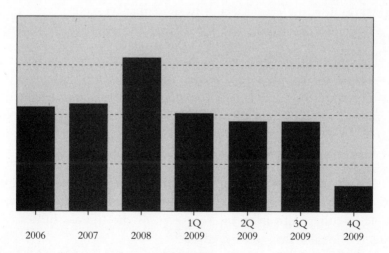

Figure 12.2 J.P. Morgan's Compensation Costs as a Share of Revenue
Data Sources: Elliott Wave International; JPMorgan Chase.

Bill Gross of Pacific Investment Management Company wrote,

Credit-default swaps are perhaps the most egregious offenders in today's banking system. Our modern shadow banking system craftily dodges the reserve requirements of traditional institutions and promotes a chain letter, pyramid scheme of leverage, based in many cases on no reserve cushion whatsoever.[18]

The world of credit default swaps is large and complex. It is unregulated. Warren Buffett called these instruments "financial weapons of mass destruction." But could government regulation have saved us from the impending doom?

Think about it like this. Math wizards, quantitative geniuses, and MBA business graduates had created these "financial weapons of mass destruction." It took them weeks, months, and years to develop and refine them.

Therefore, could the likes of Christopher Dodd, senator from Connecticut and chairman of the Senate Committee on Banking, or Congressman Barney Frank, chairman of the Financial Services Committee, understand these weapons well enough to regulate them and prevent a global financial meltdown?

The truth is these instruments were over the heads of many members of Congress. In October 2008, Eric Dinallo, the New York state insurance superintendent, gave members of Congress a guided tutorial on how the credit default swap market worked.

George Soros, chairman of Soros Fund Management, commented:

The super-boom got out of hand when the new products became so complicated that the authorities could no longer calculate the risks and started relying on the risk management methods of the banks themselves. Similarly, the rating agencies relied on the information provided by the originators of synthetic products. It was a shocking abdication of responsibility.[19]

And what about the SEC or the Federal Reserve? Could either one have saved us from 10 percent unemployment in the United States as people lost their jobs from the recession, or the trillions of dollars in retirement wealth that was wiped out?[20]

According to Gillian Tett, author of *Fool's Gold: How the Bold Dream of a Small Tribe at J.P. Morgan Was Corrupted by Wall Street Greed and*

Unleashed a Catastrophe, Masters and Demchak presented their new credit swap idea to regulators at the Federal Reserve and the Office of the Comptroller of the Currency.

Although they had never seen anything like this before, the Feds very much liked the idea. In August 1996, they wrote that banks could be allowed to reduce their capital reserves requirements by using credit derivatives.

Now the idea had the blessing of the U.S. government. If J.P. Morgan could use credit swaps to reduce its cash reserves requirements, then so too could any other banking institution. In fact, the Office of the Comptroller of the Currency reports that revenue generated by U.S. banks in their credit derivatives trading totaled $1.2 billion in the third quarter of 2009.

Of derivatives, Martin Mayer, guest scholar at the Brookings Institution writes:

> These "over the counter" derivatives—created, sold and serviced behind closed doors by consenting adults who don't tell anybody what they're doing—are also a major source of the almost unlimited leverage that brought the world financial system to the brink of disaster last fall.[21]

Playing Wall Street Russian Roulette

When the federal government took over American International Group (AIG) in September 2008, it had to do so because the insurance giant was carrying far more in credit default swaps than it could insure. AIG had become a prime player in credit default swaps.

The company knew there was no way it had enough money on hand to back the value of the swaps it was insuring. AIG was playing Russian roulette. It was betting that at any given time, only a small fraction of the credit swaps would come due.

And Wall Street firms were playing right along with AIG. They, too, like AIG, never anticipated that a large portion of the swaps would default. Not only that, but they had an incentive to stay in the game. That's because the Fed had already issued a statement that banks could reduce their capital reserve requirements by using credit derivatives.[22] So the more risks they could get off their books, the more capital they freed up.

The credit default market had grown so big, it was 50 times the size of the subprime mortgage derivatives market.[23] What makes this market more dangerous than subprime mortgage–backed securities is that, while with subprimes you can somewhat figure out the value of the property, with credit derivatives the insurer has to make a lot of assumptions, because basically they are guessing whether the company that has taken out the loan can pay it back.

To make those assumptions, the insurer has to analyze all kinds of information about the health of the company itself, how the company is managed, and the company's industry as a whole—whether it is growing or contracting, foreign competition, and a host of other factors.

Now if you were insurance giant AIG, and you wanted to make a fortune in the credit default market, because you know the fees are substantial, the easiest way to do that is to lower your assumption that a company will default. The lower the assumption for defaults, the more profits you make in the transaction.

But there's a second benefit: The lower your assumptions for default of other companies, the greater your chances of beating out competitors who are going after the same purportedly lucrative business. Now factor in that AIG had a triple-A credit rating. That meant that AIG needed only a small amount of collateral against the potential losses. So all the way around, it's a win–win scenario for AIG.

AIG's credit default swap business had grown so big that at one point it had something close to $527 billion sitting on its books.[24]

From Insurance to Credit Defaults

But how did an insurance company become a major player in the credit risk business? Look no further than the company's Financial Products division, called Capital Markets.

In 1987, three Drexel Burnham Lambert traders, led by finance scholar Howard Sosin, convinced then–AIG CEO Hank Greenberg to branch out from the company's core insurance business by creating a financial products division.

Greenberg agreed. The division was structured so that 38 percent of the revenues the group produced stay within the division, while the other 62 percent went to the AIG core group.[25] The other component of the deal was that profits would be booked up front, although they knew most of the deals the team would create would take years to pay out.

The team now heading the new Financial Products division got to work, and the first deal they put together was a $1 billion interest rate swap with the Italian government. An interest rate swap is a derivative where one party exchanges a stream of interest payments for another party's stream of cash flow.[26]

In 1993, Sosin left AIG's financial division and was replaced by Tom Savage, who would later (in 1998) head up the Financial Products division. Savage was no stranger to derivatives. He began his career at First Boston writing computer models for collateralized mortgage obligations. In fact, it was First Boston who helped create mortgage-backed securities.

By 1998, under Savage's direction, the Financial Products division had earned $500 million in revenues. But the money didn't come from credit derivatives. Derivatives didn't play a large part until later that year when none other than J.P. Morgan asked if the division would be willing to insure a portion of Morgan's corporate debt.

Of course, J.P. Morgan was more than willing to pay AIG a fee for its service. Now remember, one of the key components needed for credit swap deals to happen is a company with a strong credit rating. AIG already had an AAA credit rating.[27]

The two took full advantage of AIG's rating. AIG's Financial Products division wrote close to $80 billion worth of credit default swaps contracts. Some of the credit swaps were loaded with mortgage securities, some of them subprime loans. As the housing market fell apart, the credit derivatives declined in value. As the derivatives fell in value, the once stellar triple-A credit ratings AIG had obtained were downgraded.

The drop in AIG's creditworthiness triggered clauses in the credit default contracts that allowed the counterparties to demand the cash that backed the swaps.[28]

One of those counterparties was Goldman Sachs. In August 2007, Goldman demanded $1.5 billion in collateral from AIG to cover the mortgage-backed securities it had insured. Other counterparties demanded their cash, too. AIG didn't have sufficient funds to back all the credit swaps it had insured. That year AIG's market value crashed from $180 billion to $5 billion. Yet the demands continued.[29]

In February 2008, AIG announced it had lost $1.5 billion. The most it could manage to post in collateral for its credit swaps was $5.3 billion. That wasn't enough to cover all the credit swaps it had underwritten. The credit default swap contract states that if AIG's credit rating drops below a certain level, it would have to fork over $13 billion in collateral to the buyers of the swaps.[30]

In September 2008, AIG learned that its credit rating was about to be downgraded yet again. This would only trigger more demands for cash. But it was too late. AIG's level of exposure to its credit default swap losses was higher than anyone could have imagined.

The government had to step in to save the company. In September, the Federal Reserve gave $85 billion to AIG in bailout funds.[31] But it was too little. In November the feds coughed up another $150 billion that included a $60 billion line of credit from the Federal Reserve; $40 billion of preferred stock, making the Treasury a 70.9 percent owner of AIG; and two fed-sponsored financing vehicles that rid AIG's financial statements of about $50 billion of troubled assets.[32]

The Cancer Had Spread

But why was AIG saved and not Lehman Brothers? After all, Lehman Brothers was dealing in credit derivatives, too. There were at least 350 banks and investors linked to Lehman's credit swaps.[33]

The week leading up to AIG's rescue, credit markets froze up. Lehman Brothers was one of the first to feel the effects. It had some 900,000 credit-related derivative contracts in place and no one was extending credit. Without a source of funding, Lehman had no choice but to file bankruptcy.

Of the filing, Peter G. Peterson, co-founder of the private equity firm Blackstone Group, and who had been head of Lehman Brothers in the 1970s said, "My goodness. I've been in the business 35 years, and these are the most extraordinary events I've ever seen."[34]

When the government realized the extent of the problem related to credit default swaps, it opened its vault of bailout funds to AIG.

But those vault doors were probably nudged open by the fact that one of the companies caught in AIG's credit derivative web was none other the company Henry Paulson had once run, Goldman Sachs. The choice to save one firm over another is hard to understand.

The government insists it couldn't save Lehman Brothers because, unlike Merrill Lynch, Bear Sterns, or Wachovia, no one wanted to buy the company. In his new book, *On the Brink*, Henry Paulson blames Alistair Darling, the Chancellor of the Exchequer, for failing to allow Barclays Bank of London to buy Lehman Brothers. Paulson says, "The British screwed us."[35]

On the day Lehman Brothers filed for bankruptcy, Paulson said, "I never once considered it appropriate to put taxpayer money on the line."[36] Yet that's exactly what he used when bailing out AIG.

Treasury Secretary Timothy Geithner's explanation for not bailing out Lehman Brothers was that the government didn't have the legal authority to do so. He suggested the government would prefer to maintain the line between responsibilities and powers of the fiscal authority and those of the monetary authority.

Christopher Whalen, managing director and co-founder of Institutional Risk Analytics, suggests AIG was a prime beneficiary of bailout money because of the strong ties between Geithner and Stephen Friedman, a former Goldman Sachs executive who served on the board of the New York Federal Reserve branch, where Geithner worked before becoming Treasury secretary.[37]

What's also odd about the government's decision not to save Lehman Brothers is that, just as Goldman Sachs and J.P. Morgan had applied to become a bank holding company and received approval, Lehman did the same. But the government denied its application.

If the government didn't have the authority to save Lehman Brothers from failing, then how could it, just one day later, step in and save AIG?

Besides the obvious connection to Goldman Sachs and Paulson, AIG's counterparties were widespread, touching 25 financial institutions in the United States and at least seven other countries.[38]

Table 12.1 Companies that Received Money from AIG When It was Awarded Bailout Funds

AIG Counterparty	Maiden Lane III Payment	Collateral Payments Posted (as of 11/7)	Total
Sociètè Gènèrale	6.9	9.6	16.5
Goldman Sachs	5.6	8.4	14.0
Merrill Lynch	3.1	3.1	6.2
Deutsche Bank	2.8	5.7	8.5
UBS	2.5	1.3	3.8
Calyon	1.2	3.1	4.3
Deutsche Zentral-Genossenschaftsbank	1.0	0.8	1.8
Bank of Montreal	0.9	0.5	1.4
Wachovia	0.8	0.2	1.0
Barclays	0.6	0.9	1.5
Bank of America	0.5	0.3	0.8
The Royal Bank of Scotland	0.5	0.6	1.1
Dresdner Bank AG	0.4	0.0	0.4
Rabobank	0.3	0.3	0.6
Landesbank Baden-Wuerttemberg	0.1	0.0	0.1
HSBC Bank, USA	0.0*	0.2	0.2
Total	27.1**	35.0	62.1

*Amount rounded down to $0.
**In addition to the $27.1 billion in payments to the counterparties, AIGFP received a payment of $2.5 billion as an adjustment payment to reflect overcollateralization.
SOURCE: SIGTARP analysis of AIG and FRBNY data, www.sigtarp.com/reports/audit/2009/Factors_Affecting_Efforts_to_Limit_Payments_to_AIG_Counterparties.pdf.

AIG's annual statement revealed that about $379 billion of the $527 billion in the company's default swap portfolio "represent[ed] derivatives written for financial institutions, principally in Europe, for the purpose of providing them with regulatory capital relief rather than risk mitigation."[39] (See Table 12.1).

Lessons Not Learned

The fallout of the credit crisis was far greater than anyone calculated. The Federal Reserve suggested that financial markets would suffer a loss of around US $100 billion. But now reports are surfacing that suggest financial institutions around the globe have already written down more than US $500 billion of bad debts and investment losses. The International Monetary Fund (IMF) says the crisis will have a final price tag of over US $1.3 trillion.[40]

The Federal Reserve and J.P. Morgan bailed out the fifth-largest U.S. investment bank, Bear Stearns.[41] The fourth-largest, Lehman Brothers, filed for bankruptcy.[42] The third largest, Merrill Lynch, was acquired by the Bank of America.

Needless to say, mistakes were made on a grand scale. In cases where risk-to-reward ratios were high, assumptions were recalculated to soften the risk so that underwriting fees could prevail and Wall Street bonuses could be paid. Washington, clouded by its rose-colored visions of economic good times that wouldn't end, and the hope of more votes, sat idly by, watching the events unfold.

This isn't much different than what happened with Long Term Capital Management (LTCM) in 1998. Using computers, massive databases, and the insights of top-level theorists, LTCM suspected it could spot profit when markets deviated from normal patterns and were likely to readjust back to those normal patterns.

LTCM's staff was led by Nobel Prize–winning economists Myron Scholes and Robert Merton. Also among LTCM's team was John Meriwether, a former vice chairman of Salomon Brothers, and David Mullins, a former vice chairman of the Board of Governors of the Federal Reserve System. In fact, it is Meriwether who gets credit for founding LTCM when he was forced to leave Salomon Brothers because of the company's treasury auction rigging scandal.[43]

At its height, the fund had $5 billion in assets, controlled over $100 billion, and had positions whose total worth was over $1 trillion. The group believed that by creating hedged portfolios, any risks associated with market events could be reduced to zero.[44]

In August 1998, Russia defaulted on its debt and the financial markets unraveled. LTCM had placed big bets that the disruption the default created in the markets would eventually return to normal levels. However, the group's assumptions didn't pan out. The firm nearly went bankrupt, but the Federal Reserve Bank of New York saved the company.[45]

In many ways, derivatives were created to protect against future LTCM failures. But instead of being used as protection, Wall Street found a way to use them to escape regulations and profit handsomely.

The failure of LTCM and the damage it caused became a distant memory. And once again, the derivative frenzy on Wall Street took hold.

That frenzy cost us dearly. The IMF predicts that the world economic growth will slow from the 30-year high of around 5 percent to much lower levels. In its *Global Financial Stability Report* released in January 2009, the IMF says that despite wide-ranging policy actions by governments and central banks around the world, financial strains remain acute, pulling down the real economy.[46]

In the end, the barbarians of wealth prevailed. Just as towns and villages throughout Europe were victims of Attila's ruthless raids, the American public was the victim of modern-day financial barbarians who plundered our wealth.

No longer can we look forward to a comfortable retirement, but instead we must worry what the future holds. For now, the future outlook remains highly uncertain.

Chapter 13

The Brotherhood
of Banks

I n 1791, Robert Morris, an immigrant from England, had an idea
on how to transform the country's banking system. He proposed
his idea to the Continental Congress of the United States. Morris
was a wealthy businessman who had made his fortune capturing British
vessels and selling their bounty to the emerging colonies of the new
world.

Now, Morris wasn't just a shipping pirate, but a financier to the newly
formed government. Fifteen years earlier, Morris had loaned the Congress
$10,000 of his own money to feed, clothe, and supply the fledgling
country's troops. In fact, Morris was considered one of the nation's
wealthiest men. And he would use that wealth and the power it brought
him to his full advantage.

Morris was born in England and immigrated to the United States in
1744. He took a job as an apprentice with a local merchant. When
his employer, an exporting merchant, died, Morris entered into

a partnership with the son. His business did well for many years, which helped him earn a nice living.

But that comfortable living was in jeopardy when in 1765 the British government imposed the Stamp Act. Basically, the act forced a tax on colonial documents. Each document such as newspapers, magazines, books, and anything else printed on paper had to carry an official seal.

In Britain, stamp acts had become a very successful method of taxation. In fact, they generated over £100,000 in tax revenue with very little in collection expenses.

Unfortunately for the colonies, the tax had to be paid in valid British currency, not in colonial paper money. This posed a bit of a problem. The colonies already suffered a chronic shortage of official coins with which to carry out their everyday commercial activities.

Worse yet, there were many different forms of currency floating around. Some experts say that in North Carolina alone, there were up to 17 different forms of money being used.

Now the country already had a bank, the Bank of Pennsylvania. But it was a state bank and didn't operate in the ordinary sense of banks. It was more of an organization formed with the main purpose of financing supplies for the army. Morris, being an astute businessman and realizing the shortcomings of the Bank of Pennsylvania, presented to fellow members of the Continental Congress in 1781 his idea to establish the Bank of North America. Congress approved Morris's proposal and appointed him the first superintendent of finance.

The bank was funded with $400,000. One thousand shares were issued at a cost of $400 each. Investors could pay for the shares in gold or silver coins. The shares were available during the summer and autumn of 1791. By January 1, 1792, the country's first bank was up and running.[1]

In his proposal, Morris suggested that the Bank of North America not only serve the government but also act as a commercial bank. The Bank of North America was granted the privilege of issuing paper notes, which could be used to pay taxes.

In addition, all Congressional funds would be housed at the bank. The charter also stipulated that no other banks could issue paper notes. Basically, it was granted a banking monopoly.

Unfortunately for Morris, the states outside Pennsylvania, where the bank was headquartered, had little faith in the new paper money. By 1783, the bank's role switched to that of a state–chartered commercial bank.

Explosion in Banking Business

From 1811 to 1815, the number of banks in the United States grew rapidly from 117 to 212, roughly an 80 percent growth rate. In addition, the number of private banks blossomed in number from 208 to 246.[2] However, half the banks that opened between 1810 and 1820 had failed by 1825. But this didn't end the explosion of banks that seemed to dominate the economic landscape for many years.[3]

The Office of the Comptroller of the Currency (OCC) reports that in 1912 there were 25,176 banks in operation. That's roughly two and a half times the number of banks that existed in 1900. The OCC further states that the rate of increase in banks was almost double that of the population during the same time period. That means that there was one bank for every 3,788 citizens.[4]

However, one problem that all banks faced was maintaining the value of the notes they issued. In 1863, every bank could print money. At one point 7,000 different banknotes were in circulation.[5]

The problem of different banknotes came about because the country's infrastructure wasn't fully developed, making it difficult for people to get around. So the population worked and shopped mostly within the area in which they lived.

This meant the notes issued by the banks had a higher value in the local areas in which they were used, while notes in circulation outside of the local area depreciated much faster.

That situation gave rise to money brokers who would travel to each bank, gather up the depreciated currency, and return it to the state where it was originally issued for coin redemption. The money brokers kept journals of their redemptions. This made it much easier for the public to know the rate of exchange.

But ingenuity is always at work, and a new class of banks called *wildcat banks* sprang up around the country. As the name implies, wildcat banks were specifically located "out in the wild" and were issuing their own currency. Of the 7,000 different notes in circulation, 1,700 were notes issued by wildcat banks.[6]

Being located in areas hard to find and even more difficult to travel to made it that much harder for the money brokers to find these wildcat banks.

The truth is, banking in the early seventeenth century had a Wild West feel. It was chaotic. Systems and procedures hadn't been fully developed. Banks could arbitrarily suspend redemption of notes for coins. Bank went out of business as quickly as they opened up. But Congress settled things down when it passed the National Bank Act.

The government offered federal charters to banks that had a sufficient amount of capital on hand and would be willing to submit to restrictions set up by the government. Under the act, banks were required to purchase government bonds as a condition of start-up. As the bonds were deposited with the federal government, the bank could issue its own notes for up to 90 percent of the market value of the bonds on deposit.[7]

Congress was able to reduce the number of state banks by putting a 10 percent tax on the notes they issued. Congress curbed the growth of national banks by not allowing the banks to branch out if their state did not allow them to do so. They also couldn't branch out across state lines.

Investment Banks Blossom

Investment or merchant banks developed mostly through importing commodities that manufacturers needed and exporting the finished goods back to Europe.

Most investment banks established their own private agreements with merchants. The head of an investment bank would usually finance the deals using his own money. And since it took a lot of money to make these deals happen, wealthy businessmen owned and operated the banks.

For example, Stephen Girard, an investor in the first Bank of the United States, started the Girard Bank in Philadelphia. At the time, Stephen Girard was the richest man in the country.

Alexander Brown, an immigrant from Ireland, also a very wealthy businessman, set up a chain of investment banks in Baltimore, Philadelphia, and New York.

One of the most recognized names in banking is that of J. Pierpont (J.P.) Morgan. Morgan was the son of wealthy merchant banker Junius Spencer Morgan. His father got young Morgan a job in the New York banking firm of Duncan, Sherman & Company. At just 24 years old, J.P. set up his own bank that funded various business ventures. When his father's business partner retired, J.P. became a partner in his father's bank.

The two merged their company with a firm owned by Anthony Drexel and his brother Frank. The new company was known as Drexel, Morgan & Company. Knowing how to spot an opportunity, J.P. made millions upon the death of Cornelius Vanderbilt when Cornelius's son William hired Drexel and Morgan to sell off his inheritance.

Just as there were very few regulations and laws governing commercial banks, the same was true of investment banks. Therefore, developing strong relationships with the merchants was important to their long-term success. The better the relationships they developed, the more information they gained about other merchants, and other merchant bankers.

Having this detailed knowledge gave Drexel and Morgan a competitive advantage. It also allowed them to grow their business by lending money directly to owners of different enterprises. They knew who could repay the funds and who couldn't.

By the end of the nineteenth century, most of the merchant banks were making a large portion of their profits from the money they lent out to other commercial enterprises.

It was also around this same time period that the United States was transforming from an agriculture-dominated economy to an industrial-driven one. Capital was needed on a much grander scale. Investment bankers were becoming finance specialists.

State banks wanted a piece of the action. And although they had been prevented from formally engaging in investment banking activities through the National Bank Act, many got around the law by setting up state-chartered companies that not only provided investment banking activities but accepted deposits from customers for both checking and savings accounts.

The number of banks during this period grew like wildflowers. The Currency Act of 1900 made it much easier to fund a bank. The start-up costs dropped from $50,000 to $25,000. But this also marked the beginning of a dual banking system.[8]

Two Systems in One

Most bank customers wouldn't be able to tell you what type of charter their bank holds. Here in the United States, we operate on a dual banking system where banks can choose whether to hold a state or federal charter.

The dual banking system doesn't exit in other countries. In most countries, such as Canada, Germany, France, Japan, and the United Kingdom, four or five major banks dominate the banking industry with nationwide branches.

As the name implies, the federal system means banks are issued a federal bank charter, follow federal laws, and operate under federal rules and regulations. State banks are issued a state charter, follow state laws, and operate under state rules and regulations.

Federally chartered banks are supervised by the Office of the Comptroller of the Currency (OCC) while state banks are watched over by their state chartering authority, such as the State Banking Commissioner or the State Banking Department, and either the Federal Deposit Insurance Corporation (FDIC) or the Federal Reserve System.

Banks can choose which charter they'd like to have. But the choice of charter also determines the bank's powers, capital requirements, and lending limits. On the whole, state-chartered banks are smaller than federally chartered banks. But supervisor fees, which all banks are required to pay, are lower at the state bank level. Banks that choose a state charter claim to do so because state commissioners understand local issues better.

Why does the United States have a dual banking system while other countries do not? Most analysts and experts say having the two regulating agencies—state and federal—provides a greater checks and balance mechanism over the entire system of banking.

Former Federal Reserve Chairman Alan Greenspan has been quoted as saying:

> A system in which banks have choices, and in which regulations result from the give and take involving more than one agency, stands a better chance of avoiding the extremes of supervision.... A single regulatory, charged with responsibility for safety and soundness is likely to have a tendency to suppress risk

taking. A system of multiple supervisors and regulators creates checks on this propensity.[9]

Analysts also suggest that the dual banking system creates a more competitive environment where banks offer more products and services to their customers. But in the early part of the 1900s, this wasn't always the case.

Not Equal among Banks

In 1924, at least 18 states allowed banks to branch out to other areas of the state they served. But due to the National Banking Act of 1863, national banks weren't allowed to branch out. In fact there was no mention of branching in the legislation, which the Supreme Court, the OCC, and the Treasury interpreted as meaning it was not allowed.

This gave state banks a competitive advantage over national banks that Congressman Louis T. McFadden viewed as unfair and inadequate. McFadden had served as chairman of the Banking and Currency Committee for 10 years.

In 1922, McFadden introduced legislation that would allow national banks to enjoy the same privileges as state banks. But the bill met with strong opposition and failed.

Comptroller of the Currency D. R. Crissinger, concerned about the competitive disadvantages, issued a ruling that national banks could establish agencies or teller windows within the city of the parent bank with the sole purpose of accepting deposits and cashing checks. But this could only happen as long as state banks were permitted by their own states to operate branches in much the same manner.

Because the teller windows weren't actual offices and couldn't provide loans, in Crissinger's view these were simply convenient points of contacts for customers.

But the Federal Reserve Board members disagreed. They felt the best way to get around the competitive disadvantage the national banks faced was to restrict state-member banks from branching out at all.

Henry Daws, Federal Reserve Board member, said that unless branch banking was curbed, it would destroy national banks and thereby destroy the Federal Reserve System. The measure was voted on and won.

When Congress convened in 1927, McFadden submitted a revised version of his bill in favor of equal branch activities by all banks. By this time the number of bank failures from the Great Depression was growing at a rapid rate. The bill passed, and now national banks could branch out to wider areas of the state, enjoying the same privileges as state banks. But the bill did not allow for banks to cross state lines.

As banks went under, customers lined up outside to withdraw their money.

Banks Become Gamblers

According to FDIC numbers, in the United States, there are about 8,000 commercial banks. But there's a problem hidden in these statistics. Since the credit crisis began, the number of banks that have gone under has mushroomed.

If you look over the FDIC's list of bank failures, you'll see that between the years 2000 and 2007, there were roughly 27 bank failures.

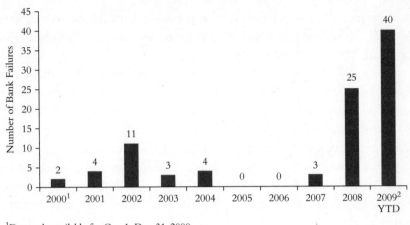

¹Data only available for Oct. 1–Dec. 31, 2000.
²As of June 19, 2009.

Figure 13.1 Dramatic Growth in Bank Failures, 2000–2009
SOURCES: CNBC.com, FDIC.

That's close to four bank failures a year.[10] Figure 13.1 provides a dramatic visual of the number of bank failures that have occurred in the United States since 2000.

The numbers change dramatically in 2008. In fact, in that year alone, 25 banks closed. That's more bank failures in one year than throughout the previous seven years.[11]

In 2009, there were a whopping 140 bank failures. That's five times the rate of banks that failed in 2008. And during the writing of this book (2010), 22 banks had already been shut down just in the first two months of the year. That brings the total number of banks that have failed because of the credit crisis to 187.[12]

Some analysts suspect the reason for such high failures is that the banking industry has endured a persistent secular decline in profitability since 2003 that may have forced banks into speculative lending practices.[13]

But the critical question is, has the problem of bank failures subsided? Not according to the FDIC. More than 700 U.S. banks are on the FDIC's problem list of banks in danger of defaulting.

Of course, this isn't the only time in history when we've experienced an outrageous number of bank failures. During the Great Depression, banks were failing at high rates as people rushed to withdraw their money. In 1921, 505 banks failed. But over the next few years, bank failures shot up from 500 to as many as 1,000 per year.[14]

Between 1929 and 1933, 9,400 banks had failed.[15] The FDIC says that from 1929 to 1933, bank failures resulted in losses to depositors of about $1.3 billion.

Now many historians say that more banks failed than necessary in many ways because of the passage of the McFadden Banking Act, which kept banks tied to their state and local economies and imposed other heavy restrictions. Whether the McFadden Act helped destroy more banks than necessary is debatable, but the failure rate was certainly alarming.

Senator Carter Glass, a representative from Virginia, and former Treasury secretary, thought the reason banks were failing had to do more with the activities they were engaged in than the restrictions that limited their ability to branch out.

Lines in the Sand

Banks, whether state or federally chartered, were free to invest in securities. You see, while the Federal Reserve Act of 1913 gave the Federal Reserve Board the power to supervise the nation's banks, it did not give the Fed any authority over the nation's stock-exchange activities.

In early 1900s, commercial banks established security affiliates that could underwrite corporate stock issues. Glass theorized that banks had manipulated the money in their accounts so that in reality they had less than the 7 percent cash required and were using the funds for what he called "maelstrom stock speculation."

Now Glass wasn't against investing altogether. He owned shares in newspapers, banks, hotels, and other types of business.

But what Glass saw as destructive to the economy was speculative stock investing. To him, it was nothing more than glorified gambling. He'd seen how this behavior was ruining America's hope for prosperity. He witnessed the money being lost by the banks with their reckless investing habits.

For example Goldman, Sachs & Company sold nearly a billion dollars' worth of securities in three interconnected investment trusts it set up: Goldman Sachs Trading Corporation, Shenandoah Corporation, and Blue Ridge Corporation.[16] As the market crashed, the values of all three depreciated to virtually nothing.

What's interesting to note about Senator Glass is that he was one of the backers of the Federal Reserve Act of 1913. However, by the time the market began to crash in October 1929, Senator Glass was already considering a banking reform bill to correct what he saw as an error in the Federal Reserve Act.

The error was related to a section of the Act that allowed the Federal Reserve to discount paper of member banks under the stipulation that the Act shall not include notes, drafts, or bills covering investments issued or drawn for the purpose of carrying or trading in stocks, bonds, or other investment securities, except bonds and notes of the government of the United States.

In other words, if banks did not include money used for investing purposes, they would have access to more capital at discounted rates from the Fed. These new funds could then be passed on to securities affiliates created by the banks, set up with the sole purpose of doing the banks' speculative investing. It was a loophole in the act that banks used to their advantage quite successfully.

Senator Glass wanted to restrict banks from dealing in and holding corporate securities altogether. So he began drafting a bill that would separate commercial banking activities from investment activities. Glass did not want securities investing to become the principal focus of commercial banks, which had already proven disastrous to the economy.

When the bill was presented to the Senate in 1932, it immediately set off debates, none of which could be settled. In June, it was removed from the Senate's calendar. It came back on the floor a year later. Meanwhile, Henry B. Steagall, a representative from Alabama and chairman of the House Committee on Banking and Currency, had proposed creating deposit insurance.

But he was getting stiff opposition. Those against his idea suggested that deposit insurance would be too expensive. The president of the American Bankers Association declared that deposit insurance was unsound, unscientific, and dangerous. Another critic of deposit insurance was Senator Glass himself.

He didn't believe it would do any good. In his opposition to federal deposit insurance, Glass pointed to the record of the defunct state insurance programs. However, Steagall, wanting his proposal passed, agreed to support Senator Glass's banking reform bill on the condition that he would amend the bill so that it permitted bank deposit insurance. Glass agreed, and the need for deposit insurance was written into the bill. In 1933 the Glass–Steagall Act was passed.

For Glass, the passage of the bill provided a mechanism that could prevent an economic catastrophe as wide-reaching and profound as the Great Depression.

Unfortunately for Americans living in the twenty-first century, our modern-day politicians turned a blind eye to the bill. They would soon become willing participants in "irrational exuberance."

Greenspan Tears Glass-Steagall into Pieces

In 1986, a funny thing happened at the Federal Reserve Board. It made a ruling in favor of easing the restrictions in the Glass-Steagall Act. In a surprising reversal, the Fed decided that language in the act that kept commercial banking and securities activities separate could suddenly be interpreted to mean "on a limited basis."

So the Fed issued a ruling allowing up to 5 percent of a bank's gross revenues be associated with investing activities. In other words, the Fed was now opening the door for commercial banks to get back into the securities market as long as it wasn't their main activity.

The Glass-Steagall Act would further be hacked into meaningless pieces with the blessing of Alan Greenspan, the new Federal Reserve chairman and former director of J.P. Morgan, already one of the country's largest investment banking firms.

Greenspan wasted no time wielding his sword. In January 1989, the Board, under Greenspan's direction, issued an order raising the limit of revenues earned from securities from 5 percent to 10 percent. In that same year, the Fed Board approved an application by J.P. Morgan, Chase Manhattan, Bankers Trust, and Citicorp to expand the Glass-Steagall ruling to include debt and other types of securities.[17]

Making sure his former company could thrive under this new expansion of the Glass–Steagall Act, the Federal Reserve Board chairman allowed J.P. Morgan to become the first bank to underwrite securities.

But Greenspan's hacking away at the Glass–Steagall Act wasn't finished. In December 1996, the Federal Reserve Board once again reviewed the language of limited basis and amended its 1989 ruling, increasing the limit to 25 percent. This now made it possible for banks to be more heavily involved in the securities market than in previous years. The only thing left of the Glass–Steagall Act was a restriction that prevented banks from owning insurance-underwriting companies.[18]

In 1997, the Federal Reserve further reduced the Glass–Steagall Act provisions to basically meaningless line items. The Fed rationalized that banks had the right to acquire securities firms outright.

Now one wonders why the Fed would do an about-face on an act that had been on the law books for the past 54 years. But its actions aren't so surprising when you consider that the Board was being pressured by the likes of J.P. Morgan, CitiBank, and Bankers Trust.

These firms were anxious to enter into the municipal bond, commercial paper, and mortgage-backed securities markets. To do so, they needed the cooperation of the Federal Reserve—and they got it.

In fact, Dr. Charles Geisst, professor of finance at Manhattan College, suggests Citibank spent $100 million on lobbying and public relations. Add in the lobbying dollars of other financial firms and it totals $200 million spent to repeal the Glass–Steagall Act. That's right, the Fed was buckling to Wall Street's huge lobby machine.[19]

But we can't tell this story without mentioning Sanford (Sandy) Weill, Citigroup creator and former CEO. Read the hundreds of articles and essays written about Weill and you'll see they arrive at the same conclusion: He was instrumental in getting Congress to completely eradicate the Glass–Steagall Act.

How could one person have such an influence? With his money and power. Weill epitomizes the rags-to-riches stories we love to read about. Except in his climb to reach the top, he stripped away the barrier that could have saved prosperity for many Americans.

Pushed by his love for money and a lavish lifestyle, he ransacked Wall Street and built one of the largest investment banks in the United

States, Citigroup. Yes, dear reader, the same Citigroup that was rescued by your taxpayer dollars to the tune of $45 billion.[20]

The Man Who Ransacked Wall Street

Weill started his investment career at Bear Sterns, working for Cy Lewis as a quote boy. Quote boys were responsible for inputting the ticker symbols of stocks into quote machines as directed by their bosses. From this entry-level position, Weill worked his way to margin clerk, where he kept track of the loans the company made to customers to buy stocks. Eventually Weill secured a position as a broker, where he developed a client list of his own.

In 1956 Weill left Bear Sterns and took his client list with him to Burnham & Company. Over time, Weill earned a good salary from his commissions. But his goal was to start his own firm. With the help of three other Wall Street brokers and friends, Arthur Carter, Roger Berlind, and Peter Potoma, Weill ventured out on his own to form Carter, Berlind, Potoma & Weill.

The team of four was doing modestly well in their new business and making a name for themselves until Potoma was accused of violating New York Stock Exchange rules. Not wanting to risk having the new firm's name damaged, Potoma was forced to resign and the firm was renamed Carter, Berlind & Weill.

The firm's big breakthrough came when it helped Saul Steinberg, head of Leasco Data Processing Equipment Corporation, take over Reliance Insurance Company out of Philadelphia. The deal netted Weill and his group $750,000 in finder's fees and $47,000 in commissions. It also earned his company a name on Wall Street. By 1969, the new company was earning $2.6 million annually.[21]

Over the years the company changed partners once again. Carter left and Arthur Levitt joined, and the firm became Cogan, Berlind, Weill & Levitt (CBWL). Weill served as the new company's chairman. This also marked the beginning of a wild buying spree of other brokerage firms, spearheaded by Weill himself.

In 1970, securities firm McDonnell & Company, with 26 branches around the country, announced it was shutting down for good. CBWL picked up the firm for pennies on the dollar. The acquisition allowed the group to rapidly expand its retail brokerage business.

However, McDonnell & Company wasn't the only company in need of a buyer. Hayden Stone & Company, with some 57,000 accounts and about $113 million in revenues, was running out of money.

Worried about the impact of such a large firm going under, the New York Stock Exchange was actively looking for a company to take it over. CBWL saw the opportunity and seized it. At the time, the deal was unlike anything seen on Wall Street, and once again, Weill grew his firm.

Now recognized as a full-fledged securities firm, in 1971 the group of four decided to sell one million shares of CBWL to the public. At the initial public offering, the shares sold for $12.50 each. Now the firm had the capital it needed for acquiring companies. And Weill wasted no time buying up Wall Street. In fact, the company was growing by leaps and bounds, and each of the partners was getting richer along the way.

Weill was obsessed with acquiring company after company. It was as if there were no wall or boundaries to stop him from buying up Wall Street itself.

Weill's next acquisitions included Shearson Hammill & Company in 1974, whereupon CBWL once again changed its name. The new company would be known as Shearson Hayden Stone. The Shearson name was kept because of its wide recognition as a major underwriter on Wall Street.

By 1977, Weill had built Shearson into the seventh-largest investment-banking firm in the country. Its revenues had more than tripled to $134 million. But Weill wasn't satisfied—he wanted more.[22]

In 1979, Weill and his gang at Shearson acquired Loeb, Rhoades, Hornblower & Company, one of Wall Street's oldest and most successful firms. This takeover now put Shearson in the position of the second-largest investment-banking firm in the world.

The company had grown so big that Weill, in a surprising move, decided to sell Shearson. In 1981, he found a buyer in American Express who was willing to pay $900 million. But Weill was cunning and clever.

Selling Shearson to American Express didn't mark the end for him. It was simply a new beginning. You see, Weill saw this as an opportunity to use American Express's capital and clout for more deal making.

In the deal, Weill agreed to hold a position behind the CEO and president of American Express, making him third man on the totem pole. He wasn't interested in running the business. Weill wanted access to the firm's capital.

He wasted no time putting American Express's money to work. In 1984, Weill acquired Lehman Brothers Kuhn Loeb for $360 million.[23] But Weill didn't have the freedom to buy all the companies on his wish list. So his buying frenzy would have to be put on hold temporarily until he could secure the top position at American Express.

Weill was unstoppable, and by 1993 he took over as president of American Express. Soon, however, his passion for buying would overtake him. In 1995 he resigned from American Express.

An aggressive businessman, it didn't take Weill long to find his next deal. In 1986, he convinced struggling Control Data Corporation to sell one of its units, Commercial Credit Company, in an initial public offering. Control Data Corporation liked Weill's idea and let him serve as lead person in the initial public offering. Weill had bought shares himself and became Commercial Credit Company's CEO.

Once again Weill began his aggressive strategy of acquiring one company after another. By 1992, he had acquired a 27 percent stake in Travelers Corporation.

In what many experts and analysts consider not only remarkable but extremely cunning, Weill regained control of Shearson, the company he had sold to American Express, through an acquisition of its retail-brokerage and asset-management operations. Immediately following this acquisition, Weill acquired the remaining 73 percent of Travelers Corporation. The company was renamed Travelers Group.[24]

With almost no end in sight for the companies Weill could acquire, he set his sights next on investment banking firm Salomon Brothers. And as usual, Weill got what he wanted. The deal was worth $9.1 billion.

Now Weiss was ready to move on to something bigger. In 1986 Weill proposed one of the most outrageous and boldest mergers ever, involving three companies. He would take insurance giant Travelers Group and merge it with Salomon Smith Barney, which was the largest investment bank on Wall Street. But that was just the beginning. He would then merge those two companies into CitiBank, the largest commercial bank in America.[25]

However, there was one problem. The merger was considered illegal in terms of the Glass-Steagall Act. But we already know that Greenspan and his group were chopping away at the language of the Glass-Steagall Act with their many revisions and exemptions that allowed banks to be involved in securities.

Now it would take an act of Congress to completely remove this final provision. But Weiss wasn't worried. He had made many friends in his journey to become the richest man on Wall Street. Remember, the world of Wall Street and Washington are heavily connected. Consider:

- Henry Paulson, former Treasury secretary, was also once head of Goldman Sachs.
- Alan Greenspan, appointed Treasury secretary in 1987, had been an executive at J.P. Morgan.
- Former Treasury secretary for President Clinton Robert Rubin was also a former Goldman Sachs partner and was then invited to join Citigroup.

Do former Wall Street executives suddenly forget about the companies they were once a part of when they are appointed to government positions such as Treasury secretary or chairman of the Federal Reserve? Do they become roadblocks, preventing their former Wall Street firms from making their fortunes?

Their decisions suggest their allegiance lies with Wall Street. In fact, in a 1995 speech to Congress, then–Treasury Secretary Robert Rubin suggested it was time to repeal the Glass-Steagall Act. Rubin told Congress:

> The banking industry is fundamentally different from what it was two decades ago, let alone in 1933. U.S. banks generally engage in a broader range of securities activities abroad than is permitted domestically. Even domestically, the separation of investment banking and commercial banking envisioned by Glass-Steagall has eroded significantly.[26]

A new bill was drafted that would destroy the last remaining line of defense in the Glass-Steagall Act. It was submitted to the Senate and House as the Financial Services Modernization Act of 1999.

The bill, also known as the Gramm-Leach-Bliley Act—named for its sponsors, Republican Senate Banking Committee chair Phil Gramm, House Banking Committee chair James Leach, and Virginia Representative Thomas Bliley—was signed into law by President Clinton on November 12, 1999.

In an ultimate slap in the American public's face, Treasury Secretary Robert Rubin, the former co-chairman of Goldman Sachs, accepted a top job at Sanford Weill's coveted, Citigroup.

America's Future Prosperity Is Destroyed

Major modifications to the Glass-Steagall Act in the new Gramm-Leach-Bliley Act were as follows:

- Title 1 facilitates affiliation among banks, securities, and insurance companies. Basically it revokes the restrictions on banks affiliating with securities that had been stipulated in sections 20 and 32 of the Glass-Steagall Act.
- Another section of the bill allows banks to create financial holding companies. The holding company can participate in financial activities including underwriting securities, merchant banking, insurance company portfolio investment activities, and any activity that is complementary to financial activities.

Amazingly but not coincidentally, after the passage of the Gramm-Leach-Bliley Act, the subprime market took off. We shouldn't forget that Commercial Credit Company, taken over by Sanford Weill in 1986, was heavily involved in subprime lending, which now rose in popularity.

Subprime loans mushroomed and grew from $65 billion in 1995 to $332 billion in 2003. The market share of the top 25 firms making subprime loans grew as well, from 39.3 percent in 1995 to over 90 percent in 2003. Through its newly formed CitiFinancial, Citigroup became the number one subprime lender in the country.[27]

Some analysts argue that the repeal of the Glass-Steagall Act had little to do with the recession of 2007. But are we to believe it is merely a coincidence that subprime securities took off after its repeal? Banks could now engage in security activities and they wasted no time in doing so.

Robert Kuttner, co-founder and co-editor of *The American Prospect* magazine, and author of *The Squandering of America*, testified before the Senate Committee on Banking and Financial Services:

> Since repeal of Glass-Steagall in 1999, after more than a decade of de facto inroads, super-banks have been able to reenact the same kinds of structural conflicts of interest that were endemic in the 1920s—lending to speculators, packaging and securitizing credits and then selling them off, wholesale or retail, and extracting fees at every step along the way.[28]

Much like the Great Wall of China, the Glass-Steagall Act stood as a defensive measure to protect Americans from the devastating tantrums of the greed-driven barbarians who sit on Wall Street.

Now that defensive measure is gone, and we are left with having to rely on our government to save us from the next Wall Street mania. May God bless our souls.

Chapter 14

Wall Street Bloodlines

On Wednesday, January 27, 2010, Secretary of the Treasury Timothy Geithner sat before the House Committee on Oversight and Government Reform to answer a few questions. Now Timothy's a smart man, so answering a few questions from a handful of politicians shouldn't prove too difficult.

Except those questions had to do with his role in the $180 billion bailout of insurance giant American International Group, Inc. (AIG). What the members of the committee wanted to know, as do most Americans, is why AIG was allowed to pass on billions of the bailout money it received to big Wall Street banks that were considered business partners.

Sitting before the House Committee on Oversight and Government Reform, Geithner insisted that he played no role in AIG's decision to pay back banks that were its business partners. Geithner also insisted that he did not withhold information from the public about the deals the firm made.

Geithner didn't seem to be phased at being on the hot seat. After all, he'd been here before. Before being confirmed as Treasury secretary,

Giethner was under fire for his failure to pay the correct amount of social security and Medicare taxes on time, and for employing a foreign housekeeper whose work authorization had expired.

Obama called it an "innocent mistake." Unfortunately, we don't know how innocent it was because the entire matter was discussed in closed-door meetings between Geithner and members of the Senate Finance panel.

His nomination was approved and on January 26, 2009, Geithner became the country's seventy-fifth Treasury secretary. However, before this appointment, Geithner had been president of the Federal Reserve Bank of New York, one of the main players in helping the government respond to the financial crisis.

Of course, one of those responses was handing AIG a huge chunk of taxpayer money. After providing the funds to AIG, Congress and the public wanted to know how the money was used. The Federal Reserve refused to publicize a list of AIG's counterparties in the credit derivatives and mortgage-backed security deals they had put together.

The American public became outraged when AIG announced it planned to pay about $165 million in bonuses to executives in the same business unit that had brought the company to its knees. Geithner insists that information on how the money would be used by AIG wasn't disclosed to him.

He would like us to believe that as president of a major Federal Reserve bank, he isn't privy to those kinds of specific details. It makes absolutely no sense. Some one from the Federal Reserve had to know.

So the attention then moved on to Ben Bernanke, chairman of the Federal Reserve, with the hope (or rather illusion) that he could provide the answers.

When questioned about the very same thing, Bernanke told the investigative panel that he was not directly involved in negotiations regarding payments from AIG to big banks such as Goldman Sachs and other Wall Street firms. Bernanke said those negotiations were handled primarily by the staff of the New York Fed.

So two very powerful and influential men—one the president of the New York reserve bank and the other, the chairman of the Federal Reserve—had not a single clue as to how the money they authorized to bail out AIG would be used.

Of course, no one should be surprised that the greedy bankers of Wall Street would simply pass the money around among their friends. As we found out later, most of the money was indeed given to AIG's counterparties, including Goldman Sachs, Merrill Lynch, Bank of America, Wachovia, and a host of others. In fact, the list totaled 25 banks that received money from AIG.[1]

Geithner and Bernanke remained tight-lipped about the situation. But the truth is, since its inception in 1913, the Federal Reserve has acted in secrecy and with very little government oversight.

Speaking about the Federal Reserve, Senator Barry Goldwater of Arizona said, "Most Americans have no real understanding of the operation of the international money lenders. The accounts of the Federal Reserve System have never been audited. It operates outside the control of Congress and manipulates the credit of the United States."[2]

Even legendary automobile maker Henry Ford recognized that few people would understand how a central bank operates: "It is well that the people of the nation do not understand our banking and monetary system, for if they did, I believe there would be a revolution before tomorrow morning."[3] Senator Charles Lindbergh (the aviator's father) called the Federal Reserve the nation's biggest money trust.[4]

Gaining access to the inner workings of that trust has been difficult. In February 2009, Ron Paul, a member of the U.S. House of Representatives, introduced bill H.R. 1207 to expand the authority of the Government Accountability Office (GAO) to audit the Fed. Specifically, the bill would authorize the GAO to audit the Fed's funding facilities, such as the Primary Dealer Credit Facility, Term Securities Lending Facility, and Term Asset-Backed Securities Lending Facility.[5]

Noted author James Grant of *Grant's Interest Rate Observer* is in full support of Mr. Paul's bill. Grant believes that if the Fed were subject to the treatment and auditing it gives other banks, it would be found insolvent.[6]

By July more than 50 Democrats and 150 Republicans were in support of H.R. 1207. It looked as if the bill would pass and the American people would know exactly what this group was doing. But the bill was defeated.

The *Huffington Post* ran an article citing Senators Christopher Dodd and Judd Gregg as the main blockers of the bill. Barney Frank told members of the House Financial Services Committee that Senate Banking Committee Chairman Chris Dodd (D-Conn.) informed him that he had assured Senator Judd Gregg (R-N.H.) that H.R. 1207's provision to audit the Fed wouldn't be a part of the bill. Gregg said, "Passage of the Paul Amendment by the House Financial Services Committee is a dangerous move . . . "[7]

Seems odd that members of Congress would not want regular audits of the Fed. Maybe Robert Heinlein, often referred to as "the dean of science fiction writers" and a man who is active in politics (he once ran for the California State Assembly), says, "Every congressman, every senator knows precisely what causes inflation . . . but can't [won't] support the drastic reforms to stop it [repeal of the Federal Reserve Act] because it could cost him his job."[8]

What the America public fails to recognize is that there is nothing *federal* about the Federal Reserve. Most people see it as a government agency that creates and overseas all of the financial activities of the United States. But the Federal Reserve is a privately run organization.

It began with approximately 300 people or member banks that purchased stock at $100 per share. The stock is not publicly traded. The shareholders of the Federal Reserve receive a guaranteed 6 percent dividend that is not taxable.

Since a Federal Reserve Bank is not a publicly traded corporation, it is therefore not required by the Securities and Exchange Commission (SEC) to publish a list of its major shareholders.

However, the Federal Reserve Act requires national banks and participating state banks to purchase shares of their regional Federal Reserve Bank upon joining the system, thereby becoming *member banks*. The act also stipulates that the number of shares a member bank can purchase must be in proportion to the bank's size.

If you look up the top banks in the United States on Usabanks.org, you'll find that Bank of America tops the list with $2.2 billion in assets, J.P. Morgan comes in second with $2.0 billion, Citigroup is third with $1.8 billion, Wells Fargo is fourth at $1.2 billion, and Goldman Sachs comes in fifth at $882 million.

Cross-reference this list with the Federal Reserve's statistical release; you'll see that J.P. Morgan, Bank of America, CitiGroup, Wells Fargo Bank, and Wachovia are all Federal Reserve member banks. We can assume, then, that these banks own the greatest amount of shares in the Federal Reserve System.

If we cross-reference this list against banks that received bailout funds, we find that Wells Fargo received $25 billion, Bank of America received $2 billion, J.P. Morgan received $25 billion, Citigroup received $25 billion, Morgan Stanley received $10 billion, and Goldman Sachs received $10 billion.

So the largest member banks of the Federal Reserve System also received the largest amounts of bailout funds.[9] Take at look at Table 14.1, and you'll also see that these same banks were loaded with toxic assets, with J.P. Morgan sitting on $81 billion.

But where things get really interesting is the intersection of Wall Street and Washington. The line between the two is quite blurred.

The Family Ties of Wall Street and Washington

As it turns out, at one time or another executives of some of the companies on Wall Street also held major Washington positions or are linked to someone who did. Take Timothy Geithner, who worked for Robert Rubin when Rubin was secretary of the Treasury.

There are some who say it was Rubin who got Geithner the job as president of the New York Federal Reserve Bank and who also introduced him to Obama when the newly elected president was forming his administration. One could naturally conclude it was that introduction that swayed Obama to pick Geithner for the position of secretary of the Treasury.

But Geithner isn't the only Robert Rubin protégé. There's Michael Froman, whom President-elect Obama appointed as part of his transition team to the White House. Later Froman received an appointment from the president as international finance adviser for both the National Economic Council (NEC) and the National Security Council (NSC).

Now, Froman and Obama aren't strangers. They knew each other when working at the *Harvard Law Review*. That is nothing to raise an eyebrow over, but throw in the fact that before accepting a position on Obama's team, Froman was a high-ranking executive at Citigroup, the same Citigroup founded by Sanford Weill.

Table 14.1 Top Banks Loaded with Toxic Assets

Rank	Bank Name	State	Total Assets	Total Derivatives	Total Futures (Exch. Tr.)	Total Options (Exch. Tr.)	Total Forwards (OTC)	Total Swaps (OTC)	Total Options (OTC)	Total Credit Derivatives (OTC)	Spot Fx
1	J.P.Morgan Chase Bank NA	OH	$1,688,164	$81,161,463	$1,015,753	$2,115,326	$8,285,777	$51,383,402	$10,861,241	$7,499,964	$725,944
2	Goldman Sachs Bank USA	NY	161,455	39,927,511	459,854	86,185	109,941	33,485,299	4,523,808	1,262,424	609
3	Bank of America NA	NC	1,434,037	38,864,033	1,326,649	526,908	4,301,359	26,905,515	3,937,263	1,866,339	137,739
4	Citibank National Assn.	NV	1,143,561	29,618,659	280,724	561,805	4,181,828	16,140,102	5,767,006	2,687,194	395,223
5	HSBC Bank USA National Assn.	VA	1,77,778	3,454,013	42,098	103,062	582,290	1,630,104	182,070	914,389	38,323
6	Wachovia Bank National Assn.	NC	579,258	3,393,720	156,443	47,894	328,652	2,181,876	370,150	308,705	10,790
7	Wells Fargo Bank NA	SD	552,170	1,869,881	182,918	1,584	885,021	622,887	175,839	1,632	11,018
8	Bank of New York Mellon	NY	163,006	1,153,880	24,928	39,423	370,497	413,454	304,457	1,121	35,360
9		MA	142,458	645,128	2,378	2,000	570,719	24,379	45,480	170	27,506

State Street
Bank &
Trust Co.

	Bank	State									
10	Suntrust Bank	GA	174,237	292,928	24,497	39,903	36,517	152,984	37,509	1,518	381
11	PNC Bank National Assn.	PA	140,011	143,677	6,318	3,000	5,379	112,021	12,450	4,499	957
12	Keybank National Assn.	OH	95,515	124,338	15,688	640	8,014	83,473	9,380	7,142	561
13	Northern Trust Co.	IL	65,796	123,814	0	0	116,003	7,424	202	186	13,483
14	National City Bank	OH	146,013	114,220	25,118	1,150	23,052	46,782	16,028	2,090	253
15	U S Bank National Assn	OH	258,527	105,621	994	5,000	35,738	52,445	8,917	2,527	551
16	Regions Bank	AL	137,000	86,324	8,034	3,500	2,858	69,554	1,779	599	7
17	Branch Banking & Trust Co.	NC	139,275	79,208	4,607	0	20,010	48,921	5,619	51	39
18	Fifth Third Bank	OH	68,458	70,383	69	0	11,956	46,448	11,556	353	630
19	RBS Citizens National Assn.	RI	134,826	51,728	0	0	5,755	44,111	1,613	249	55
20	Morgan Stanley Bank NA	UT	66,742	41,306	0	0	0	11,511	0	29,795	0
21	GMAC Bank	UT	36,366	40,738	0	0	19,863	1,422	19,453	0	0

(*Continued*)

Table 14.1. (Continued)

Rank	Bank Name	State	Total Assets	Total Derivatives	Total Futures (Exch. Tr.)	Total Options (Exch. Tr.)	Total Forwards (OTC)	Total Swaps (OTC)	Total Options (OTC)	Total Credit Derivatives (OTC)	Spot Fx
22	UBS Bank USA	UT	33,958	40,315	0	0	0	40,315	0	0	0
23	Citibank South Dakota NA	SD	84,228	36,685	0	0	0	16,685	20,000	0	0
24	Union Bank National Assn.	CA	68,255	35,319	4,174	0	3,469	19,788	7,887	0	370
25	Bank of Oklahoma NA	OK	16,389	27,285	477	184	19,033	6,217	1,373	0	1
	Top 25 commercial banks and trust companies with derivatives		$7,707,483	$201,502,177	$3,581,720	$3,537,564	$19,923,734	$133,547,122	$26,321,089	$14,590,948	$1,399,798
	Other commercial banks and trust companies with derivatives		2,786,837	462,035	2,988	1,406	70,399	314,890	56,198	16,153	1,045
	Total commercial banks and trust companies with derivatives		10,494,320	201,964,212	3,584,708	3,538,970	19,994,133	133,862,012	26,377,287	14,607,101	1,400,844

SOURCE: Marketoracle.com.

Froman was in charge of Citibank's Alternative Investments group that eventually was forced to write down almost $11 billion in losses stemming from subprime mortgage–backed securities.[10] Froman remained in the employ of Citigroup for two months, even as he helped Obama appoint the people who would shape the future of his own firm.

Froman's Citigroup not only received bailout money from his friends at the Fed, but his former employer was also allowed an exemption from paying millions of dollars in taxes on that money. On December 16, 2009, the *Washington Post* reported that the Internal Revenue Service had issued an exception to long-standing tax rules for the benefit of Citigroup. As a result, Citigroup was allowed to retain billions of dollars worth of tax breaks.[11]

The ties between Wall Street and Washington are deep. From 1993 to 1995, Froman worked at the National Safety Council and National Economic Council in a number of capacities. He then joined the Clinton Treasury Department in 1995 as a deputy assistant secretary for Eurasia and the Middle East for two years. In 1997, Froman became Treasury Secretary Robert Rubin's chief of staff at the Treasury Department.

Coincidentally, after leaving the Treasury Department, Froman found work at Citigroup. That work was probably easier to get because when his former boss Robert Rubin left the Treasury, he, too, went to work for Citigroup as a member of the firm's advisory board. It's nice to have friends in high places.

While Froman wasn't directly involved with mortgage-backed securities trading at Citigroup, Rubin certainly was. In fact, during his tenure at Citigroup, Rubin served as senior adviser to former Citigroup CEO Sanford Weill, who pushed the firm into the mortgage-backed securities business.

But let's not forget that Weill was one of the primary crusaders for the repeal of the Glass–Steagall Act. It was during this time that Rubin served as Treasury secretary. Initially Rubin had been on the fence about the repeal, but suddenly he changed his mind. Perhaps knowing he'd have a job at Citigroup when he left his post as Treasury secretary made changing his mind that much easier.

After serving as Weill's adviser, Rubin became Citigroup chairman for about a month following the ouster of then–chairman and CEO

Charles Prince in November 2007. When a new CEO was found, Rubin took a position as a senior counselor to Citigroup.

Of course, things didn't work out well for Citigroup, which had subprime loans in excess of $55 billion. Citigroup was one of the most active investment banks in the subprime mortgage–backed securities market, buying billions of dollars worth of mortgages and then selling them to international investors.

In January 2009, amid finger-pointing for Citigroup's subprime losses, Rubin resigned his post. But don't feel bad for Rubin. He had made close to $110 million during his stint at Citigroup, while shares fell from above $50 to below $5, wiping out billions of dollars of shareholder wealth in the process, as he became richer.[12]

In an article for the *Huffington Post*, Charles Gasparino wrote, "For anyone who thinks that big Wall Street and Big Government aren't joined at the hip, promoting policies and laws that keep each other fat and happy often at the expense of the American taxpayer, consider the career of Robert Rubin."[13]

Rubin's Wall Street heritage can be traced back to Goldman Sachs, where he served as co-chairman. Rubin joined Goldman Sachs in 1966 as a junior arbitrage trader and five years later was named partner of the firm. During the 1980s, Rubin headed up the firm's risk arbitrage group. He left Goldman in 1995 to become the country's seventieth Treasury secretary.

The press dubbed his financial policies "Rubinomics." Not only that, but Rubin was a big proponent of deregulation—specifically, deregulation of the financial industry.

But now, Rubin is taking a bashing for the demise of Citigroup, and rightly so. While Weill may have opened the door for Citigroup to step into mortgage-backed securities by having the Glass-Steagall Act repealed, Rubin served as lead adviser for the firm the entire time the company was involved in the risky securities.

Blood Lines Run Deep

Goldman Sachs executives are no strangers to Washington, either. Former Treasury Secretary Henry (Hank) Paulson served as Goldman's CEO for seven years. While Paulson would love to go down in history as one of the brightest and greatest Treasury secretaries, he'll be remembered for the massive bailouts he engineered for top Wall Street firms.

President Bush picked Paulson to serve as the new Treasury secretary in 2006. CNN Money says Paulson's influence in the White House might have been helped by the fact that Josh Bolten, the White House chief of staff, served as executive director of legal and government affairs for Goldman Sachs' London office for five years before joining the Bush campaign for president in 1999.[14]

Goldman Sachs did well under Paulson's guidance. The stock rose 175 percent from August 1999 to May 2006, when he stepped down. The year before he left to serve as Treasury secretary, the company reported $5.6 billion in earnings. Paulson himself made $38 million that year. However, in 2005, his Goldman stock ownership was worth just under $700 million.

Before the credit crisis, Paulson's role as Treasury secretary was uneventful. It was indeed the crisis that would make him a household name. In July 2008, Paulson asked Congress for the authority to use government money to help firm up companies suffering huge losses from the mortgage-backed securities that were poisoning their balance sheets.

It's not as if Paulson was a stranger to mortgage-backed securities. In April 2006, while still employed as chairman of Goldman Sachs, the company sold $494 million of mortgage-backed securities to institutional investors, offering yields somewhat above those available on U.S. Treasuries.

Goldman did so well with trading securities that roughly 75 percent of its revenue came from trading (not banking). But as the credit crisis took hold, Goldman would need bailout money from Uncle Sam. And who better to ask than its former chairman, Hank Paulson.

Of course, Paulson had to get the money from Congress first. So he told Congress he would use the money to buy troubled assets off banks' books. But just days after Congress passed the legislation creating the Troubled Asset Relief Program (TARP), Paulson changed direction, using most of the money as a capital infusion into banks and other financial institutions, an action that was criticized as a bait-and-switch.[15]

Paulson is also taking criticism for the bailout funds he issued to J.P. Morgan and Goldman Sachs. Bloomberg documented the fact that a report written by Jeffrey Rosenberg, Bank of America's head of credit strategy research, shows that the big investment firms benefited the most from the bailout funds. His report specifies that the benefits of the bailout funds are largely limited to investment banks and other banks that have aggressively written down the value of their holdings and have already recognized the attendant capital impairment.[16]

The criticisms of Paulson don't end there. Paulson is also getting heat for his decision to let Lehman Brothers collapse and instead choosing to help Bear Sterns. Paulson says Lehman had to fail because a buyer couldn't be found. That might seem like a reasonable justification, but then why did Paulson reach out to Bear Stearns and find a buyer in J.P. Morgan?

In March 2008, investment bank Bear Stearns was on the verge of utter collapse until the Federal Reserve stepped in and extended the company emergency loans. Then just two days later, with Paulson's blessing, the government put $30 billion of taxpayer money on the line so that Bear Sterns could be sold to J.P. Morgan. In essence, Paulson helped bring the two together.

His deal making didn't end there. Paulson was also instrumental in brokering a deal between Merrill Lynch and Bank of America. So that begs the question, why couldn't he broker a deal for Lehman Brothers as he had done for J.P. Morgan and Bank of America?

The Merrill Lynch–Bank of America deal alone seemed to alarm and surprise analysts. *Business Insider* says the reason the deal drew so much attention was that Bank of America had been regarded as a lead contender for acquiring Lehman Brothers as part of a government-orchestrated rescue. Another reason for surprise was that Merrill's troubles were not regarded as being as urgent as Lehman's.[17]

In Plain Sight

There is an oddity in this collusion of Wall Street and Washington. In September 2008, Lehman Brothers was forced to file bankruptcy. This was the largest bankruptcy proceeding ever filed. Unlike its counterparts, Lehman Brothers would receive no bailout money. One wonders why Lehman Brothers was allowed to fail and not rescued by the government as was its counterpart, Bear Sterns.

After all, Lehman was part of the Wall Street good old boy network. The CEO sits as a board member of the New York Federal Reserve Bank. And the company has been in the thick of things for quite some time. In the early days, Lehman Brothers provided the financing to build America's railroads. It funded American mom-and-apple-pie businesses such as Sears Roebuck, Woolworth's, B.F. Goodrich, and RCA.

In 1984 American Express, then led by Sanford Weill, founder of Citigroup, acquired Lehman Brothers. But in 1994, after being spun off from American Express, Lehman once again became an independent company.

Between 1994 and 2007, Lehman Brothers' market cap grew from $2 billion to $445 billion. And during this time, the share price went from $5 to $86.[18]

Why was Lehman Brothers allowed to fail? In a *60 Minutes* interview, Fed Chairman Ben Bernanke was asked this question. Bernanke responded by explaining that the Fed could make the loans based on good collateral in American International Group's (AIG) portfolio. And based on that "good collateral," the Fed loaned $85 billion to a company that wasn't even a bank.

But AIG was just as involved in backing risky mortgage investments as were Lehman Brothers and many other major firms on Wall Street. Yet Bernanke insists that with Lehman Brothers, the Fed couldn't risk giving it any money.[19]

While Lehman Brothers didn't receive bailout money, it did receive something else, something only its Washington cronies could provide: the gift of looking the other way as Lehman hid $50 billion of troubled assets.

You see, as part of the bankruptcy proceedings the Bankruptcy Court appointed an examiner to investigate certain aspects of the Lehman Brothers bankruptcy. That court-appointed examiner was Anton R. Valukas, a former federal prosecutor, expert in white-collar crime, and chairman of the Chicago law firm Jenner & Block.[20]

After Valukas was done his examination, he submitted a 2,000-page report that offers some insight into special accounting practices Lehman Brothers used.

The report calls into question Lehman Brothers' use of what are called "Repo 105" transactions. In early 2000, a new accounting practice was adopted that involved the standards for accounting for the repurchase of securitizations and other transfers of financial assets.

Under this new standard, classified as SFAS 140, repurchase agreements could be accounted as true sales but only if certain conditions proved that the transferer had given up control of the asset.

Using this new accounting revision, Lehman Brothers decided it would book its repurchase agreements as sales rather than temporary transactions. Lehman's argument was that the higher-than-usual fees associated with the securities were enough to meet the conditions set forth in SFAS 140.

But to make the accounting magic work, it needed the blessing of a lawyer. It couldn't get that blessing from its U.S. law firm, so the investment bank turned to its London-based law firm, Linklaters. Linklaters signed off on the accounting scheme. In essence, booking repurchase agreements as sales allowed Lehman Brothers to massage its balance sheet.

Valukas writes in his report that Lehman funded itself through the short-term repo markets and had to borrow tens or hundreds of billions of dollars in those markets each day from counterparties to be able to open for business.[21]

So how does Washington tie into this accounting gimmick? Well, in testimony before the House Committee on Oversight and Government Reform, Lehman Brothers CEO Richard Fuld, Jr. stated that "throughout 2008, the SEC and the Federal Reserve actively conducted regular, and at times, daily oversight of both our business and balance sheet."[22]

Fuld further states that representatives from the SEC and Fed were in Lehman Brothers' offices on a regular basis, monitoring the firm's activities. He also told the panel that Lehman Brothers had created a specific team to work with the SEC and the Fed to take them through the company's finances and answer any and all of their questions.

In that same testimony, Fuld says, "Quarter to quarter, month to month, regulators saw how we reduced our commercial real estate holdings; how we increased our liquidity pool, how we decreased leverage and strengthened our capital levels. They saw how we arrived at our valuations, including our mortgage and commercial real estate valuations."

Is it possible the SWAT team of investigators appointed by the Fed and SEC missed this accounting magic altogether? Not likely. Geithner and his team of financial experts devised a series of bank stress tests to determine a bank's health. These tests should have found some type of misuse of Repo 105, but they failed to uncover any wrongdoings.

Yves Smith, the author of *ECONned: How Unenlightened Self Interest Undermined Democracy and Corrupted Capitalism*, writes on her blog, "Even though Lehman dressed up its accounts for the great unwashed public, it did not try to fool the authorities. Its game-playing was in full view."[23]

Andrew Sorkin, writing for the *New York Times*, says, "There's a lot riding on the government's oversight of these accounting shenanigans. If Lehman Brothers executives are sued civilly or prosecuted criminally, they may actually have a powerful defense: a raft of government officials from the SEC and Fed vetted virtually everything they did."[24]

These clever accounting maneuvers show the level of deceit modern-day barbarous bankers will use, regardless of their supposedly good intentions to protect the public. And the government seems to be in on it or at least willing to excuse the behavior.

Bernanke and his man Geithner say they were doing all they could to save the economy. But how is it possible that their own team of auditors, appointed to Lehman Brothers since March 2008, could miss this kind of accounting "error" that had been in practice for years?

According to the *Financial Times*, Bernanke and Geithner and other members of the Fed were given advance warning about Lehman's accounting shenanigans. The article contends that former Merrill Lynch officials said they contacted regulators about the way Lehman measured its liquidity position for competitive reasons. The Merrill officials said they were coming under pressure from their trading partners and investors, who feared that Merrill was less liquid than Lehman.[25]

Has our government gotten so inept that it can't isolate accounting errors? Or does it choose to ignore these practices, letting Wall Street do as it pleases? The answer to the latter is a resounding yes.

Not only were regulators given warnings about Lehman's accounting practices, but consider the number of warnings the SEC received concerning Bernie Madoff's Ponzi scheme.

Harry Markopolos, an independent financial fraud investigator, says he repeatedly warned the SEC that Bernard Madoff was perpetrating a massive investment fraud. Markopolos says, "The SEC is also captive to the industry it regulates and it is afraid of bringing big cases against the largest, most powerful firms."[26]

Markopolos began contacting the SEC at the beginning of the decade to warn that Madoff was a fraud. He sent detailed memos, listing dozens of red flags, laying out a road map of instructions for SEC investigators to follow, and even listing contacts and phone numbers of Wall Street experts who he said would confirm his findings.

In fact, a ProPublica article says that Madoff even filled out required SEC forms stating how much money he was managing and the number of people employed by his firm.[27] According to reports, the SEC didn't bother to check his filing documents or even inspect Madoff's firm, which was originally registered as an investment adviser in September 2006. The SEC claims it doesn't have the resources and tends to target firms that use high-risk investment strategies.

Tends to target firms that use high-risk investment strategies? That's just about every firm on Wall Street, especially those that were bailed out by the government. It was indeed risky credit derivatives and mortgage-backed securities that brought down most of the major players on Wall Street and stifled the global economy.

The Working Group

The truth is that Washington and Wall Street are tied together not just by who worked where and when, but also by a government order. On March 18, 1988, Ronald Reagan signed an executive order to create the President's Working Group (PWG) on Financial Markets.

As the book *Bailout Nation* explains, the goal of the PWG was to enhance the integrity, efficiency, orderliness, and competitiveness of our nation's financial markets while maintaining investor confidence.[28]

The members of the PWG include the secretary of the Treasury, the chairman of the Board of Governors of the Federal Reserve System, the chairman of the Securities and Exchange Commission, and the chairman of the Commodity Futures Trading Commission (CFTC).

This group was given the authority to implement government actions that are appropriate to carry out their recommendations. The members of the group can consult with representatives of various exchanges, clearinghouses, self-regulatory bodies, and with major market participants to determine private-sector solutions wherever possible. Section 3 of the order establishing the PWG authorizes the Department of the Treasury to provide the group with funds and administrative support to perform its functions.

The authors of *Bailout Nation* dismiss the idea that this secret group has any impact on the markets. But Bryan Bottarelli of Bottarelli Research sees it entirely differently. In the early days of July 2009, Bryan spotted what he sees as intervention of the PWG. Figure 14.1 shows the S&P before any actions taken by the PWG.

Now, Bryan is an expert on candlestick charting, which he uses to identify major moves on market exchanges. A head-and-shoulders formation is one of the oldest and most reliable of all chart formations. The formation usually takes place after a trend has been established and

Figure 14.1   S&P 500 before Working Group
SOURCE: Bottarelli Research.

in place for some time. The formation carries a high degree of accuracy and usually indicates a major change in direction is occurring.

Bryan's charting showed that, based on the formation of the head-and-shoulders pattern on July 9, 2009, the SPX was likely to break its trend. In this case, the peak of the head was formed at 956, and the neckline was established right around 875. That's a difference of 81 points. The downside price target is calculated by subtracting the price at which the pattern breaks the neckline (SPX 875) by the difference between the head and the neckline (81).

Based on this configuration, one could correctly predict that in a matter of days the SPX was headed down to 794 points, representing an 11 percent drop.

To put this in context, on September 29, 2008, after the House rejected the government's $700 billion bank bailout plan, the DOW lost 777.68, surpassing the 684.81 loss that occurred on September 17, 2001. But the SPX index lost 8.8 percent, its seventh worst day ever on a per-centage basis and the biggest one-day percentage drop since the crash of 1987, when it lost 20.5 percent.[29]

However, this time the market didn't drop as anticipated. And that's when Bryan suspected that the PWG had stepped in to avoid another major market meltdown. Bryan points to July 13, 2009, when influ-ential analyst Meredith Whitney upgraded Goldman Sachs to a "buy." This caused a market rally.

Of Whitney's comments, Bryan explains:

> Her upgrade was featured on every major financial program in America, which was very, very odd. After all, Goldman Sachs was scheduled to report earnings the very next day. Therefore, for an analyst to come out and publicly upgrade the company *one day* before their earnings release is highly suspect. You generally never see an upgrade the day before earnings are released. It happens after earnings reports.[30]

Bryan believes that Whitney's deliberate comments interrupted the head-and-shoulders formation of the SPX. But that's not all. He also says that at or around the same time, Art Cashin made live comments on CNBC regarding huge buying surges in stocks. Those comments were related to "offshore" buying on the S&P 500 futures.

Bryan asserts this offshore buying can be interpreted as the work of the PWG. He says the sole purpose of these massive cash dumps by the PWG on the S&P futures was to make the markets look good.

Then hedge funds picked up on it and piled into the markets on a massive buying spree. The major media began declaring a bull market on Wall Street. Investors' confidence was restored. The PWG had done its job. On July 24, 2009, just 10 days later, the head-and-shoulders formation was broken, as demonstrated in Figure 14.2.

Longtime Wall Street Friend

Of course, we can't tell the story of Wall Street and Washington bloodlines without taking a look at former Federal Reserve Chairman Alan Greenspan.

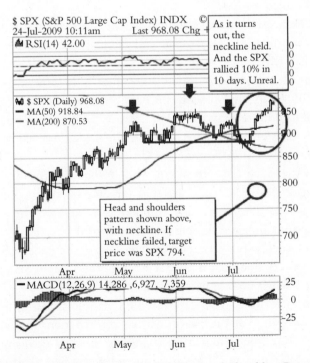

Figure 14.2 Working Group Breaks the Head and Shoulders Pattern
SOURCE: Bottarelli Research.

Greenspan's first introduction to politics was when he served as director of domestic policy research for Richard M. Nixon's successful presidential campaign. He also served on the president's transition team.

From 1981 to 1983, during Ronald Reagan's first term in office, Greenspan served as chairman of the National Commission on Social Security Reform. When Paul Volker resigned his post as chairman of the Federal Reserve, Reagan nominated Greenspan for the job. On August 11, 1987, Greenspan took office as head of the Federal Reserve.[31]

Prior to his time in Washington, Alan was a partner in an economic consulting firm, Townsend-Greenspan, which he started with William Townsend. Some of the firm's clients included U.S. Steel and J.P. Morgan.

But according to an article in the *New York Times*, some of those clients posed a potential conflict of interest. One in particular is J.P. Morgan. On documents he submitted to the White House and Congress just prior to his approval as Fed chairman, Greenspan listed his 10 years as a director of Morgan and its banking subsidiary, the Morgan Guaranty Trust Company.[32]

Mr. Greenspan declined to discuss the document. Of course, to secure his nomination, Greenspan said he'd sit out on discussions that involved J.P. Morgan so as to avoid a conflict of interest.

Greenspan's circle of business colleagues isn't limited to those he knew at J.P. Morgan. Growing his economic consulting firm enabled Greenspan to build a network of Wall Street heavy hitters. For example, in the early days of building his business, Greenspan was well acquainted with Sanford Weill, the founder of Citigroup.[33]

That's the same Sanford Weill who pushed for the repeal of the Glass-Steagall Act—the same act that Greenspan, during his reign as chairman, gradually and steadily chipped away at with the exceptions and exemptions he gave the big investment banks.

When Greenspan left his post as chairman of the Federal Reserve in 2006, he was considered a master at steering the United States through some of the worst economic times the country had seen.

But oh, how things change. Now he's being blamed for leading the economy into the worst recession we've ever experienced. Peter Schiff, author of *Crash Proof: How to Profit from the Coming Economic Collapse*, says of Alan Greenspan, "He's not just the worst Fed chairman we've ever had, he's the worst American we've ever had."[34]

At the heart of the matter is this: Relaxed regulations created an environment for Wall Street fat cat bankers to bend rules, overlook safety nets, and push derivatives to their limits. But that environment was fostered by Greenspan's easing of interest rates, which made credit easy to get for anyone for anything.

Greenspan admits that letting bankers regulate themselves was a mistake. But he takes no other blame for the economic mess we're in. Greenspan defends his actions by suggesting that rising nations such as China and India created a competitive environment for the United States, which forced his hand.

According to the National Council of Applied Economic Research (NCAER), in 1984 through 1985, India's middle class constituted less than 10 percent of the population. Since then it has more than tripled.[35]

China's middle class is growing as well. Shaun Rein, founder of the Shanghai-based China Market Research Group, says, "The emergence of a solid middle class, in cities and towns across the country, will transform the Chinese market."[36] China's middle class has grown from 65.5 million in January 2005 to 80 million in January 2007 and is forecast to expand to 700 million by 2020.[37]

Greenspan argues that in order to keep inflation from rising from the pressures of this type of aggressive competition, he had to keep interest rates low. In 1989 a series of 23 rate cuts began in June and continued until September 1992, taking the fed funds rate to 3 percent from almost 9.75 percent. The last series of cuts began January 3, 2001, and ended in June 2003. The rate dropped to 1 percent from 6.5 percent.[38]

Greenspan says lowering interest rates did not cause the housing bubble. But the fact is that the fed funds rate does have an impact on various sectors of the economy.

You see, as people deposit and withdraw money from banks on a daily basis, some banks wind up having more money on hand than they need, while other banks wind up not having enough money. So banks lend each other money overnight. The federal funds rate is the target rate for this overnight lending. The cheaper it is for banks to borrow money, the cheaper they can loan it out to other banks.

If the Fed increases the federal funds rate, then banks are going to raise the interest rate they charge one another for overnight lending. If you apply for a mortgage and are borrowing the money from a bank, that bank is going to charge a slightly higher interest rate because it is paying a higher rate to borrow the money.

When Greenspan cut the federal funds interest rate down to 1 percent, that meant lower rates on mortgages. While Greenspan would like to pretend he didn't cause the housing boom, it's simply not true. His monetary policy decisions—interest rate cuts—had a huge impact on the housing boom.

But there's a more serious reason why we can put the blame squarely on Greenspan's shoulders. In 1994, Congress enacted the Home Ownership and Equity Protection Act, which gave the Fed the authority to oversee mortgage loans.

The bill, known as H.R. 1728, would place a number of new federal restrictions on mortgage loan providers, servicers, brokers, and third parties who buy or sell mortgages on secondary securities markets, as well as appraisers. The bill also holds creditors liable if they do not comply with the new regulations.[39]

But Greenspan, believing bankers could regulate themselves, didn't set any regulations or rules for the industry to follow. Greenspan had his chances and blew it *big-time*.

Looking back on the mess, Greenspan admits he didn't understand all the economic shifts that were taking place in the economy. In his blog for Amazon, Greenspan writes:

> At the Fed, I had at first focused primarily on monetary policy— interest rates and the forces that determined their appropriate levels. But as the years rolled on, it became increasingly clear to me that we needed to understand an entirely new range of factors to implement policy effectively ... as I raced from one policy meeting to another, I never had time to sit back and think about all this.[40]

Too bad for the American public that Greenspan didn't have time to do his job properly.

After an 18-year reign, on January 31, 2006, Alan Greenspan stepped down as chairman of the Federal Reserve. But his legacy of low interest rates would live on through his protégé, Ben Bernanke. You can see in Figure 14.3 that the federal funds rate has trended on the low side, with the exception of 1982.

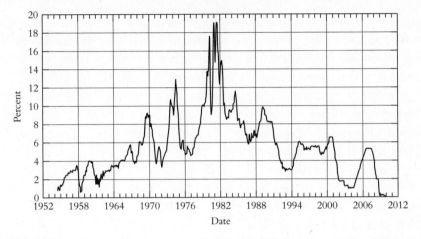

Figure 14.3 Ups and Downs of Federal Funds Rate, July 1954 to December 2009
SOURCE: answers.com.

Greenspan's Legacy Lives

In 2009 *Time* magazine named him Person of the Year. Of the nomination, *Time* wrote, "Bernanke is the 56-year-old chairman of the Federal Reserve, the central bank of the U.S., the most important and least understood force shaping the American—and global—economy."[41]

Time magazine couldn't have said it any better: The Federal Reserve is the least understood force shaping our economy. And Bernanke is the man steering the ship.

Bernanke is a Harvard graduate where he earned an economics degree and graduated summa cum laude before heading to the Massachusetts Institute of Technology, where he got a Ph.D. in economics in 1975. Before joining the Fed, Bernanke spent his early years teaching economics at major universities including Princeton and Stanford.[42]

Prior to being named chairman in 2006 and again in 2010, he was a member of the Board of Governors of the Federal Reserve System from 2002 to 2005. Bernanke echoed Greenspan's beliefs in low interest rates.

In 2003, when Bernanke was a governor of the Federal Reserve, the Fed cut the short-term interest rate to 1 percent. The result was a free-money lending binge that led to outrageous excesses in the subprime mortgage business.

But the Fed favored a low-interest-rate policy. Bernanke was an advocate of easing rates. The *Washington Post* says Bernanke even expressed openness to cutting rates toward zero, even if doing so meant the Fed would need to find new tools to stimulate the economy.[43]

It didn't matter to Bernanke, as it didn't matter to Greenspan, that lowering the federal funds rate would stimulate a housing bubble. And just as Greenspan denies that low rates fueled one of the biggest housing booms of all times, Bernanke, too, denied that the Fed's policy decisions had any impact.

In a speech made at the annual meeting of the American Economic Association, Bernanke argued that the housing bubble began before the Fed pushed interest rates low.[44]

The sad fact is this: Economic experts such as Greenspan and Bernanke both say it wasn't interest rate policies that caused the housing bubble and widespread misuse of mortgage-backed securities. Both say they could not foresee the problems that came to fruition in 2007.

In recent speeches, Bernanke tells the American public we are out of the woods. Yet there has been no major overhaul of the financial system. The systemic risk associated with mortgage-related securities still exists. No reforms or regulations have been made to curb the abuse of these securities that started on Wall Street and became a part of almost every pension fund you can name.

Banks considered too big too fail, such as Goldman Sachs and J.P. Morgan, now have direct access to government funds at ridiculously low interest rates. With the Fed's help, J.P. Morgan not only bought out Bear Stearns but also bought $30 billion in toxic assets that J.P. Morgan wouldn't have touched on his own. The Fed stepped in to save Fannie Mae and Freddie Mac and now holds about $34.5 billion in mortgage-backed investments that are not guaranteed by either firm.[45]

The government is now in the same situation as the banks it bailed out. It now has to deal with a huge portfolio of loans and properties that have lost their value. This will be Bernanke's biggest challenge. For the American people, it is our biggest nightmare.

Part Four

POLITICAL BARBARIANS

Chapter 15

The Monied-Class Rulers and Demigods

On May 10, 1775, the Second Continental Congress convened in Philadelphia, Pennsylvania, with representatives from 12 of the 13 colonies present. There were 56 delegates in all, including notable names such as John Hancock and George Washington.

This Congress would declare war on the British and become the sole governing body of what would become the United States of America.

It's an inspiring story. One that you can't help but feel proud of . . .

But this first congress of independence wasn't quite open to just any American—as the new Constitution would declare 13 years later. This was a close-knit elite (and elitist) group that was far more inclined to be elected by birthright than by character.

"There was room for bright young men to rise into it, so that there were always a few lowborn men in public office," wrote Christopher and James Lincoln Collier, authors of *Decision in Philadelphia: The Constitutional Convention of 1787.* "But as often as not, the people in control of the states were born to their stations and went on to college to prepare themselves for their roles."[1]

Most of the delegates were white Protestants, landowners, and wealthy merchants. Most had served in some office before, and were lawyers—statesmen. They were the monied class. Need I say that they were male? "Only two of them were small farmers, from the class that made up 85 percent of the white population," report the Colliers.[2]

These guys were power players. This group of congressmen would manage the revolution, adopt the Declaration of Independence, and ratify the Articles of the Confederation—the predecessor to the Constitution. And they would do so for their own benefit first. Let me explain . . .

The evolution of Congress's power came out of necessity. They had no power to tax the people, and the States were enjoying their new-found freedom from a central government. But Congress had a war to fund, and only about 6 percent of total revenues came from taxes, as states sent money only when they felt like it.[3]

Much of the funding for the revolution came from borrowing—from wealthy Americans, and from France and Holland—and from stealing. John Steele Gordon, author of *An Empire of Wealth: The Epic History of American Economic Power*, wrote, "During the course of the war, American privateers seized some two thousand British vessels, worth, together with their cargoes, some 18 million pounds."[4]

And, of course, the Continental Congress had control of the printing press.

The common practice at the time was for sovereign countries to hold all the wealth—including gold and coinage. That means the American colonies were cash poor, as nearly all the minted money was held in Britain.

Individual colonies started printing bills of credit in the late seventeenth century because coinage was so scarce, and Congress started issuing bills of credit in 1775. They were called Continentals, and in the four years after their origination, Congress had issued $225 million worth of them.[5]

We need to put this in perspective, because this is an extraordinary sum when compared to the American economy at that time. In 1700,

Carolina rice production added about a million pounds a year to the British Empire's GDP.[6] In dollars, that's roughly $1.5 million (using modern-day exchange rates). So the bills of credit issued by Congress equated to 170 years' worth of Carolina rice production!

This, of course, caused inflation, which made prices climb tenfold between 1779 and 1781. In order to staunch the bleeding, Congress revalued its Continentals to a mere 2.5 percent of their face value.[7] How's that for an investment?

This type of borrowing has always led to trouble, it would seem. And some of America's brightest politicians initially despised the practice. Jefferson believed that debt and borrowing divided citizens into two categories: taxpayers and interest collectors.[8] Government in early America was not that different from the Hunnic society, or Charlemagne, in regards to the concentration of money and power.

According to Robert Hormats, author of *The Price of Liberty: Paying for America's Wars from the Revolution to the War on Terror*, Jefferson believed that wars inevitably gave power to those of the "monied classes."[9]

Here's why: In order to fund the war, government took on a huge amount of debt. And who bought that debt? The already rich and powerful. These folks, many of whom were already in government positions, could exercise their power to place the cost of repaying that debt on the shoulders of the working class—in other words, heavy taxation.

Of course, at this point in American history—and to a great extent today, one could argue—the monied classes and Congress were one and the same. After its creation, and throughout the Revolutionary War, up until the writing of the Constitution, Congress did not have the power to tax. The evolution of Congress didn't give them this authority until later. Power is another story.

Congress had created the Articles of Confederation to replace the Second Continental Congress in 1781, but power was still concentrated within this elite governing body, whose delegates were appointed by the state governments.

The Articles of Confederation was an imperfect agreement, and some states elected to stay out of the whole process. When Congress came to try to collect revenue, some states would refuse to pay, sparking a domino effect, and in the end, Congress would go deeper into debt.

When the Confederation called a convention in 1786 to determine better regulations of commerce, delegates from only five states showed up. Numbers were so few that the group in effect rescheduled the meeting for May 1787 in Philadelphia. This time, people showed up— and they were some of the most powerful people in the country.

Demigods

At the Constitutional Convention on May 25, 1787, 55 of the 74 hand-picked delegates from 12 of the 13 states showed up at the State House in Philadelphia. George Washington, Robert Morris, James Madison, George Mason, Benjamin Franklin, and Alexander Hamilton were present, just to name a few. Christopher and James Lincoln Collier's research for their book, *Decision in Philadelphia: The Constitutional Convention of 1787*, found:

> More than half were lawyers; another quarter were owners of large commercial farms or plantations. All of them had held public office. Three of them were governors of their states, and four others had been. At least eight were judges, forty-two had been congressmen, most had served in their state governments, and a sprinkling had been speakers of their state legislatures. Eight had signed the Declaration of Independence, thirty had served in the army during the Revolution, some fifteen had seen serious action, and several were authentic battlefield heroes.[10]

Thomas Jefferson, who was the minister to France at the time, called the meeting of delegates an assembly of "demigods."[11] It was the minds of these demigods, the upper echelon of American society, that drew up our Constitution.

One of the most contentious topics was how to fill Congress. Some delegates backed the "New Jersey Plan," and wanted each state to have one representative, which would give smaller states, like Delaware, the same amount of power as a large state like New York. This idea wasn't much different than what was already in place according to the Articles of Confederation—and it didn't sit well with the delegates from the more populous states of the Union.

Other delegates backed the "Virginia Plan," which favored representation based on population.

In the end, there was a compromise. It's called the Connecticut Compromise or the Great Compromise because it balanced both the Virginia and New Jersey plans. One house of Congress would adopt the Virginia plan, based on population, and the other house would provide equal representation. The other interesting compromise was that the individual state legislatures would elect the senators to Congress.

That's because the senators were concerned about letting average Americans into their circle. They'd rather strut around garnering support from the common man than elevate him to their intellectual—and financial—equal.[12]

This method was apparently designed to keep the elite in power and the common man in his place. John Steele Gordon notes, "People in government will always try to help those who are powerful at the expense of those who might become so. What-is can always wield influence that what-might-be cannot match, regardless of any campaign finance laws that may be in place."[13]

This was one way of assuring that the *right* people got into Congress. The Colliers wrote, "These were members of the establishment and they did not come to Philadelphia to overthrow the system."[14]

Robert Morris: The Viking

One of those right people was Robert Morris, the second senator ever elected. He was from Pennsylvania, and he was of the Pro-Administration party, meaning that he was in favor of bigger government, but only a certain kind of government.

The Senate Historical Office says of Morris, "Robert Morris was a wealthy Philadelphia merchant who distrusted governments based on popular choice."[15] He was a wealthy merchant who had served in the Continental Congress and signed the Declaration of Independence. He was also the national superintendent of finance from 1781 to 1784 and helped establish the Bank of North America.[16] In other words, he was regarded as the second most powerful figure in America, after George Washington.

He was a consummate businessman, advocating for free trade, partially because his business was hurt by the tariffs on slave importation in Pennsylvania. His import/export business (with partner Thomas Willing) was one of the most prosperous in the state.

He was known as the "financier of the American Revolution" and loaned the government $10,000 to pay his friend Washington's troops. This was the first of many efforts to fund American troops, and "Morris notes" made it possible for Washington to continue the war.

According to Clarence L. Ver Steeg, author of *Robert Morris: Revolutionary Financier*, Morris lent $1.4 million of his own credit to move Washington's army from New York to Virginia. In one year, 1783, when New Hampshire gave $3,000 to the Revolutionary War efforts, Morris put up $14.9 million. But the revolution was a boon to Morris.[17]

His wealth flourished because he owned many privateer ships that seized British cargo ships. *Privateer* is just another word for *pirate* at this point in time, no matter the nobility of the intent.

Morris, it's been reported, captured 1,500 British vessels, and he also helped sell off the booty as they came into port. These weren't new tactics for Morris, either. He'd been pirating ships long before the war, which gave him one of the largest personal navies in the war.

It also made him one of the richest men in America. George Washington even nominated him to the secretary of the Treasury for his administration, a post Morris declined. Perhaps that was because he had other things in mind. According to the Senate Historical Office, "One of the nation's richest men, Morris saw nothing wrong with using privileged government information to shape his personal investment strategy."[18]

This is a statement that rings true even today. Just consider how much money some of the richest companies in our country spend on lobbying members of Congress on legislation that favors them.

Eliza Krigman, writing for the Open Secrets blog, says, "The ability to effect change appears easiest for those who have the financial resources to reach and influence lawmakers."[19]

In the days of the early Congress, lawmakers didn't need lobbyists. The early Congress was made up of rich men, Morris being the richest.

In fact it's the distinctive title "First Political Barbarian of Early Congress" that we bestow on Morris. In the late 1770s, Thomas Paine and other contemporaries accused Morris of war profiteering and improper financial transactions. He was acquitted in 1779 by a congressional committee, but the stigma continued. And so did Morris's practices. "People with an economic advantage, however 'unfair' that advantage may be, will always fight politically as hard as they can to maintain it," comments Gordon.[20]

Some of Morris's more positive economic and financial ideas stuck around, too. As superintendent of finance, Morris proposed the idea of a national bank in 1781—nearly a full decade before Alexander Hamilton founded the First Bank of the United States.

In 1782, the Bank of North America was founded in part with a loan from France, and its purpose was to fund the Revolutionary War—at first. It was the first private charter bank of the United States, and in essence became the country's central bank.

At the time, Congress had stopped issuing Continentals and was deeply in debt. Alexander Hamilton wrote of Morris, under a pseudonym, in *The Continentalist* in late August 1781, "He has very judiciously proposed a National Bank, which, by uniting the influence and interest of the moneyed men with the resources of government, can alone give it that durable and extensive credit of which it stands in need."[21]

Back in 1776, Congress spent $14 million. And by 1781, the Treasury was in debt by $25 million. Hamilton wrote, "It cannot be denied that there was a want of order and economy in the expenditure of public money."[22] This is his way of supporting the idea of a National Bank, and of putting control of money in the hands of Congress.

Congress did approve Morris's plan for the Bank of North America, and he funded it with gold and silver, as well as loans from France and the Netherlands, who had previously allied themselves with the Americans against the British in the revolution. Thomas Goddard dubbed him "the father of the system of credit, and paper circulation, in the United States."[23]

But after only three years, on September 13, 1785, the bank's charter was revoked under suspicion of "alarming foreign influence and fictitious credit." The state banks of Pennsylvania claimed that the Bank of North America was giving preferential treatment to foreigners and wasn't competing fairly.[24]

So not only was Robert Morris one of the first political barbarians of the early Congress, he was one of the first barbarians of money, too. Add in Morris's privateering of British ships during the war and you've got an eighteenth-century Viking running the early American economy.

And get this: Morris's old business partner, Thomas Willing, was the first president of the bank, and after its charter was revoked, Willing was named president of Alexander Hamilton's First Bank of the United States in 1792.[25]

Talk about keeping it in the family. This cronyism typifies the behavior of the early Congress, and you can expect nothing less in today's political system. Congress even allowed Morris to continue his personal business endeavors while serving as the superintendent of finance and having executive authority over marine policies (read: trade routes).

By creating a national bank and funding it with his own monies and loans from friendly countries, Morris boosted the United States' credit, and money could start flowing again. This was a massive change for the government, and not everyone was a fan.

Hormats wrote in his book *The Price of Liberty*, "[Thomas Jefferson] had written that if he could 'add a single amendment' to the Constitution, it would be one 'taking from the federal government the power of borrowing.' "[26]

Two of the other reforms Morris suggested during his stint as superintendent of finance were to demand financial support from the states and to create a national mint. Now, the U.S. Mint wasn't established until 1792, under Alexander Hamilton's pressures, but financial support from the states—well, that was a big new change for the federal government when the Constitution was signed.

The Creation of Taxes and the Booty of Credit

The U.S. Treasury Department's fact sheet "History of the Tax System" says, "The Constitution endowed the Congress with the power to '... lay and collect taxes, duties, imposts, and excises, pay the Debts and provide for the common Defense and general Welfare of the United States.' "[27]

After the Revolutionary War, the government used taxes and tariffs to pay down debt. The government taxed things like alcohol, tobacco, sugar, and some real estate property, and Congress passed the Tariff and Tonnage Acts in 1789 that imposed a 6-cent duty per ton on American ships entering U.S. ports and a 50-cent duty on foreign ships.[28] And later, in the 1790s, the government instituted direct taxes on houses, lands, slaves, and estates. Thomas Jefferson abolished these when he was elected president in 1802, but they were not to be gone forever.

In just 10 years, the United States would be involved in another war, the War of 1812, and the federal government would need to raise more funds.

It did so by imposing additional taxes and issuing Treasury notes. The country's national bank, instituted by Alexander Hamilton in 1792 as the First Bank of the United States, was an unpopular idea in the president's mind, and apparently half the minds of the House of Representatives. The bank's charter was allowed to expire on January 24, 1811. President James Madison, elected in 1809, held similar views to those of Thomas Jefferson. Let's contrast the two ideas.

Alexander Hamilton wanted to use America's national debt to create a larger and more flexible money supply. This is how it would work. Hamilton suggested paying interest on debt bought by investors. This meant that banks holding government bonds could issue banknotes backed by them, and that bonds could be used as collateral for loans.

Also, according to John Steele Gordon, "Hamilton also wanted the federal government to assume the debts that had been incurred by the various states in fighting the Revolution."[29] That seems fair since the first centralized government, the Second Continental Congress, assumed control of the war.

But Hamilton may have done this for another reason. His own father held $60,000 in government securities.[30] Not only that, but he was the founder of the Bank of New York (in 1784), and New York was the first to hear about Hamilton's "Report on Public Credit" in 1790 where he proposed to Congress his idea of issuing new bonds to redeem old government debt. As a result, New York was able to get in on the ground floor with cheap old debt.

The northern states still had a large amount of debt from the Revolutionary War, while most southern states had already paid back their debt.

That's why Thomas Jefferson and James Madison, both from Virginia, were against Hamilton's plan. The northern states, in essence, would be able to transfer their war debts to the federal government. In a compromise—as Jefferson and Madison could rally enough votes to block the plan—Hamilton suggested locating the country's new capital in Philadelphia. The deal was agreed upon, and the government bonds sold out within weeks.[31]

Indeed, U.S. debt went from being worthless to having the highest credit rating in Europe. And some of its bonds were going for 10 percent over par![32]

Hamilton also sought to establish a national bank, the First Bank of the United States. It was created with the concept of handling the financial needs of the government. Now, there were some important issues that a national bank would solve. The most important was money supply. State banks could issue printed money, but nothing was uniform.

In the last decade of the eighteenth century, there were no less than 50 different currencies in circulation. This made it easy for speculators to bank on the instability of the system (or lack thereof). For example, once Hamilton's debt plan was known, speculators bought up bonds for 15 cents on the dollar, but got paid the full dollar once Hamilton's plan was in place.[33]

A national bank would create a stable currency and lessen speculation. It would also create a way for the government to establish credit. The catch, though, was that the bank would be held in private hands, with the government holding 20 percent of the bank's stock, but the government could not afford to buy $2 million worth of the bank's stock. Hamilton suggested that the bank loan the government the money to buy its stock, and that the government would pay back that money in 10 annual installments.[34]

Jefferson, however, felt that a national bank would be unconstitutional. In his "Opinion against the Constitutionality of a National Bank," from Volume III of *The Writings of Thomas Jefferson*, then–Secretary of State Jefferson wrote:

I consider the foundation of the Constitution as laid on this ground: That "all powers not delegated to the United States, by the Constitution, nor prohibited by it to the States, are reserved to the States or to the people." To take a single step beyond the boundaries thus specially drawn around the powers of Congress, is to take possession of a boundless field of power, no longer susceptible of any definition. The incorporation of a bank, and the powers assumed by this bill, have not, in my opinion, been delegated to the United States, by the Constitution.[35]

Jefferson had more personal feelings about banks. In a letter to John Adams, he wrote, "I have ever been the enemy of banks.... My zeal against those institutions was so warm and open at the establishment of the Bank of the U.S. that I was derided as a Maniac by the tribe of bank-mongers, who were seeking to filch from the public their swindling, and barren gains."[36]

He might as well have called Hamilton's idea of a national bank a barbaric shift in financial ideology for the new United States.

James Madison was a staunch ally of Jefferson's, and agreed with him on the bank's unconstitutional nature. While president, Madison let the bank's charter expire. Perhaps one of his reasons was the rampant speculation in bank stocks on the securities markets in New York and Philadelphia. As we learned in Chapter 5, a former U.S. Treasury Department employee, William Duer, was speculating in the banking sector that had substantial growth. During that time, the number of banks in the United States grew from 3 to 29 in just 10 years.

That's an incredible 866 percent growth rate, one that Duer couldn't resist. However, Duer's scheming landed him in prison for the rest of his life, and landed the rest of Wall Street in hot water. "The next day," reports Gordon, "twenty-five failures were reported in New York's still tiny financial community."[37]

The Panics of the Markets

It would seem that the connection between government and the financial system leads to scandals and rumors of impropriety. This is evidenced by the financial connections between Morris as super-intendent of finance and his old business partner Thomas Willing as president of the Bank of North America, whose charter was revoked under suspicion of fictitious credit.

Even today, with our modern political and financial barbarians, we see this same type of cronyism. Take, for example, the U.S. secretary of the Treasury under President Obama, Timothy Geithner. He is a former president of the Federal Reserve Bank of New York, and during his stint there, his practices forged close ties with Wall Street. The *New York Times* reported, "His actions, as a regulator and later a bailout king, often aligned with the industry's interests and desires, according to interviews with financiers, regulators and analysts and a review of Federal Reserve records."[38]

The Federal Reserve Bank of New York is supposed to curb risk in the banks it oversees, but it also answers to a board filled with many CEOs of the very banks it's supposed to be holding in check! Talk about a conflict of interest.

That appears to have filtered into his role as U.S. Treasury secretary, too. Geithner's detractors were outraged that AIG was allowed to use billions in bailout money to pay off bonuses. But that's just the tip of the iceberg with AIG.

In a Hamilton-esque bailout, the taxpayer money issued to shore up AIG was dispensed to banks with AIG "counterparty insurance contracts" (read: credit default swaps). Some $62.1 billion was divided between 16 banks. These banks got 100 percent of what they were owed, despite the fact that most of the assets had crumbled in value.[39]

Does this remind you of Hamilton's issuance of government bonds to replace debt at full value?

What this means is that some banks were able to take far greater risks than they could afford, and not pay any penalty for their misguided actions. And Timothy Geithner was in charge of AIG's rescue.

The next stage of this barbaric bailout showed a cover-up, with reports that AIG was instructed to conceal the "counterparty" data. It did so by hiding e-mails. Bloomberg reported on January 7, 2010, "The Federal Reserve Bank of New York, then led by Timothy Geithner, told American International Group Inc. to withhold details from the public about the bailed-out insurer's payments to banks during the depths of the financial crisis, e-mails between the company and its regulator show."[40]

And here's another government connection: One of those 16 banks that received 100 cents on the dollar for those credit default swaps was

Goldman Sachs, whose former CEO, Henry Paulson, was none other than Timothy Geithner's predecessor to the Treasury secretary cabinet position.

Some things never change. Wall Street and government have always formed these cadres, these bands of financial and political barbarians, where the rich get richer at the expense of the masses—in other words, taxpayers: you and me.

This is exactly what Madison feared as he let the charter for Hamilton's First Bank of the United States expire. But the War of 1812 forced anticredit politicians to cave in and charter the Second Bank of the United States in 1816 to stabilize the credit system and combat the severe inflation that followed the war.

You see, after the First Bank was closed, the number of private banks soared, and each was printing its own banknotes. But the government itself couldn't finance its war debts, so the Second Bank was created.[41]

Of course, after the war, the country was in a period of economic prosperity as France had been decimated by England in the Napoleonic Wars. This made trade with the United States extremely important, and U.S. merchants and the economy as a whole benefited greatly—perhaps too greatly. The banks became overextended, prices started to bubble, and fraud became rampant.[42]

In one fell swoop, banks started calling in the loans they'd made, which brought land sales nearly to a halt and slowed the production boom. This became the first major financial crisis of the United States. It's known as the Panic of 1819. Bankruptcies exploded, unemployment in major cities climbed to catastrophic levels (75 percent in Philadelphia), people were thrown into debtors prison ... [43] People went to pull their money out of banks, only to find there was none left.

The panic lasted three years. The Second Bank of the United States would last 20. Like the First Bank, its charter would not be renewed.

But the economy would go on to experience boom and bust cycles,[44] as well as two more panics before the Civil War. The next panic was in 1837, and it was also built on speculation.[45]

So the political invention of a financial system was riddled with fraud and excess, while the hands-off, antibank approach let free markets create and destroy whole economies. We've had barbarians on either side of the gate ever since the founding of this country.

Chapter 16

Barbarians in the Lobby

Barbarians attract barbarians. Think of Charlemagne's political and military prowess holding together a confederation of petty kingdoms through only the promise of wealth and plunder. Think of Robert Morris's election to the Senate even though his contemporaries thought he was a slimy businessman. He had personally backed the Revolutionary War, and that kind of money talks.

As long as there has been wealth in the United States Congress, there have been people with their hands out. Today, they are called lobbyists, and some of them are just as ruthless as Attila and his Huns demanding tribute from Rome.

A lobbyist's job is to woo congressmen (and their friends, even their families) in order to gain money or favors for a certain interest.

The exchanges between Congress and lobbyists have a long and ruthless history, and one filled with many scandals. But interestingly, it's taken about 200 years for a president to order every appointee in the executive agency to take an ethics pledge.

Here's one of the sections:

Lobbyist Gift Ban. I will not accept gifts from registered lobbyists or lobbying organizations for the duration of my service as
an appointee.[1]

The federal government, in the Code of Federal Regulations, says
a "gift includes any gratuity, favor, discount, entertainment, hospitality,
loan, forbearance, or other item having monetary value. It includes
services as well as gifts of training, transportation, local travel, lodgings
and meals, whether provided in-kind, by purchase of a ticket, payment
in advance, or reimbursement after the expense has been incurred."[2]

But this isn't the most important section of the pledge. Those
signing this pledge cannot work for a lobbyist group for two years after
their employment ends. Furthermore, those coming into office cannot
participate in matters in which they have lobbied in the two prior years
to their appointment.

This executive order tries to close the revolving door between
Congress and K Street, the barbarian's not-so-secret lair—but it doesn't.
It covers the executive agency only, and that leaves the door wide open
for barbarians in the legislature and barbarians in the lobby.

At the start of Congress, as we saw with Pennsylvanian Senator
Robert Morris, there wasn't much difference between a congressman
and a businessman. There weren't any laws that obligated public ser-
vants to quit their day jobs, as it were. And the government itself was
complicit in some corporate manipulations, opening the doorway for
lobbyists to elicit favors, votes, and money from congressmen in
exchange for kickbacks.

John Steele Gordon, author of *An Empire of Wealth: The Epic History
of American Economic Power*, wrote, "Immediately after the [Civil] War,
however, nothing characterized American politics and thus the American economy so much as corruption."[3] In fact, in 1868, the New York
State Congress passed a law that essentially legalized bribery. The law
read, "No conviction shall be had under this act on the testimony of the
other party to the offense, unless such evidence be corroborated in its
material parts by other evidence."[4]

So long as the congressman took his bribes in easily hid cash
(with no witnesses), there would be no evidence with which to

convict him—even if his co-conspirator stepped forward to unveil the corruption.

Government and Corporate Scandals

One of the best-known barbaric episodes of government and corporate scandals in the early days of our country was the Crédit Mobilier scandal first exposed by the *New York Sun* in 1872.

This scandal was the result of an ambitious plan for a transcontinental railroad, the construction of which was backed by Congress with the Pacific Railroad Acts of 1862 and 1864, and by 30-year government bonds, massive land grants, and the creation of the Union Pacific Railroad company, the first corporation chartered by the government since the Second Bank of the United States nearly 50 years prior.[5]

The government-sponsored company issued 100,000 shares at $1,000 apiece, raising $100 million, an immense sum of money, but not nearly enough to fund the project. To subsidize costs, the company would receive $16,000 to $48,000 in government bonds, and 6,400 acres of land for every mile of track built. But that's not all. In 1864, the government said that the Union Pacific Railroad (along with Central Pacific) was allowed to sell mortgage bonds on that land, and increased the land allotment to 12,800 acres per mile.[6]

Yet even these subsidies weren't enough, in Union Pacific's mind, to secure profits. The project was one on par with the Panama Railroad in 1855 and surpassed the Erie Canal built in the 1820s. Union Pacific laid more than 1,000 miles of track through harsh and demanding land. It was no small feat, and the construction was expensive.

And here's where the scandal comes in.

Union Pacific's top investor was Thomas Clark Durant. He was the controlling partner and president of the line. Under his direction, Union Pacific set up a construction company, owned by itself, with a fancy French name, Crédit Mobilier, and hired it to build the railroad. Needless to say, it charged the railroad top dollar, and often then some, for its services.

Although the chief engineer, Peter Dey, had estimated that the initial section, west of Omaha, could be built for an average of $30,000 a mile, when Crédit Mobilier asked for $60,000, the president of the line, Thomas C. Durant, ordered Dey to resubmit his proposal, making the sum needed $60,000 a mile.[7]

Gordon reports that Peter Dey resigned. But that didn't stop Crédit Mobilier and Union Pacific from milking as much money as they could from the government—and from Wall Street.

Durant was a smart barbarian. He began as a cotton smuggler in the 1850s with his partner Greenfield Dodge, but he quickly moved up the scale, founding the Missouri & Mississippi (M&M) Railroad with his ill-gotten gains.

As president of the government-chartered Union Pacific line, he spread rumors about where the line would connect, buying up shares of other railroads as the speculation climbed.

PBS's *American Experience* said of Durant:

> Durant announced that the Union Pacific would connect to his own M&M line, causing M&M stock to rise sharply. He sold his shares discreetly and bought stock in the competition. A new announcement declared the connection would be the Cedar Rapids & Missouri line. Investors flocked to that company and divested themselves of M&M, which Durant bought back at low cost.[8]

Dodge's brother said of the scheme, "In other words, he gets back home and makes in the roundtrip for him and his friends $5,000,000. It is the smartest operation ever done in stocks and could never be done again."[9]

Of course, we've seen higher-netting scandals resulting in tens of millions of dollars for lobbyists, but we'll get to Jack Abramoff in a minute.

Durant learned to manipulate the game, but after his cool $5 million, he stepped a little into the background, though his insidious whispers still resulted in the unprecedented Crédit Mobilier scandal uncovered in 1872.

This scandal rivaled even Abramoff's infamous plunder of the Indian tribes, and the *Encyclopedia Americana* called it "the most tremendous legislative scandal in American history,"[10] although this was published in 1918.

Durant and his fellow barbarians hatched a brilliant, if fiscally diabolical, conspiracy. Stephen E. Ambrose exposes the plot in his book,

Nothing Like It in the World: The Men Who Built the Transcontinental Railroad, 1863–1869.

Union Pacific (UP) paid Crédit Mobilier by check, with which Crédit Mobilier purchased from UP stocks and bonds—at par, which is the trick to the whole thing—and then sold them on the open market for whatever they would fetch, or used them as security for loans.[11]

The *Encyclopedia Americana* reports that the U.S. government paid $94,650,287.28 to Union Pacific and $50,720,958.94 to Crédit Mobilier. Do the math. That means there was $43,929,328.34 in profits (including the stocks and bonds the construction company paid itself), and Crédit Mobilier reported a cash profit of only $23,366,319.81. These numbers, though certainly understated, were partially the result of government collusion.[12]

And there was another level here that's missing—namely Oakes Ames, a congressman from Massachusetts and a stockholder of Crédit Mobilier. This congressman was the architect of the Pacific Railroad Act provision that allowed Union Pacific to issue mortgage bonds that equaled, dollar for dollar, the government bonds backing the project.

Additionally, Union Pacific could issue these bonds 100 miles in advance of construction, and issue the mortgage bonds ahead of the government bonds, putting all the risk in the government's hands.

It was an attractive offer, and the only way Union Pacific could sell its stock, because the government backing in excess of costs was the only thing attracting subscribers. But it also left a lot of money on the table—too much. Something needed to be done, and Ames was the guy to do it. That's how Crédit Mobilier came into being in the first place.

"To gain possession of the balance," says the *Encyclopedia Americana*, "it was decided to form the stockholders of the Union Pacific into a duplicate corporation under another name, as a construction company, to which the railroad company should turn over its bonds and stocks as payment for work and supplies."[13]

Crédit Mobilier did all the work, and Union Pacific was a railroad corporation in name only. That's how we find the profit of more than $43 million, after duplicate payments to both Crédit Mobilier and Union Pacific.

And who came up with this barbaric plan? Congressman Oakes Ames was the chief of the enterprise.

So why would a congressman get his hands dirty in this shell company? Simple greed. The scam was making so much money that everyone had their hands out. That's what eventually got the company—and Congressman Ames—in trouble.

To keep Crédit Mobilier moving forward required some legislation, and Ames thought he could buy off other congressmen to grease the wheels. In 1867, Ames came to Washington with 343 shares of the company that were trading at a 100 percent premium, and sold them at par in order to keep things on the right track.[14]

Ames had lots of big names involved in his bribery scandal: folks like Schuyler Colfax and Henry Wilson, who would both become vice presidents; James Garfield, who would become president; and James G. Blaine, who would be the Republican nominee for president in 1884.[15]

It wasn't long before a disgruntled stockholder raised the alarm with a lawsuit saying he'd been cheated. The story became headline news—front page, even.

The *New York Sun* ran a six-column headline reading:

THE KING OF FRAUDS
HOW THE CREDIT MOBILIER BOUGHT ITS WAY
THROUGH CONGRESS
Colossal Bribery[16]

There must have been madness in Congress, with expulsions galore, right?

Not so much.

A congressional committee was formed in December 1872 to investigate how far the fraud went, and actually recommended Oakes Ames and one other congressman be expelled. But the House did not expel them—only censured them![17]

This scandal did nothing but ensure that the Republicans lost control of the House during the next election cycle. There were reforms put into place after the scandal, but the problem was, the financial system was outrunning the law. The lawmakers could not keep up with the wealth that the economic expansion of the late nineteenth century brought to the table.

Political Corruption

It would be easy—and wrong—to say that Congress has wised up in the past 150 years. At the turn of the millennium, we still had government and business holding hands, and shoving no-bid contracts under the table and behind closed doors. To wit, Dick Cheney and Halliburton.

One example? As secretary of defense in 1991, Cheney gave millions of dollars worth of contracts to Halliburton, and when he left office in 1995, he served as CEO of Halliburton until he was chosen by George Bush to be the vice presidential candidate. Cheney resigned his post as CEO, of course, but as vice president, he again gave hundreds of millions of dollars worth of contracts to Halliburton during the Gulf War in 2003. We later learned that at least some of these contracts were noncompetitive.

And we also learned that Halliburton was accused of overcharging the government, thanks to Bunnatine Greenhouse, a whistle-blower in the Army Corps of Engineers who was, as a result, demoted.

A *New York Times* article by Erik Eckholm in late August 2005 reported:

> Ms. Greenhouse's lawyer, Michael Kohn, called the action an "obvious reprisal" for the strong objections she raised in 2003 to a series of corps decisions involving the Halliburton subsidiary Kellogg Brown & Root, which has garnered more than $10 billion for work in Iraq.[18]

The issue was a noncompetitive contract worth up to $7 billion for the reconstruction of Iraq's oil operations. But Halliburton was also accused in 2003 of overcharging the government by $61 million for transporting fuel from Kuwait to Iraq. The *New Yorker* reported, "Halliburton charged the United States as much as $2.38 per gallon, an amount that a Pentagon audit determined to be about a dollar per gallon too high."[19]

It's not the first time a government official abused his station, nor was it the last. And the barbarians are on both sides of the aisle.

Take Democratic Senator Christopher Dodd of Connecticut. He was the chairman of the Banking Committee before he was forced to resign because of the Countrywide financial scandal.

The more benign part of this scandal was the realization that Countrywide provided VIP loans that waived points and fees that saved Dodd and other government officials thousands of dollars.

The shocking part was the blatant disregard for company borrowing rules.

For example, James Johnson, a former chief executive of government-sponsored mortgage reseller Fannie Mae, received a $3 million loan for a second home, even though the amount exceeded Countrywide's limit for such a loan. He also received favorable interest rates on two of his other properties which he refinanced through Countrywide.[20]

What's really so bad about all this?

It was the financial system's overextension and poor loan decisions that nearly collapsed the global economy. In fact, Countrywide nearly went bankrupt during the crisis, and saw its share price plummet from $45 a share in February 2007 to less than $5 a share less than a year later. Bank of America picked up the company for a cool $4 billion in a stock swap.[21] (See Figure 16.1.)

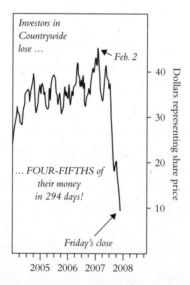

Figure 16.1 As Countrywide's Shares Plummet, Investors Lose Money
DATA SOURCE: MarketOracle, article 2890. www.marketoracle.co.uk/index.php?name=News&file=article&sid=2890 Nov 26, 2007.

And here's the rub—and why congressmen like Christopher Dodd are the new barbarians of wealth: "The growing scandal surrounding the 'friends of Angelo' loans (so-called by company employees, referring to Countrywide CEO Angelo Mozilo) should serve as a political wake-up call," reported the *Wall Street Journal* on June 18, 2008. "Yet the Senate appears intent on pushing forward legislation, co-authored by Sen. Dodd, that would bail out the worst actors in the subprime mortgage banking industry."[22]

Why would Dodd support such legislation?

We know he saved tens of thousands of dollars on his loans. Senator Dodd received two loans in 2003 through Countrywide's VIP program. He borrowed $506,000 to refinance his Washington townhouse, and $275,042 to refinance a home in East Haddam, Connecticut. Countrywide waived three-eighths of a point, or about $2,000, on the first loan, and one-fourth of a point, about $700, on second, according to internal documents. Both loans were for 30 years, with the first 5 years at a fixed rate.

The interest rates on the loans, originally pegged at 4.875 percent, were reduced to 4.25 percent on the Washington home and 4.5 percent on the Connecticut property by the time the loans were funded. The lower rates would save the senator about $58,000 on his Washington residence over the life of the loan, and $17,000 on the Connecticut home.[23]

But maybe there was something else behind this. Perhaps it was because Countrywide had contributed $21,000 to his campaign fund since 1997.[24] In fact, according to the *Wall Street Journal*, Senator Dodd's last campaign "war chest" was made up mostly of donations from banks, and finance and real estate companies![25]

And who else besides Countrywide was a big donor? None other than AIG.

The *Washington Post* reported on March 30, 2009, that AIG donated more money to Senator Dodd than to any other American politician, and that Dodd's wife was actually employed by an AIG subsidiary from 2001 to 2004. What did these donations buy? Dodd's amendment to the stimulus bill that ensured executives could still collect their bonuses even if their companies were bailed out by the government.[26]

This scandal involved some heavy hitters, key banking players like Dodd and Johnson, and Senate Budget Committee Chairman Kent

Conrad. But none was so big as one of the most well-known, and hardest-hit, men in Congress, Tom DeLay, the twenty-fourth majority leader of the House of Representatives.

Tom DeLay has been implicated in a number of lobbyist scandals, not the least of which was the Abramoff scandal, for which two of his top aides have already been convicted, and for which he himself was charged by a Texas court with criminal violations of campaign finance laws and money laundering.

But Abramoff wasn't the only barbarian in DeLay's company. And in fact, DeLay should be considered one of Congress's most infamous barbarians.

Robert Kaiser, author of *So Damn Much Money: The Triumph of Lobbying and the Corrosion of American Government*, relates the following story:

> In the mid-1990s DeLay and his colleagues in the Republican leadership had struck a bargain with Washington's lobbyists that was both brazen and remarkably successful: if the lobbyists would help raise hundreds of millions of dollars to support Republicans and help preserve their majority in Congress, DeLay would invite them into the legislative process, and allow them to propose entire bills and suggest changes to legislation proposed by others.
>
> Both sides fulfilled this understanding with gusto. The Republican National Committee and the party's House and Senate campaign committees, which collected $358 million in contributions in the two years prior to the 1994 elections when Republicans won control of Congress for the first time since 1952, reported contributions of $782 million a decade later in 2003–2004—a 220 percent increase. Lobbyists and their clients helped make that possible. And lobbyists for corporate interests won countless legislative provisions from the Republican House and Senate favoring their clients.[27]

But how could this happen? Wasn't this barbaric plan so transparent that even a five-year-old could see through it?

The answer is yes, but why this was allowed to continue unabated was due to the bribery and ethics laws in place. It has to do with one vague but key word in the law that makes charges of bribery difficult to stick. That word is *corruptly*.

Kaiser explains that this word speaks to intent, but has no clear definition. [28] So just like in the mid-nineteenth century, if you didn't have direct evidence that a lobbyist's money bought results, you didn't have a case. See how far our Congress has come?

Political Scoundrel

Let's not forget, however, that bribery is a two-way street. The lobbyists are waving fistfuls of cash, too—and raking in even more. So let's talk about Jack Abramoff.

This guy is one of the slimiest barbarians yet, a double-timing, money-laundering, millions-skimming scoundrel whose schemes brought down some big names in Congress. His largest was the Indian lobbying scandal that saw Abramoff and his fellow barbarian lobbyists double-deal Native American tribes, flipping tens of millions of dollars through backdoors and into legislators' pockets—his own (and those of his partner in crime, Michael Scanlong) were stuffed with $85 million dollars.

Here's how he did it.

In the mid-1990s, Jack Abramoff started representing Indian gambling interests as a lobbyist for Preston Gates Ellis & Rouvelas Meeds LLP. As power changed hands in Congress from the Democrats to the Republicans, the Native American tribes felt like they were losing influence, and sought out someone who could gain the ears of the new leadership.

Abramoff had some sharp connections that he had no problem flaunting to his prospective clients. He employed former (and sometimes current) congressional aides who would give him connections to the congressmen themselves, like Tony Rudy, senior aide for our good friend Tom DeLay. And we know that DeLay was implicated in the Abramoff scandal.

Washington Post reporter James Grimaldi said in an interview with Ray Suarez on *NewsHour with Jim Lehrer*:

> Tom DeLay is probably the biggest name that's been mentioned. He was described—he described Jack Abramoff as his—one of his closest and dearest friends. Our investigation showed

that they may not have been personal buddies but they certainly were political allies. And Tom DeLay actually took a trip to Scotland with Jack Abramoff that came right before a vote that was unusual for Tom DeLay.

He voted against an anti-gambling bill that one of Jack Abramoff's clients, actually a couple, wanted to kill. And most of the Republican caucus actually voted for that bill. Mr. Delay says that there was no quid pro quo. He said that he voted against that bill because it had loopholes in it.[29]

So it was friends with influence like Tom DeLay, Bob Ney (R-Ohio), John Doolittle (D-California), Byron Dorgan (D-North Dakota), J. D. Hayworth (R-Arizona), J. Steven Griles (deputy U.S. secretary to the interior), David Safavian (Office of Management and Budget's chief procurement officer), and even Harry Reid (D-Nevada), who swayed Native American tribes to throw money at Abramoff and his barbarian lobbyists in order to win friendly legislation for Indian casinos.

And boy, did they ever!

The Mississippi Choctaws were the first to employ Abramoff in 1995, and by 1999, they had paid him $1.3 million. Abramoff and his crew funneled that money to one Ralph Reed, former head of the Christian Coalition and one-time runner for lieutenant governor of Georgia. Abramoff got Preston Gates to hire Reed for a $20,000-a-month retainer fee.[30] Reed's job was to mobilize the Christian Right in Alabama to ensure that a gambling bill that would put some games in dog racing tracks wouldn't pass. The Choctaws were afraid this competition would eat into their profits. The bill was scuttled.

Time and time again, Abramoff's services were used by Native American tribes: the Mississippi Band of Choctaw Indians, Coushatta Tribe of Louisiana, Saginaw Chippewa Tribe of Michigan, Agua Caliente Band of Cahuilla Indians, Ysleta del Sur Pueblo (Tigua), and the Pueblo of Sandia of New Mexico. Sometimes he even pitted them against each other.

Between 2001 and 2003, Abramoff and Scanlon collected about $66 million in fees from these six tribes![31]

Of course, they did get legislation passed on the tribes' behalf, but it was at a huge cost. Some accounts show that tribes were overbilled for services and also billed for services never performed.[32]

For example, Michael Scanlon offered the tribes political database services as part of Abramoff's pitch. In one instance, he charged the Coushatta Tribe of Louisiana $1,345,000 for this service, but he spent only $104,560 on its development and operation. The remaining $1,240,440 was split between Scanlon and Abramoff.[33]

But that money wasn't just going into Abramoff's and his cronies' coffers. Some of that money found its way into congressmen's campaign funds.

The lobbyist and his partners also coordinated political donations worth $1.7 million to more than 200 members of Congress on behalf of clients such as the Choctaw Indian tribe in Mississippi, the U.S.–administered Northern Mariana Islands in the Pacific, and Russian oil magnates.

Legislation passed by Congress in recent years directly benefited those clients, and the Justice Department's ethics division is now seeking to prove that those votes were bought.[34]

But sometimes, what tribes donated to certain congressmen was passed off as contributions from Abramoff and his lobbyists. He had an "entertainment program" that wined and dined congressmen and their families and friends. We're talking about skyboxes at big games, VIP treatment at his New York restaurant, even overseas trips, with all expenses paid by Abramoff.[35]

Needless to say, the intricacies of Jack Abramoff's Indian lobbying scandal fairly boggle the average American's mind. With so many third-party corporations funneling money among each other to deliberately disguise both the origins and destinations of the bribes, understanding all the moving parts is nearly impossible, and it took a congressional investigation to uncover all the partners.

But while this scandal was unfolding in the papers, American's weren't paying much attention to these new barbarians of wealth.

"Fewer than one in five Americans, 18 percent, say they are paying very close attention to the scandal around Abramoff," reported *USA Today* on January 11, 2006, "who pleaded guilty and is cooperating in a wide-ranging probe that could involve up to 20 members of Congress and their aides, according to the Pew Research Center for the People & the Press."[36]

USA Today found that 81 percent of those surveyed think that bribing members of Congress is fairly common in the nation's capital.

They're not wrong. Even the insiders are claiming bribery is commonplace.

Take Brent Wilkes, an American defense contractor who came clean about the lobbying and bribery business after a conviction for his involvement in the Duke Cunningham defense contracting scandal back in 2007.

The *New York Times* ran a lengthy article about Wilkes' introduction to the business.

In 1992, Brent R. Wilkes rented a suite at the Hyatt Hotel a few blocks from the Capitol. In his briefcase was a stack of envelopes for a half-dozen congressmen, each packet containing up to $10,000 in checks.

Mr. Wilkes had set up separate meetings with the lawmakers, hoping to win a government contract, and he planned to punctuate each pitch with a campaign donation. But his hometown congressman, Representative Bill Lowery of San Diego, a Republican, told him that presenting the checks during the sessions was not how things were done, Mr. Wilkes recalled.

Instead, Mr. Wilkes said, Mr. Lowery taught him the right way to do it: Hand over the envelope in the hallway outside the suite, at least a few feet away.[37]

According to Wilkes, campaign contributions were required if you wanted to receive a federal contract. Indeed, as Wilkes learned the ropes, he and his associates gave more than $706,000 to federal campaigns, and his company received about $100 million in federal contracts.[38]

Even congressmen are speaking out about how blinded its members are becoming to the color green. Chuck Hagel, the Republican senator from Nebraska between 1997 and 2009, said, "There's no shame anymore. We've blown past the ethical standards, we now play on the edge of the legal standards."[39] Nothing was getting done unless money was greasing the wheels.

Kenneth Schlossberg, another barbaric lobbyist insider, wrote an article for the *New York Times* on May 14, 1986—yes, *1986.* In it he wrote:

The truth is that money has replaced brains and hard work as the way for a lobbyist to get something done for his client....

Nobody can say when all the small cracks created by legal corruption in our legislative and administrative processes will create a disaster.[40]

These new barbarians of wealth are growing in number. Between 2000 and 2006, the number of companies with registered lobbyists climbed 58 percent. The Cato Institute found that lobbyists spent more in that time, too: $2.1 billion, up from $1.5 billion.[41]

And that's just what's reportable. That doesn't count some things, like those special skyboxes that Abramoff made available to congressmen, or those cheap loans and waived fees that Countrywide gave its VIPs.

Robert Kaiser calls these barbarian lobbyists "a new class in Washington, hustlers who exploited the public policy-making process for profit."[42]

We call them modern-day Attilas, and the new barbarians of wealth.

Unfortunately, these problems aren't confined to the borders of the United States. There are other barbarians of wealth gathering power and money, and sometimes, they're running countries.

Chapter 17

Global Barbarians

When Genghis Khan united the tribes on the steppes of Asia to become the Golden Horde, he did so by establishing a rule of law—the Yassa—by which all Mongols would live, sometimes under pain of death.

His barbaric campaigns that expanded into Europe and down through to Southeast Asia brought more goods and natural resources under his control, and more people under his Yassa. Long swaths of the Silk Road passed through Mongol lands, and it made many barbarians rich.

Today, and in recent times, we're seeing other barbarians grasp global resources with both meaty fists.

Hu Jintao, of China, has been buying up the world's resources in places like Australia and Africa. Umaru Musa Yar'Adua, along with his predecessors in Nigeria, has allowed the administration to lock up the wealth from the oil industry from its citizens. And we've also seen Hugo Chávez in Venezuela taking over the country's resource sector and expelling all foreign corporations.

But no global barbarian of wealth can compare with Russia's Vladimir Putin.

Putin "Khan," as we like to call him, famously said, "Comrade wolf knows whom to eat—he eats and does not listen to anyone."[1] He was speaking about U.S. foreign policy, but this ideology is found throughout his own policies as well.

Putin is as unyielding as concrete, and just as dispassionate. He is the Stalin-era concrete gulag that says, "I am here. You have built me." And that indeed is what has happened.

Putin's rise to power was a surprise. He was a run-of-the-mill KGB man who worked his way into politics in St. Petersburg, becoming deputy mayor of the city. And he had a nickname . . .

Although St. Petersburg never grew to become the financial powerhouse that many had hoped, its fortunes improved as many foreign investors moved in, such as Coca-Cola and Japanese electronics firm NEC. Putin gained the nickname "the gray cardinal" in response to his behind-the-scenes influence and low profile.

He was investigated in the early 1990s for allegations of favoritism in granting import and export licenses, but the case was dismissed due to lack of evidence.[2]

Not exactly an awe-inspiring leader—but he was eventually taken under the Kremlin's wing. In 1996, President Boris Yeltsin made him deputy to the chief administrator, Pavel Borodin. In 1998, he became the head of the Federal Security Service, the organization that replaced the KGB. In all aspects he was a lawman.

In 1999, Yeltsin appointed him prime minister. It was clear that Putin was now being groomed for the presidency, and in December, when the very ill Yeltsin stepped down as president, Putin stepped up as acting president.

Putin was seen as devoutly loyal to Mother Russia and to his own allies, which made him the perfect successor to Yeltsin and his family, who, like every other passing president, feared charges of corruption would be brought once he relinquished his post.[3]

But as prime minister, Putin earned his stripes with the second war in Chechnya.

The first lasted two years, and showed little progress with the rebellious region. Putin orchestrated a six-month campaign that brought

Chechnya to heel. The turmoil in Chechnya is long and tragic. All the atrocities that happened are too many to be listed in these pages.

In a brief summary, Chechnya—a small republic in the Caucasus region—sought independence after the fall of the Soviet Union in 1991, but the Russian Federation, under the rule of Boris Yeltsin, argued that Chechnya had not been an independent state within the Soviet Union, and therefore did not have the right to secede.

Need it be said that Chechnya was an important hub for Russia's oil and energy infrastructure?

The situation exploded in 1994 when Russian forces attempted to take the mountainous regions back from Chechen guerillas. Despite their overwhelming man- and fire-power, they were unsuccessful for two long years. Meanwhile, the Chechen separatists resorted to terrorist attacks like the Budyonnovsk hospital hostage crisis in 1995 that resulted in between 105 and 166 hostages' deaths.

Yeltsin and Chechen leaders agreed to a ceasefire in 1996 and signed a peace treaty a year later after tens of thousands were dead. Chechnya's economy and its physical cities were destroyed and the new leader, Aslan Maskhadov, lobbied for Moscow's help in rebuilding. Russia sent money but most of the funds found their way into the pockets of the Chechen warlords and the new authorities. This meant that much of the republic's population saw little aid from Russia, with the result that tensions against the motherland began to climb again and more and more militants and religious extremists became active.

In 1999, a second war broke out. Chechnya was aiding a rebellion in the Russian republic of Dagestan, and had been accused of carrying out three separate apartment building bombings in Russia, including one in Moscow. In response, Russia launched a devastating air campaign against Chechnya in late August.

Reports of tens of thousands of refugees fleeing the region appeared, and one report said that 300 civilians were killed in the capital as a result of Russian bombings.[4]

On October 1, 1999, Putin Khan took over the war effort. Also on October 1, land troops entered Chechnya. By October 5, they'd pushed as far as the Terek River. This created a buffer zone that was meant to protect Russia from Chechen attacks. But when it became clear that this zone wasn't effective, Putin crossed the river. His forces had already taken civilian lives.

According to the *Guardian*, a Russian tank shell hit a bus carrying refugees, killing 11.[5] The *Independent* reported that Russia dropped 30 bombs on the village of Elistanzhi in the foothills of the Caucasus Mountains, killing dozens of civilians.[6] But Russia denied both incidents.

The *Independent* article says:

> Villagers were bitter that Vladimir Putin, the Russian Prime Minister, had said that no Russian planes had flown on the day Elistanzhi was attacked.... In theory the raids are targeted on "terrorist" bases of Chechen leaders blamed by Russia for the bomb attacks which killed 300 people in apartment buildings in Moscow and elsewhere. In practice, since the Chechen guerrillas do not have fixed bases, this means the bombing of any area where they are known to have once been present. There were no signs of any military installations in Elistanzhi.[7]

Once the Russians were across the Terek River, they turned their offensive towards Grozny, the capital of Chechnya. People were fleeing before the Russian army, which was slowly eating up the land around the capital.

On October 21, 1999, Russia fired short-range ballistic missiles that killed more than 140 people. Missiles struck the capital's marketplace and near the president's building. The Russians said the marketplace was targeted because it was being used by the rebels as an arms bazaar.[8]

The U.S. Holocaust Memorial Museum put Chechnya on its Genocide Watch List. It reported in 2001, "Chechnya was devastated, including the almost complete destruction of Grozny, the Chechen capital. Russian artillery and air indiscriminately pounded populated areas. Human rights organizations also documented several massacres of civilians by Russian units."[9]

In fact, in 2005, the European Court of Human Rights found the Russian government guilty of violating the right to life, freedom from torture or inhuman or degrading treatment, and the right to seek remedy for injustice, according to the Institute for War & Peace Reporting. Six Chechen civilians had filed the suit, and were awarded 135,000 euros plus court costs.[10]

Many such rulings have followed this first landmark case, but has Vladimir Putin been tried for war crimes? No, and even after his presidency ended, he was once again appointed prime minister, the same role in which he conducted the Second Chechen War.

So what was behind such barbaric vehemence? Was it just the mud on the face of the motherland after Chechnya wanted to break from the Russian Federation? That certainly played a part. Russian loyalty and Russian pride are two important qualities, particularly important to Putin Khan, just like Genghis.

This is evidenced by Robert Service, author of *A History of Modern Russia: From Tsarism to the Twenty-First Century.* "He had left nothing to chance against challengers who matched his zeal to promote Russian state interests and national pride,"[11] he said, and that included eliminating those who defaced Russia and her actions.

Loyalty was rewarded, and talk against the State was punished. This included journalists and former government officials alike. In 2006, journalist Anna Politkovskaya was shot execution style, and former KGB officer Alexander Litvinenko was poisoned. Steve LeVine, author of *Putin's Labyrinth: Spies, Murder, and the Dark Heart of the New Russia*, wrote:

> I had been under no illusions about Putin. His bare-knuckle approach to governing Russia has been apparent for some time. But now it was hard to avoid the conclusion that something more ominous was happening. What I was seeing in Russia went beyond the question of leadership style. Putin had set about restoring the legacy of brute Russia.[12]

The death of investigative journalist Anna Politkovskaya in October 2006 hit the world like a bombshell. She wrote about war in Chechnya with a critical eye toward Russia. She was dogged in reporting the atrocities of the Russian campaign.

But that wasn't the only politically motivated killing during Putin Khan's reign. Alexander Litvineko, an associate of Boris Berezovski who criticized Russian authorities, was poisoned with polonium–210 in the United Kingdom, and countless others were murdered, harassed, tortured, beaten . . .

Robert Service wrote:

> A gang of unidentified thugs had crushed the fingers of Yabloko leader Grigori Yavlinshi's pianist son in Yeltsin's time. . . . Garry

Kasparov was temporarily thrown into gaol merely for campaigning for justice and civil rights. The FSB was given license to act outside the law in defense of the whole state order.... Russia sank deeper and deeper into a pit of authoritarian rule backed by criminality.[13]

When Putin was first elected, PBS interviewed a number of Russian journalists, and specialists on Russian politics. One Yevgenia Albats essentially said that compared to Yeltsin, who was sick and nearly a puppet leader, Putin was the guy you wanted to lead you. She said, "And all you have to do is just to grab this hand and say, 'Guy, take me in this bright future. I want to go there with you, whatever it takes. And if on your way to this bright future, you need to create another Gulag, that's fine with me, as long as you lead me.'"[14]

It seemed as though there were many anti-Putin activists headed for much worse fates.

Government Thugs

Russia was fast becoming a gangland, where the biggest band of thugs was the government itself. These barbarians intimidated, threatened, stole, killed, and more in the name of keeping an ordered state. This is nothing new for Russia, though, whose history has such ruthless notables as Lenin and Stalin.

But in today's Russia, the barbarians have their grubby hands on the economy. Consider the article from the National Review Online titled, "Putin and Chávez's Slow Descent: Russian, Venezuelan Presidents' Dictatorships Are Doomed." Here's the bit that deserves attention:

He still enjoys the gratitude of the Soviet voters for making them richer and ending the chaotic "robber capitalism" of the later Yeltsin years—even if "robber capitalism" has ended only through the KGB state's elimination of rival robbers and world oil markets deserve the credit for Russia's temporary prosperity.[15]

But we're getting ahead of ourselves. Let's get to what this national pride—and violence in its name—means for Russia's natural resources.

Here's where the global barbarian of wealth becomes worthy of the name Putin Khan. All you had to do was look at the headlines of the time to see that something was wrong.

The *New York Times* reported in 2002 that U.S. officials "have growing doubts about the nature of [Putin's] leadership."[16]

Inside Russia, the *Moscow Times* stated in 2003 that "Russia is full of fear. Businessmen and politicians are afraid of Vladimir Putin. [Putin] relishes the fear. The greater the fear, the stronger his power."[17]

And in 2007, *USA Today* confirmed these statements and said that Putin "is now showing his true—and very Soviet—colors."[18]

Most particularly telling is the United Kingdom's report from the oldest and most respected newspaper, *The Daily Mail*, calling Putin a "brutal despot who is dragging the West into a new Cold War."[19]

And one of its deadliest weapons is its abundant natural resources.

Less then 10 hours after the 2007 G8 Summit with President Bush and other major leaders in Germany ended, Vladimir Putin made his cutthroat intentions known to the world.

"The world is changing before our eyes," he said before 200 corporate leaders at the International Economic Forum in St. Petersburg.[20] Global financial institutions like the World Trade Organization and the IMF were, according to Putin, "archaic, undemocratic and inflexible." They didn't, he said, "reflect the new balance of power."

And Putin left little doubt as to where this new balance of economic power would be centered. "The new architecture of economic relations requires a completely new approach," he stated defiantly. "Russia intends to become an alternative global financial center and to make the ruble a reserve currency for central banks."[21]

This was more than just a warning shot. It was a blazing opening salvo that caught the United States, and the rest of the world, for that matter, totally off guard. But this move wasn't half as strong as Russia's energy extortion with Europe and international companies.

Putin's grand empire accounts for over 20 percent of the world's oil and natural gas reserves. That makes them virtually energy independent from the rest of the world. Russia also holds huge reserves of countless raw materials including iron ore, manganese, chromium, nickel, platinum, titanium, copper, tin, lead, tungsten, diamonds, phosphates, and gold, and the forests of Siberia contain an estimated one-fifth of the world's timber supply!

They're a rogue nation, the largest in the world in fact, that owes allegiance to no one but themselves.

"Some believe that we are too lucky to possess so much natural wealth, which they say must be divided. These people have lost their mind." Putin said.[22]

This kind of rhetoric is par for the course when it comes to Putin Khan. His nationalistic ideology ranged from killing off anti-State journalists to hoarding billions of barrels of oil and gas, ready to cut off supplies at the drop of a hat.

Russia's iron fist did not make many friends. Robert Service said, "Russia caused fear without gaining friends or admirers. It also worried potential investors. Despite its petrochemical riches, it needed help in modernizing its drilling and refining facilities—and the Russian government's bullying of foreign companies was scarcely going to hasten this process."[23]

That means that the oil and gas industry and the government were in bed together. "Occasional information trickled out about the wealth of ministers. Public office became a ticket to vast wealth," wrote Service.[24] That's no surprise, but with Putin, the knife cut both ways.

From Steve LeVine:

> ...Russia's richest man [Mikhail Khodorkovsky], who was arrested in 2003 by masked federal agents aboard his private plane on the tarmac of Siberia's Novosibirsk Airport. He was sentenced to eight years in prison, and his oil company, Yukos, was systematically dismantled and taken over by two state-controlled companies, Gazprom and Rosneft.[25]

Khodorkovsky did nothing more than finance Putin's political opponents, seeking to put an oppositional bloc of politicians in parliament.

Those in the State who were loyal, however, were rewarded. For example, Gazprom, Russia's behemoth state-owned gas firm, was chaired by First Deputy Prime Minister Dmitry Medvedev, who became Putin's presidential successor.

Rosneft, another state-owned oil firm, was chaired by Igor Sechin, the Kremlin deputy chief of staff. Rosneft forced a sale of Yuganskneftegaz, the production arm of rival Yukos, below market price.

Russian state diamond monopoly, Alrosa, was headed by Alexei Kudrin, former minister of finance, who hypocritically called for less government control over the economy.[26]

Former German Chancellor Gerhard Schröder was rewarded for his support with a directorship of Gazprom. Coincidentally, Gazprom was the company building a pipeline to transport gas directly from Russia to Germany.[27]

Other government officials were controlling the oil and gas sector, too, in Putin's time.

Arial Cohen wrote in his Heritage Foundation article titled "Putin's Legacy and United Russia's New Ideology" that Russian leaders believe that by controlling natural assets, they can distribute wealth to the Russian population.[28]

But that's not really what Putin said. He said that if you believe in dividing that wealth, you've lost your mind. Was he talking about sharing profits with international companies, or with his own people? You can never tell with this type of barbarian.

Clearly Putin favors some Russians over others, and always those loyal to the State.

Service noted that Putin restricted access to the Council of the Federation, where local leaders would be able to affect the passage of legislation, and in 2004, he gave himself the power to appoint new regional governors without an election.[29]

All this power and control made Putin Khan a wealthy and dangerous man—and that combination can lead to barbaric results.

Controlling the Pipeline

Putin knew that his path to power was littered with desperate commodity buyers—and they were all playing resource roulette against the house. It was a simple strategy, really: Either fall in line and comply with Putin's demands or find somewhere else to buy your oil, natural gas, or any other resource for that matter.

And in that frenzied buyers' market, finding another seller was next to impossible. On New Years Day 2006, Gazprom, Russia's massive nationalized LNG company, cut off any and all gas supplies to the Ukraine when it failed to comply with Gazprom's price demands.

The message was loud and clear: Putin has the power and he's more than willing to use it.

"Putin could flip a switch and families from Paris to Milan would go to sleep with their coats on tonight," said James Verini for *Condé Nast Portfolio* magazine.[30]

That wasn't the only incident where Russia held Europe hostage with its energy resources in the dead of winter. Even as Putin handed his presidency over to Medvedev, and was given the appointment of prime minister (again), Russia was still lording its energy wealth over Europe— and even former Soviet states.

In early January 2010, another quarrel broke out. This time the quarrel was between Russia and Belarus. Russia halted deliveries to refineries in Belarus on New Year's Eve. The two were supposed to have reached a new agreement for pricing for the new year but failed to do so.

Belarus said Moscow was pressuring too hard over a preferential tariff, which is applied to Russian oil passing through Belarus.

The BBC said, "Russia says it is prepared to sell oil to Belarus duty-free for domestic consumption but wants to charge the tariff for oil that Belarus exports."[31]

Sounds reasonable, but what might not be reasonable was the immediate supply cut that ensued on New Year's Eve after no decision had been reached between Russia and Belarus.

It's a good thing that Belarus had a week's supply in its inventories, because Germany gets between 10 and 15 percent of its oil needs from Belarus, and Poland relies on the country for 75 percent of its oil consumption.

Belarus has threatened to increase its transit fees in retaliation for Russia shutting down its supply.

A full 400,000 barrels of oil a day is shipped through the Druzhba pipeline to European countries, making it one of the world's biggest. This move (if it comes to pass) might help mitigate some of the costs of a preferential tariff, which some experts estimate would have ranged in the neighborhood of about 10 percent of the country's GDP, or about $5 billion.[32]

Not surprisingly, Belarus has tipped its hand a little.

The country has threatened to cut off electricity supplies to the Russian enclave of Kaliningrad.

This is a tricky situation, as Kaliningrad is the only Russian port on the Baltic that is ice-free all year, meaning winters make Kaliningrad's port very important for both economic and military reasons.

Kaliningrad was also seriously considered—until January 2009—as a site for a missile installation, as the United States was in talks with neighboring Poland for the development of a missile shield.

On Monday, January 5, 2010, at 6:30 P.M. in Kaliningrad, it felt like 11 degrees Fahrenheit. In Minsk, Belarus, it felt like minus 5.

So energy becomes a bargaining chip, particularly as harsh winter weather makes its way into the region. No one knows this game better than Russia. Even up-and-coming global barbarian Hugo Chávez can't play as well as Putin Khan.

The energy war over Russia's natural resources was so wrapped up in Putin's nationalistic ideology that his relations with the West were as sour as Genghis Khan's fermented yak milk.

Max Hastings, writing for the *Guardian*, said, "A few months ago I heard a cluster of diplomats lament the difficulties of doing business with the Russians. 'They still see negotiation in the old cold-war way, as a zero-sum game,' said one. 'If the West wants something, it must be bad for Moscow.'"[33]

Putin even teams up with other global barbarians, like Chávez in Venezuela and Castro in Cuba, trying to broker deals with the corrupt nation of Nigeria,[34] and even going so far as to block certain sanctions against Iran.[35]

This all adds up to nation building—imperialism. Putin wanted Russia to regain its superpower status, and his best bargaining chip was its natural resources. That's why Putin realized that his only way of becoming a force in the world again was to keep control of its resource industry with the State, and to put his own cronies in positions of power.

But as we've said before, this kind of control keeps wealth in the hands of the powerful barbarians already in charge—even as it's doubled Russia's GDP per capita between 2000 and 2004.[36]

Cohen wrote, for the Heritage Foundation, "However, income inequality in the Russian Federation remains remarkably high. Energy superpower status certainly benefits Russia as a whole, but it benefits members of the political-bureaucratic-security elite with access to government-controlled resources far more than it benefits others."[37]

And Putin guarded this wealth—and the energy plunder sopped up by his oligarch friends. In a barbaric world where *disloyalty* (a.k.a. speaking out against the State and/or its policies) could get you killed, Putin reigned supreme.

Max Hastings noted, "Putin cannot shrug off a simple truth about his society: his friends and supporters walk the streets in safety and wealth; his foes perish in horrible ways, with dismal frequency. The murder of one Russian journalist critical of his regime might be dismissed as mischance. The deaths of 20 mock Kremlin protestations of innocence."[38]

In fact, Russia was ranked 131st in a world ranking of countries according to how peaceful they were.[39] This may have been due in part to the ongoing turmoil over Chechnya, but even aside from that violence, crime and repression were climbing in Russia—and the money spent on the military climbed right on with it.

Putin is virtually untouchable and he's got his own country on a complete lockdown, the likes of which we haven't seen since Joseph Stalin. The air of fear and paranoia running through the country is as potent as 100-proof vodka.

Not since the days of Adolph Hitler (who shares with Putin the distinction of being named *Time's* "Man of the Year") have we seen a leader quite so dangerous.

The *Washington Post* goes so far as to say that Putin is "imposing dictatorship the old-fashioned way."[40]

Putin's iron-fisted control over Russia's resource riches has sent him on a power trip worthy of Alexander the Great.

Putin governed Russia with a philosophy the Kremlin called "Managed Democracy"—which is code for "barbaric nationalism."

Just a few examples are all it takes to make the hairs on the back of your neck stand up.

- He seized controlling interest of Gazprom, Russia's largest energy company and the biggest extractor of natural gas in the world.
- He ruthlessly dismantled Gazprom's biggest non-State energy competitor, Yukos Oil, by charging it over $7 billion in back taxes

and then throwing its CEO into a Siberian prison to rot. He then proceeded to sell Yukos at a fire-sale price to a company he owns 20 percent of.

- Putin's secret police force is suspected in the murders of three Russian journalists, all of whom were working on stories exposing corruption inside his administration. When a former official came forward and accused Putin of the killings, he was soon found dead as well.
- Putin is followed devotedly by an almost cult-like youth movement called the Nashi. Putin often visits their training camps and rallies, including a recent one next to the Kremlin attended by over 20,000 Nashi members, to deliver fiery anti-Western rants and speeches.[41]

Putin's second term as president thankfully ended in 2007. But not so fast: He has assumed the position of prime minister immediately following his presidency, all but ensuring that his reign over the country will continue for years to come.

That means that while the West is held hostage by Russia's energy power, Putin and his minions get rich. For every $1 per barrel rise in oil prices, approximately $3.4 billion pours into the Russian treasury![42]

Max Hastings wrote, "The tools of success in Putin's universe are corruption, violence, vice, and licensed theft on a colossal scale."[43]

Robert Service likened Putin Khan to a hunter when he took office, "eyeing the trees on either side of him for quarry."[44] He is still hunting . . .

The conflict between Russia and Chechnya is still ongoing. On March 29, 2010, two separate suicide bombers targeted busy metro stations in Moscow during rush hour. Chechen rebels claimed responsibility.[45]

The war over Russia's energy resources is not over, either. The West is seeing to build a new natural gas pipeline that would bypass Russia, getting energy from places like Turkmenistan and Azerbaijan in the Caspian region, with the pipeline route circling through Turkey and a number of Eastern European (former Soviet bloc) countries.

Russia is countering with two pipelines that would route natural gas around the troublesome Eastern European countries (like Ukraine, whose energy war with Russia included shutting down shipments in one of Europe's coldest winters).

Europe and the West are being forced to deal with this global barbarian of wealth. Russia and Putin Khan will continue meddling in affairs beyond its borders, one hand on the oil trigger, the barrel pointed at Western Europe's head. This Putin Khan may still be the most dangerous man in the world.

Part Five

PROTECTION STRATEGIES

Chapter 18

Diversification: The Key to Wealth Protection

Now, there are lots of sneaky ways that these modern-day Attilas can get their hands on your money, from trifling credit card fees to full-blown trillion-dollar bailouts. They'll be underhanded and shady, and they'll be bold and unapologetic.

Today's barbarians of wealth are addicted to power and the color green. They'll do anything for money—even if it's yours.

And history has shown that it *is* yours.

You have two choices: to do nothing about it, or to do something about it.

Doing something about it doesn't have to mean grabbing a pitch-fork or ax and storming the castle. You don't have to incite riots or rebellions shouting, "Down with Goldman Sachs!" or "Get your hands out of my pockets!" though there are plenty of opportunities to join with protestors nowadays.

Doing something about it can be as simple as putting your money out of reach of today's most notorious barbarians.

You can preserve your wealth with gold, silver, or other precious metals.

You can stave off an attack by getting your money out of the U.S. dollar and into an appreciating currency.

Or you can protect your capital by investing in prosperous countries and international companies.

We'll talk about each of these three strategies in later chapters, but the main thrust of these tactics is diversification, and to diversify before it's too late. Asset allocation is key in preserving wealth.

Imagine you're in a monastery in Ireland during the Viking Age, when suddenly you see a forest of ship masts with full sails rounding into your bay. Is that the time you say to yourself, "Man, we should've sent some of our treasures to our brothers in France!"?

No, certainly not. The time to be diversified is *before* something happens, because you rarely have enough time to react to preserve your wealth.

Think you're safe holding your wealth in cash? Think again. Cash isn't safe anymore, particularly if you're under attack. You can't just stuff $10,000 under your mattress and expect it to all be there when you need it.

Here's an example. If you had stuffed $10,000 under your mattress at the start of 2009, you'd really have only $9,398 left at the end of the year. That's how much the U.S. dollar suffered.

The U.S. Dollar Index weighs the value of the greenback against a basket of other major currencies. The U.S. Dollar Index read 83 in January 2009, and 78 in December 2009. That's a 6.02 percent drop in one year.[1] (See Figure 18.1.)

And that's with the country recovering from the recession!

Don't get us wrong, though. We're not against cash (though we've got some strong reservations about certain currencies). We're not against any asset, per se. What we are against is putting all your eggs in one basket.

So let's talk a little about asset allocation.

Asset Allocation

One of the most popular—and fairly proven—theories of portfolio management is the *permanent portfolio*. This idea was created by one

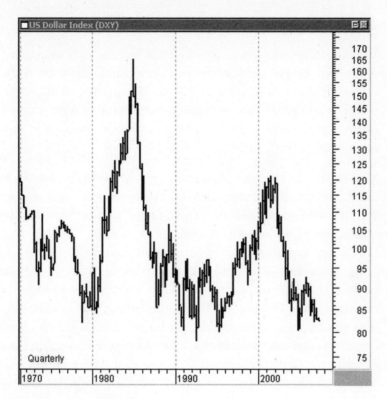

Figure 18.1 U.S. Dollar Index
SOURCE: maoxian.com/us-dollar-Index.

Harry Browne, a free market investment analyst and two–time Liber-tarian nominee for president of the United States. He wrote a book titled *Fail-Safe Investing: Lifelong Financial Security in 30 Minutes.*

The gist of his permanent portfolio strategy, which, incidentally returned on average 9.7 percent a year between 1970 and 2003,[2] was this:

Asset Allocation	**Four Equal Components**
25% stocks	Would thrive with economic prosperity
25% long-term bonds	Would balance deflation
25% gold (bullion)	Counters inflation
25% cash (Treasury bill money-market fund)	Safety[3]

In his book, Browne wrote:

When you depend upon one investment, one institution, or one person to see you through, you must constantly worry that your one source of security might fail. But when you diversify across investments and institutions—and keep things simple enough to manage yourself—you can relax, knowing that no one event can do you in.[4]

You could also take this allocation one step further and make sure you have diversification within these four components. You don't want all of your stocks to be held in the tech sector, and perhaps you don't want all of your cash in the U.S. dollar.

Nowadays, you might not even want all your gold in, well, gold. Other precious metals are proving to be hedge-worthy, and some exchange-traded vehicles are backed by the actual metals, so technically you are still buying bullion. We'll talk more about that in Chapter 19.

The one sector that Browne doesn't hit much on is the commodity sector, though you can certainly add commodity-based companies (a.k.a. miners and producers) to the stock component of your portfolio.

This sector has a strong impact on markets, both domestic and global.

Take energy, for a quick example. The transportation industry, the refining industry, the utilities industry, and a number of others watch the price of oil, natural gas, coal, and other energy commodities very closely.

The airline industry buys oil options so it can guarantee fuel prices months down the road. These commodities have a huge effect on markets and companies.

To be fair, Browne's permanent portfolio was designed to be put on autopilot, so that you, the investor, don't have to think much about your investments unless the components become unbalanced. Browne's suggestion:

If any of the four investments has become worth less than 15 percent, or more than 35 percent, of the portfolio's overall value, you need to restore the original percentages. Otherwise, you'll be relying too much on the most successful investment to continue being successful, and you'll be leaving some other investment with too small a share to carry the portfolio when its time comes to pull the load.[5]

This method certainly helps preserve wealth. The back-testing of this strategy back to 1970 shows that no single year lost more than 6 percent.[6]

At the same time, however, this portfolio might leave some gains on the table. Safety is Browne's goal, along with steady gains. By incorporating some other portfolio strategies, you may be able to win back some of the wealth today's Attilas have stolen from you.

And the fact is, you can do *that* through diversification, too. The whole point of asset allocation is to make opportunistic moves.

Reasons for Shifting Your Portfolio

Robert Hagin, author of *Investment Management: Portfolio Diversification, Risk, and Timing—Fact and Fiction*, wrote, "The tactical part of an asset allocation strategy, which has some similarity to market timing, involves making opportunistic shifts above or below the strategic, or normal percentages."[7]

For example, a tactical shift might involve pulling money from riskier assets, like stocks, and putting them into safer investments, like Treasury bills, during times of economic hardships. This might help you preserve your wealth. A shift from safety to a riskier asset during times of prosperity might help you grow your wealth faster than Browne's permanent portfolio.

You just have to know which asset class to invest in, and when.

And that's where the barbarians of wealth love to take your cash. Leave a chink in your armor, and a Hunnic arrow will pierce your nest egg. An unrepaired crack in your portfolio's castle wall leaves you vulnerable to Charlemagne's trebuchets.

After the financial crisis, many investors were left with cracks in their portfolios, and were left to do battle with notched swords and rusted armor. But now's the time to start repairing the damage, and rebuilding what the greedy hordes have torn down.

Were you overextended in the real estate market? Did you let a small fortune ride the commodity wave? Did you eye up investment banks like they were huge cuts of wagyu beef? Lots of people did. That's what the barbarians wanted you to do. They didn't care about the bubble that was growing out of control, as long as they were raking in more of your cash.

Now you've seen some of the weapons these guys are using. Now you can start to protect yourself.

"A good portfolio is more than a long list of good stocks and bonds," wrote Harry Markowitz in his book *Portfolio Selection: Efficient Diversification of Investments*. "It is a balanced whole, providing the investor with protections and opportunities with respect to a wide range of contingencies."[8]

How you balance your portfolio—what weight you give each of your investment components—is determined by how much risk you're willing to take.

If you're an aggressive investor, you're willing to take on more risk in order to get a bigger reward. This balance could help you win back some of your wealth.

If you're a more conservative investor, you're not willing to take on more risk, and you're more comfortable with smaller, more consistent gains. Your safer investments help preserve the wealth you have.

In either category, it's diversification that provides the balance. You can arrange your portfolio to suit your needs.

Also in either category, you're up against risk. And while diversification helps lower your risk of losses, nothing can eliminate it. (Even if you're just deciding to hold cash, as we've already noted.)

Investopedia.com identifies two types of risk: systematic and unsystematic. In its article "The Importance of Diversification," these two types of risk are defined as undiversifiable and diversifiable.

- *Undiversifiable*. Also known as *systematic* or *market risk*, undiversifiable risk is associated with every company. Causes are things like inflation rates, exchange rates, political instability, war, and interest rates. This type of risk is not specific to a particular company or industry, and it cannot be eliminated or reduced through diversification; it is just a risk that investors must accept.
- *Diversifiable*. This risk is also known as *unsystematic risk*, and it is specific to a company, industry, market, economy, or country; it can

be reduced through diversification. The most common sources of unsystematic risk are business risk and financial risk. Thus, the aim is to invest in various assets so that they will not all be affected the same way by market events.[9]

For example, if we go back to Browne's permanent portfolio components, we note that the risk in stocks is both diversifiable and undiversifiable. And you can help mitigate that risk by investing in things like cash, bonds, and gold.

But that doesn't mean a balanced portfolio of cash, bonds, and gold is completely safe. Another layer of diversification is geographic.

Let's look at cash specifically. There might be international currencies that are climbing in relation to those that are falling. For example, during Greece's debt crisis in early 2010, the euro traded down sharply against the U.S. dollar, meaning the U.S. dollar gained value comparatively.

But during the global financial crisis, other currencies, like the Australian dollar, were climbing as the U.S. greenback lost value. (See Figure 18.2.)

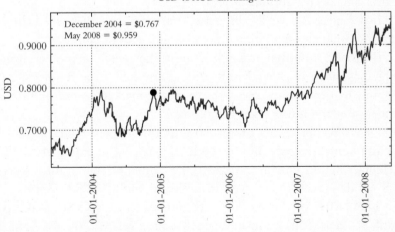

Figure 18.2   Strength of Australian Dollar
SOURCE: http://staypuff.net/?p=2321.

Therefore, it might be wise to hedge your cash position with a balancing international currency. We'll talk about ways to do just that in Chapter 20.

But international diversification has many more aspects than just a different currency.

And investing in international markets doesn't have to mean buying up some obscure bonds in Malaysia. Global investing is just like domestic investing. There are levels of risk associated with different types of international investing.

The first obvious way to break down the global investment scene is by an economy's classification. Is it a developed economy like the United States, Japan, or France? Or is it an emerging market, like China and India?

The bigger, more developed economies are considered less risky than emerging economies—kind of like how large-cap companies are considered safer than small-cap companies. At the same time, some emerging markets will offer better returns than will developed economies.

Michael Schmidt, a chartered financial analyst and editor for Investopedia.com, wrote, "Constructing a portfolio of non-U.S.-based assets, particularly in developed stock markets, has both increased total returns and decreased volatility."[10]

In Chapter 21, we'll talk about four principals that will help you determine which international markets you should consider.

But there's another thing your portfolio needs to protect against: unpredictability. In other words, no one can know the future. We can certainly make educated guesses as to where markets and economies are headed, but the future itself is unknown.

Diversification helps protect against unforeseen events. Take the environmental tragedy in the Gulf of Mexico in April 2010. This accident killed 11 people and caused the biggest oil spill in the history of U.S. oil disasters—bigger even than Exxon Mobil's Valdez spill.

The owner of the oil rig is Transocean, Ltd. (NYSE: RIG). On April 21, 2010, this company's stock traded for $90.37. By April 30, shares were trading for $72.32, a 19.97 percent loss.[11]

This event was certainly unforeseen, and RIG wasn't the only oil driller hit. The whole sector fell as a result. A portfolio heavily invested in drilling and exploration companies would have taken huge losses. But gold prices climbed significantly over this same time frame.

On April 21, gold for June 2010 delivery traded for $1,140.40 an ounce. By April 30, gold was trading for $1,180.70, a 3.53 percent gain.

So let's see what a $10,000 portfolio would have done in two different situations. If it was fully invested in RIG, the portfolio would have been worth, on April 30, 2010, $8,003. If the portfolio was half invested in RIG and half invested in gold, the portfolio would have been worth $9,178 on April 30, 2010. You've just turned a 19.97 percent loss into an 8.22 percent loss.

That's some serious protection!

So you can see where diversification can really cut risk and exposure to unforeseen events.

Gold and other precious metals are particularly helpful in balancing your portfolio against unforeseen events, and against often overlooked risks like inflation.

Let's start there, then, and take a look at how diversification into gold and silver can benefit your portfolio.

Chapter 19

Precious Metals: Inflation Protection Strategies

As you've seen from previous chapters, as the total supply of dollars grows, each individual dollar becomes worth less and less. But in addition to a growing supply of money, we have to be concerned with inflation.

In 2007 inflation was running between 2.0 and 2.78 percent. But as the market tanked, inflation shot up as high as 4.3 percent. It slowly came back down. In 2008, inflation averaged 3.85 percent (according to Inflationdata.com).

As the economy struggled to recover in 2009, we had little inflation. But already in 2010, inflation is sitting at 2.63 percent. It's likely to go higher. In fact some economists are already warning we could again see inflation levels of the 1970s. In 1974, inflation ran as high as 11 percent. (See Figure 19.1.)

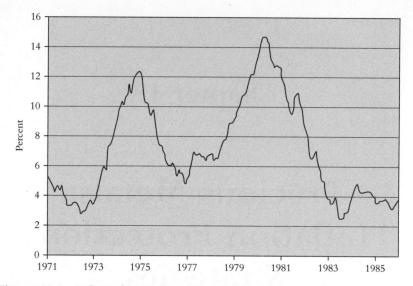

Figure 19.1 Inflation Rates Based on Consumer Price Index, Year-to-Year Changes in Monthly Levels, 1971–1985
SOURCES: Inflationdata.com, St. Louis Federal Reserve.

Rising inflation is dangerous to the economy. If the Fed had to raise interest rates to attract buyers of its debt (which we've seen has become a huge problem), that move would threaten recovery. Not only would it threaten worldwide recovery, but inflation would also rob you of your hard-earned wealth. That's why you need inflation protection strategies.

In March, the National Inflation Association (NIA) released a statement citing its concerns related to inflation. The statement read:

> The United States today is in a short-term deflationary phase caused by forced liquidations, de-leveraging, going out of business sales, and other temporary factors. It is our belief that the monetary policies of the Federal Reserve and United States Treasury will soon put an end to this deflationary phase, and we will see massive inflation in the U.S. that could ultimately lead to Zimbabwe-style Hyperinflation.[1]

The NIA also says we haven't even begun to feel the inflation that is coming from President Obama's $787 billion in stimulus money.

Arun Motianey of Roubini Global Economics says we're headed for an inflationary world. In a recent Moneynews.com article, Motianey was quoted as saying, "Deflation is a very serious risk [but] inflation is a greater likelihood."[2]

Martin Feldstein, writing for the *Financial Times*, agrees that the United States is headed for inflation. In his April 19, 2009, article, "Inflation Is Looming on America's Horizon," Feldstein says, "The unprecedented explosion of the U.S. fiscal deficit raises the spectre of high future inflation."[3]

Feldstein argues that the potential inflationary danger is that the large U.S. fiscal deficit will lead to an increase in the supply of money. He says that when deficits do not lead to an increased supply of money, evidence shows that they do not cause sustained price increases.

Feldstein points to 1980 as an example of low inflation because the money supply was not increased. In the United States in the early 1980s, at the same time that fiscal deficits were rising rapidly, inflation fell because the Federal Reserve tightened monetary conditions and allowed short-term interest rates to rise sharply.

But now the large U.S. fiscal deficits are being accompanied by rapid increases in the money supply and by even more ominous increases in commercial bank reserves that could later be converted into faster money growth.

Today most people pay little attention to inflation. They don't realize the danger it possesses. Inflation erodes the purchasing power of assets and incomes. For example, an item that costs $40 in 1973 would cost you $100 in 1983. The truth is, since 1971 the dollar has lost 82 percent of its value.

Because inflation is so powerful, investors need to be aware of its ongoing damage to their portfolios. They need to look beyond investing in equities. That's because inflation destroys shareholder value as well.

Most investors believe that as long as companies can pass increased costs on to their customers, they can keep inflation from destroying shareholder value.

But as the *McKinsey Quarterly* points out in a recent report, to prevent inflation from eroding shareholder value, earnings must grow much faster than inflation, a target that most companies typically don't hit.

The McKinsey study found that during the 1970s to the 1980s, U.S. companies managed to increase their earnings per share at a rate roughly equal to that of inflation of around 10 percent. But in order to preserve shareholder value, companies would have had to increase their earnings growth by around 20 percent.[4]

That's difficult to do, especially in an economy that is struggling to recover from the recession of 2007. So instead of choosing equities, we recommend putting your money in inflation-protection investments such as gold and silver.

Hedging against Inflation

With U.S. government debt continuing to set record highs, low interest rates, and a huge boost to the monetary base in recent months, the easiest way to protect yourself from inflation as well as make excellent returns is to invest in gold.

Precious metals act as a hedge against market downturns. For example, when the Dow Jones Industrial Average dropped 380.48 points and fell below 8,000 on February 10, 2009, gold futures climbed $21.40 in a single day. And since then, gold futures have topped $1,000 an ounce.

As of the writing of this book, gold came close to surpassing $1,050 an ounce. Gold is reacting to investors' increasing fear that inflation will rise. Gold, after all, is a leading indicator of inflation.

In a report for the World Gold Council, David Ranson of H.C. Wainwright & Co. says that gold doesn't just act as a hedge against inflation; it also indicates when inflation is coming. In his study, Ranson found that changes in the price of gold bear a 0.50 correlation with consumer-price inflation 12 months down the road.[5]

Ranson says, "Inflation is a monetary phenomenon, by which we mean it is governed by the purchasing power of a currency in terms of 'hard money' benchmarks. How to tell whether government actions are combating or accommodating inflation? Watch gold, not oil."[6]

If the increase in the price of gold is a precursor to inflation, it also stands to reason that the increase indicates a decline in the value of the dollar.

Demand for gold is widespread. East Asia, the Indian subcontinent, and the Middle East accounted for 70 percent of world demand in 2008. The five countries that make up most of the demand are India, Italy, Turkey, the United States, and China.[7]

Most of the demand for gold can be traced to jewelry and industrial use. However, the largest increase in demand for gold comes from investors. Since 2003 investment has represented the strongest source of growth in demand, with a value increase through 2008 of around 412 percent. Investment attracted net inflows of approximately US$32 billion in 2008.[8]

Investors buy gold mainly for three reasons:

1. As a hedge against inflation
2. As a hedge against a falling dollar
3. For protection against rising political and economic crises

Over the years, gold has steadily risen in price. Take a look at Figure 19.2.

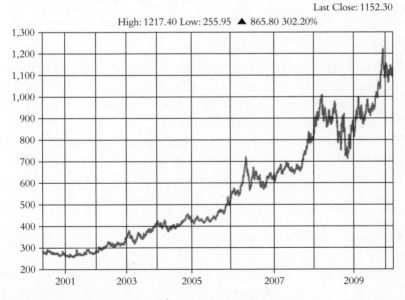

Last Close: 1152.30
High: 1217.40 Low: 255.95 ▲ 865.80 302.20%

Figure 19.2   Ten-Year Gold Price in U.S. Dollars per Ounce
SOURCE: goldprice.org.

Anthony Mirhaydari, writing for MSN Money, says that through-out all the tumult of the past 10 years—the bubbles, the recessions, the wars, the bank failures, and the bailouts—one asset class has outshone all others: gold.

There are a few ways you can invest in gold. These include buying and storing the metal yourself, investing in gold coins, and investing in exchange-traded funds (ETFs).

Of course, another way to invest in gold is by buying shares of gold mining companies. Mining companies can range from large businesses with massive gold reserves all the way down to the tiny development-stage company that owns some land but doesn't even know what's in the ground yet.

Mining companies have to deal with all different kinds of costs, like energy and equipment, mining licensing, labor, and any number of other things. But that doesn't mean mining companies can't be a good investment option.

In fact, some companies can offer you tremendous gains that surpass the hedging and safety potential of buying the actual precious metals. Here are three factors to look at if you're considering investing in gold mining companies, aside from actual reserves in the ground and amount being produced, which are a must.

1. *Cost of extraction.* First and foremost, you need to compare mining companies' cost of extraction, meaning how much money it takes to get an ounce of gold out of the ground. For the most part, the lower the costs, the higher the profits.

   For example, a company that can extract gold at a cost of only $300 an ounce will have a distinct cost advantage over a miner with extraction costs at $420 an ounce. (These extraction numbers are only an example and are not representative of true extraction costs.)

2. *Leverage.* Second, you need to look at leverage, which has a direct effect on earnings multiples—which affects how much money investors should expect to make in the future. Any increase in gold prices affects the percentage profits of a mining company, but for higher-cost companies, profits jump by a higher percentage than for lower-cost companies.

For example, if gold climbs from $800 an ounce to $850 an ounce, lower-cost miners see their profits rise from $500 to $550, or 10 percent. Higher-cost companies see their profits rise from $380 to $430, or 13.2 percent. That means that higher-cost companies should see a bigger rise (32 percent bigger) in their share prices compared to the lower-cost companies' shares.

3. *Hedging.* Lastly, look at a mining company's hedging policies. Hedging means a mining company enters a contract to sell its gold or silver to someone for a fixed price, no matter what the actual price might be at the time of the sale. Companies that hedge most of their production are severely limiting their leverage, which, as we've said, can have a strong effect on earnings multiples and share prices.

So, for example, let's assume a company with an extracting cost of $400 an ounce hedges production at $800 an ounce, meaning they've entered a contract to sell their gold for $800 an ounce. If gold continues to rally past $800 to $900, they've eliminated a massive chunk of their profit potential, capping their leverage at $800 and profit at $400 an ounce. An unleveraged company with the same extracting costs can ride that profit all the way up to $500 an ounce—or 25 percent more than its competitor.

Mining companies worth considering include Newmont Mining (NEM), Barrick Gold (ABX), Agnico-Eagle Mines (AEM), and Gold-corp (GG).

Before you decide to delve into every mining company's leverage and hedging strategies, let's look at some other precious metal investing options, like exchange-traded funds (ETFs).

Alternative Investments Offer Strong Returns

An ETF is simply a collection or *basket* of securities that trades like an ordinary stock. It's a bit like an index or mutual fund. ETFs are also traded at or close to their underlying net asset values.

ETF Daily News reports that by the end of the first quarter of 2009, the global ETF industry had 1,635 ETFs with 2,857 listings, $633.55 billion in assets, and 87 providers on 43 exchanges globally.

In Figure 19.3, you can easily see the huge increase and interest in ETFs as an investment of choice.

ETF Trends says analysts are calling for a $3 trillion growth spurt over the next three years as a number of new providers are entering the industry and new products are launching.

Tom Lydon, founder of ETF Trends, says:

> Five years ago, ETFs were not a threat to the mutual fund industry. Today, it's more of a reality that ETFs may be digging into the market share of the more conventional mutual funds. If you are a middle of the road mutual fund company and you have so-so performance, and average or above-average fees, as time goes on, ETFs will be a bigger and bigger threat to you.[9]

Exchange-traded funds hold advantages over mutual funds that are worth considering. For example, investors can redeem mutual funds (for their net asset value) at the end of the trading day. But ETFs trade like stocks, which means they can be bought and sold anytime the market is open.

Many mutual funds require a minimum investment to get in, whereas ETFs have no minimum investment.

Exchange-traded funds, unlike mutual funds, offer more flexible investing methods including the use of options. ETFs can even be sold

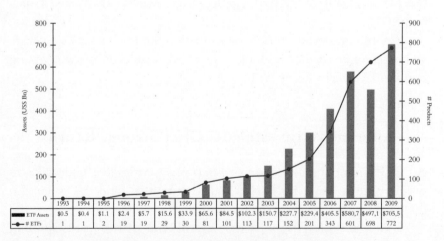

Figure 19.3   U.S. ETF Asset Growth as of December 2009
DATA SOURCES: ETF Research and Implementation Strategy Team, BlackRock, Bloomberg.

short, which allows the investor to bet on a price decline on the index itself.

Lastly, returns on gold-related ETFs are much higher than gold-related mutual funds. Gold ETFs provided investors with 29 percent returns in 2008 and 8 percent in 2009. Gold mutual funds haven't fared as well, offering investors negative returns.[10]

A gold ETF fund purchases a large amount of gold and maintains that supply in storage. The ETF will then issue shares in baskets with the idea that the value of those shares will increase alongside the price of gold. For example, if the price of gold goes up by 10 percent, then individual shares of the ETF would increase in value by the same 10 percent.

Now, in the gold sector, the ETF we recommend you consider is the SPDR Gold Shares ETF (NYSE: GLD). There are others, but this is one of the most liquid.

The ETF tracks the share price of gold and is backed by the actual metal itself. In fact, the ETF is backed by more than $40 billion in physical gold. This is the largest ETF with approximately 62 percent of gold ETF holdings.

There are a few other ETFs available, including iShares Comex Gold Trust (IAU), Physical Swiss Gold Shares (SGOL), the Power-Shares DB Gold (DGL), and UBS E-Tracs Gold Total Return (UBG).

ETFs offer investors the ability to move in and out of gold like stocks, while profiting from the price moves of gold and silver without worrying about costs, like energy and equipment, mining licensing, and labor, all of which are concerns with mining companies.

That also means that investing in these ETFs is a great way to hedge against a falling dollar. Figure 19.4 compares the progress of the GLD against a U.S. dollar ETF.

With ETFs, liquidity is one of the things investors need to take into account. A track record of a large amount of trades ensures that investors can buy or sell that ETF without any difficulty. It also suggests that the fund will be around for a long time. This is great for long-term investors, particularly in the gold sector.

And for faster-moving traders, the GLD offer options, which can mean even more leverage for aggressive investors—and greater potential gains of 100 percent, 200 percent, or even more.

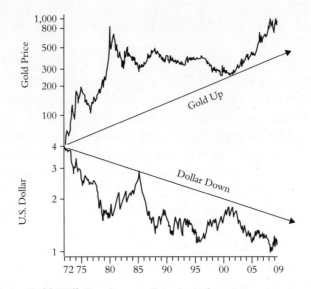

Figure 19.4   Gold Will Continue to Rise in Value
DATA SOURCE: usrarecoins.com.

Gold Fund

Besides investing in mining companies or gold-related ETFs, yet
another choice for investors is a gold fund. One that is not well known
by American investors is the Central Fund of Canada, quoted on the
Toronto Stock Exchange and having the symbol CEF on the American
Stock Exchange.

Philip M. Spicer founded the Central Fund of Canada in 1961.
It doesn't mine for gold. It is a closed-end investment management
company. The company stores gold and silver bullion in the highest-
rated-security treasury vaults at a Canadian chartered bank on an insured
basis.

At least 90 percent of the Central Fund's assets are made up of gold
and silver. An investment in CEF provides share ownership in gold and
silver bullion. As of April 2010, the Central Fund held $1.5 billion
worth of gold or 1.3 million ounces. The total value of the fund's assets
including silver and cash holdings is $2.8 billion.

It's hard to beat CEF for safety and value. The company mandates
that its storage of gold and silver bullion be audited on a semiannual

basis. But it also updates its financial information on a regular basis through its web site, which is open to anyone.

In addition, the Central Fund has managed to post some very strong numbers. In fiscal 2009, net assets as reported in U.S. dollars increased by $1,178.3 million or 97.9 percent.[11]

In 2009 the company increased the amount of gold and silver it has on hand. The Central Fund used approximately $248,376,698 of its money to purchase 271,705 ounces of gold bullion, and another $178,962,947 was used to purchase 13,588,255 ounces of silver.[12]

But the company also increased its net earnings. Net income of $728,638,579 was reported for the 2009 fiscal year, compared to the 2008 net loss of $352,572,657. The increase in net income for 2009 was primarily the result of appreciation of holdings during the year.[13]

There are several advantages to investing in CEF. The shares trade in the same fashion as any other stock, and all you need is a broker, just as if you were buying shares of a regular company.

You don't have to store the gold yourself. There aren't any extra hidden fees (other than the fees you would pay your broker). The fund's profits generally increase as the price of gold increases.

The CEF is a great way to invest in gold without actually owning the physical metal and still be able to hedge against inflation.

Silver ETFs

Another hedge against inflation is silver. Silver has always been an effective tool to offset inflation. In 1979 silver prices had risen as high as $15 and $25 an ounce, mostly on concerns of rising inflation. Only eight years earlier, silver was selling at roughly $1.55 an ounce.

Silver has long had a reputation for extreme volatility and lightning-fast gains. For example, after topping out in 1979, as inflation concerns eased, silver prices dropped.

However, in late 1982, investor interest in silver was rekindled. The international financial panic led investors to turn to silver. Others were attracted by what they saw as unsustainably low prices. This renewed interest was reflected in silver prices, which rose from the June 1982 low of $4.98 to a peak of $14.72 in March 1983.[14]

In the late 1990s and early 2000s, silver prices had declined and were trading in the range of $4.88 and $5.79 an ounce.[15] Prices rallied in 2006 because of the successful launch of Barclays' Global Investors iShares Silver Trust exchange-traded fund, which was introduced in late April of that same year. Led by strong investor demand coupled with industrial demand, silver rallied to $13.38 an ounce in 2007.[16]

During the first half of 2008, investors drove the silver price up above $20 an ounce. But economic outlook deteriorated rapidly, and silver, as well as other metal prices, slumped. However, silver's price in the first third of 2009 recovered a good part of the lost ground.[17]

By April 2009 silver hit a high of $19.29 an ounce. By April 2010, silver prices had stabilized at around $18 an ounce. That's a 210 percent increase since silver's low in the late 1990s.[18]

Unlike gold, silver is constantly used for manufacturing purposes such as medical devices, flat-screen televisions, cell phones, and other high-tech gadgets. Gold is mostly preserved.

An important factor in silver fundamentals is that U.S. government stockpiles are now officially depleted. In 1960, the U.S. government held the single largest amount of silver on hand: 3.5 billion ounces. But by late 2008, only 20 million ounces of silver were left in the U.S. government's stockpile.[19]

Today, government stockpiles around the world hold only 0.016 percent of the original 3.5 billion ounces that the U.S. government used to hold.[20] As the world economy emerges from the recession of 2007, we're likely to see an increase in demand for silver as manufacturing picks up the world over. But significant shortages of silver will cause a dramatic rise in prices.

Investing in silver, especially a silver ETF, makes perfect sense. The best silver ETF is the iShares Silver Trust (NYSE: SLV). It is the largest silver ETF. The fund actually owns silver bullion.

The returns on this ETF have been quite remarkable. As of December 31, 2009, the fund's one-year annualized returns were 56.6 percent. Since its inception (April 2006) the ETF has returned 8.87 percent.[21] Figure 19.5 shows the rapid appreciation of the silver shares ETF.

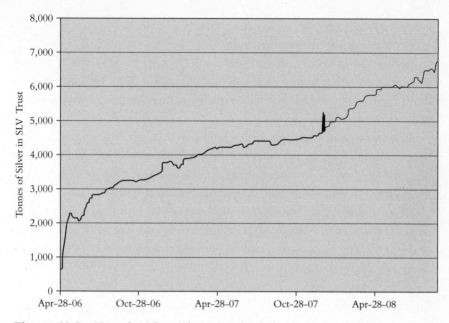

Figure 19.5   How the Silver iShares Has Performed over the Years
SOURCE: Seekingalpha.com.

Silver and Gold Futures

Another way investors can protect themselves from inflation is investing in gold or silver futures. This type of investing is not for the faint of heart, nor the shallow-pocket investor. With futures, you take on the risk of the commodity price moving drastically against you, and you can incur significant losses.

But the rewards can also be significant.

Here's how it works. According to the World Gold Council, "Gold futures contracts are firm commitments to make or take delivery of a specified quantity and purity of gold on a prescribed date at an agreed price."[22] So if you're buying a futures contract, you can expect to be holding that gold or silver in your hand someday.

The World Gold Council further explains, "Futures prices are determined by the market's perception of what the carrying costs—including the interest cost of borrowing gold plus insurance and storage charges—ought to be at any one time. The futures price is usually higher than the spot price for gold."[23]

When an investor buys a futures contract, the cash deposit is only a fraction of the price of that quantity of gold. That means investors don't have to pay for the full value of the futures contract until they take delivery of the actual gold.

In most instances, the physical gold doesn't actually change hands. That happens only when the contract expires or if the contract specifies "physical delivery of gold." However, most contracts are settled in cash, which means they are bought or sold on the open market before expiration date.

If the price of gold (or silver, in the case of silver futures) climbs higher than the price of the futures contract, then the investor has made a profit without forking over a lot of cash. That's great if the value of that gold or silver has climbed, but not so great if gold or silver prices fall.

Here's an example. If you buy a gold futures contract at $950 an ounce, and gold rallies to $1,000 an ounce, you've just made $50 on every ounce that you bought (and most contracts are traded in bundles of 100, just like options). But if gold falls to $900 an ounce, you just lost $50 on every ounce you purchased, and you still have to pay the full value of the futures contract.

You can see that an investor can really take it on the chin if prices move drastically against him.

That kind of risk isn't for the everyday investor. But one method for investing in gold and silver that can be used by every investor is simply buying gold and silver outright.

Physical Gold and Silver

Be it bars, bullion, or coins, this surefire way of investing in gold and silver cuts out all the worry. You don't have to pay any fees, like you do with the gold and silver ETFs; you don't have to pay for a mining company's energy costs; and you don't have to buy 100 ounces in a futures contract if you don't want to.

Let's talk about coins specifically, because here's where things get interesting. In addition to the actual gold or silver value of the coin, you can also take advantage of the demand for and rarity of certain coins.

Here's a specific example: U.S. Mint Silver Eagles.

In 2008 alone, the U.S. Mint shattered its previous sales record of 10.4 million by selling almost 20 million Silver Eagles—and demand still hasn't cooled off.[24] The premiums folks are paying are staggering—some of the highest premiums ever recorded for Eagles.

That means investors are paying more for this coin than the actual value of the silver in the coin. And the U.S. Mint Silver Eagle isn't even a rare coin. When high demand meets rarity, that's when premiums skyrocket, sometimes even doubling the initial price of the coin.

Want another example? How about the 1994 Viking Gold Noble? This coin was authorized by the Pobjoy Mint for the Isle of Man, but it was never minted.

In other words, this coin has never existed—until now.

In fact, it's the first Gold Noble minted in 544 years, making the coin extremely rare and unusual. No more than 10,000 of these coins were allowed to be made.

The design features a proud Viking longship complete with fierce dragon prow and the distinctive diamond-patterned sail.

The mint has struck these coins in a full gem proof finish, with a frosted design against a glittering mirror background. Each contains a tenth of an ounce of fine 99.99 percent 24K gold and is official legal tender of the Isle of Man, but you may want to hold on to it.[25]

The fact that this coin is unlisted in any catalog, and that you will be among the first to own it, creates a unique market opportunity. Firsts, such as China's first Gold Panda, can be highly sought after. In fact, 13,532 China one-ounce Gold Pandas were issued in 1982, but today sell for as much as $2,999 each.[26]

So coins are an easy way to buy into the gold and silver sector, and they offer the additional benefit of "consumer interest leverage." More than just demand for safety or a portfolio hedge, collectors' interest in gold and silver coins can really boost an investor's profits.

Every Portfolio Should Have Gold or Silver

There are a number of different ways you can invest in gold and silver—through mining companies; exchange-traded funds; futures; options on stocks, funds, and futures; and through buying bars, bullion, and coins.

Each offers its own advantages and risk profiles, and investors can tailor their investments to their own portfolios.

But whichever method you use to get invested in gold and silver, keep in mind that any allocation to precious metals can offer a safety net that's much needed in today's markets.

Talk to your broker about these strategies, or get involved with a coin distributor to snap up the next U.S. Mint Silver Eagle or Viking Gold Noble that could double, even triple in value.

Chapter 20

Barbarians of Wealth, Castles of Currency

The foreign currency marketplace (FOREX) is utterly enormous. It is a vast international network of traders bound to one another by computer screens and telephone links. FOREX is open 24 hours a day, six days a week, and trades an astounding $3.2 trillion each day as money moves around the world, changing from euros to dollars to yen to francs—on and on. But $3.2 trillion every day! That makes it the largest and most liquid market in the world, according to the Bank for International Settlements.[1]

In fact, this market is greater than one-fifth of the United States' entire GDP! It's big enough to write a $10,500 check to each and every American, and still have enough left over to buy the CME Group ($20.4 billion), Intercontinental Exchange ($8.4 billion), NYSE Euronext ($7.5 billion), and the NASDAQ OMX Group ($4 billion). Oh, and you can throw in AIG ($4.85 billion) and still have over $5 billion left, according to market cap data from May 21, 2010.

And here's the important thing to understand: Because of its sheer size, liquidity, and speed, even tiny fluctuations in the currency markets can result in staggering profits.

Let me repeat that, because it is very important:

The FOREX market is so big—and so liquid—even tiny, almost imperceptible moves can result in million-dollar profits, literally overnight.

Here's an example of what I'm talking about. Back in 1991, George Soros made $1 billion in one day trading the British pound. Now, that sounds incredible, doesn't it? An amazing amount of money to make in a single day.

But $1 billion is a mere .03 percent of the daily FOREX volume.

That's less than one-tenth of 1 percent. It's nothing—a drop in the bucket.

Most people assume that for Soros to make his billion-dollar fortune, the market had to move in big leaps and bounds. But it didn't. His fortune was created on a tiny move.

Imagine a coin maker back in Roman times, nipping a bit of a coin while his master's not looking. A tenth of an ounce isn't much on its own, but now imagine he can nip a bit of every coin in the Roman Empire. That adds up, now doesn't it?

That's essentially what happens every minute of every day in the currency market. Traders determine how much a particular currency is worth in relation to another currency. Take, for example, the situation in Greece in the first half of 2010. The country had been lying about its debt and was on the verge of defaulting when the European Union's heavy hitter came up with a $1 trillion bailout (€750 billion).

That number is made up of emergency loans that will help Greece's government pay out its issued bonds.[2] But it's not real cash. It's the promise of cash, and that's not the same thing. This obligation made the euro drop in value, and on Tuesday, May 11, 2010, the euro traded down to $1.27 against the U.S. dollar, down from $1.2804 the previous day.[3]

Now, a 1.04-cent move may not seem like a lot, but consider the size of the market. Just like that Roman coin maker, the nips add up. So for investors, ignoring the currency market means letting money sit on the table. That can be a big mistake.

Think back to Browne's permanent portfolio. He suggested holding 25 percent of your entire portfolio in cash. For most U.S. investors, that means holding U.S. dollars. In today's environment of ubiquitous barbarians of wealth, nearly nonexistent interest rates, and trillion-dollar bailouts, the value of the greenback is in jeopardy. But also in today's market, you have a lot more choices at your fingertips.

With so many choices comes the need to make sharp and savvy decisions.

Technical traders base their trading decisions exclusively on price charts. Basically, they analyze chart patterns to determine entry and exit points for each trade. *Fundamental* traders base their trading decisions on an array of economic data and news that reflect the political and economic health of countries around the world.

Fundamental data include things like interest rates, monetary policy, elections, and trade balances. For example, if Great Britain announces higher interest rates, this action will impact the price of the pound. If the United States raises interest rates, this will impact the price of the U.S. dollar. If Japan enforces trade embargoes against Canada, this will impact the price of the yen. In other words, you need to know what today's barbarians are doing to global economies.

Now, most currency traders are technical traders and insulate themselves from fundamental data. They don't even consider world events when making trading decisions. Their argument is that all the information clouds their thinking. Instead, they rely on price charts (technical data) to make their trading decisions.

This is a mistake.

Pricing charts are a powerful way to determine entry and exit points, but they can't tell traders where the most lucrative opportunities will emerge.

All Currencies Follow Fundamentals

Imagine being a Silk Road trader back when the Mongols nearly ruled the world. Now imagine if you knew ahead of time that the Mongols were going to attack the Persian city of Samarkand in modern-day Uzbekistan. This city was rich in the thirteenth century.

Samarkand was a city of great opulence and great marvels. In its factories were woven gold and silver lamé. . . . It was said that when Muhammad and his entourage went hunting, the men wore cloth of gold and brought along their tame cheetahs.[4]

This city lies right on the Silk Road between China and the Mediterranean. Tons of wealth flowed through here, and made the Persian leaders very rich indeed. According to Thomas J. Craughwell, author of *The Rise and Fall of the Second Largest Empire in History: How Genghis Khan's Mongols Almost Conquered the World*, the city held nearly half a million inhabitants. To give you a sense of just how big that was at the time, thirteenth-century London had about 40,000 residents and Paris had fewer than 80,000.[5]

As a trader, you'd be out of your mind not to deal with the Samarkand market.

But if you knew that in a few short days the weight of the Mongol army would rip Samarkand to shreds and make its rich Persian ruler nothing more than a beggar with a price on his head, would you bring your caravans anywhere near Samarkand?

Absolutely not. It's far too risky.

All currency trends flow from fundamental data.

Currency movements are driven by geopolitical events, government actions, economic reports, and so on. What happens in Europe impacts how the euro trades against the U.S. dollar. What happens in Japan determines how the yen trades against the euro. And what happens in Canada impacts how the Canadian dollar trades against every other currency on the planet.

So what is it about our current economic situation that makes currencies a valuable tool in combating today's barbarians of wealth?

Let's start with debt—the United States' national debt in particular. Here's a primer, from Investopedia.com:

The federal government generates a budget deficit whenever it spends more money than it brings in through income-generating activities such as taxes. In order to operate in this manner, the Treasury Department has to issue treasury bills, treasury notes and treasury bonds to compensate for the difference. By issuing these types of securities, the federal government can acquire the cash that it needs to provide governmental services. The national debt is simply the net accumulation of the federal government's annual budget deficits.[6]

And we've seen what both budget and national deficits can do to a government.

After years of mismanagement and cheating on its budget reporting (sound familiar?), Greece was facing a total economical collapse in the first half of 2010. And it wasn't just Greece. The turmoil was spreading to other countries, including Spain, Portugal, and Ireland.

There's no doubt that debt has a huge impact on an economy, and on individual investors, but one way that goes directly to the argument for a portfolio of international currencies is inflation. Inflation is, in its simplest form, an excess of dollars. Too much money for too few goods produced means the value of a dollar is diminished.

When the United States went into a recession in 2007, the government took on an unprecedented role in the economy. It increased spending drastically to make up for the falling private sector. It sold billions of dollars in Treasury bonds and flipped the switch on the printing press.

The U.S. government was printing money like mad—anything to staunch the flow of the bleeding economy.

But this created an oversupply of U.S. dollars, and to top it off, the increase in the debt burden through issuing the Treasury bonds leaves less money to support the economy. Milton Friedman, the American economist who inspired Fed Chairman Ben Bernanke to unleash the low-interest credit era, even says, "There's no doubt that one of the ways to avoid inflation was to finance as large a fraction of current spending with tax money as possible."[7]

So flooding the market with cheap credit makes buying our bonds less attractive to investors. What happens if they stop buying?

This is really a benign way of asking, "Uncle Sam is busy bailing out Wall Street, but who's gonna bail out Uncle Sam?"

What if we can't make good on our debts? Will our entire nation fold in default?

USA Today notes, "Even the most casual observers know the federal government has a serious debt problem that's propelling the USA towards the same cliff as Greece."[8]

We have a massive mound of debt—about $8.5 trillion, or 58 percent of our entire economy. But some estimates put the numbers much higher. If you take away the Social Security trust fund surplus, you've got a figure of about $13 trillion, or 90 percent of the economy.[9]

According to data compiled by the CIA, that puts the United States right behind Greece on the list of the world's highest public debt as a percentage of the economy.

Another key issue for the currency market is a country's interest rate. For the present economic situation, as the world recovers from its recession, the United States' interest rate set by the Federal Reserve is the weightiest issue. In fact, the national debt and the key interest rate kind of go hand in hand.

We've already told you how the government created a monopoly on money by taxing state banks for printing cash, but not national banks. The manipulation of interest rates is the barbarians' coup d'état, except this blitz was decades in the making. It starts with liquidity, or how many dollars are in the system.

At the end of 1979, the M3 money supply, the total quantity of dollars in circulation (or the total liabilities of the Fed), was $1.8 trillion and the amount of gold the government held was $142 billion. This meant that gold backed only 7.85 percent of the value of the dollar. By mid-2003, the amount of gold assets was valued at $91 billion, while the M3 was valued at $8.757 trillion, putting gold's backing of the dollar at a paltry 1.04 percent.[10]

"The U.S., following the every-possible-mistake script, is managing to both debase and inflate the dollar simultaneously," explain James Turk and John Rubino in *The Collapse of the Dollar and How to Profit from It: Make a Fortune by Investing in Gold and Other Hard Assets*. "Just as a coin is debased by reducing its gold content, the dollar can also be debased by reducing its gold backing."[11]

Fed Barbarians Withhold Key Numbers

Want to know how many dollars and promises are in the system now? So do we.

As it turns out, on March 23, 2006, the Federal Reserve discontinued the release of its M3 statistics. In its H.6 Release, the Fed stated, "M3 does not appear to convey any additional information about economic activity that is not already embodied in M2 and has not played a role in the monetary policy process for many years. Consequently, the Board judged that the costs of collecting the underlying data and publishing M3 outweigh the benefits."[12] The last number released was for February 2006, where the amount of dollars totaled $10.2987 trillion.[13]

Through the stimulus packages (the first during the Bush administration, the second on Obama's watch) there could be trillions more to add to the pile.

You see, the United States has been lulled into believing that high debt is a good thing. The dollar's preeminence created a demand for the currency, which the United States was only too happy to fulfill with Treasury bonds. It was also allowed to run huge deficits with its trading partners because the dollar was so stable and trustworthy. J. Anthony Boeckh says this climate was like a "free lunch" for the United States. But there's always a catch.

"The downside of this free lunch, like all free lunches, is that it created bad habits. The United States has been able to pursue policies that have been far more inflationary than they would otherwise have been."[14]

Of course, it's worse than a bad habit, because if we quit cold turkey, we'll still have $4 trillion worth of debt to pay back to the rest of the world. Think your Visa credit card associates are good at harassing you for late payments? *These* debts could start wars.

And we haven't even started talking about interest rates. Here's where these factor into the picture.

In times of economic growth, interest rates tend to rise, as the government wants to keep rising prices (a.k.a. inflation) in check. But in times of economic doubt, and even recession, lower interest rates help keep credit flowing. If money is cheap to borrow (because of low interest rates), then the likely effect is that more people will borrow money.

To see how interest rates have affected our current economy, we need to go back a couple decades. So let's take a look at Greenspan's legacy. The Maestro is hailed as a genius, but what he really did was set up one of the biggest bubbles this country has ever seen.

To be sure, the mid-1990s were very turbulent for markets. The global economy was shaken by a number of emergencies; everything from the Asian contagion to the Y2K computer bug hacked away at the global economy. In response Greenspan cut rates, making cash cheap and markets liquid. Cutting rates got the world through some pretty tough times.

But cutting rates is just a patch job, a Band-aid.

James Turk and John Rubino, in their book *The Collapse of the Dollar and How to Profit from It*, explain:

> The lesson the Maestro took from all this is that financial bubbles happen, and the way to keep them from impacting the broader economy is to provide the system with plenty of cheap credit.[15]

This is a falsehood.

Just to give you an example of how drastically Greenspan cut rates, let's look specifically at the economy after the tech bubble and 9/11. After the tech bubble burst in March 2000, interest rates were between 6 and 6.5 percent for the rest of the year. But heading into 2001, the NASDAQ continued to fall, and the Fed started to intervene. In December 2000, the rate stood at 6.51 percent. January saw the rate drop to 5.74 percent; in April, the rate was 4.71 percent. In August, right before the attacks, the Fed had the rate at 3.54 percent.

And then the terrorists struck, and put our economy in a tailspin. Greenspan started slashing rates like mad. By November, the rate was 2.03 percent, and as we moved into 2002, the rate was a mere 1.70 percent. And here's where Greenspan dropped the ball. The rate did not get above 2 percent until November 2004![16] But by then, the Fed had to play catch-up. The real estate market was booming. In December 2002, the average home price in the United States was $237,800. By December 2003, that price had climbed to $253,900. A year later, it was $284,300. At its peak, the average home price in the United States was at $329,400 in March 2007.[17] The Fed's rate had climbed back to 5.23 percent, but the pace of rates did not affect the price of housing fast enough. By the time rates became more effective, housing prices had already started plummeting.

Now, all those variable mortgages were starting to climb, and all those folks who bought their snazzy McMansions on cheap credit couldn't pay the piper now that rates had caught up to them. The inevitable pop brought the global economy to its knees.

An Admission of Guilt

Greenspan admitted, "While I was aware a lot of these practices were going on, I had no notion of how significant they had become until very late. I really didn't get it until very late in 2005 and 2006."[18]

But by that time, average housing prices has climbed more than 22 percent, and in hot spots around the country (New York, California) they had climbed even more.

It was clear that poor rate policy had a major effect on the housing industry, and on how the economy behaved after the bubble popped. As the Federal Reserve saw a changing of the guard in early 2006 from Greenspan to Ben Bernanke, economic pundits were wondering how monetary policy would change.

Bernanke has written extensively about the Great Depression. And here he was, standing on the brink of what could be the next black hole. He turned to history for an answer. He turned to American economist Milton Friedman, whose theory held that the Great Depression was the result of the Federal Reserve's action to reduce monetary supply and tighten credit policy.[19]

So he did the opposite.

"Bernanke has repeatedly invoked the late libertarian economist in support of lowering interest rates to zero, bailing out banks, and pumping untold trillions of dollars into the financial system," wrote Penn Bullock for *Reason* magazine.[20] Indeed, rates dropped from 5.23 percent at the peak of housing prices in March 2007 to 0.19 percent in the beginning of 2009, a faster and much sharper drop than anything Greenspan could have conceived.

Rates have continued to stay near zero as the Fed tries to stoke growth with no fear of inflation.

This is utterly ridiculous.

Turk and Rubino think all the pieces are in place for a cataclysmic currency event on the scale of a full collapse, like Weimar Germany, or

1990s Argentina. If that happens, they suggest, the world could lose confidence in all fiat currencies.[21] The phrase "Your money's no good here" takes on a whole new meaning. The barbarians in the Federal Reserve will have effectively kneecapped the entire global economy.

And that could be just where we're headed. According to Charles Goyette, a *New York Times* best-selling author and a libertarian/conservative talk-radio show host:

> Alchemists of antiquity, who spent their entire lives trying but were never able to "goldify the lead," would have been in awe at the way modern central bankers "monetize the debt." This process of turning debt into money is truly an act of central banking wizardry.
>
> The government runs deficits by spending more money than it has. The government's debts are then used as collateral for the creation of new money. . . . The greater the government's debt, the more money the Fed can create.
>
> This system of creating money is so incredible it seems as though it were designed to hide the inflation process from the public.[22]

He asserts that the U.S. dollar's "King of Currencies" status is starting to be questioned—and rightly so. "Ninety-six cents of the value of every dollar has vanished on the Fed's watch," he says, "and we've seen the worst depression and the worst bank failures in the nation's history, massive malfunctions in the credit markets, bubbles and busts, all under the great money and credit engineers of the central bank. It's been a costly affair, the infatuations of nineteenth-century intellectuals notwithstanding."[23]

In essence, what has happened is the U.S. government has taken on the debt of the private sector through bailouts and handouts, stimulus packages and subsidization. And that means our tax dollars have gone to pay off the modern-day Attilas who plundered everyone's wealth in the first place. To add insult to injury, what money we do have left is being made worthless by the Federal Reserve in order to help keep these debt hordes afloat.

There is no good solution to this problem.

In fact, the only way to deal with today's barbaric financial institutions is to counter the aftermath of the siege. Dollar falling? Euro imploding? Invest in other currencies.

Use Their Weapons against Them

The good news is that today's barbarians have gotten so greedy that they've created investment products that can be used against them. One of these weapons is a currency ETF.

Here's a primer from Goyette:

> In the typical structure of a currency ETF, each share represents one hundred units of the underlying currency. The funds will commonly invest in foreign short-term investment-grade money market securities in the country concerned. In so doing, the currency shares earn interest at the prevailing overnight rates in the countries involved. That yield can be used to offset the funds' fees.[24]

For example, if the currency rate for the euro versus the dollar is $1.33, then the price of a euro-based currency ETF or exchange-traded note (ETN) would be at or near $133. That means an investor can profit off the moves in exchange rates. If the euro rate versus the dollar changes to $1.39, then the ETF or ETN would be trading for $139.

The best thing about currency ETFs is that they simplify the Forex market. There is no centralized exchange, like the New York Stock Exchange or the IntercontinentalExchange (ICE). That means there's no one in charge who would technically guarantee the trading going on there. Trading is done, mostly, bank to bank—or barbarian to barbarian. These ETFs put currencies on your traditional exchanges, giving you the power to take advantage of the trades these barbarians make. With these new products you can invest in the movements of many global currencies, from the Swiss franc to the Chinese renminbi to the South African rand. And there are even funds that allow you to short a currency. In other words, you make money when a specific currency declines.

Here's how it works.

Obviously, interest rates differ from country to country depending, on a country's specific economic situation. If the value of a specific currency appreciates too quickly, the country's central bank raises rates. Sometimes, though, a quick rise means the country is less stable than countries whose currency appreciates in a steady fashion. But with more risk comes more reward, if you're on the right side of the trade. "The yield is higher in currencies thought to represent less stability and more risk; the return is lower in currencies believed to be safer," says Goyette.[25]

By following the fundamentals of a particular country, you can determine if its currency is a good investment for your portfolio. We'll get into some specific principles to determine whether a country's currency is strong and growing in Chapter 21.

Adding international currencies can be a great balance to the rest of your portfolio, too, not just a hedge against the dollar (or your home currency). John Jagerson, in his article "Currency ETFs Simplify Forex Trades," writes, "Different currencies benefit from some of the same things that may hurt stock indexes, bonds or commodities and can be a great way to diversify a portfolio."[26] What does he mean by that?

Remember when we talked about the difference between systematic risk and unsystematic risk, in Chapter 18? Systematic risk is caused by things like inflation rates, exchange rates, political instability, war, and interest rates. It's not tied to a specific company or industry. That means if a country descends into a recession, it will affect all stocks within that market, the country's bonds and (potentially) debt ratings, and its currency. But when one market falls, many times, another market rises in relation to it.

This lets currency traders make significant gains in playing these moves. But it also allows currency ETF investors to balance the currency portion of their portfolio with international opportunities. These ETFs can also boost your portfolio gains.

In Chapter 21, we compare debt to the hordes of invaders that wiped out whole economies. And in Chapter 19, we talked about inflation's natural hedge against the dollar's devaluation: precious metals. But now we want to talk about how to use the currency market to help protect your portfolio against the falling greenback.

International currencies have been experiencing surprising growth. Investopedia notes, "Many of the countries that ran current account deficits in the 1990s (deficits accompanied by high inflation and weak domestic financial positions) moved into trade surpluses during this time and built up sizable foreign exchange reserves. Countries such as Brazil, which allowed its currency to float, have seen their local currencies appreciate dramatically against the U.S. dollar."[27]

In fact, most currency market transactions involve the dollar, whether traders are betting for or against it. But the other side of the bet is another currency, and these bets can really pan out. For example, back in 2000, the U.S. dollar was worth about 1.25 euros, but just four years later, one dollar was only worth 0.73 euros—a 40 percent decline.[28] Even annualized (at 10 percent) this drop is steep!

Maneuverability Will Keep You Alive

With currency ETFs that trade like stocks, you can easily move between investments. But not all currency investments are the same. Some hold the actual underlying currency while others hold non-U.S. money market securities. Some even hold debt securities from other countries, so you have to know what you're looking for. Since we're talking about cash here, let's take a look at the different currency ETFs available on the market now that are backed by the actual currency.

Most of those ETFs are available through Rydex CurrencyShares funds. Of course, you shouldn't construe this discussion as an endorsement of the company or any of its funds, just the cleanest comparison to the currencies themselves. While the different ETFs and ETNs have an incredibly high correlation, there are differences in price movements. Let's compare the Currency Shares Euro Trust (FXE) to the WisdomTree Dreyfus Euro Fund (EU) (see Figure 20.1) and the EUR/USD Exchange Rate ETN (ERO) (see Figure 20.2).

The FXE correlates most closely with the euro–U.S. dollar exchange rate.

When the U.S. government allowed Lehman Brothers to go bankrupt back on September 15, 2008, the U.S. dollar was worth 70.290 euros. A week later, a dollar would buy only 69.150 euros. And as we've said, little nips can make big money. At the same time, the FXE ticked up from $142.20 to $145.28.

Of course, as the turmoil began over Greece's "Debt-gate" scandal, the euro took another turn, this time down versus the dollar. On April 23, 2010, Greece asked the European Union and the International Monetary Fund for a multibillion-euro bailout. On April 27, 2010, Greece's debt rating fell to junk status, and the euro plummeted. The

Figure 20.1 Comparison between Three Euro-Based ETFs: FXE, EU, ERO
SOURCE: Created by Yahoo! Finance's Yahoo! Interactive Charting System.

euro bought US$1.3343. Two weeks later, the euro bought only $1.2781. Now that's more than a little nip.

Maneuvering through the currency ETFs could have allowed you to profit from these global fluctuations. With the drop in the euro, the FXE fell from $132.51 to $127.51. However, at the same time, the

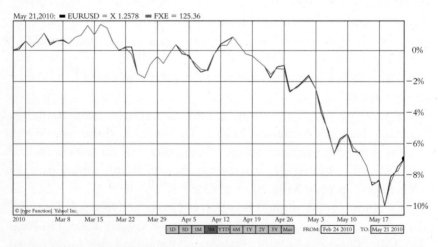

Figure 20.2 The FXE Is Closely Correlated with the Euro Exchange Rate to the Dollar
SOURCE: Created by Yahoo! Finance's Yahoo! Interactive Charting System.

CurrencyShares Japanese Yen Trust (FXY) ticked up from $106.08 to $106.29; and the PowerShares DB U.S. Dollar Index Bullish (UUP) rose from $23.95 to $24.64.

Aside from the FXE and the FXY, CurrencyShares offers ETFs in the Australian dollar (FXA), the British pound sterling (FXB), the Canadian dollar (FXC), the Mexican Peso (FXM), the Russian ruble (XRU), the Swedish krona (FXS), and the Swiss franc (FXF). That's a fair amount of geographic diversity.

Of course, there are many more exchange-traded funds and notes than those offered by CurrencyShares. WisdomTree offers several choices in emerging markets, like the WisdomTree Dreyfus Brazilian Real Fund (BZF), the Chinese Yuan Fund (CYB), the Indian Rupee Fund (ICN), and the South African Rand Fund (SZR), along with choices for the euro, yen, and New Zealand dollar.

In general, all currency ETFs and ETNs move like their represented currencies, so from an investment perspective, these products really expand your opportunities in the currency market. Also, with the ability to enter and exit these investment vehicles like stocks, you can move with the markets.

Jagerson notes, "Unlike the stock market, which has a long-term propensity to rise in value, currencies will often channel in the very long term. Stocks are driven by economic and business growth and tend to trend. Conversely, inflation and issues around monetary policy may prevent a currency from growing in value indefinitely."[29]

It's also important to know that currencies are affected by the same things that affect their countries' economies. If an economy's growth is tied to oil, like Norway, for example, the price movements of crude could affect the value of its currency. If an economy relies on trade, like Hong Kong, changes in imports and exports can impact its currency's value.

With influences like commodity prices and trade, it's imperative to keep your finger on the fundamental pulse. Thinking of grabbing a piece of the Australian dollar? You should know when the last time was that the interest rate changed, and where oil prices are trading. According to Jagerson, the Swiss franc is particularly sensitive to the Treasury's 10-year T-note. "When bond yields are rising, the Swissie falls, and vice versa," he writes. "Depending on interest rates, the value of the Swissie will frequently rise and fall with bond yields."[30]

The takeaway? Nothing is fixed. If you think you're holding cash, and its value won't change, you're wrong. Nearly every currency is floating, and fiat. That means movement—movement you can bank on.

In Standard & Poor's *Guide to Money and Investing*, you'll read, "Currency values of even the most stable economies change over time as traders are willing to pay more—or less—for dollars or pounds or euros or yen. For example, great demand for a nation's products means great demand for the currency needed to pay for those products."[31]

But as we've seen, even small moves can make investors big money—or they could be a prime way to protect your castle of wealth from modern-day barbarians.

Now that you know how currencies can fortify your portfolio, you'll need to know where to look. There are certain characteristics that you should be looking for in a currency, and they all deal with how rich an economy is.

Conversely, you need to know which ones to avoid . . .

Chapter 21

Arm Yourself with Ultra-Resource-Rich Countries

Four years ago, we pioneered a brand-new newsletter for the Taipan Publishing Group called *Material Profits*. It combined fundamental company analysis with the dynamic intricacies of the commodities markets. We found some companies that were absolutely stunning investors with their growth.

We pegged massive rises in the refining sector, noted extraordinary growth in the alternative energy industry, and unraveled the cyclical nature of agricultural companies. As the years went by, we noticed that more of the companies we found to be great recommendations were international companies—Canadian mining companies, Norwegian oil companies ... These were areas that some investors were overlooking, and that some analysts didn't understand.

We started adding these companies to our portfolio, and they provided great opportunities for gains. But we also noticed they were a natural hedge when the U.S. dollar started losing ground against the euro two years ago.

That's why we changed direction from a solely commodity-based focus to a global investment concept. To give you a sense of where the world is now, let's equate what happened in the financial world with what happened in the barbaric Dark Ages.

In 2008, a debt horde invaded the United States.

Pre-horde, the environment supported huge empires, like hedge funds, private equity funds, and big investment banks. Post-horde, all these leveraged realms are now dying. The aftermath of this debt-horde invasion led to global plundering and raiding of leveraged kingdoms all over the planet.

This is why the view from now looks so bleak. Almost everything looks beaten down because the U.S. debt horde has raided everything.

If we had to pick a specific date for when the U.S. debt horde invaded, it would probably be September 14, 2008. That was the day Lehman Brothers hurtled into bankruptcy, setting off a margin call to the system that led to global panic.

As credit markets froze and investors fled, almost every major asset class got crushed. The Dow Jones World Stock Index, the Reuters-CRB commodity index, the MSCI Emerging Markets Index, and West Texas Intermediate Crude all give example of the carnage.

The landscape also looks bleak because the mighty U.S. consumer has finally thrown in the towel.

We can see this from U.S. retail sales, which showed the sharpest annual decline since the government started keeping records in 1992.[1] (See Figure 21.1.)

The media was also filled with headlines like "More Americans Joining Military as Jobs Dwindle,"[2] "U.S. Loses Most Jobs since 1945,"[3] and "Struggling Retailers Press Struggling Landlords on Rent."[4]

Since the U.S. debt horde covered the globe with barbaric bands of pirates, anything with a direct link or a deep dependence on the free-spending, easy-credit, oxygen-rich conditions of the past is in peril.

Depressing stuff, no doubt. But the good news is, the news is not all gloomy!

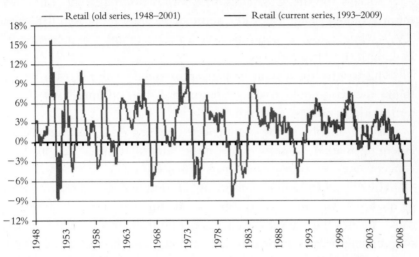

SA 3mo Moving Avg January 2008 to June 2009

——— Retail (old series, 1948–2001)   ——— Retail (current series, 1993–2009)

Figure 21.1 Retail Sales Year-to-Year Percent Change, 1948–2008
SOURCE: Shadow Government Statistics, Recessional Special Report, August 1, 2009, via the St. Louis Federal Reserve, www.shadowstats.com/article/depression-special-report.pdf.

Debt Horde Invasion Clears the Way for Real Wealth

Remember that after the Vikings came the age of trade expansion. To a certain extent, the old world of fat, elite financial empires had to crumble before the new world of lean, real wealth could rise.

So the thing to do now is get past the carnage, sift through the ash and debris, and identify the opportunities set to thrive in the next cycle—the age that is about to begin.

Because the U.S. consumer is still so burdened with debt, odds are many of these opportunities will arise outside the United States.

Curtis Mewbourne is a managing director with PIMCO, an investment management firm with close to $800 billion in assets. Mewbourne believes that emerging market countries can be divided up into "strong" and "weak" categories, and that the outlook for the stronger countries is bright.[5]

In contrast to the deeply indebted United States, the savers in the strong emerging markets (EM) category are still candidates for upgrading their standard of living.

"Success for the U.S. consumer," Mewbourne points out, "will mean avoiding losing his or her home or recently purchased flat-screen TV," while Chinese consumers, who have ample savings, are still looking to buy those things.

This is why for certain strongly positioned countries Mewbourne thinks the crisis could actually fast-forward their advance toward western world standards of wealth.

As we highlight the differences between U.S. consumers and emerging market consumers, it's important to revisit a key investing concept: the idea of *impaired* versus *unimpaired*.

The dictionary defines *impaired* as "Diminished, as in strength, value, or quality." An easy way to think about this is in terms of bouncing back. Areas of the market with permanent impairment have little chance of bouncing back. Unimpaired areas, in contrast, have the potential to come back even stronger than before.

In an interview with *Fortune* magazine, legendary investor Jim Rogers talked about his view of "impaired" versus "unimpaired" opportunities.

"Historically," Rogers said, "the way you make money in times like these is that you find things where the fundamentals are unimpaired. The fundamentals of GM are impaired. The fundamentals of Citigroup are impaired. . . .

"Virtually the only asset class I know where the fundamentals are not impaired—in fact, where they are actually improving—is commodities. . . .

"Farmers cannot get a loan to buy fertilizer right now. Nobody's going to get a loan to open a zinc or a lead mine. Meanwhile, every day the supply of commodities shrinks more and more."[6]

Like Mewbourne, Rogers is also bullish on China and Chinese stocks.

There is no question of China's gravity in the international scene. Demand there is so strong and relentless that you absolutely can't talk about international investing without talking about China.

There has already been a massive amount of money made from domestic-demand-linked China plays. Everything from oil and coal to life insurance and casinos has given investors something to smile about. Those kinds of play do often come from outside of China, particularly from commodity-based economies, like steel from Brazil, coal from Australia, oil from Canada.

There are many great equity opportunities in these unimpaired countries ... But given the huge sweep of what's happened, one of the most powerful ways to take advantage would be through a basket of countries and/or currencies.

Ultra-Resource-Rich Investments

It's simple, really. Commodity prices have bubbled in the past decade. Oil went from less than $12 a barrel in 1998 to more than $147 in 2008. Copper went from about $0.73 per pound to nearly $4.00 a pound. Wheat jumped from around $120 per metric ton to an astonishing $439 in 2008. (See Figure 21.2.)

What do these price increases mean for producers? Easy money. Countries like Norway, Australia, and Canada have been raking in the dough, and socking it away in massive foreign exchange reserves.

And when a country has significant reserves saved, its economy is considerably healthier and can weather a crisis better than other countries. So if we translate that strength into the performance of a country's currency, we notice that strong foreign exchange reserves equate to a stronger currency.

Figure 21.2   CRB Spot Index Shows Prices Have Risen
SOURCE: SeekingAlpha.com, September 22, 2008.

A basket of currencies based on this principle would be a fantastic way to both stay invested in the market and preserve your wealth. In fact, such a basket already exists. It's offered through Everbank and it's called the Ultra Resource Index CD. (See Figure 21.3.)

If Jim Rogers is right, and commodities are one of the few areas where the long-term fundamentals are unimpaired in terms of demand and the ability to bounce back, then that logic should apply to the currencies of these resource-rich countries, too.

One of the surprising aspects of the 2008 meltdown was a sharp rise in the U.S. dollar, as panicked U.S.-based investors sold their international investments.

This massive selling led to a short squeeze that pushed the dollar and Treasury bonds to sky-high levels. But we know that this period of artificial dollar strength cannot last.

Even more reason to look at the currencies of resource-rich countries with strong cash balances. They will be the true champions in the landscape ahead.

Here are some other reasons to look at international markets.

Diversification is the same thing as saying "Don't put all your eggs in one basket." Basically, if you're only invested in one thing, and something happens to negatively affect that investment, there's only one result—you lose money.

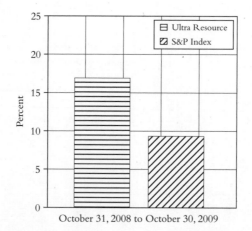

Figure 21.3   Performance of Ultra Resource Index CD Compared to S&P
Source: Everbank.com.

There's a popular investment education website called Investopedia. A recent article talked about diversification. It said, "The time to practice disciplined investing with a diversified portfolio is before diversification becomes a necessity. By the time an average investor 'reacts' to the market, 80 percent of the damage is done."[7]

A smart way to diversify is to incorporate some international investments into your portfolio, and we'll talk about a couple specific ideas to help you further vary the types of investments for your portfolio. International markets can also provide above-average returns.

For example, one of our group's international financial trips was to Spain, where we'd set up an interview with the country's second-largest bank, BBVA Group (NYSE: BBVA).

In the interview, we learned that Spanish banks didn't buy up those toxic subprime derivatives that helped cause the global financial crisis. We also learned that BBVA Group had great exposure to emerging markets in Latin America—in countries that were still growing through the crisis.

That's why, when share prices across the financial sector got whacked, we saw that BBVA Group's stock was becoming undervalued. We first told our readers about this company in late October 2008 at a time when most analysts were telling investors to run from financial stocks. BBVA Group was trading for $10.86 a share. A year later, it was trading for $19.78, a gain of more than 82 percent.

Just to give you a comparison of how this international company performed in that year, Bank of America (NYSE: BAC) lost some 37 percent and Citigroup (NYSE: C) lost more than 65 percent.

QVM Group, an investment adviser, says that emerging markets "handily outperformed" the United States for the 20 years leading up to the financial crisis. Their research found that "$1 invested in emerging markets on December 31, 1987, would have been worth $10.89 as of December 31, 2007. The same $1 would have grown to $5.69 invested in the U.S. market."[8]

That means that global markets can actually be a hedge against downturns in the U.S. market. What's a hedge? It's an investment that reduces the risk of adverse price movements in an asset.

For example, gold is considered a hedge against the U.S. dollar. When the value of the dollar falls, the value of gold climbs. Some international currencies are viewed the same way, because when the dollar falls, other currencies appear to climb in value.

So how do you know where to start looking? That QVM Group research also said that "the same $1 would have grown only to $3.01 if invested in the entire world excluding the U.S."

That means that not every international market is a good place to invest. Here are some things to look for in a stable international market.

Four Principles of Rich Countries

There are four principles of rich countries.

1. *Resource rich.* You want to know that a country is resource rich—fossil fuels, timber, uranium, base metals, and the like. Commodities are one of the few areas where the long-term fundamentals are unimpaired in terms of demand and the ability to bounce back. Resource-rich countries raked in the dough, and socked it away in massive foreign exchange reserves.

2. *Finance rich.* In the twenty-first century, new financial hubs will rise and old financial hubs will fall. The world's center of gravity will shift toward Asia, as new wealth is created and dynamic growth unfolds. This will benefit two currencies specifically, one associated with one of the most powerful free-market cultures on earth and the other belonging to the "Switzerland of Asia."

3. *Freedom rich.* Each year, the Heritage Foundation and the *Wall Street Journal* compile a ranking of the world's freest countries, in terms of political and economic freedom. The amount of freedom an economy has to be creative and innovative goes a long way to help countries and markets adjust to financial crises.

4. *Cash rich.* In a world where debt is a burden, cash is king. While the countries we look at in this chapter can be considered rich in many unconventional ways, they are rich in the old-fashioned way, too. More than one of them have powerful sovereign wealth funds with anywhere from tens of billions to hundreds of billions in cash, which adds to the attractiveness of these countries' currencies and overall economic health.

We've chosen five countries that represent the best of these qualities: Canada, Norway, Australia, Hong Kong, and Singapore. Let's take a look.

These five countries were chosen because they rank very highly in one or more of our four principles of rich markets. This is by no means an exhaustive list, and you'll notice that traditional emerging markets aren't on this list, like Brazil and India.

Emerging markets have their place in a diverse portfolio, but some might come with more risk than a traditional investor is looking for. Some might have smaller markets. Some might have high inflation. Some might have geopolitical issues that make the economy more volatile.

If you're interested in emerging markets, you should keep these in mind. In this chapter, we'd like to address a safer way to invest internationally.

O, Canada: Land of Rich Resources

Canada—our neighbor to the north. Canada has a very similar economy to that of the United States, but there are some big differences. The United States is Canada's largest trading partner, and the largest supplier of foreign energy. In fact, the United States consumes about 80 percent of Canada's exports.[9]

At first glance, you might think that this was a bad thing, since the United States went into a recession and demand for many things fell drastically.

But Canada is incredibly resource rich, and demand from outside the United States has helped to pull the country back up. Additionally, according to the CIA's World Factbook, "Canada's major banks, however, emerged from the financial crisis of 2008–2009 among the strongest in the world, owing to the country's tradition of conservative lending practices and strong capitalization."[10]

Over 3.6 trillion cubic feet of natural gas is exported every year. Nickel is a top metallic mineral produced, with shipments valued at $7.6 billion. Copper production is over $2.03 billion, and gold exports top $8.2 billion.

In total, $103 billion worth of mineral production takes place in Canada, when we include smelting and refining of domestic and imported ores and concentrates, recycling, steel and aluminum production, and oil sands mining.[11]

Because these resources attract buyers around the world—including, of course, the United States—Canada has about C$56.7 billion (US $56.57 billion) in foreign exchange reserves and assets (as of April 2010).[12] That provides for some great capitalization, and allows the country to come out of the financial crisis without having to print new money.

What does this mean for the country's currency? The Canadian dollar has had a nice appreciation compared to the U.S. dollar—25.9 percent from March 2009 through March 2010, and 15.7 percent between April 1, 2009 and June 1, 2009 alone.[13] (See Figure 21.4.)

Canada has the lowest net debt-to-GDP ratios of all the G8 members. That means that the country doesn't have to print its way out of an economic crisis.

It has taken measures to ensure bank liquidity, but not by injecting newly minted money into the system. It's bought up $75 billion of insured mortgages, for one thing, generously cut interest rates, and increased access to longer-term financing.[14]

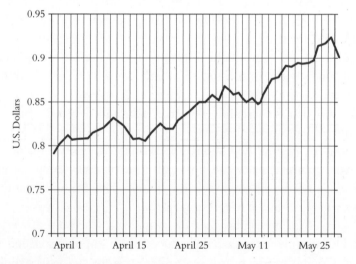

Figure 21.4 Canadian Dollar Soars
SOURCE: CBCnews.com.

These points set up a nice strength argument for the economy and its currency.

Norway: Former Vikings Turned Safe Haven

Norway is an interesting mix of free markets and government intervention. The government controls the oil sector, as it contributes about 30 percent to the country's revenue.[15] But Norway saves that revenue in a sovereign wealth fund that now reaches into the hundreds of billions of dollars.

That means that when oil prices fell and the economy took a tumble, Norway was able to help mitigate the economic costs, and keep its market and financial system very liquid.

The country also decided to stay out of the eurozone—the monetary union that adopted the euro as its currency—but it is a member of the European Economic Area, which means large amounts of trade flow between Norway and Europe. It uses the krone as its currency.

Norway is the world's seventh-largest oil exporter and, as noted before, the petroleum industry accounts for more than 30 percent of its GDP. It has natural gas fields, high hydropower capacity, and an abundance of forests, minerals, and fish. Norwegians enjoy the fifth-highest GDP per capita in the world, mainly due to the massive oil revenues the country sees each year.[16] Those oil revenues have given the international reserve assets and gold worth NOK 293.2 billion (US $49.23 billion) at the end of February 2010.[17]

Falling oil prices and inflation negatively affect this oil-export economy. Even though the krone exchange rate had been weaker than expected, its low value has helped to mitigate the effects of the international downturn on the country's economy.

Norges Bank's executive board decided in mid–December 2008 to reduce its key policy rate by 1.75 percentage points to 3 percent. This was in the heart of the panic, and it wasn't the only cut. At a low, Norway cut rates to 1.5 percent. Since then, Norway has followed Australia and has begun to raise rates again. In mid–December 2009, the country raised rates to 1.75 percent.[18]

That said, the Norwegian krone appreciated nicely against the U.S. dollar between March 2009 and March 2010, and also had a significant pullback. But oil prices are back on the rise. They topped $85 a barrel in early April, which will help both this currency and Norway's market. Still, the currency climbed 18.6 percent against the U.S. dollar.[19] That helped the country's market perform very well in the same time frame.

Australia: Boy Wonder of the Natural World

Now let's move on to Australia. It's one of our favorite markets to talk about, because there are so many things going for this country.

The CIA's *World Factbook* says, "Emphasis on reforms, low inflation, a housing market boom, and growing ties with China were key factors over the course of a 17-year economic expansion that ended with the recent global financial crisis."[20]

But what's really changed? While things were worse during the financial crisis, economic data shows that Australia is in a good place. Australia still has strong ties with China, and they're continuing to grow. Inflation fell to 1.9 percent last year from 4.4 percent in 2008.[21] There is still room for improvement: unemployment jumped in 2009, along with public debt.

There are some other good things going for Australia. It is a massive exporter of coal, iron ore, gold, uranium, and nickel. The country also was the first to start raising interest rates after the global financial crisis, which allows for currency strength and stability. And Australia has $44.4 billion (US$41.23 billion) in foreign exchange and gold reserves.[22]

Here are the statistics:

- *Coal*: Largest exporter of coal and fourth-largest producer of coal behind China, United States. and India.
- *Iron ore*: Third-largest supplier after China and Brazil.
- *Gold*: Fourth-largest producer after China, South Africa, and the United States.
- *Uranium*: Second-largest supplier after Canada.
- *Nickel*: Third-largest producer after Russia and Canada.[23]

While the commodity boom was in full swing, Australia's economy was growing at an average rate of 3.6 percent a year. With that rise came the appreciation of the Australian dollar.

Of course, when commodity prices tumbled, this currency also fell. When financial institutions around the world seized up, Australia was forced to use some of its currency reserves to inject liquidity into its system. Australia also started slashing its interest rates, which had been steadily climbing along with its currency.

That might have done the job, though, and late last year, Australia became the first country to begin raising its rates after the financial crisis. No doubt that's due to its strong currency reserves and massive commodity reserves.

And this is the result: The Australian dollar has rocketed higher against the U.S. dollar, up 41 percent from March 2009 through March 2010.[24] And that, in turn, translates to a higher market.

Hong Kong: King of the Asian Financial World

Moving on to Hong Kong, the *World Factbook* says, "Hong Kong has a free market economy highly dependent on international trade and finance—the value of goods and services trade, including the sizable share of re-exports, is more than four times GDP."[25]

What are *re-exports*? Re-exports are foreign goods exported in the same state as previously imported. Hong Kong is a through port for many goods. There's so much traffic that Hong Kong is the world's eleventh-largest trading entity. This tiny island is only 426 square miles, less than half the size of Rhode Island.

As you might expect, the global downturn hit Hong Kong pretty hard. This export-based economy saw exports drop more than 10 percent last year. But guess what? Hong Kong's largest trading partner is China, and China continued to grow through the global economic crisis, and is expected to grow even faster this year.

Here are the statistics released by the Hong Kong Monetary Authority:

- *Services industry*: 92.3 percent of GDP.
- *Industry*: 7.6 percent of GDP.

- *Inflation*: −0.3 percent.
- *Unemployment*: 5.9 percent.
- *Forex reserves and assets*: $255.8 billion.[26]

Hong Kong is a highly capitalistic economy, and has been ranked as the freest economy in the world in the Index of Economic Freedom for 16 consecutive years.[27]

As previously stated, Hong Kong is the world's eleventh-largest trading entity.[28] The country is so small and has so few natural resources of its own, it must import most of its food and raw materials.

Being the site of a large number of corporate headquarters and the Hong Kong Stock Exchange for the Asia-Pacific region, this area has become an important center for international finance and trade. And with $258.2 billion in foreign exchange reserves and assets (at the end of March 2010), Hong Kong is uniquely equipped to handle the current economic crisis.[29]

Hong Kong has an incredibly stable currency, which may be one of the reasons the Hong Kong dollar is the ninth-most-traded currency in the world.[30]

But it's different from the other countries highlighted in this chapter. The Hong Kong Monetary Authority rigidly manages the exchange rate using an automatic interest rate adjustment mechanism.

Recently, Hong Kong has been dropping interest rates to limit demand growth in its currency. Rates will automatically increase if demand drops, thereby creating stability and limiting speculation.[31] The difference between the highest point and the lowest point from March 2009 to March 2010 is less than 0.4 percent. That's stability.[32]

The result of all the trade that passes through Hong Kong is a robust stock market. Interestingly, this market also gives international investors access to Chinese companies. Many Chinese companies list shares on both the Hong Kong exchange and the Shanghai exchange. This has also boosted Hong Kong's market higher.

Singapore: The Switzerland of Asia

Lastly, we look at Singapore. As small as Hong Kong is, Singapore is even smaller—only 274 square miles, less than the size of Memphis, Tennessee.

For all that, Singapore is one of the most successful free-market economies in the world. What's even more interesting is the lack of corruption in the government and the financial system.

But like Hong Kong, Singapore is a champion of trade. Singapore has no natural resources of its own and has turned itself into a highly developed market-based economy, which revolves around extended trade.

It's the middleman with the one of the busiest ports in the world, and a significant amount of the country's GDP depends on exports from the refining of imported oil and from manufactured goods.

But Singapore has been rated as the most business-friendly economy in the world, with thousands of foreign expatriates working in multinational corporations—and that's making the country one of the biggest financial hubs in Asia. Additionally, advances in technology have put Singapore on the cutting edge of innovation.

Here's a closer look at Singapore's statistics:

- One of the busiest ports in the world with connections to over 600 other ports in 123 different countries[33]
- Handles one-fifth of the world's shipping containers[34]
- Rated most business-friendly economy in the world and second-freest economy in the world[35]

Interestingly, Hong Kong is Singapore's largest export partner.

The city-state is also the fifth-wealthiest economy in the world in terms of purchasing power, and holds $196.4 billion in Forex reserves and gold (as of March 2010).[36]

The Singapore economy has weakened over the course of 2008 and into 2009, alongside the turmoil in financial markets and a severe drop in global economic activity and trade.

The Monetary Authority of Singapore has adopted a policy stance of zero percent appreciation of the Singapore dollar exchange rate.[37] This means that in a situation where inflation is dropping, as it is now in Singapore, its currency will maintain strength and stability, without putting exporting power in jeopardy.

But as you can see in Figure 21.5, Singapore's currency has been appreciating—10.9 percent between March 2009 and March 2010.[38] That's mainly because the U.S. dollar has been underperforming other currencies.

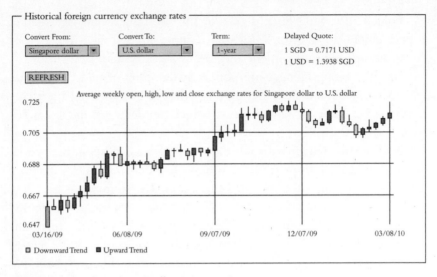

Figure 21.5   Singapore Dollar Rises
SOURCE: Everbank, www.everbank.com/002CurrencySingapore.aspx.

One of the ways to keep its currency from appreciating too quickly is to cut interest rates, which the country has been doing for the past couple years.

How to Play Ultra-Resource-Rich Countries and Currencies

Now that we've armed you with the four principles of rich countries, and told you about five specific countries that fit these characteristics, what investments are available to take advantage of this information?

The good thing is that there are a number of new and easy ways to invest internationally. Some are easier and less risky than others. First, let's revisit exchange-traded funds (ETFs).

What is an ETF? It's a security that tracks an index, a commodity, or a basket of assets like an index fund, but trades like a stock on an exchange. Over the past few years, the number of ETFs that pull together international companies has grown, and there are even a number of country-specific ETFs. The most well-known country-specific ETFs come from a company called Invesco PowerShares. And some of the countries examined in this chapter are represented through country-specific ETFs.

The EWC is the iShares MSCI Canada Index Fund. The fund tracks the performance of the Canadian equity market. It does this by putting together a basket of public Canadian companies—100 to be exact. The EWA follows Australia, the EWH follows Hong Kong, and the EWS follows Singapore.

There are also ETFs that invest in multiple countries and emerging markets. You can find a list of these on Yahoo! Finance, or on specific fund sites like iShares.com and PowerShares.com.

There are also currency ETFs that follow the performance of specific currencies. Many are offered by a company called CurrencyShares, like the FXA that tracks the Australian dollar, or the FXC that tracks the Canadian dollar. There are others, of course, and you can also find them at Yahoo! Finance.

Then there are American Depositary Shares (ADSs) and American Depositary Receipts (ADRs). These are international companies listed on a U.S. exchange.

Sometimes these ADRs and ADSs represent more than one share of the company, so do your homework as to what you're actually buying. For example, BHP Billiton, Australia's well-known mining company, offers its ADR at a ratio of 1 to 2, meaning that every share of BHP you buy on the New York Stock Exchange actually represents two shares of the company. By contrast, Statoil, a Norwegian oil company, has a 1 to 1 ratio.

A good resource that you can use to search for ADRs in a number of countries is, simply, ADR.com, run by J.P. Morgan.

Other choices for investors include international currency-based CDs, currency futures, and currency options. These investments can be very expensive, and both futures and options can be fairly risky.

The number of methods for U.S. investors to diversify with international investments grows every year. That means two things: lots of opportunity and lots of risk. But you can use the four principles of rich countries as a guide to selecting strong and growing countries.

Notes

Introduction

1. Daniel Wagner and Dan Strumpf, "Goldman E-mails Show How Crash Turned into Cash," Yahoo Finance, April 24, 2010.

2. Ibid.

3. Sun Tzu, *The Art of War*, trans. Lionel Giles (El Paso, TX: El Paso Norte Press, 2009), 6.

Chapter 1 Attila the Hun: The Scourge of God

1. Christopher Haas, "Embassy to Attila: Priscus of Panium," Fragment 1, Villa-nova University, www29.homepage.villanova.edu/christopher.haas/embassy .htm; based on C. W. Müller, ed., *Fragmenta Historicorum Graecorum, by Priscus of Panium* (Paris, 1848–1853).

2. Edward Gibbons, "The Character, Conquests, and Court of Attila, King of the Huns.—Death of Theodosius the Younger.—Elevation of Marcian to the Empire of the East," ch. 34 in *The History of the Decline and Fall of the Roman Empire* (New York: Penguin Books, 2001).

3. Patrick Howarth, "Life of Saint Hypatius, Callinicus of Rufinianae," in *Attila, King of the Huns: Man and Myth* (New York: Barnes and Noble, 1995), 49.

4. Richard Gordon, "Battle of Châlons: Attila the Hun Versus Flavius Aëtius," *Military History* magazine, December 2003.

373

5. Patrick Howarth, *Attila, King of the Huns* (New York: Barnes & Noble, 1995), 191–192.

6. Gibbons, "Character, Conquests, and Court of Attila."

7. Gordon, "Battle of Châlons."

8. Christopher Haas, "Embassy to Attila: Priscus of Panium," Fragment 1b, Villanova University, www29.homepage.villanova.edu/christopher.haas/ embassy.htm; based on C. W. Müller, ed., *Fragmenta Historicorum Graecorum, by Priscus of Panium* (Paris, 1848–1853).

9. Gibbons, "Character, Conquests, and Court of Attila."

10. Haas, "Embassy to Attila," Fragment 5.

11. Ibid.

12. Gibbons, "Character, Conquests, and Court of Attila."

13. Justin Fox, "Henry Paulson—Person of the Year 2008," *Time* magazine, December 17, 2008, Time.com.

14. Sara Lepro, "Documents: Paulson Forced 9 Bank CEOs into Bailout," Associated Press, *San Francisco Chronicle*, June 14, 2009.

15. David Ellis, "Citigroup Suffers $7.6 Billion Loss," CNNMoney.com, January 19, 2010, http://money.cnn.com/2010/01/19/news/companies/citigroup/ index.htm.

16. Edward Gibbons, "Invasion of Gaul by Attila.—He Is Repulsed by Aëtius and the Visigoths.—Attila Invades and Evacuates Italy.—The Deaths of Attila, Aëtius, and Valentinian the Third," ch. 35 in *The History of the Decline and Fall of the Roman Empire*, (New York: Penguin Books, 2001).

17. Ibid.

18. Ibid.

19. "US Faces Global Funding Crisis, Warns Merrill Lynch," *Daily Telegraph*, July 16, 2008, www.telegraph.co.uk/finance/newsbysector/banksandfinance/2793309/ US-faces-global-funding-crisis-warns-Merrill-Lynch.html.

20. Zhao Yidi and Kevin Hamlin, "China Shuns Paulson's Free Market Push as Meltdown Burns U.S.," *Bloomberg*, September 24, 2008. www.bloomberg .com/apps/news?pid=20601087&sid=aCl7bFUJzWRk.

21. Gibbons, "Invasion of Gaul."

22. Gordon, "Battle of Châlons."

23. Gibbons, "Invasion of Gaul."

24. Gordon, "Battle of Châlons."

25. Charles Christopher Mierow, trans., *The Gothic History of Jordanes* (Cambridge: Speculum Historiale, 1966), ch. 40, 209.

26. Gibbons, "Invasion of Gaul."

27. Johann Peter Kirsch, "Pope St. Leo I (the Great)," *The Catholic Encyclopedia*, vol. 9 (New York: Robert Appleton Company, 1910), retrieved from New Advent, www.newadvent.org/cathen/09154b.htm (accessed March 9, 2010).

28. John Man, *Attila: The Barbarian King who Challenged Rome* (New York: Thomas Dunne Books, 2005), 264.

29. Haas, "Embassy to Attila," Fragment 23.

30. Hector Munro Chadwick, *The Heroic Age* (London: Cambridge University Press, 1926), 39, n. 1.

31. Michael Babcock, *The Night Attila Died: Solving the Murder of Attila the Hun* (New York: Berkley Publishing Group, 2005).

Chapter 2 Charlemagne: The Clandestine Barbarian

1. Samuel Epes Turner, trans., *Einhard: The Life of Charlemagne* (New York: Harper & Brothers, 1880), ch. 23; retrieved from Internet Medieval Sourcebook, www.fordham.edu/halsall/basis/einhard.html (accessed January 1999).

2. "Battle of Tours," *Britannica Online Encyclopedia*, wwwa.britannica.com/eb/article-9060566 (accessed February 25, 2010).

3. Derek Wilson, *Charlemagne: A Biography* (New York: Vintage Books/Random House, 2005), 27.

4. Edward Gibbons, "Invasion of Gaul by Attila.—He Is Repulsed by Aëtius and the Visigoths.—Attila Invades and Evacuates Italy.—The Deaths of Attila, Aëtius, and Valentinian the Third," ch. 35 in *The History of the Decline and Fall of the Roman Empire* (New York: Penguin Books, 2001).

5. Wilson, *Charlemagne: A Biography*, 21.

6. Thomas Shahan and E. Macpherson, "Charlemagne," in *The Catholic Encyclopedia* (New York: Robert Appleton Company, 1908), New Advent: www.newadvent.org/cathen/03610c.htm (accessed February 25, 2010).

7. Robert Levine, trans., "A Thirteenth-Century Life of Charlemagne," vol. 3, ch. 2 of *Les Grandes Chroniques* (Boston University, 1991), www.bu.edu/english/levine/charles3.htm.

8. E. S. Browning, "Exorcising Ghosts of Octobers Past," *Wall Street Journal*, October 15, 2007, C1–C2, http://online.wsj.com/article/SB119239926667758592.html?mod=mkts_main_news_hs_h.

9. Ibid.

10. Federal Reserve, "30-Day AA Nonfinancial Commercial Paper Interest Rate," www.federalreserve.gov/releases/h15/data/Monthly/H15_NFCP_M1.txt.

11. Edward Gibbons, "Introduction, Worship, and Persecution of Images.—Revolt of Italy and Rome.—Temporal Dominion of the Popes.—Conquest of Italy by the Franks.—Establishment of Images.—Character and Coronation of Charlemagne.—Restoration and Decay of the Roman Empire in the West.—Independence Of Italy.—Constitution Of The Germanic Body," ch. 49 in *The History of the Decline and Fall of the Roman Empire* (New York: Penguin Books, 2001).

12. Wilson, *Charlemagne: A Biography*, 6.

13. Susan Wise Bauer, *The History of the Medieval World: From the Conversion of Constantine to the First Crusade* (New York/London: W.W. Norton, 2010), 376.

14. Wilson, *Charlemagne: A Biography*, 41.

15. Turner, *Einhard: The Life of Charlemagne*, ch. 6, "Lombard War."

16. Richard Eskow, "Greenspan's Testimony: Will the 'Maestro' Face the Music?" *Huffington Post*, April 2, 2010. www.huffingtonpost.com/rj-eskow/greenspans-testimony-will_b_526403.html.

17. Charles Henry Robinson, *The Conversion of Europe* (New York: Longmans, Green, and Co., 1917), 389

18. Wilson, *Charlemagne: A Biography*, 41.

19. Ibid.

20. Ibid., 79.

21. Will Durant, "Charlemagne the King," from *History of Civilization, Vol. III: The Age of Faith* 1950), retrieved at the Knighthood, Chivalry, & Tournaments Resource Library, 2000, www.chronique.com/Library/MedHistory/charlemagne.htm

22. Robert Collins, *Charlemagne* (London: Macmillan 1998), 153.

23. A.J. Grant, ed. and trans., *Early Lives of Charlemagne by Eginhard and the Monk of St. Gall* (London: Chatto & Windus, 1926), ch. 26, 90.

24. Quoted in Sewell Chan, "Bill Offered to Restrict Big Banks," *New York Times*, March 4, 2010, http://query.nytimes.com/gst/fullpage.html?res=9802E1D8173CF937A35750C0A9669D8B63&sec=&spon=&pagewanted=2.

25. Durant, "Charlemagne the King."

26. Charles Cawley, "Medieval Lands," Foundation for Medieval Genealogy, http://fmg.ac/Projects/MedLands/CAROLINGIANS.htm#_ftnref91.

Chapter 3   The Vikings: Savage Pirates, Savvy Traders

1. Thomas J. Craughwell, *How the Barbarian Invasions Shaped the Modern World: The Vikings, Vandals, Huns, Mongols, Goths, and Tartars who Razed the Old World and Formed the New* (Beverly, MA: Fair Winds Press, 2008), 131–132.

2. Ibid., 131.

3. Derek Wilson, *Charlemagne: A Biography* (New York: Vintage Books/Random House, 2005), 123.

4. Craughwell, *How the Barbarian Invasions Shaped the Modern World*, 136.

5. Ibid., 131.

6. Jonathan Clements, *A Brief History of the Vikings: The Last Pagans or the First Modern Europeans?* (Philadelphia/London: Running Press, 2005), 52.

7. Robert Ferguson, *The Vikings: A History* (New York: Viking/Penguin Group, 2009), 64–65.

8. Clements, *A Brief History of the Vikings*, 9.

9. Craughwell, *How the Barbarian Invasions Shaped the Modern World*, 171.

10. David Willis McCullough, *Wars of the Irish Kings: A Thousand Years of Struggle, from the Age of Myth through the Reign of Queen Elizabeth I* (New York: Three Rivers Press, 2002), 86.

11. Craughwell, *How the Barbarian Invasions Shaped the Modern World*, 149.

12. Ibid., 152.

13. George Holmes, *The Oxford History of Medieval Europe* (Oxford/New York: Oxford University Press, 2001), 101.

14. Craughwell, *How the Barbarian Invasions Shaped the Modern World*, 177.

15. Thomas Cahill, *Mysteries of the Middle Ages: And the Beginning of the Modern World* (New York: First Anchor Books/Random House, 2006), 105.

16. Alistair Horne, *The Fall of Paris: The Siege and the Commune 1870–1871* (London: Pan, 2002).

17. Craughwell, *How the Barbarian Invasions Shaped the Modern World*, 177.

18. Ibid., 231.

Chapter 4   Genghis Khan: Mighty Warrior

1. Thomas J. Craughwell, *The Rise and Fall of the Second Largest Empire in History: How Genghis Khan's Mongols Almost Conquered the World* (Beverly, MA: Fair Winds Press, 2010), 33.

2. Ata-Malik Juvaini, *Genghis Khan: The History of the World Conqueror*, trans. J. A. Boyle, Manchester, UK: Manchester University Press, 1958, 1997), 36.

3. Sir Henry Howorth, Preface in *History of the Mongols: From the 9th to the 19th Century* (London: Longmans, Green and Co., 1876), x.

4. "Genghis Khan." *Encyclopædia Britannica*, 2010, Retrieved from Encyclopædia Britannica Online, www.britannica.com/EBchecked/topic/229093/Genghis-Khan (accessed April 2, 2010).

5. Juvaini, *Genghis Khan*, 21.

6. Craughwell, *The Rise and Fall*, 37.

7. Ibid., 47.

8. Ibid., 60.

9. Leo de Hartog, *Genghis Khan: Conqueror of the World* (London/New York: Tauris Parke Paperbacks, 2004, 2006), 140.

10. Edward Gibbons, "Conquests of Zingis Khan and the Moguls from China to Poland.—Escape of Constantinople and the Greeks.—Origin of the Ottoman Turks in Bithynia.—Reigns and Victories of Othman, Orchan, Amurath the First, and Bajazet the First.—Foundation and Progress of the Turkish Monarchy in Asia and Europe.—Danger of Constantinople and the Greek Empire," ch. 64 in *The History of the Decline and Fall of the Roman Empire* (New York: Penguin Books, 2001).

11. Craughwell, *The Rise and Fall*, 68.

12. Paul Ratchnevsky, *Genghis Khan: His Life and Legacy*, trans. and ed. Thomas N. Haining (Oxford: Blackwell, 1991), 152.

13. George Lane, *Genghis Khan and Mongol Rule*, (Westport, CT: Greenwood Press, 2004), 30.

14. David Morgan, *The Mongols*, 2nd ed. (Malden, MA: Blackwell Publishing, 2007), 55.

15. Craughwell, *The Rise and Fall*, 18.

16. Amy Chua, *Day of Empire: How Hyperpowers Rise to Global Dominance—And Why They Fall* (New York/Toronto: Anchor Books/Random House, 2007), 89.

17. John Masson Smith Jr., "The Mongols and the Silk Road," in *Silk Road Newsletter*, www.silk-road.com/newsletter/volumeonenumberone/mongols.html.

18. Ibid.

19. Lane, *Genghis Khan and Mongol Rule*, 29.

20. Morgan, *The Mongols*, 54.

21. Ratchnevsky, *Genghis Khan: His Life and Legacy*, 152.

22. Bret Stephens, "For the Sake of One Man," *Wall Street Journal*, July 17, 2007.

23. Ata-Malik Juvaini, *Genghis Kahn*, 22.

24. George R. Goethals, Georgia Sorenson, and James MacGregor Burns, Encyclopedia of Leadership, Volume 1 (Thousand Oaks, CA, and London, UK: Berkshire Publishing Group, 2004), 570.

25. Gibbons, "Conquests of Zingis Khan and the Moguls from China to Poland."

Chapter 5 The Brotherhood of Power

1. E. Michael Gerli and Samuel G. Armistead, Medieval Iberia: An Encyclopedia, (Routledge, 2003), 143.

2. Ibid.

3. Stephen Quinn and William Roberds, "The Bank of Amsterdam and the Leap to Central Bank Money," American Economic Review Papers and Proceedings, (2007).

4. John Sandrock, "The Currency Collector, Ancient Chinese Cash Notes — The World's First Paper Money," Part II, The Currency Collector, www .thecurrencycollector.com/pdfs/Ancient_Chinese_Cash_Notes_-_The_Worlds_ First_Paper_Money_-_Part_II.pdf, 1.

5. Bamber Gascogione, "History of Money, Better Than Barter," HistoryWorld 1, www.historyworld.net/wrldhis/PlainTextHistories.asp?historyid=ab14.

6. Riksbank.com, "History," Sveriges Riksbank (March 23, 2009), 1, www.riksbank .com/templates/Page.aspx?id=9159.

7. Eric D. Butler, "The Enemy Within the Empire: A Short History of the Bank of England," Australian League of Rights. New Times, 1941.

8. Bank of England, "History," www.bankofengland.co.uk/about/history/ index.htm.

9. R. O. Roberts, "Financial Crisis and the Swansea 'Branch Bank' of England, 1826," National Library of Wales Journal, Vol. XI/1, 1959.

10. "The Rothschild Story: A Golden Era Ends for A Secretive Dynasty," The Independent UK, April 16, 2004.

11. http://quotes.liberty-tree.ca/quote/nathan_mayer_rothschild_quote_4f94.

12. Nicolas Apostolou and D. Larry Crumbley, "The Tally Stick, The First Internal Control," ACFEI News.

13. "The Personal Rule of Charles 1, By Act of Oblivion," Allempires.com Online History Community.

14. Rob Kirby, "G20 U.S. Dollar Fiat Currency Smoke and Mirrors Manipulation," MarketOracle.com, April 3, 2009.

15. "John Law," Columbia Encylopedia, 6th ed., 2008, www.encyclopedia.com/ topic/John_Law.aspx.

16. "Episodes of Hyperinflation," San Jose State University, Department of Economics, www.sjsu.edu/faculty/watkins/hyper.htm.

17. Jon Moen, "John Law and the Mississippi Bubble: 1718–1720," Mississippi Historical Society, October 2001, http://mshistory.k12.ms.us/articles/70/john-law-and-the-mississippi-bubble-1718-1720.

18. John E. Sandrock, "John Law's Banque Royale and the Mississippi Bubble," The Currency Collector, http://www.thecurrencycollector.com/pdfs/John_Laws_Banque_Royale.pdf.

19. Garrett Johnson, "That's Not How Bubbles Work," *Huffington Post*, July 20, 2009.

20. Sandrock, "John Law's Banque Royale."

21. Ibid.

22. Sseezi-Cheeye Teddy, "The Uganda Tax Base is Not Sufficient to Sustain Its Economy," *Economist*, May 22, 2008.

23. www.revolutionary-war-and-beyond.com/thomas-jefferson-quotes-5.html.

24. University of Virginia, "Thomas Jefferson on Politics & Government: Money and Banking," compiled by Eyler Robert Coates Sr., http://etext.virginia.edu/jefferson/quotations/jeff1325.htm.

25. Ibid.

26. Ibid.

27. "A History of Central Banking in the United States," The Federal Reserve Bank of Minneapolis.

28. "Bank of the United States," Answers Corporation, 2010.

29. David Cowen, "The First Bank of the United States," Economic History Services, EH.net, Net, March 2, 2010.

30. Robert Wright and David. J. Cowen, *Financial Founding Fathers: The Men Who Made America Rich*, chapter 2: "The Creator: Alexander Hamilton" (Chicago: University of Chicago Press, 2006).

31. "William Duer," *Virtualology*, 2001. http://virtualology.com/apwilliamduer/.

32. John P. Foley, ed., *The Jeffersonian Cyclopedia, A Comprehensive Collection of the Views of Thomas Jefferson*, Funk & Wagnalls (1900) 668.

Chapter 6   Race to the Bottom Line

1. Luke Burgess, "How to Profit from U.S. Inflation," *Wealth Daily*, October 9, 2009.

2. Eric Dash and Andrew Ross Sorkin, "Government Seizes WaMu and Sells Some Assets," *New York Times*, September 25, 2008.

3. Bill Ganzel, "Bank Failures," *The Ganzel Group*, 2003, www.livinghistoryfarm.org/farminginthe30s/money_08.html.

4. Burgess, "How to Profit."

5. Jill Konieczko, "The 10 Biggest Bank Failures," *U.S. News and World Report*, July 15, 2008.

6. Ajay A. Palvia, "Management Turnover, Regulatory Oversight, and Performance: Evidence From Community Banks" Office of the Comptroller of the Currency, Economics Working Paper, 2008-1, http://docs.google.com/viewer?a=v&q=cache:AMMCcCEMXIsJ:www.occ.treas.gov/ftp/workpaper/wp2008-1.pdf+Office+of+the+Comptroller+of+the+Currency+report+on+bank+failures+1979+to+1989&hl=en&gl=us&pid=bl&srcid=ADGEESjLcQp-HJIIz6nDrmM7QdeR4t0xLbrvux-Y-lgXQDeOo69aM0FGonqMYBnh0yWh2_BXL0UKD5JHHm5bRJb8nGIHoZE_97usOBasyiAnaptx2vq3_I4sfl2WI2Y8AE-d4YfQG9Qpv&sig=AHIEtbRm6UERJTwA7SI3wM_ hroG1tJTefw.

7. Michael E. Collins, "Supervision Spotlight on the Root Causes of Bank Failures," *SRC Insights*, Fourth Quarter 2009, Federal Reserve Bank of Philadelphia, www.philadelphiafed.org/bank-resources/publications/src-insights/2009/fourth-quarter/q4si2_09.cfm.

8. Ibid.

9. Brenda Cose, "The History of Money Market Funds," eHow Inc., www.ehow.com/about_5171321_history-money-market-funds.html.

10. Bert Ely, "Savings and Loan Crisis," Library of Economics and Liberty, www.econlib.org/.

11. Timothy Curry and Lynn Shibut, "The Cost of the Savings and Loan Crisis: Truth and Consequences," *FDIC Banking Review*, 2000.

12. Ely, "Savings and Loan Crisis."

13. George G. Kaufman, "The U.S. Banking Debacle of the 1980s: A Lesson in Government Mismanagement," *The Freeman* 45 (4) (April 1995), www.thefreemanonline.org/featured/the-us-banking-debacle-of-the-1980s-a-lesson-in-government-mismanagement/.

14. Mark J. Perry, "Due North: Canada's Marvelous Mortgage and Banking System," American Enterprise Institute, February 26, 2010.

15. Andrew Coyne, "Is Canada's Banking System Really So Smart," Historica Foundation, April 13, 2009, http://thecanadianencyclopedia.com/index.cfm?PgNm=TCE&Params=M1ARTM0013368.

16. "25 Biggest Bank Failures in History," *Business Pundit*, May 7, 2009.

17. Edward M. Shepard, "The Panic of 1837," in *Life of Martin Van Buren* (Boston: Houghton, Mifflin Company, 1888), http://answers.yahoo.com/question/index?qid=20071001164354AAApUblE.

18. "Encyclopedia: Panic of 1837," NationMaster.com, http://search.nationmaster.com/cgi-bin/search.cgi?query=panic+of+1837.

19. Ibid.

20. Historian.net, Rise of the West 1819-1829, "Chapter IX. The Crisis of 1819 and Its Results," Frederick Turner, http://historion.net/rise-new-west-1819-1829/chapter-ix-crisis-1819-and-its-results-1819-1820?page=3.

21. "Encyclopedia: Panic of 1837," NationMaster.com.

22. "Economic Crisis of 1837," Economy-point.org, 2006, www.economypoint.org/e/economic-crisis-of-1837.html.

23. David A. Skeel Jr., "Bankruptcy Act of 1841," Encyclopedia.com, 2004.

24. U.S. History.com, Sherman Silver Purchase Act, Acts, Bills, and Laws, 1890, www.u-s-history.com/pages/h762.html.

25. "Philadelphia and Reading Railroad Company," Scripophily.com, www.scripophily.net/phandrecoph1.html.

26. "Public Opinion: A Comprehensive Summary of the Press Throughout the World," Public Opinion Company, Vol. 25, July 1989–December 1989, http://books.google.com/books?id=RKVAAAAAMAAJ&printsec=frontcover&dq=Public+Opinion:+A+Comprehensive+Summary+of+the+Press+Throughout+the+World&source=bl&ots=-AIOA4rJks&sig=8HA8PDBDRY VA06XJoKIk0bjHs4o&hl=en&ei=SAB0TLHTLIKClAeZsOzHCA&sa=X&oi=book_result&ct=result&resnum=1&ved=0CBIQ6AEwAA#v=onepage &q&f=false.

27. *Atlantic Reporter* 33, West Publishing Company, 1896.

28. *Public Policy* 3, Public Policy Publishing Co., 1900.

29. J. Kingston Pierce, "Panic of 1893: Seattle's First Great Depression," HistoryLink.org, 1999, www.historylink.org/index.cfm?DisplayPage=output.cfm&File_Id=2030.

30. "Panic of 1893," History Central, www.u-s-history.com/pages/h792.html.

31. Matthew Josephson, *The Robber Barons* (Harvest/Harcourt Brace & Co., 1995).

32. "An Era of Economic Instability, 1879–1920," *Gale Encyclopedia of U.S. Economic History*, Gale Group, 1999.

33. Ibid.

34. American History, "Herbert Hoover Address Accepting Republican Presidential Nomination" *New York Times Company* http://americanhistory.about.com/library/docs/blhooverspeech1932.htm.

35. Scot J. Paltrow, "Merrill Lynch Posts Loss of $361 Million in 4th Quarter," *Los Angeles Times*, January 23, 1990.

Chapter 7　Say Goodbye to Gold

1. Only Gold, A Brief History of Gold, Tutorial Pages, www.onlygold.com/tutorialpages/historyfs.htm.

2. John Blair and Nigel Ramsay, *English Medieval Industries: Craftsmen, Techniques, and Products*, (Continuum Publishing Group, 2001) pg. 107.

3. British Banking History Society, "A History of English Clearing Banks," www.banking-history.co.uk/history.html.

4. Paul Vallely "The Rothschild Story: A Golden Era Ends For a Secretive Dynasty," *The Independent*, April 16, 2004.

5. *Encyclopedia Americana*: A Library of Universal Knowledge, (Encyclopedia Americana Corp., 1919), 22.

6. Ibid., 712.

7. Ibid., 23.

8. Ibid., 23.

9. "The Comstock Lode," OnLine Nevada Encyclopedia, www.onlinenevada.org/comstock_lode.

10. John Dryfhout, *The Work of Augustus Saint Gaudens* (Lebanon, NH: UPNE, 2008), 35.

11. Steve Peters, *Buy Gold Like an Insider: The Guide to Insiders' Secrets* (Apple Valley, MN: SCP Associates, 2010), 115.

12. J. Bradford DeLong, "Slouching Towards Utopia?: The Economic History of the Twentieth Century-XIV. The Great Crash and the Great Slump" University of California, Berkeley, February 2003.

13. The American Presidency Project, www.presidency.ucsb.edu/ws/index.php?pid=14611.

14. Jimbovard.com, "The Great Gold Robbery," James Bovard, December 6, 2006, http://jimbovard.com/blog/2006/12/06/the-great-gold-robbery/.

15. Quotationspage.com, Quotation #37700, The Thomas Jefferson Encyclopedia, Thomas Jefferson, www.quotationspage.com/quote/37700.html.

16. "Major Foreign Holders of Treasury Securities," www.ustreas.gov/tic/mfh.txt.

17. Quoted in John Waggoner, "U.S. Dollar Is Still the World's Most Trusted Currency," *USA Today*, March 13, 2010.

18. Ambrose Evans-Pritchard, "China Alarmed by U.S. Money Printing," *UK Telegraph*, March 15, 2010.

19. Judy Shelton, *Money Meltdown* (New York: Free Press, October 1998), 284.

20. John Koning, "The Losing Battle to Fix Gold at $35," Mises.org, February 18, 2009.

21. GoldSeek.com, "Gold Headed to $200 or $10, Part II," Eric Hommelberg, May 15, 2009, http://news.goldseek.com/EricHommelberg/1242397613.php.

22. "Money: DeGaulle vs. the Dollar," *Time*, February 12, 1965.

23. "Money Supply and Purchasing Power," *Financial Sense*, February 2009.

24. Kosuke Takahashi, "Gas and Oil Rivalry in the East China Sea," *Asia Times Online*, July 27, 2004.

Chapter 8 The Gatekeepers

1. *Investor's Business Daily*, March 11, 2010.

2. Scribd.com, Knickerbocker Trust Company, www.scribd.com/doc/34983602/The-Dynamics-of-a-Financial-Dislocation-The-Panic-of-1907-and-the-Subprime-Crisis.

3. Underground Politics: Federal Reserve History and Conspiracy, September 4, 2009.

4. FDIC.gov, About FDIC, Learning Bank, www.fdic.gov/about/learn/learning/when/19-1919.html

5. Victor Germack, "Top 50 Banks Aren't Healthy," January 26, 2010, www.legalservicesmag.com/news/2010/0116/1000015240070.htm.

6. "Of Course We Won't Use Bailout Money to Make Loans," *Business Insider*, October 25,2008

7. U.S. SBA Office of Advocacy, Frequently Asked Questions, 2009. www.sba.gov/advo/stats/sbfaq.pdf.

8. Tyler Bagwell, Jekyll Island History, www.jekyllislandhistory.com/federalreserve.shtml.

9. Deuteronomy 23:19–20, New Living Translation, www.biblegateway.com/passage/?search=Deuteronomy%2023:19-20&version=NLT.

10. "International Jewish Bankers Between 1850 and 1940: An Example of Internationalization Along Ethnic Lines," Huibert Schijf, July 22–26, 2002, http://eh.net/XIIICongress/cd/papers/10Schijf205.pdf.

11. "The Rothschild Story, A Golden Era Ends for A Secretive Dynasty," *The Independent*, April 16, 2004.

12. Kuhn, Loeb & Company home page, www.kuhnloeb.com/.

13. Naomi Weiner Cohen, *Jacob H. Schiff: A Study in American Jewish Leadership* (Lebanon, NH: UPNE, 1999), 17.

14. Rabbi Elchonon Oberstein, "Jacob Schiff, Portrait of A Leader," *Where What When*, www.wherewhatwhen.com/read_articles.asp?id=584.

15. Ibid.

16. T. Cushing Daniel, *Real Money versus False Money: Bank Credits* (Amsterdam, The Netherlands: The Minerva Group, Inc., 2004), 208.

17. Ibid., 218.

18. Paul Warburg, "Defects and Needs of Our Banking System," *New York Times*, January 6, 1907.

19. Ibid.

20. The Federal Reserve, Jekyll Island, Chapter 1.

21. Roger Johnson, *Historical Beginnings, The Federal Reserve* (Boston: Federal Reserve Bank, 1999), 20.

22. Verle B. Johnson, Ideas.repec.org,The Aldrich Plan, January 6, 1984, San Francisco, CA, http://ideas.repec.org/a/fip/fedfel/y1984ijan6.html.

23. Johnson, *Historical Beginnings*, 20.

24. J. Bradford DeLong, "Did J.P. Morgan's Men Add Value?" NBER Working Paper 3246, August 1990, 3.

25. "Louis Brandeis," Jewish Virtual Library, www.jewishvirtuallibrary.org/jsource/biography/Brandeis.html.

26. Stephen M. Axinn and Norman Yoerg, *Interlocking Directorates under Section 8 of the Clayton Act*, (American Bar Association, 1984), 4.

27. Testimony in the Money Trust Investigation, Subcommittee of the Committee on Banking and Currency, 1913.

28. Abram Piatt Andrew, *Some Facts and Figures Related to The Money Trust Inquiry* (GPO. 1913), 10.

29. Rixey Smith and Norman Beasley, *Carter Glass: A Biography* (New York: Longman, Green & Co., 1939), 28.

30. SEMP Library, "Carter Glass and the Federal Reserve Act," Biot Report 605, March 25, 2009, www.semp.us/publications/biot_reader.php?BiotID=605.

31. Ibid.

32. Smith and Beasley, *Carter Glass: A Biography*, 89.

33. SEMP Library, "Carter Glass and the Federal Reserve Act."

34. Smith and Beasley, *Carter Glass: A Biography*, 99.

35. Ibid., 104.

36. Eustace Mullins, *Secrets of the Federal Reserve: The London Connection* (Bankers Research Institute, 1985), 25. www.apfn.org/apfn/reserve.htm.

37. Smith and Beasley, *Carter Glass: A Biography*, 104.

38. Mullins, *Secrets of the Federal Reserve*, 20.

39. Suzanne Phillips, "Heal the Money System, Heal Society," www.federalreserve.net/.

40. *Merriam-Webster Dictionary*, www.merriam-webster.com/dictionary/inflation.

41. Lawrence H. White, "Inflation and the Federal Reserve: The Consequences of Political Money Supply," Cato Institute, April 15, 1982, www.cato.org/pubs/pas/pa008.html.

42. Michael Edwards, "The Battle America Lost in 1913," AFN Organization, www.afn.org/~govern/battle.html.

43. Economic Expert.com, "Federal Reserve Act," www.economicexpert.com/a/Federal:Reserve:Act.html.

44. Mullins, *Secrets of the Federal Reserve*, 29.

45. Ibid., 28.

46. Ibid., 33.

47. Adam Lass, memo to author.

48. Ibid.

49. James Turk, "The Barbarous Relic: It's Not What You Think," Kitco Metals, Kitco.com, September 2005.

Chapter 9   Money for Nothing

1. Josh Clark, "How Stuff Works: How Much Money There Is in The World," money.howstuffworks.com/how-much-money-is-in-the-world.htm.

2. Ibid.

3. Ibid.

4. Jim Jubak, "Fed Kills a Key Inflation Gauge," MSN Money, March 31, 2006.

5. John Williams, "Financial Sense Editorials: Near Record Money Growth Threatens Monetary Inflation," January 14, 2008. www.financialsensearchive.com/editorials/williams_j/2008/0114.html.

6. Ibid.

7. Economics.arawakcity.org, famoushistorical quotes related to money and banking, part 1, www.economics.arawakcity.org/node/26.

8. Justice Litle, "The Banks Will Bring Us Hyperinflationary Depression," *Taipan Daily*, Taipan Publishing Group, December 19, 2009.

9. "How Financial and Economic Crisis Is Related to Healthcare," *Resource Economics* January 1, 2010.

10. "Can The Wealth of Our Foundations Cause Hyperinflation?" The China Foundation, November 16, 2009, http://webcache.googleusercontent.com/search?q=cache:sQUM8-meSbkJ:www.thechinafoundation.org/documents/Hyperinflation_FAQs.pdf+In+1922,+inflation+in+Austria+reached+1,426% 25+percent.+From+1914+to+January+1923,+the+consumer+price+index+rose+by+a+factor+of+11,836 &hl=en&gl=us.

11. Mark Skousen, *The Making of Modern Economics: The Lives and Ideas of Great Thinkers* (Armonk, NY: M.E. Sharpe, April 2001), 289.

12. Ibid.

13. School of Mathematics and Statistics, University of St. Andrews, Scotland, Simon Newcomb Biography, www-history.mcs.st-andrews.ac.uk/Biographies/Newcomb.html.

14. Litle, "The Banks Will Bring Us Hyperinflationary Depression."

15. "Businesses and Banks Hoarding Cash," *Times Dispatch*, March 24, 2010.

16. Larry Doyle, "New York Fed and Treasury Tell Banks to Hold Cash," Sense on Cents, March 10, 2010.

17. Liz Moyer, "Banks Promise Loans But Hoard Cash," *Forbes*, February 2, 2009.

18. Bradley Keoun, "Pandit Near Death Hoard Signals Lower Profits," Bloomberg, November 2, 2009.

19. "Small Businesses: Banks Not Lending," *Huffington Post*, March 12, 2010.

20. Small Business Administration, Frequently Asked Questions, www.sba.gov/advo/stats/sbfaq.pdf.

21. Justin Baer and Francesco Guerrera, "Regulators Tell US Banks to Hold Funds," *Financial Times*, March 9, 2010.

22. Ibid.

23. The Compliance Exchange, Goldman Sachs Posts Record Profit, January 21, 2010 compliancex.typepad.com, http://compliancex.typepad.com/compliancex/2010/01/goldman-sachs-posts-record-profit-on-bonus-pool-cuts.html.

24. "JP Morgan Profit Rises," *New York Times*, January 15, 2010.

25. The Federal Reserve Board, Remarks by Governor Ben Bernanke, November 21, 2002.

26. Mike Whitney, "Greenspan's Cheap Money Role in the US Housing Crash of 2007," MarketOracle.com, February 7, 2007.

27. St. Louis Federal Reserve, Newsroom, Speches, March 24, 2009, www.stlouisfed.org/newsroom/speeches/2009_03_24.cfm

28. Thorsten Polleit, "Bad News for Our Money," Ludwig von Mises Institute, June 4, 2009. http://mises.org/daily/3494.

29. Ibid.

30. Seeker 401, "Follow the Money, Biggest Holder of US Government Treasury Debt," http://seeker401.wordpress.com/2009/04/14/the-biggest-holder-of-us-government-debt-treasuriesbonds/

31. FedUpUSA.org, http://fedupusa.org/ http://fedupusa.org/2010/01/08/federal-reserve-purchased-80-of-treasury-issues-in-2009/.

32. Robert Shapiro, "How and Why National Debt Doesn't Matter to Progressives," NDN, March 11, 2010, http://ndn.org/blog/2010/03/how-and-why-rising-national-debt-matters-and-doesnt-progressives.

33. PolitiFact.com, "$5 Trillion Added to National Debt Under Bush," January 18, 2009, www.politifact.com/truth-o-meter/statements/2009/jan/22/rahm-emanuel/5-trillion-added-national-debt-under-bush/.

34. Nouriel Roubini, "No Greece in the American Machine," *Forbes*, March 25, 2010

35. "Stocks Down in Early Trading on US Debt Rating Worry," *Investment News*, March 15, 2010.

36. Jeff Cox, "Why US Debt Rating Poses Such a Big Worry to Investors," CNBC, May 22, 2009.

37. Shawn Tully, "The Next Great Crisis: America's Debt," *CNN Money*, June 11, 2009.

38. The Cato Project on Social Security Privatization, Social Security: Facing the Facts, by Mark Weinberger, April 10, 1996, www.socialsecurity.org/pubs/ssps/ssp3.html.

39. The Economic Collapse, "It's Now Mathematically Impossible to Pay Off the U.S. Debt," http://theeconomiccollapseblog.com/archives/it-is-now-mathematically-impossible-to-pay-off-the-u-s-national-debt.

40. David Lindsey, *H. Clay/Andrew Jackson: Democracy and Enterprise* (Cleveland: Howard Allen, 1962), 79.

41. Jay Cooke, *How Our National Debt Can Be Paid: The Wealth, Resources and Power of the People of the United States* (Philadelphia: Sherman, 1865).

42. Gerald Prante, "Summary of the Latest Individual Income Tax Data," Tax Foundation, July 20, 2009.

43. Congressional Budget Outlook, "The Budget and Economic Outlook: Fiscal Years 2009 to 2019," www.cbo.gov/ftpdocs/99xx/doc9958/01-08-Out-look_Testimony.pdf.

44. James Quinn, "Citizens of the United States Welcome to Animal Farm 2009," MarketOracle.com, July 25, 2009.

Chapter 10   The Barbarians' Powerful Ally

1. Jody Shenn, "Moody's May Lower $43.4 Billion of Older Jumbo-Mortgage Bonds," *BusinessWeek*, April 16, 2010.

2. Ibid.

3. Edward Manfredonia, "Goldman Sachs: The Great Deceiver," Blackstarnews .com, April 26, 2010.

4. Thismatter.com, "Bond Ratings and Credit Risk," http://thismatter.com/money/bonds/bond_ratings_and_credit_risk.htm

5. Frank Partnoy, *Infectious Greed, How Deceit and Risk Corrupted the Financial Markets* (New York: Times Books, 2003), 66.

6. Marcus Hartwall and Christian Pettersson, "Reformation of the Credit Industry—Is There a Need?" Institute of Business Studies, June 2005.

7. John O'Connell, "Update 2—EU Says Will Probe Rating Agencies After Greece," John O'Donnell, Reuters.com, May 4, 2010.

8. Lawrence White, Roundtable to Examine Oversight of Credit Agencies. Arlington, VA: Mercatus Center, George Mason University, April 15, 2009.

9. Jay Cochran, "An Economic Analysis of the SEC's Nationally Recognized Statistical Rating Organization Standard" (working paper, Mercatus Center, George Mason University, Arlington, VA, August 2005).

10. "Rebecca Mark's Exit Leaves Azurix Treading Deep Water," *Wall Street Journal*, August 28, 2000.

11. "Kenneth Lay Biography," Encyclopedia of Business, References for Business .com, www.referenceforbusiness.com/biography/F-L/Lay-Ken-1942.html.

12. Ibid.

13. Sam Jones, "When Junk Was Gold," *Financial Times*, October 17, 2008.

14. Howard Kurtz, "The Enron Story That Waited to Be Told," *Washington Post*, January 18, 2002.

15. Justine Blau, "WorldCom Malfeasance Revealed," CBS News, June 13, 2003.

16. Charles Haddad, Dean Foust, and Steve Rosenbush, "WorldCom's Sorry Legacy," *BusinessWeek*, July 8, 2002.

17. Scott Reeves, "Lies, Damned Lies and Scott Sullivan," Forbes.com, February 17, 2005.

18. Jennifer Bayot and Roben Farzad, "Ex-WorldCom Officer Sentenced to Five Years in Accounting Fraud," *New York Times*, August 12, 2005.

19. "Bond Ratings and Credit Risk," ThisMatter.com., http://thismatter.com/money/bonds/bond_ratings_and_credit_risk.htm.

20. Lorraine Woellert and Dawn Kopecki, "Moody's, S&P Employees Doubted Ratings," Bloomberg, October 22, 2008.

21. Ibid.

22. Ibid.

23. Kevin Hall, "How Moody's Sold Its Ratings and Sold Out Investors," McClatchy, October 18, 2009.

24. Jeremy Warner, "Credit Rating Agencies, the Untouchable Kings of Finance," *UK Telegraph*, December 11, 2009.

25. Ibid.

26. Gary Ater, "Credit Rating Agencies Need More than Just a 'Slap on Hands,'" *American Chronicle*, March 22, 2010.

27. Consumer Federation of America, "The Need for Credit Agency Regulatory Reform," position paper, www.consumerfed.org/elements/www.consumerfed.org/File/CFA_Position_Paper_Credit_Rating_Agencies_FINAL.pdf.

28. Generational Dynamics, "Moody's and Other Rating Agencies Made Money Overrating CDOs," February 5, 2008.

29. "Who's Guarding the Gate?" *Vermont Law Review* 33:585.

30. Manfredonia, "Goldman Sachs: The Great Deceiver."

31. Docs.govdoc.org, hearing, "The Role of Credit Agencies in the Structured Finance Market," September 27, 2007, http://docs.govdoc.org/us/legi/house/cfs/hearings/HHRG-110-0062.pdf.

32. Generational Dynamics, "Moody's and Other Rating Agencies."

33. Viktoria Baklanova, "Credit Rating Litigation, Some Unintended Consequences of Preserving the Freedom of Speech for Market Players," http://westminster.academia.edu/documents/0011/3114/Credit_Rating_Litigation_1.23.09.ppt.

34. Moody's.com, "Company History, A Century of Market Leadership," http://v3.moodys.com/Pages/atc001.aspx.

35. Richard Cantor and Frank Packer, "The Credit Rating Industry, Richard Cantor and Frank Packer," *FRBNY Quarterly Review*, Fall 1994.

36. "Moody's Reports Results for First Quarter," CNBC, April 21, 2010.

37. "SEC Finds Shortcomings in Credit Rating Agencies Practice and Disclosure to Investors," U.S. Securities and Exchange Commission, July 2008.

38. Ronpaul.com, "The SEC Is A total Failure and Part of the Problem," April 19, 2010, www.ronpaul.com/2010-04-19/ron-paul-the-sec-is-a-total-failure-and-part-of-the-problem.

Chapter 11 The Scourge of Wall Street

1. Gretchen Morgenson and Don Van Natta, Jr., "Paulson's Calls to Goldman Tested Ethics," *New York Times*, August 8, 2009.

2. "Economic News Release," United States Department of Labor, 2010.

3. Christine Harper, "Goldman Sachs Stock Sale, TARP Repayment, Might Pressure Rivals," Bloomberg, April 10, 2009.

4. Federal Reserve, Periodic Public Report, April 27, 2009, www.federalreserve.gov/monetarypolicy/files/129periodicupdate04272009.pdf.

5. The Bowery Boys.com, "Goldman Sachs: Things Were Much Simpler Then," April 2010, http://theboweryboys.blogspot.com/2010/04/goldman-sachs-things-were-much-simpler.html.

6. Tom Bawden and Susan Thompson, "Goldman Sachs Makes $4bn Profit on Daring Sub-Prime Bet," *The Times*, December 15, 2007.

7. Allan Slone, "Junk Mortgages Under the Microscope," *Fortune*, October 16, 2007.

8. Ibid.

9. Standard & Poor's, "A History of Standard & Poor's," www.standardandpoors .com/about-sp/timeline/en/us/.

10. "Ratings Direct," Standard & Poor's, 2007.

11. Politico.com, "Anthony Weiner: The Republican Party Is a Wholly Owned Subsidiary of an Insurance Giant," *New York* magazine, February 24, 2010, www.politico.com/blogs/glennthrush/0210/No_One_Silences_Anthony_ Weiner.html.

12. Stevenson Jacobs, "Goldman Sachs Profits Hit $4.8B, Pay Up 47 Percent Over 2008," *Huffington Post*, January 21, 2010.

13. Jeannine Aversa, "Fed Says Recession Wiped Out $1.3 Trillion in Personal Wealth," *Spokesman-Review*, June 11, 2009.

14. Edmund Conway, "WEF 2009: Global Crisis 'Has Destroyed 40pc of World Wealth,'" Telegraph Media Group, January 28, 2009.

15. FundingUniverse.com, "The Goldman Sachs Inc., History," www.funding universe.com/company-histories/The-Goldman-Sachs-Group-Inc-Company-History.html.

16. Ibid.

17. Matt Taibbi, "Inside the Great American Bubble Machine," *Rolling Stone*, July 2, 2009.

18. Nina Munk, "It's the I.P.O., Stupid," *Vanity Fair*, January 2000.

19. Ibid.

20. Tony Long, "March 10, 2000: Pop!" *Wired*, March 10, 2007.

21. Malcolm Wheatley, "Investing Lessons From the Dot Com Crash," *Yahoo! Finance*, March 11, 2010.

22. Christopher Byron, "Salon.com Typifies Demise of 'Content' IPOs," Bloomberg, June 20, 2000.

23. FundingUniverse.com, "Goldman Sachs."

24. Office of the Attorney General, Media Center, February 4, 2010, www.ag.ny .gov/media_center/2010/feb/feb04a_10.html.

25. Bradley Keoun, "Merrill Posts Record Loss on $16.7 Billion Writedown," Bloomberg, January 17, 2008.

26. Securities Arbitration.blogspot.com, "Merrill Lynch's Illiquid Assets," http:// securitiesarbitration.blogspot.com/2008_05_01_archive.html.

27. "Bank of America to Repay TARP Funds; Move Will Free Bank From Executive Pay Restrictions," *Business News*, December 2, 2009.

28. Stevenson Jacobs, Martin Crutsinger and Daniel Wagner, "Emergency Capital Injections Provided to Support the Viability of Bank of America, Other Major Banks, and the U.S. Financial System," SIGTARP, 2009.

29. Crocodyl.org, Company Profile, Merrill Lynch, January 19, 2010, www .crocodyl.org/wiki/merrill_lynch.

30. Merrill Lynch & Co, Answers.com, "Company history," www.answers.com/topic/merrill-lynch-co-inc-2.

31. Ibid.

32. James Sterngold, "Merrill Lynch Puts Bond Loss at $250 Million," *New York Times*, April 30, 1987.

33. Diana Henriques, "Merrill Lynch Settles Claims From $250 Million '87 Loss," *New York Times*, August 28, 1990.

34. John Furrier, "M&A: Frank Quattrone & Qatalyst Scores Win With Dell 3Par Deal," SiliconAngle.com, August 16, 2010.

35. Kurt Eichenwald, "Company News; First Boston in Accord to Revise Sealy Debt," *New York Times*, September 19, 1991.

36. Leah Nathans, "Raging Bull," *BusinessWeek*, November 25, 1991.

Chapter 12   Epic Tool of Destruction

1. Exxon Valdez Oil Spill Trustee Council, "Details about the accident," State of Alaska, February 1990, www.evostc.state.ak.us/facts/details.cfm.

2. "The Exxon Valdez Oil Spill Disaster," *ExploreNorth*, March 1999, http://explorenorth.com/library/weekly/aa032499.htm.

3. "Exxon Valdez Oil Spill," *OnLine Highways LLC*, www.ohwy.com/ak/n/nocomfrt.htm.

4. Cutler Cleveland, "Exxon Valdez Oil Spill," National Oceanic and Atmospheric Administration, 2008.

5. "Exxon Valdez Oil Spill Disaster," *ExploreNorth*.

6. "Exxon Valdez Oil Spill," *OnLine Highways LLC*.

7. PrimerOnMoney.com, "Reserve Requirements Ratios," www.primeronmoney .com/reserverequirements.html.

8. "Exxon Valdez Oil Spill Disaster," *ExploreNorth*.

9. John Porretto, "Exxon Mobil Reports Record $45.2 Billion Profit for 2008," *Huffington Post*, January 30, 2009.

10. Securities Industry and Financial Markets Association, Research Report, November 2008, www.sifma.org/research/pdf/RRVol3-10.pdf.

11. Gerald Epstein, *Financialization and the World Economy* (Northampton, MA: Edward Elgar, 2005), 149.

12. The Federal Reserve.gov, Remarks by Chairman Alan Greenspan, March 19, 1999.

13. National Public Radio, Fool's Gold: The Banking World's Responsibility, March 14, 2009, www.npr.org/templates/story/story.php?storyId=104130944

14. Gillian Tett, "Fool's Gold," *Free Press*, May 12, 2009.

15. "The J.P. Morgan Guide to Credit Derivatives," Risk, www.investing inbonds.com/assets/files/Intro_to_Credit_Derivatives.pdf.

16. Jesse Eisinger, "The $58 Trillion Elephant in the Room," Portfolio.com, October 15, 2008, www.portfolio.com/views/columns/wall-street/2008/10/15/Credit-Derivatives-Role-in-Crash/#ixzz0xXNTJkjw

17. Megan Carpenter, "Is the Greco-European Financial Crisis Goldman's Fault Too?" *Washington Independent*, February 10, 2010.

18. Caroline Salas, "Credit Derivatives May Lose $250 Billion," Bloomberg, January 8, 2008.

19. George Soros, "The Worst Crisis in 60 Years," GeorgeSoros.com, January 23, 2008, www.georgesoros.com/articles-essays/entry/the_worst_market_crisis_in_60_years/.

20. "United States Unemployment Rate," *Trading Economics*, August 6, 2010.

21. Martin Mayer, "The Dangers of Derivatives," Brookings Institution, April 2010, www.brookings.edu/~/media/Files/rc/papers/2010/0407_derivatives_litan/0407_derivatives_litan.pdf.

22. Ellen H. Brown, "Credit Where Credit Is Due: The Direct Way to Fix the Credit Crisis," Webofdebt.com, January 11, 2009, www.webofdebt.com/articles/creditcrunch.php.

23. Daniel R. Amerman, "AIG's Dangerous Collapse & Credit Derivatives Risk Primer," Financial Sense University, September 17, 2008.

24. John Carney, "Here's the Untold Story of How AIG Destroyed Itself," *Business Insider*, March 3, 2010.

25. Zachary Roth and Ben Buchwalter, "The Rise and Fall of AIG's Financial Products Unit," TPM Media LLC, March 20, 2009, http://tpmmuckraker.talkingpointsmemo.com/2009/03/the_rise_and_fall_of_aigs_financial_products_unit.php.

26. Ibid.

27. Ibid.

28. Ibid.

29. Carol Loomis, "AIG's Rescue Has a Long Way to Go," Cable News Network, December 29, 2008.

30. Paul Kiel, "AIG's Spiral Downward: A Timeline," Pro Publica Inc., 2008.

31. Matthew Karnitschnig, Deborah Solomon, Liam Pleven, and Jon E. Hilsenrath, "U.S. to Take Over AIG in $85 Billion Bailout; Central Banks Inject Cash as Credit Dries Up," *Wall Street Journal*, September 16, 2008.

32. Hugh Son, Craig Torres, and Erik Holm, "AIG Gets Expanded Bailout, Posts $24.5 Billion Loss," Bloomberg, November 10, 2008.

33. Shannon D. Harrington and Neil Unmack, "Lehman Credit-Swap Auction Sets Payout of 91.38 Cents," Bloomberg, October 10, 2008.

34. Megan Carpentier, "Lehman Bankruptcy Report Illuminates Need for Derivatives Regulation," *Washington Independent*, March 15, 2010.

35. Henry Paulson, *On the Brink: Inside the Race to Stop the Collapse of the Global Financial System* (New York: Grand Central Publishing, February 2010).

36. Martin Crusinger, Associated Press, "Paulson: 'Never Once' Considered Lehman Bailout," *New York Sun*, September 15, 2008.

37. Pension Pulse, "Are Pension Fund Managers Paid Too Much?" January 21, 2009, http://pensionpulse.blogspot.com/.

38. Carol J. Loomis, "Revealed: 15 AIG Bailout Counterparties," Cable News Network, March 9, 2009.

39. Lucid-minds.com, "The Real AIG Crimes," March 23, 2009, www.lucid-minds.com/Karl/two/p15.htm.

40. Choi Wing Hung, "The Aftermath of Subprime and Credit Crisis—The World Economy Needs Profound Adjustments," Hong Kong Trade Development Council, 2008.

41. Joseph Giannone and Dane Hamilton, "Fed Comes to Bear Stern's Rescue," Thomson Reuters, March 15, 2008.

42. Katy Marquardt, "FAQ on Investment Banks," *U.S. News and World Report*, March 17, 2008.

43. David Shirreff, "Case Set Up, Lessons From the Collapse of Hedge Fund, Long Term Capital Management," Risk Institute, http://riskinstitute.ch/146490.htm.

44. Ibid.

45. "Case Study: LTCM—Long Term Capital Management," *Sungard*, 2010, www.erisk.com/learning/CaseStudies/Long-TermCapitalManagemen.asp.

46. IMF.org,External Pubs, Global Financial Stability Report, January 2009, www.imf.org/external/pubs/ft/fmu/eng/2009/01/pdf/0109.pdf.

Chapter 13   The Brotherhood of Banks

1. O. M. Powers, "Banking in the United States. Colonial Period; Bank of North America; Hamilton's Views; First United States Bank; State Banks," ch. XXII in *Commerce and Finance* (Powers & Lyons, 1903).

2. Bill Meridian, "The Inflation War of 1812," BillMeridian.com, www.bill meridian.com/articles-files/inflation.htm

3. John Steele Gordon, "A Short Banking History of the United States," *Wall Street Journal*, October 10, 2008.

4. A. Piatt Andrew, *Some Facts and Figures Relating to the Money Trust Inquiry* (Washington, DC: Government Printing Office, 1913), 5.

5. Rixey Smith and Norman Beasley, *Carter Glass: A Biography* (New York: Longman, Green & Co., 1939), 95.

6. Ibid.

7. Michael Malloy, "What Was the National Bank Act?" eNotes.com, www .enotes.com/major-acts-congress/national-bank-act.

8. John R. Walter, "Depression-Era Bank Failures: The Great Contagion or the Great Shakeout?" *Economic Quarterly—Federal Reserve Bank of Richmond*, 2005.

9. "The Benefits of Charter Choice, Dual Banking System as a Case Study," Office of the State Bank Commissioner, June 24, 2005.

10. FDIC.gov, FDIC history, www.fdic.gov/bank/analytical/firstfifty/.

11. Ibid.

12. Ibid.

13. "Top 50 Regional Banks Aren't Healthy and Hoarding Cash," CDTV, January 27, 2010, www.cdtv.net/newswire/content/top-50-regional-banks-arent-healthy-nor-lending-hoarding-cash-ratefinancials-study.

14. Walter, "Depression-Era Bank Failures."

15. Research Department, Federal Reserve Bank of San Francisco, The McFadden Act: A Look Back, April 1982, http://docs.google.com/viewer?a=v&q= cache:ZARXV0dO7I8J:www.frbsf.org/publications/economics/letter/1983/ el83-33.pdf+Between+1929+and+1933,+9,400+banks+had+failed& hl=en&gl=us&pid=bl&srcid=ADGEESgLGFIVnGCuTSjXI7QiiXrNeY TrWCo5HGsrLuXxefUKQNG5Vh8mc9Oi8xJVcjoLfJgvOylHBdDg5rOg ZcRVCMPjO_o2oeEz8RLjZvMDSIxFgMcXmQ4yIBGKUP8dHHH4 Rodaok9k&sig=AHIEtbSM24-Oq5ZMZMrJRePaR87t4oryWg.

16. John Kenneth Galbraith, "The Days of BOOM and BUST," American Heritage.com, www.americanheritage.com/articles/magazine/ah/1958/5/ 1958_5_28.shtml.

17. Henry C. K. Liu, "Bank Deregulation Fuels Non-Bank Financial System," *Asia Times Ltd.*, 2007.

18. FederalReserve.gov, "Federal Reserve Board, history," www.federalreserve .gov/aboutthefed/default.htm.

19. StrangeDeathofLiberalAmerica.com, "Bill Clinton, Glass-Steagall and the Current Financial and Mortgage Crisis, Part Two of an InDepth Investigative Report," 2008, http://thestrangedeathofliberalamerica.com/bill-clinton-glass-steagall-and-the-current-financial-and-mortgage-crisis-part-two-of-an-indepth-investigative-report.html.

20. Jim Puzzanghera, "Citigroup Chief Thanks Taxpayers for $45 Billion Bailout," *Network Journal*, 2010.

21. Monica Langley, "Tearing Down the Walls: How Sandy Weill Fought His Way to the Top of the Financial World ... And Then Nearly Lost it All," *Wall Street Journal*, 2003.

22. "Shearson Lehman Brothers Holdings Inc.," *International Directory of Company Histories*, St. James Press, 1994.

23. Answers.com, "Company History: Shearson Lehman Brothers Holdings Inc," Answers Corporation, 2010, www.answers.com/topic/shearson-lehman-brothers-holdings-inc.

24. Michael Tsang, Crag Trudell, and Michael J. Moore, "Primerica Discounted in IPO as Citigroup Unravels Weill Deals," Bloomberg, 2010.

25. American Academy of Achievement, "Sanford Weill Biography: Financier and Philanthropist," American Academy of Achievement, 2009, www.achievement.org/autodoc/page/wei0bio-1.

26. All Business, "Rubin Calls for Modernization of Glass-Steagall Act," May 1, 1995, www.allbusiness.com/government/business-regulations/500983-1.html.

27. Souphala Chomsisengphet and Anthony Pennington-Cross, "The Evolution of the Subprime Mortgage Market," *Federal Reserve Bank of St. Louis Review*, 2006.

28. Generational Dynamics, "American Prospect's Robert Kuttner Compares 2007 to 1929," October 2007.

Chapter 14   Wall Street Bloodlines

1. Mary Walsh, "A.I.G. Lists Banks It Paid With U.S. Bailout Funds," *New York Times*, March 15, 2009.

2. Liberty Tree Quotes, Barry Goldwater, http://quotes.liberty-tree.ca/quotes_by/barry+goldwater.

3. Barefoot's World, "Quotes On Banking and the Federal Reserve System FRAUD," www.barefootsworld.net/banking-fed-quotes.html.

4. James Perloff, "Our Monetary Mayhem Began with the Fed," *The New America*, April 2, 2009.

5. GovTrak.us, "Congress Legislation," www.govtrack.us/.

6. *Huffington Post*, "Bill to Audit Fed Sponsored by More than Half the House," July 17, 2009.

7. Ibid.

8. Barefoot's World, "Quotes on Banking."

9. Comptroller of the Currency, OCC's Quarterly Report on Bank Trading and Derivatives Activities, First Quarter 2009, p. 22, http://webcache.google usercontent.com/search?q=cache:rNl_0822H68J:www.occ.treas.gov/ftp/ release/2009-72a.pdf+top+25+commercial+banks+and+trusts+companies +in+derivatives+as+of+march+31,+2009&hl=en&gl=us

10. Eric Jackson, "Citi Ex-CEO Prince: Blinded by Hubris," Breakout Performance blog, April 28, 2010. http://breakoutperformance.blogspot.com/ 2010/04/citi-ex-ceo-prince-blinded-by-hubris.html.

11. Binyamin Applebaum, "U.S. Gave Billions in Tax Money in Deal for Citigroup's Bailout Repayment," *Washington Post*, December 19, 2009.

12. Charles Gasparino, "Robert Rubin's Agony," *The Daily Beast*, www.thedaily beast.com/blogs-and-stories/2009-08-19/robert-rubin-in-hell/.

13. Charles Gasparino, "Robert Rubin: The Man at the Nexus of Big Business and Big Government," *Huffington Post*, November 11, 2009, http://www .huffingtonpost.com/charles-gasparino/robert-rubin-the-man-at-t_b_353571 .html.

14. Chris Isidore, "Goldman's Chief to Take on Treasury," CNN Money, May 30, 2006.

15. WhoRunsGovernment.com, "Hank Paulson: Why He Matters," www .whorunsgov.com/Profiles/Henry_Paulson.

16. Jody Shenn, "Paulson Debt Plan May Benefit Mostly Goldman, Morgan," Bloomberg, September 22, 2008.

17. John Carney, "Blood in the Streets: JP Morgan Pushed Merrill Lynch into Bank of America Merger," *Business Insider*, October 7, 2008.

18. Richard S. Fuld Jr., Testimony before United States House of Representatives Committee on Oversight and Government Reform, October 6, 2008.

19. CBS, "Ben Bernanke's Greatest Challenge," *60 Minutes*, June 7, 2009.

20. Michael Hiltzik, "Lehman's Collapse Was All Its Own Fault," *Los Angeles Times*, March 17, 2010.

21. Robert Butche, "Financial Markets Rest Substantially, If Not Entirely on Fraud," *Newsroom Magazine*, March 24, 2010.

22. Richard S. Fuld, Jr., Testimony Before the United States House of Representatives Committee on Oversight and Government Reform, October 2, 2008.

23. Yves Smith, "NY Fed Under Geithner Implicated In Lehman Accounting Fraud Allegation," Naked Capitalism.com, March 1, 2010, www.nakedcapitalism.com/2010/03/ny-fed-under-geithner-implicated-in-lehman-accounting-fraud.html.

24. Andrew Sorkin, "At Lehman Watchdogs Saw It All," *New York Times*, March 15, 2010.

25. Henry Sender, "Rival Warned Regulator Over Lehman," *Financial Times*, March 18, 2010.

26. Allan Chernoff, "Madoff Whistleblower Blasts SEC," CNN Money, February 4, 2009.

27. Jake Bernstein, "Madoff Client Jeffry Picower Netted $5 Billion—Likely More Than Madoff Himself," ProPublica.com, June 23, 2009, www.propublica.org/article/madoff-client-jeffry-picower-netted-5-billion.

28. Barry Ritholtz, *Bailout Nation: How Greed and Easy Money Corrupted Wall Street and Shook the World* (Hoboken, NJ: John Wiley & Sons, 2009), 56.

29. CNN Money, September 28, 2008.

30. Bottarelli Research, August 2009 Chicago Conference.

31. Investing Value, "Alan Greenspan Biography," www.investingvalue.com/investment-leaders/alan-greenspan/index.htm.

32. Nathaniel Nash, "Greenspan Says He'll Sit Out on Some Fed Votes," *New York Times*, July 11, 1987.

33. Justin Martin, *Greenspan: The Man Behind the Money* (Cambridge, MA: Perseus, 2000), 63.

34. http://themessthatgreenspanmade.blogspot.com/2010/03/peter-schiff-on-alan-greenspan.html.

35. Gurcharan Das, "India's Growing Middle Class," *The Globalist*, theglobalist.com.

36. Peter Ford, "Consumer Tidal Wave on the Way: China's Middle Class," *Christian Science Monitor*, January 2007, christiansciencemonitor.com.

37. An Hodgson, "China's Middle Class Reaches 80 Million," *Euromonitor*, euromonitor.com, July 25, 2007.

38. Elizabeth Stanton, "History Points to Another Rate Cut Before January," TBO.com, January 25, 2007.

39. GOP.gov, *Legislative Digest*, H.R. 1728.

40. Amazon.com, Alan Greenspan's Amazon Blog, August 31, 2007.

41. "2009 Person of the Year," *Time*, December 16, 2009.

42. FederalReserve.gov, Board of Governors of the Federal Reserve, www.federalreserve.gov/.

43. Neil Irwin, "Bernanke Favored Rate Cuts Tied to Bubble," *Washington Post*, May 7, 2009.

44. "Better Regulation, Not Better Monetary Policy Is the Key To Preventing Bubbles," Transcript of Ben Bernanke Speech, *Business Insider*, January 3, 2010.

45. Daniel Wagner, "Fed Reserve Discloses Toxic Assets It Bought to Rescue Banks," *Insurance Journal*, April 2, 2010.

Chapter 15   The Monied-Class Rulers and Demigods

1. Christopher and James Lincoln Collier, *Decision in Philadelphia: The Constitutional Convention of 1787* (New York: Ballantine Books, 2007), 21.

2. Ibid., 20.

3. John Steele Gordon, *An Empire of Wealth: The Epic History of American Economic Power* (New York, London, Toronto, Sydney: Harper Perennial, 2004), 60.

4. Ibid.

5. Ibid.

6. Ibid., 26.

7. Ibid., 60.

8. Robert D. Hormats, *The Price of Liberty: Paying for America's Wars from the Revolution to the War on Terror* (New York: Times Books, Henry Holt and Company, 2007), 30.

9. Ibid.

10. Collier, *Decision in Philadelphia*, 103.

11. Hormats, *Price of Liberty*.

12. Gordon S. Wood, *Empire of Liberty: A History of the Early Republic, 1789–1815* (New York: Oxford University Press, 2009), 57.

13. Gordon, *Empire of Wealth*, 67.

14. Collier, *Decision in Philadelphia*, 104.

15. "The First Two Senators—An Odd Couple," Senate Historical Office, United States Senate, www.senate.gov/artandhistory/history/minute/The_First_Two_Senators_-_An_Odd_Couple.htm.

16. "Morris, Robert (1734–1806)," from the Biographical Directory of the United States Congress, 1774–Present, http://bioguide.congress.gov/scripts/biodisplay.pl?index=M000985.

17. Clarence L. Ver Steeg, *Robert Morris, Revolutionary Financier* (Philadelphia: University of Pennsylvania Press, 1954).

18. "The First Two Senators."

19. Open Secrets, "Races to Watch V̇: Lobbyist Favor Candidates," September 30, 2008, www.opensecrets.org/news/2008/09/races-to-watch-v-lobbyists-fav.html.

20. Gordon, *Empire of Wealth*, 55.

21. Alexander Hamilton, "The Continentalist," in *The Works of Alexander Hamilton*, ed. Henry Cabot Lodge (Federal ed.) (New York: G.P. Putnam's Sons, 1904). In 12 vols. Vol. 1 [1774]. Online Library of Liberty, http://oll.libertyfund.org/title/1378/64156 (accessed on 2010-07-30).

22. Ibid.

23. Thomas H. Goddard, *History of Banking Institutions of Europe and the United States* (Carvill, 1831), 49.

24. Ibid., 48–50.

25. "Willing, Thomas (1731–1821)," from the Biographical Directory of the United States Congress, 1774–Present, http://bioguide.congress.gov/scripts/biodisplay.pl?index=W000556.

26. Hormats, *Price of Liberty*, 3031.

27. "History of the U.S. Tax System," from the United States Department of the Treasury, www.ustreas.gov/education/fact-sheets/taxes/ustax.shtml.

28. Gordon, *Empire of Wealth*, 73.

29. Ibid., 74.

30. Ibid.

31. Ibid., 74–75.

32. Ibid., 75.

33. Ibid., 73.

34. Ibid., 77.

35. Yale Law School, "The Avalon Project, Jefferson's Opinion on the Constitutionality of a National Bank: 1791," http://avalon.law.yale.edu/18th_century/bank-tj.asp.

36. Gordon, *Empire of Wealth*, 78.

37. Ibid., 80.

38. Jo Becker and Gretchen Morgenson, "Geithner, as Member and Overseer, Forged Ties to Finance Club," *New York Times*, April 26, 2009, www.nytimes.com/2009/04/27/business/27geithner.html.

39. Jennifer Liberto, "Bernanke: Bring on AIG scrutiny," CNNMoney.com, January 19, 2010, http://money.cnn.com/2010/01/19/news/economy/Fed_AIG/index.htm.

40. Hugh Son, "Geithner's Fed Told AIG to Limit Swaps Disclosure (Update3)," Bloomberg Press, January 7, 2010, www.bloomberg.com/apps/news? pid=newsarchive&sid=afBRd2IifYuw.

41. Gordon, *Empire of Wealth*, 121.

42. Sidney Ratner, James H. Soltow, and Richard Sylla, *The Evolution of the American Economy: Growth, Welfare, and Decision Making* (New York: Macmillan, 1993), ch. 7.

43. Mintz, S. "The Era of Good Feelings: The Growth of Political Factionalism and Sectionalism," Digital History, 2007, www.digitalhistory.uh.edu/database/ article_display.cfm?HHID=574 (accessed July 30, 2010).

44. Gordon, *Empire of Wealth*, 81.

45. Richard H. Timberlake, Jr., "Panic of 1837," in *Business Cycles and Depressions: An Encyclopedia*, ed. David Glasner and Thomas F. Cooley (New York: Garland Publishing, 1997), 514–516.

Chapter 16 Barbarians in the Lobby

1. The White House, "Ethics Commitments By Executive Branch Personnel: Executive Order," President Barack Obama, January 21, 2009, www .whitehouse.gov/issues/ethics/.

2. GPO Access, Electronic Code of Federal Regulations, July 28, 2010, http://ecfr .gpoaccess.gov/cgi/t/text/text-idx?type=simple;c=ecfr;cc=ecfr;sid=a0dcdfe51d 08338cbc20ea46d2089b92;idno=5;region=DIV1;q1=2635.203%20b%20;rgn =div6;view=text;node=5%3A3.0.10.10.9.2.

3. John Steele Gordon, *An Empire of Wealth: The Epic History of American Economic Power* (New York, London, Toronto, Sydney: Harper Perennial, 2004), 207.

4. Ibid., 208.

5. Ibid., 217.

6. Ibid., 217–218.

7. Ibid., 218.

8. "People & Events: Thomas Clark Durant (1820–1885)," *American Experience*, PBS, www.pbs.org/wgbh/amex/tcrr/peopleevents/p_durant.html.

9. Ibid.

10. *The Encyclopedia Americana: A Library of Universal Knowledge*, vol. 8 (New York, Chicago: The Encyclopedia Americana Corporation, 1918), 173.

11. Stephen E. Ambrose, *Nothing Like It in the World: The Men Who Built the Transcontinental Railroad 1863–1869* (New York: Touchstone, Simon & Schuster, 2000), 93.

12. *Encyclopedia Americana*, vol. 8, 173.

13. Ibid.

14. Ibid.

15. Gordon, *Empire of Wealth*, 219.

16. Ibid., 220.

17. *Encyclopedia Americana*, vol. 8, 173.

18. Erik Eckholm, "Army Contract Official Critical of Halliburton Pact Is Demoted," *New York Times*, August 29, 2005, www.nytimes.com/2005/08/29/international/middleeast/29halliburton.html?_r=1.

19. Jane Mayer, "Contract Sport: What Did the Vice President Do for Halliburton?" *New Yorker*, February 16, 2004, www.newyorker.com/archive/2004/02/16/040216fa_fact.

20. Daniel Golden, "Countrywide's Many 'Friends,'" Portfolio.com, June 12, 2008, www.portfolio.com/news-markets/top-5/2008/06/12/Countrywide-Loan-Scandal.

21. Ibid.

22. Dick Armey, "Congress and the Countrywide Scandal," *Wall Street Journal*, June 18, 2008, http://online.wsj.com/article/SB121375337067183049.html.

23. Golden, "Countrywide's Many 'Friends.'"

24. Ibid.

25. Armey, "Congress and the Countrywide Scandal."

26. Kevin Rennie, "Sen. Dodd's Cavalcade of Scandal," *New York Post*, March 30, 2009, www.nypost.com/p/news/opinion/opedcolumnists/sen_dodd_cavalcade_of_scandal_GCPyPGbBRoHvSSUkutf3LP.

27. Robert G. Kaiser, *So Damn Much Money: The Triumph of Lobbying and the Corrosion of American Government* (New York: Random House, 2009), 4.

28. Ibid.

29. "Rise and Fall of Jack Abramoff," *NewsHour with Jim Lehrer*, interview of James Grimaldi by Ray Suarez, December 30, 2005, www.pbs.org/newshour/bb/congress/july-dec05/abramoff_12-30.html.

30. "'Gimme Five'—Investigation of Tribal Lobbying Matters" (PDF), Senate Committee on Indian Affairs, June 22, 2006, 41, www.indian.senate.gov/public/_files/Report.pdf

31. Ibid., 23.

32. James V. Grimaldi, "Lobbyists, Clients Undeterred by Scandal: Alumni of Abramoff's 'Team' Still Collecting Fees, Trying to Influence Government," *Washington Post*, Sunday, June 26, 2005, http://www.washingtonpost.com/wp-dyn/content/article/2005/06/25/AR2005062500983_pf.html.

33. "Gimme Five," 25.

34. "Lobbyist to Reveal All in Congress Bribes Scandal: Senior Politicians Alleged to Have Accepted Favours," Citizens for Responsibility and Ethics in Washington, via Julian Borger, Guardian Unlimited, January 5, 2006, www.citizensforethics.org/node/23466.

35. "Rise and Fall of Jack Abramoff."

36. "Poll Finds Few Captivated by Washington Lobbyist Scandal," USAToday.com, January 11, 2006, www.usatoday.com/news/washington/2006-01-11-poll washington_x.htm.

37. David Johnston and David D. Kirkpatrick, "Deal Maker Details the Art of Greasing the Palm," New York Times, August 6, 2006, www.nytimes.com/2006/08/06/washington/06wilkes.html?_r=2&oref=slogin&oref=slogin.

38. Ibid.

39. Kaiser, So Damn Much Money, 19.

40. Kenneth Schlossberg, "The Greening of Washington," New York Times Editorial Desk, May 14, 1986, Late City Final Edition, Section A, 27.

41. David Boaz, "The Lobbyist Scandals," Cato Institute, January 15, 2006, www.cato.org/pub_display.php?pub_id=5382.

42. Kaiser, So Damn Much Money, 22.

Chapter 17   Global Barbarians

1. Ariel Cohen, "Putin's Legacy and United Russia's New Ideology," The Heritage Foundation, June 1, 2006, www.heritage.org/Research/Reports/2006/06/Putins-Legacy-and-United-Russias-New-Ideology.

2. "Biography: Vladimir Putin," Answers.com, 2006, www.answers.com/topic/vladimir-putin.

3. Steve LeVine, Putin's Labyrinth: Spies, Murder, and the Dark Heart of the New Russia (New York: Random House, 2009), 16.

4. "Russia Launches More Air Strikes against Chechnya," RTE News, September 27, 1999, www.rte.ie/news/1999/0927/russia.html.

5. Amelia Gentleman and Ian Traynor, "Russia Blamed for Attack on Refugee Bus," Guardian, October 8, 1999, www.guardian.co.uk/world/1999/oct/08/russia.chechnya.

6. Patrick Cockburnin, "Russian Warplanes Kill Dozens of Villagers," The Independent, October 11, 1999, www.independent.co.uk/news/world/europe/russian-warplanes-kill-dozens-of-villagers-740254.html.

7. Ibid.

8. "Second Chechnya War—1999–???," GlobalSecurity.org, August 15, 2006, www.globalsecurity.org/military/world/war/chechnya2-5.htm.

9. "Preventing Genocide: Cechnya, Russia Overview," United States Holocaust Memorial Museum, www.ushmm.org/genocide/take_action/atrisk/region/chechnya-russia/.

10. European Court Rules Against Moscow, Institute for War and Peace Reporting, CRS Issue 276, November 17, 2005, http://iwpr.net/report-news/european-court-rules-against-moscow.

11. Robert Service, *A History of Modern Russia: From Tsarism to the Twenty-First Century*, 3rd ed. (Cambridge, MA: Harvard University Press, 2009), 547.

12. LeVine, *Putin's Labyrinth*, xix–xx.

13. Service, *History of Modern Russia*, 557.

14. Yevgenia Albats interview on *Frontline*'s "Return of the Czar: Who Is Putin?," May 2000, www.pbs.org/wgbh/pages/frontline/shows/yeltsin/putin/putin.html.

15. "Putin and Chávez's Slow Descent: Russian, Venezuelan Presidents' Dictatorships Are Doomed," National Review Online, December 6, 2007, www.cbsnews.com/stories/2007/12/06/opinion/main3584158.shtml.

16. Steven R. Weisman, "Bitter Outburst by Putin a Sign U.S.-Russian Relations Cooling," *New York Times*, September 12, 2004, http://seattletimes.nwsource.com/html/nationworld/2002033535_usrussia12.htm.

17. Vladimir Gusinsky, "Putin's Reign of Fear," *Moscow Times*, November 10, 2003, www.eng.yabloko.ru/Publ/2003/PAPERS/11/031110_mt.html.

18. "In Cold War Flashback, Putin Flexes Russia's Muscles," *USA Today*, February 12, 2007, http://blogs.usatoday.com/oped/2007/02/post_26.html.

19. Edward Lucas, "Putin: The Brutal Despot Who Is Dragging the West into a New Cold War," *Daily Mail*, January 18, 2008, www.dailymail.co.uk/pages/live/articles/news/worldnews.html?in_article_id=509177&in_page_id=1811.

20. Mike Whitney, "Putin's War-Whoop: The Impending Clash with Russia," Information Clearing House, June 21, 2007, www.informationclearinghouse.info/article17912.htm.

21. Ibid.

22. Gary Peach, "Putin Warns of Outside Forces that Wish to Split Russia and Take Over its Natural Resources," *AP Worldstream*, November 4, 2007, www.highbeam.com/doc/1A1-D8SMVBA80.html.

23. Service, *History of Modern Russia*, 561.

24. Ibid.

25. LeVine, *Putin's Labyrinth*, xx–xxi.

26. Cohen, "Putin's Legacy."

27. Max Hastings, "Corruption, Violence, and Vice Have Triumphed in Putin's Russia," *Guardian*, November 27, 2006, www.guardian.co.uk/comment isfree/2006/nov/27/comment.russia.

28. Cohen, "Putin's Legacy."

29. Service, *History of Modern Russia*, 551–552.

30. James Verini, "Putin's Power Grab," *Condé Nast Portfolio*, November 19, 2007, www.portfolio.com/news-markets/international-news/portfolio/2007/11/19/Sakhalin-Island-Oil.

31. "Belarus Warns Russia of Power Cut," BBC News, January 4, 2010, http://news.bbc.co.uk/2/hi/europe/8439745.stm.

32. Tim Webb, "Dispute Looms as Russia Suspends Belarus Energy Supplies," *Guardian*, January 3, 2010, www.guardian.co.uk/business/2010/jan/03/russia-suspends-belarus-energy-supplies.

33. Hastings, "Corruption, Violence and Vice."

34. Robert Amsterdam, "Gazprom Looks to Capture Nigerian Gas," *Perspectives on Global Politics and Business*, January 4, 2008, www.robertamsterdam.com/2008/01/gazprom_looks_to_capture_niger.htm.

35. David Blair, "Russia Blocks Sanctions against Iran," *Telegraph*, August 26, 2006, www.telegraph.co.uk/news/1527325/Russia-blocks-sanctions-against-Iran.html.

36. Cohen, "Putin's Legacy."

37. Ibid.

38. Hastings, "Corruption, Violence, and Vice."

39. Service, *History of Modern Russia*, 562–563.

40. Robert Kagan, "Stand Up to Putin," *Washington Post*, September 15, 2004, A25, www.washingtonpost.com/wp-dyn/articles/A21853-2004Sep14.html.

41. Adi Ignatius, "Person of the Year 2007: A Tsar Is Born," *Time*, December 19, 2007, www.time.com/time/specials/2007/personoftheyear/article/1,28804,1690753_1690757_1690766,00.html.

42. Verini, "Putin's Power Grab."

43. Hastings, "Corruption, Violence, and Vice."

44. Service, *History of Modern Russia*, 547.

45. "Moscow Metro Hit by Deadly Suicide Bombings," BBC News, March 29, 2010, http://news.bbc.co.uk/2/hi/europe/8592190.stm.

Chapter 18 Diversification: The Key to Wealth Protection

1. "2009 U.S. Dollar Index Historical Prices," http://futures.tradingcharts.com/hist_US.html.

2. Aryeh Katz, "Permanent Portfolio Locks In Long-Term Profits," Investopedia .com, 2009, www.investopedia.com/articles/financial-theory/09/wisdom-permanent-portfolio.asp.

3. Ibid.

4. Harry Browne, *Fail-Safe Investing: Lifelong Financial Security in 30 Minutes* (New York: St. Martin's Press, 1999), 37.

5. Ibid., 47.

6. Katz, "Permanent Portfolio."

7. Robert Hagin, *Investment Management: Portfolio Diversification, Risk, and Timing—Fact and Fiction* (Hoboken, NJ: John Wiley & Sons, 2004,) 204.

8. Harry Markowitz, *Portfolio Selection: Efficient Diversification of Investments* (Malden, MA: Blackwell Publishing, 1991), 3.

9. "The Importance of Diversification," Investopedia.com, November 15, 2002, www.investopedia.com/articles/02/111502.asp.

10. Michael Schmidt, "Does International Investing Really Offer Diversification?" Investopedia.com, 2009, www.investopedia.com/articles/financial-theory/ 09/wisdom-permanent-portfolio.asp.

11. Yahoo! Finance, "Transocean, Ltd., Historical Prices," http://finance.yahoo .com/q/hp?s=RIG&a=03&b=21&c=2010&d=03&e=30&f=2010&g=d.

Chapter 19 Precious Metals: Inflation Protection Strategies

1. PR NewsWire, "NIA Warns Massive Inflation Could Hit US," March 12, 2010.

2. Julie Crawshaw, "Roubini Economist: We're Headed for World of Inflation," Moneynews.com, March 17, 2010.

3. Martin Feldstein, "Inflation Is Looming on America's Horizon," *Financial Times*, April 19, 2009.

4. Marc Goedhart, Timothy Koller, and David Wessels, "How Inflation Can Destroy Shareholder Value," *McKinsey Quarterly*, February 2010.

5. Adrian Ash, "Investing in Gold: A Short History of Monetary Mistrust," MarketOracle.com, March 25, 2007. www.marketoracle.co.uk.

6. Ibid.

7. World Gold Council, "Investing in Gold: Demand and Supply," www.invest .gold.org/sites/en/why_gold/demand_and_supply/

8. Ibid.

9. Matthew Scott, "Rapidly Growing ETF Industry May Need Its Own Trade Group," *Daily Finance*, January 6, 2010.

10. Money Control, "Gold ETFs Outperform Gold Mutual Funds," News Center February 26, 2009, www.moneycontrol.com/news/mf-analysis/gold-etfs-outperform-gold-mutual-funds_386961.html.

11. Central Fund of Canada, CEF Financial Press Release, December 15, 2009, http://google.brand.edgar-online.com/EFX_dll/EDGARpro.dll?FetchFiling HTML1?ID=6941900&SessionID=fY_wHSHpJOYgAl7.

12. Ibid.

13. Ibid.

14. The Silver Institute, "Price History: 1980 to 1991," www.silverinstitute.org/silver_history.php.

15. Ibid.

16. Silver Institute.org, "History of Silver."

17. Ibid.

18. The Silver Institute, "Price History, 2000 to Present," www.silverinstitute.org/2000pres.php.

19. "How Much Has the Silver Stock Pile Been Depleted?" *Contrarian Investor's Journal*, June 5, 2009.

20. Ibid.

21. iShares.com, "Silver Trust," http://us.ishares.com/product_info/fund/overview/SLV.htm.

22. World Gold Council, "Investing in Gold," www.invest.gold.org/sites/en/how_to_invest/exchange_traded_gold/

23. Ibid.

24. CMI Gold and Silver, "American Silver Eagle Coins," www.silvercoinguide.com/SilverCoins/silver-eagle-coins.php.

25. Kitcomm.com, "Why Are 22K American Eagles Worth More than a 24 oz Maple?," www.kitcomm.com/archive/index.php?t-42162.html.

26. PandaCollector.com, "Gold Panda Coins of China," www.pandacollector.com/gold-pandas-1b.html.

Chapter 20   Barbarians of Wealth, Castles of Currency

1. "Triennial Central Bank Survey: Foreign Exchange and Derivatives Market Activity in 2007," Bank for International Settlements, December 2007, 1, www.bis.org/publ/rpfxf07t.pdf?noframes=1.

2. Verena Schmitt-Roschmann, "Euphoria over Euro Rescue Fades," Associated Press, May 11, 2010, http://finance.yahoo.com/news/Euphoria-over-euro-rescue-apf-146190100.html?x=0.

3. Ibid.

4. Thomas J. Craughwell, *The Rise and Fall of the Second Largest Empire in History: How Genghis Khan's Mongols Almost Conquered the World* (Beverly, MA: Fair Winds Press, 2010), 126.

5. Ibid.

6. Troy Adkins, "What the National Debt Means to You," Investopedia.com, 2010, www.investopedia.com/articles/economics/10/national-debt.asp.

7. Milton Friedman, "Best of Both Worlds," *Reason* magazine interview with Brian Doherty, June 1995, http://reason.com/archives/1995/06/01/best-of-both-worlds.

8. "Debate on the Other Debt Crisis, Our View: Ugly Truth about State Pensions Begins to Emerge," *USA Today*, May 2, 2010, www.usatoday.com/news/opinion/editorials/2010-05-03-editorial03_ST_N.htm.

9. "Our View on the World Economy: Greek Debt Crisis Offers Preview of What Awaits U.S.," *USA Today*, May 6, 2010, www.usatoday.com/news/opinion/editorials/2010-05-06-editorial06_ST_N.htm?loc=interstitialskip.

10. James Turk and John Rubino, *The Collapse of the Dollar and How to Profit from It: Make a Fortune by Investing in Gold and Other Hard Assets* (New York: Doubleday, Random House, 2004), 65–66.

11. Ibid., 63–64.

12. "H.6 Money Stock Measures: Discontinuance of M3," Federal Reserve Statistical Release, March 9, 2006, www.federalreserve.gov/releases/h6/discm3.htm.

13. "Table A: M3 and Non-M2 M3," Federal Reserve, March 23, 2006, www.federalreserve.gov/releases/h6/hist/h6hista.pdf.

14. J. Anthony Boeckh, *The Great Reflation: How Investors Can Profit from the New World of Money* (Hoboken, NJ: John Wiley & Sons, 2010), 192.

15. Turk and Rubino, *Collapse of the Dollar*, 34.

16. "30-Day AA Nonfinancial Commercial Paper Interest Rate," Federal Reserve, www.federalreserve.gov/releases/h15/data/Monthly/H15_NFCP_M1.txt.

17. "Median and Average Sales Prices of New Homes Sold in United States," U.S. Census Bureau, www.census.gov/const/uspricemon.pdf.

18. Mark Felsenthal, "Greenspan Says Didn't See Subprime Storm Brewing," Reuters, September 14, 2007, www.reuters.com/article/idUSL1426151220070914?sp=true.

19. Penn Bullock, "Friedman Economics: Is Fed Chairman Ben Bernanke a Follower of John Maynard Keynes or Milton Friedman?," *Reason*, September 1, 2009, http://reason.com/archives/2009/09/01/friedman-economics.

20. Ibid.

21. Turk and Rubino, *Collapse of the Dollar*, 38.

22. Charles Goyette, *The Dollar Meltdown: Surviving the Impending Currency Crisis with Gold, Oil, and Other Unconventional Investments* (New York: Portfolio, The Penguin Group, 2009), 72.

23. Ibid., 81.

24. Ibid., 223.

25. Ibid.

26. John Jagerson, "Currency ETFs Simplify Forex Trades," Investopedia.com, 2007, www.investopedia.com/articles/forex/07/currency-ETFs.asp.

27. Katrina Lamb, "Investing In Emerging Market Debt," Investopedia.com, 2007, www.investopedia.com/articles/bonds/07/emerging-market-debt.asp.

28. Brian Bloch, "Exploring Non-Dollar Currencies for Forex Trading," Investopedia.com, 2007, www.investopedia.com/articles/forex/07/non-dollar.asp.

29. Jagerson, "Currency ETFs Simplify Forex Trades."

30. Ibid.

31. Virginia B. Morris and Kenneth M. Morris, *Standard & Poor's Guide to Money and Investing* (New York: Lightbulb Press, 2005), 18.

Chapter 21 Arm Yourself with Ultra-Resource-Rich Countries

1. "Economy: Retail Sales Down, Jobless Claims Up," Associated Press, January 14, 2010, www.courierpress.com/news/2010/jan/14/economy-retail-sales-down-jobless-claims/.

2. Lizette Alvarez, "More Americans Joining Military as Jobs Dwindle," *New York Times*, January 18, 2009, www.nytimes.com/2009/01/19/us/19recruits .html?ei=5124&en=19d2055be915ebb4&ex=1390107600&exprod= digg& pagewanted=all.

3. Krishna Guha, Andrew Ward, and Edward Luce, "U.S. Loses Most Jobs since 1945," *Financial Times*, January 9, 2009, www.ft.com/cms/s/0/07402ca6-de50-11dd-8372-000077b07658.html?ftcamp=rss.

4. Kris Hudson, "Struggling Retailers Press Struggling Landlords on Rent," WSJOnline, January 7, 2009, http://online.wsj.com/article/SB123129 342324759689.html.

5. Curtis Mewborne, "Emerging Markets Watch: Rewind or Fast Forward," Pimco.com, January 2009, http://australia.pimco.com/LeftNav/Featured+ Market+Commentary/EMW/2009/Emerging+Markets+Watch+January+ 2009+Mewbourne+Rewind+or+Fast+Forward.htm.

6. Jim Rogers, "8 Really, Really Scary Predictions," CNNMoney.com and *Fortune*, 2008, http://money.cnn.com/galleries/2008/fortune/0812/gallery.market_gurus.fortune/5.html.

7. James E. McWhinney, "Introduction to Diversification," Investopedia.com, 2005, www.investopedia.com/articles/basics/05/diversification.asp.

8. Richard Shaw, "History of Emerging Markets vs. US and World," QVM Group LLC, *Perspectives on Return and Risk Management*, February 18, 2008, www.qvmgroup.com/invest/archives/344.

9. Central Intelligence Agency, *The World Factbook: Canada*, www.cia.gov/library/publications/the-world-factbook/geos/ca.html.

10. Ibid.

11. *Canadian Minerals Yearbook*, www.nrcan-rncan.gc.ca/mms-smm/busi-indu/cmy-amc/2008cmy-eng.htm.

12. Department of Finance Canada, "Official International Reserves," April 7, 2010, www.fin.gc.ca/n10/10-028-eng.asp.

13. Yahoo! Finance, "CAD/USD (CADUSD=X)," http://finance.yahoo.com/echarts?s=CADUSD=X#chart3:symbol=cadusd=x;range=20090302,20100401;indicator=volume;charttype=line;crosshair=on;ohlcvalues=0;logscale=off;source=undefined.

14. "Federal Government Buying $50B More in Mortgages," CBC News, November 12, 2008, www.cbc.ca/canada/story/2008/11/12/flahertyloans.html.

15. Central Intelligence Agency, *The World Factbook: Norway*, www.cia.gov/library/publications/the-world-factbook/geos/no.html.

16. Ibid.

17. Norges Bank, "Norges Bank Balance Sheet Figures," February 2010, www.norges-bank.no/upload/78415/balance_2010_02.pdf.

18. Norges Bank, "Key Policy Rate," June 29, 2004, http://www.norges-bank.no/templates/article_____41194.aspx.

19. Yahoo! Finance, "NOK/USD (NOKUSD=X)," http://finance.yahoo.com/echarts?s=nokusd%3Dx#chart2:symbol=nokusd=x;range=20100301,20100401;indicator=volume;charttype=line;crosshair=on;ohlcvalues=0;logscale=off;source=undefined.

20. Central Intelligence Agency, *The World Factbook: Australia*, www.cia.gov/library/publications/the-world-factbook/geos/as.html.

21. Ibid.

22. Reserve Bank of Australia, Statement of Liabilities and Assets, www.rba.gov.au/statistics/frequency/stmt-liabilities-assets.html.

23. *Canadian Minerals Yearbook*, Catalogue no. M38-5/57-PDF, Natural Resources Canada, September 2009, www.nrcan-rncan.gc.ca/mms-smm/busi-indu/cmy-amc/2008cmy-eng.htm.

24. Yahoo! Finance, "AUD/USD (AUDUSD=X)," http://finance.yahoo.com/echarts?s=audusd%3Dx#chart2:symbol=audusd=x;range=20100301,20100401;indicator=volume;charttype=line;crosshair=on;ohlcvalues=0;logscale=off;source=undefined.

25. Central Intelligence Agency, *The World Factbook: Hong Kong*, www.cia.gov/library/publications/the-world-factbook/geos/hk.html.

26. Hong Kong Monetary Authority, "Economic and Financial Data for Hong Kong," www.info.gov.hk/hkma/eng/statistics/index_efdhk.htm.

27. 2010 Index of Economic Freedom, "Top Ten of 2010," www.heritage.org/index/TopTen.aspx.

28. Trading Economics, "Hong Kong Balance of Trade," http://tradingeconomics.com/Economics/Balance-Of-Trade.aspx?Symbol=HKD.

29. Honk Kong Monetary Authority, "Data Template on International Reserves/Foreign Currency Liquidity," February 28, 2010, www.info.gov.hk/hkma/eng/press/2010/attach/20100331e4a1.xls.

30. Powerset, "Hong Kong Dollar," www.powerset.com/explore/go/Hong-Kong-dollar.

31. Hong Kong Monetary Authority, "Currency Board System: Linked Exchange Rate System," August 10, 2009, www.info.gov.hk/hkma/eng/currency/link_ex/index.htm.

32. Yahoo! Finance, "HKD/USD (HKDUSD=X)," http://finance.yahoo.com/echarts?s=hkdusd%3Dx#chart2:symbol=hkdusd=x;range=20100301,20100401;indicator=volume;charttype=line;crosshair=on;ohlcvalues=0;logscale=off;source=undefined.

33. PSA Singapore, "About Us," www.singaporepsa.com/aboutus.php.

34. Ibid.

35. Central Intelligence Agency, *The World Factbook: Singapore*, www.cia.gov/library/publications/the-world-factbook/geos/sn.html.

36. Monetary Authority of Singapore, "Official Foreign Reserves," www.mas.gov.sg/data_room/reserves_statistics/Official_Foreign_Reserves.html.

37. Monetary Authority of Singapore, "Monetary Policy Statement," October 12, 2009, www.mas.gov.sg/news_room/statements/2009/Monetary_Policy_Statement_12Oct09.html.

38. Yahoo! Finance, "SGD/USD (SGDUSD=X)," http://finance.yahoo.com/echarts?s=sgdusd%3Dx#chart2:symbol=sgdusd=x;range=20100301,20100401;indicator=volume;charttype=line;crosshair=on;ohlcvalues=0;logscale=off;source.

About the Authors

Sandy Franks is the executive publisher of the Taipan Publishing Group, which has been providing readers with insightful and actionable financial information for over 20 years.

Sandy has nearly 23 years of publishing experience, and her background encompasses a variety of fields including finance, health, and business.

She has worked alongside some of the country's best-selling authors, such as Michael Masterson, personal wealth coach; Addison Wiggin, co-author of the best-selling book *Empire of Debt* (John Wiley & Sons, 2006); and William Bonner, president of Agora Publishing, one of the country's largest newsletter publishers.

Sara Nunnally is the senior research director and global correspondent for Taipan Publishing Group. She travels all over the world in search of the best investment opportunities to recommend to her readers. Her diverse resume includes studies in history, art, computer science, financial research, and a master's degree from the University of Baltimore in publication design and creative writing. She has appeared in business news media such as *Forbes on Fox*, *Fox News Live*, Bloomberg, and CNBC's *Squawk Box*, as well as numerous radio shows around the country. Sara Nunnally currently resides in Milwaukee, Wisconsin.

Index